T0305397

The Controller's Function

The Controller's Function

The Work of the Managerial Accountant

FOURTH EDITION

STEVEN M. BRAGG

WILEY

For general information on our other products and services or for technical support, please contact our Customer Care Department within the United States at (800) 762-2974, outside the United States at (317) 572-3993 or fax (317) 572-4002.

Wiley also publishes its books in a variety of electronic formats. Some content that appears in print may not be available in electronic books. For more information about Wiley products, visit our web site at www.wiley.com.

Library of Congress Cataloging-in-Publication Data:
Bragg, Steven M.
   The controller's function : the work of the managerial accountant. — 4th ed. / Steven M. Bragg.
      p. cm.
   Rev. ed. of: The controller's function / Janice Roehl-Anderson, Steven M. Bragg. 3rd ed.
   Includes index.
   ISBN 978-0-470-93742-6 (hardback); ISBN 978-1-118-00141-7 (ebk);
ISBN 978-1-118-00142-4 (ebk); ISBN 978-1-118-00143-1 (ebk)
   1. Managerial accounting. 2. Controllership. 3. Auditing. 4. Budget in business.   I. Roehl-Anderson, Janice M. Controller's function.   II. Title.
   HF5657.4.R63 2011
   658.15′11—dc22
                                                                            2010037967

Printed in the United States of America.
10 9 8 7 6 5 4 3 2 1

Contents

Preface

THIS REVISED EDITION OF *The Controller's Function* is a complete operations reference manual for the corporate controller. Within these pages the reader will find a comprehensive discussion of how to manage all major aspects of the controller's job, including strategic and annual planning, financial reporting, and managing all aspects of the accounting department, as well as peripheral issues such as control systems, the fast close, filings with the Securities and Exchange Commission cost reduction analysis, software selection and implementation—and much, much more.

This book was written in response to the growing realization that the controller is no longer being called on just to process accounting transactions and issue financial statements, tasks requiring detailed technical knowledge but no considerable management or analysis skill. Instead, the modern controller must exhibit additional mastery of a multitude of management skills, so that the accounting department runs in an efficient and effective manner, offers a detailed analysis of financial statement results, recommends improvements, monitors the activities of other departments, and perhaps even manages the computer systems in a smaller organization. This book gives considerable attention to the most recent advances in all these areas of responsibility, so that the controller will be fully capable of installing and using them to improve his or her company's level of competitive advantage. Included in our coverage of these advances are the use of target costing, activity-based costing, and throughput analysis.

In addition to these more advanced categories, the book also includes such bread-and-butter topics as cash management, internal control systems and fraud prevention, accounts receivable collections, inventory valuation, budgeting, taxes, insurance, and capital budgeting. Because basic and advanced accounting management topics are combined in one volume, the reader has access to the complete reference for mastering the controller's function.

Steven M. Bragg
Centennial, Colorado
July 2011

CHAPTER ONE

The Controller's Job

TODAY'S CORPORATION OPERATES IN an increasingly complex environment, where there are far too many activities for a chief executive officer (CEO) to keep track of. To an increasing degree, this monitoring function falls on the shoulders of the controller, who must keep the CEO apprised of the performance of all departments, product sales, costs and profits, control issues in a variety of transaction processing systems, and the impact of new government taxes and other regulations on the conduct of the business. Thus, the controller can reasonably be compared to the ship's navigator, who warns the captain of current or foreseeable problems in the shoals of the business environment that lie ahead and on all sides. In this chapter, we explore the main functions of the controller, what kind of background a controller should have, the positions reporting to the controller, and the role of ethics in the conduct of the job.

 ## MAIN JOB FUNCTIONS

The controller has a number of distinct job functions. The first four are ones that can be ascribed to any manager in any department. The last two are more specialized and do not refer to management skill. The six functions are:

1. *Planning.* The controller is responsible for determining who does the work, what work is to be done, and the timing of work completion in the accounting department, especially in regard to the timely processing of transactions and the issuance of accurate financial statements. This also extends to the budget, where the controller guides the budgeting process through other departments.
2. *Organizing.* The controller is responsible for obtaining and keeping the services of experienced and well-trained accounting personnel; this is by far the most important organizational task. This also involves obtaining sufficient floor space, office equipment, and computer hardware and software to complete all assigned work.
3. *Directing.* The controller is responsible for ensuring that all employees in the department work together in an orderly manner to achieve the controller's plans.
4. *Measuring.* The controller is responsible for measuring the performance of all key aspects of the department to ensure that performance matches or exceeds standards and that errors are caught and corrected.
5. *Financial analysis.* The controller is responsible for the review, interpretation, and generation of recommendations related to corporate financial performance. This requires excellent communication skills (both written and oral), so that the controller's information is properly and effectively conveyed to the other members of the management team.
6. *Process analysis.* The controller is responsible for periodically reviewing and evaluating the performance of each major process that is involved in the completion of transactions, with the dual (and sometimes conflicting) objectives of maintaining tight financial controls over processes while also running them in a cost-effective and efficient manner.

JOB DESCRIPTION

The controller has one of the most complex job descriptions of all company managers because there are so many functional areas for which he or she is responsible. This section provides a detailed job description that is sorted by general category in alphabetical order. The controller's responsibilities are:

Auditing

▪ The scheduling and management of periodic internal audits, as well as the preparation of resulting audit reports and the communication of findings and recommendations to management and the board of directors.
▪ The preparation of work papers for the external auditors and the rendering of any additional assistance needed by them to complete the annual audit.

Budgeting

▪ The coordination of the annual budgeting process, including maintenance of the company budget, and the transfer of final budget information into the financial statements.

Control Systems

▪ The establishment of a sufficiently broad set of controls to give management assurance that transactions are processed properly.

Cost Accounting

▪ The coordination of periodic physical inventory counts.
▪ The periodic analysis and allocation of costs based on activity-based costing pools and allocation methods.
▪ The continual cost review of products currently under development, using the principles of target costing.
▪ The periodic compilation and evaluation of inventory costs.

Financial Analysis

▪ The periodic comparison of actual to budgeted results and the communication of variances to management, along with recommendations for improvement.
▪ The continuing review of revenue and expense trends and the communication of adverse trend results to management, along with recommendations for improvement.
▪ The periodic calculation of a standard set of ratios for corporate financial performance and the formulation of management recommendations based on the results.

Financial Statements

- ▪ The preparation of all periodic financial statements, as well as their accompanying footnotes.
- ▪ The preparation of an interpretive analysis of the financial statements.
- ▪ The preparation and distribution of recurring and one-time management reports.

Fixed Assets

- ▪ The annual audit of fixed assets to ensure that all recorded assets are present.
- ▪ The periodic recording of fixed assets in the financial records and their proper recording under the correct asset categories and depreciation methods.
- ▪ The periodic review of fixed assets to determine the existence of any impairment.
- ▪ The proper analysis of all capital expenditure requests.

Policies and Procedures

- ▪ The creation and maintenance of all policies and procedures related to the control of company assets and the proper completion of financial transactions.
- ▪ The training of department personnel in the use of accounting policies and procedures.
- ▪ The modification of existing policies and procedures to match the requirements of government regulations.

Process Analysis

- ▪ The periodic review of all processes involving financial analysis to see if they can be completed with better controls, lower costs, or greater speed.

Record Keeping

- ▪ The proper indexing, storage, and retrieval of all accounting documents.
- ▪ The orderly planning for and scheduling of document destruction, in accordance with the corporate document retention policy.

Tax Preparation

▪ The timely preparation and filing of tax returns, as well as the supervision of all matters relating to corporate taxation, such as conducting an effective tax management program, and both providing and enforcing policies and procedures related to the compliance of all corporate personnel with applicable government tax laws.

Transaction Processing

▪ The timely completion of all accounting transactions at the intervals and in the manner specified in the accounting policies and procedures manual.
▪ The proper completion of all transactions authorized by the board of directors or in accordance with the terms of all authorized contracts.
▪ The proper approval of those transactions requiring them, in accordance with company policy.

This list may appear overwhelming, but just because the controller is responsible for all of the listed areas does not mean that this person must actually do each one. Instead, the controller is mostly involved in the six job functions noted in the preceding section; in other words, the controller primarily manages the work of other people and ensures that they complete most of the tasks just listed. In particular, a controller can rely on the services of assistant controllers who are responsible for smaller portions of the accounting department.

 ## JOB QUALIFICATIONS

To undertake the job description just described, the controller should have a number of qualifications, which are outlined in this section. Although not all controllers will possess these skills, it is most important to have those related to transaction processing and the production of accurate financial statements because these two areas remain the core of the accounting function. The key job qualifications are:

▪ *Analysis of information.* The controller must be sufficiently comfortable with financial information to readily understand the meaning of a variety of ratios and trends and what they portend for a company.

- *Communication ability.* A key component of the controller's function is compiling information and communicating it to management. If the compiling part of the job goes well, but management does not understand its implications, then the controller must improve his or her communication skills in order to better impart financial information to the management team.
- *Company and industry knowledge.* No accounting system is completely "plain vanilla," because the companies and industries in which it operates have a sufficient number of quirks to require some variation from the typical accounting system. Accordingly, the controller must have a good knowledge of both company and industry operations to know how they impact the operations of the accounting department.
- *Management skill.* The controller presumably will have a staff and, if so, will have considerable control over the productivity of that group. Accordingly, the controller must have an excellent knowledge of the planning, organizational, directing, and measurement functions needed to manage the accounting department.
- *Provision of timely and cost-effective services.* The controller must run the accounting department as if it were a profit center, so that the most efficient methods are used to complete each task and the attention of the department is focused squarely on the most urgent tasks.
- *Technical knowledge.* Creating an accurate financial statement, especially one for a publicly held company, requires a considerable knowledge of accounting rules and regulations. Accordingly, a controller should be thoroughly versed in all generally accepted accounting principles (GAAP). Also, if the controller's company deals with international financial reporting standards (IFRS), a knowledge of IFRS will also be necessary.

ORGANIZATIONAL STRUCTURE OF THE ACCOUNTING DEPARTMENT

The controller does not operate alone to complete all the tasks outlined through the last few sections. On the contrary, quite a large accounting staff may complete the bulk of the work. In this section, we review the structure of the typical accounting department and the tasks completed by each part of it.

The controller is usually helped by one or more assistant controllers who are assigned different sets of tasks. For example, one may be in charge of the more technically difficult general ledger, tax reporting, financial analysis, cost accounting, and financial reporting tasks, while another covers the major transactions, which are accounts payable, accounts receivable, payroll, and cash application. For smaller organizations, there may also be managers for the human resources and MIS functions who are at the assistant controller level and who also report to the controller. Below these managers are a number of subcategories, staffed either by clerks or degreed accountants, who are responsible for specific tasks. These subcategories are:

- *Cost accounting.* This position is filled by a degreed accountant who conducts job or process costing and verifies the inventory valuation.
- *Financial analysis.* This position is filled by a degreed accountant who compiles both standard and special-request analysis reports.
- *Financial reporting.* This position is filled by either a degreed accountant or a senior-level bookkeeper who prepares the financial statements and accompanying footnotes, as well as other periodic reports for public consumption if the company is publicly held.
- *General ledger accounting.* Frequently combined with the financial reporting function, this is staffed by similar personnel and is involved with the review and recording of journal entries and summary entries for subsidiary journals.
- *Payroll processing.* This position is filled by clerks who calculate pay levels and hours worked and generate payments to employees.
- *Tax form preparation and filing.* This position is filled by a degreed accountant, frequently with tax experience in a public accounting background, who completes and files all government tax forms.
- *Transaction processing.* This position is filled by clerks (usually comprising the bulk of all department headcount) who process all accounts payable, accounts receivable, and cash application transactions in accordance with rigidly defined procedures.

The positions most likely to be needed by a controller are those responsible for transactions, which are the clerks responsible for billing, collections, payables, and payroll. Here are the job requirements for these positions:

Billing Clerk: This position is accountable for creating invoices and credit memos, issuing them to customers by all necessary means, and updating customer files. Principal accountabilities are:
- Issue invoices to customers
- Issue monthly customer statements

- Update customer files
- Process credit memos
- Update the customer master file with contact information
- Track exceptions between the shipping log and invoice register
- Enter invoices into customer invoicing web sites
- Submit invoices by electronic data interchange

Collections Clerk: This position is accountable for collecting the maximum amount of overdue funds from customers, which may include a variety of collection techniques, legal claims, and the selective use of outside collection services. Principal accountabilities are:

- Stratify collection activities to maximize cash receipts
- Issue dunning letters to overdue accounts
- Contact customers regarding overdue accounts
- Issue payment commitment letters
- Negotiate the return of unpaid merchandise
- Monitor cash on delivery or COD roll payments
- Issue credit hold notifications
- Recommend that accounts be shifted to a collection agency
- Process small claims court complaints
- Recommend bad debt write-offs

Payables Clerk: This position is accountable for verifying proper payment approval, processing payments in a timely manner, and ensuring that discounts are taken. Principal accountabilities are:

- Match supplier invoices to authorizing purchase orders and proofs of receipt
- Take all economical supplier discounts
- Obtain payment approvals for non–cost of goods sold invoices
- Process expense reports
- Process procurement card payments
- Issue stop payments and void checks
- Issue reminders to suppliers regarding uncashed checks
- Pay supplier invoices when due
- Research supplier requests for payment
- Process value-added tax reclamations
- Monitor supplier W-9 form submissions

▪ Issue positive pay data to the bank

▪ Update the supplier master file

Payroll Clerk: This position is accountable for collecting timekeeping information, incorporating a variety of deductions into a periodic payroll, and issuing pay and pay-related information to employees. Principal accountabilities are:

▪ Collect and summarize timekeeping information

▪ Obtain supervisory approval of time card discrepancies

▪ Obtain overtime approvals

▪ Calculate commissions

▪ Process garnishment requests

▪ Process employee advances and paybacks

▪ Process and close periodic payrolls

▪ Print and issue paychecks

▪ Process direct deposit payments

▪ Process paycard payments

▪ Calculate and deposit payroll taxes

▪ Process employment verifications

▪ Process and issue annual W-2 forms to employees

In a smaller company, the controller may also inherit all the finance and office management functions, which means that some of the staff will be responsible for analyzing and monitoring customer credit, investing funds, supervising risk management, monitoring the phone system, and arranging for the repair of office equipment. Conversely, a larger company will not only separate these added functions, but may also move the financial analysis function under the control of the chief financial officer. Thus, the exact layout of the accounting department will depend to a large extent on the size of the company and the presence of other managers.

There can be several levels of controller within a company. The corporate controller is located at the corporate headquarters, while each division may have its own controller. There will likely be plant controllers at each location, as well. In most organizations, the controller reports directly to the most senior on-site executive. For example, the plant controller reports to the plant manager, the division controller reports to the division manager, and the corporate controller reports to the chief financial officer or president. All three levels of controllership noted here have many of the same functional responsibilities that the corporate controller has on a company-wide basis.

The corporate controller must decide if accounting operations through all company locations are to be centralized, decentralized, or occupy a position somewhere in between. Many controllers favor centralization because they can more tightly manage the function and have fewer worries about accounting control issues arising at some far-off company location. However, not all aspects of the accounting function are so amenable to centralization. Some of the reasons why decentralization should at least be considered as an option are:

■ The local organization and retention of accounting information avoids some excuses for inactivity or poor performance because "the report was late" or "the report was wrong."

■ The information sent to a central location often is duplicated at the local site; that duplication can be avoided by processing it locally.

■ The widespread distribution of accounting responsibility in the field allows a company to more quickly train promising accounting managers and evaluate them for promotion.

■ The presence of a local accountant can assist in the rapid investigation and resolution of problems that would be impossible from a central location.

Offsetting these arguments in favor of decentralization are a number of factors in favor of centralization. The primary reasoning behind the bulk of the pro-centralization approach is that the efficient use of employees to complete a high volume of transactions will keep accounting costs down to a bare minimum. The reasons are:

■ The accounting staff can be shifted between tasks to meet peak workloads.

■ The use of centralized transaction processing may have a sufficient amount of volume to justify the use of expensive computer hardware and software that will considerably improve efficiency, though it would be cost-prohibitive for a smaller division to use.

■ The use of a centralized staff may allow for the added expense of a tailored training program for accountants that will increase their efficiency, but which would be too expensive to create for the smaller numbers of accountants at a single division location.

■ The use of a centralized operation may allow for the hiring of more experienced (and expensive) accounting personnel who can do a better job of managing the department.

Thus, the controller has arguments for using either approach to organizing the department. If a company has a highly diversified group of divisions, then their transactions, chart of accounts, and processes may differ so wildly from each other that it makes no sense to centralize the accounting department. However, a company with cookie-cutter divisions that are essentially identical in their operating characteristics may be ideal for accounting centralization. In many cases, though, the correct method is to opt for a slightly more expensive middle ground, using a centralized transaction processing organization, but also paying for a small local staff that can process exception transactions, investigate variance problems on behalf of the central organization, and also be a training ground for junior accounting managers from the central accounting office.

 ETHICS

The controller is in the uniquely difficult position of having a significant impact on the level of ethics practiced throughout a company. If the controller tends to wink at monetary indiscretions or alter the timing or amount of accruals or other transactions in order to influence reported financial results, then this attitude gradually will percolate down through the organization, until management suddenly finds that the entire company is rife with ethical problems of all kinds. The alternative approach is for the controller to adopt a methodical and rigorous approach to ethical problems, as is outlined in this section.

The first step by the controller is to convince the management team, and the president in particular, that the company must adopt a written ethical standard and force the rest of the organization to adhere to it through regular audits. Once the code of ethics and all related standards of conduct are complete, the management team as a whole must present them to employees and continue to reiterate, both by example and communication, that these principles are a significant foundation underlying all company operations.

Using these preliminary guidelines, the controller can then expand the concept and promulgate a series of additional guidelines in specific areas related to accounting. Some of them are:

- Attaining annual business plan objectives
- Compliance with Securities and Exchange Commission (SEC) and other securities laws and regulations
- Employee discrimination

- Gifts and payments of money for no return consideration
- Leave for military or other federal service
- Meals and entertainment expense reporting
- Period-end accounting adjustments
- Political contributions
- Preservation of assets
- Restrictive trade practices
- Use of the company car
- Workplace safety

Only by adhering closely to these ethical guidelines, and by clearly communicating to the accounting staff that they are the corporate law, will the controller alter the mind-set of the company as a whole (and the accounting department in particular) in the direction of using the highest possible ethical standards.

CHAPTER TWO

Internal Control

ERHAPS THE MOST IMPORTANT function of the controller is to create and maintain the corporate financial control system. Doing so involves documenting the existing control structure, eliminating redundant controls, and adding new controls to cover potential risks arising out of new business situations. In order to properly assess risks, the controller must have a firm grasp of the general types of fraud and how to prevent them. This knowledge should extend to legally required controls over assets, such as those listed in the Foreign Corrupt Practices Act and the Sarbanes-Oxley Act. This chapter provides an overview of these topics.

 ## BASIC ELEMENTS

Many policies and procedures have been established to achieve the specific objectives of an organization. This set of procedures is called the internal control structure. Technically, appropriate control procedures apply to every function, to every activity of the enterprise. The emphasis in this chapter is on those controls relevant to a proper recording of transactions (income, expenses, assets, liabilities, and net worth) and the proper reporting thereof, together with safeguarding the assets of the business. The applicable control objectives, discussed later in this chapter, are a basic concern of the controller.

The controller should be aware of the various types of controls that must be interlinked to create a control system that adequately safeguards the company assets: accounting controls, administrative controls, and primary operational controls.

Accounting controls are defined as the plan of organization and all methods and procedures that are concerned with the safeguarding of assets and the reliability of the financial records. They generally include such controls as the systems of authorization and approval; separation of duties concerned with record-keeping and accounting reports from those concerned with operations or asset custody; physical controls over assets; and internal auditing. It was these controls with which historically the independent accountant was primarily concerned.

Administrative controls comprise the plan of organization and all methods and procedures that relate to operational efficiency and adherence to managerial policies and that usually are concerned only indirectly with the financial records. Included would be such controls as statistical analyses, time and motion studies, performance reports, employee training programs, and quality control.

Primary operational control concerns the establishment of policy and basic guidelines by which an enterprise will be directed as a means of achieving the business objectives.

Given the recent broadening of the traditional definition of controls, and the various statements on the subject, it facilitates discussion if the internal control structure of an entity is divided in two parts:

1. Control environment
2. Accounting systems

Control Environment

A company's control environment is the corporate atmosphere in which the accounting (and other) controls exist and in which the financial statements are prepared. It reflects management's commitment to an effective system of internal control. The control segment has recently been given increased importance in general analysis of controls. It represents the collective effort of many factors, including:

- *Management philosophy and operating style.* This factor concerns "the tone at the top" and includes a broad range of topics that influence the control environment, including:
  - Emphasis on meeting profit goals, targets, or budgets
  - Basic attitude about risk taking
  - Attitude about the need for controls
  - Attitude about the importance and sanctity of the financial statements, both internal and published
- *Organization structure.* How are the organizing, planning, directing, and controlling of operations handled? On a decentralized basis? Does strong central control exist? Does one person or do a few individuals dominate the company?
- *Functioning of the board of directors and the board committees.* Does the board exert influence or largely follow the dictates of the CEO? Does it examine or discuss important policies and procedures? Does an audit committee composed of outside directors exist? Does it oversee accounting policies and procedures, including controls? Does it meet independently with the outside auditors and with internal auditors?
- *Methods of assigning authority and responsibility.* Are policy matters such as ethical standards, conflicts of interest, and competitive response discussed?
- *Management control methods.* This category involves the heart of operational control—how management delegates authority to others and effectively supervises all company activities—and includes:
  - The planning system, both short and long term
  - The measurement system, comparing actual with planned performance, and communication of the results to appropriate individuals
  - The methods of taking timely and corrective action to bring actual performance at least to budgeted levels
  - The methods of developing procedures, modifying systems, and monitoring systems and procedures
- *The existence and effectiveness of an internal audit function.* Included in the audit function are the proper authority, organization structure and status, properly qualified personnel, and adequate resources.
- *Personnel policies and procedures.* This category includes policies and procedures for hiring, training, evaluating, promoting, and compensating personnel so that a proper and adequate corps of employees is available and permitted to carry out their assigned responsibilities.
- *Influence of external factors.* Although external influences are largely outside the control of an organization, how management monitors and

deals with outside influences, such as legislative and regulatory bodies, international events, and economic trends, and how it complies with the requirements, is germane to accomplishing the company's objectives.

How management copes with these factors reveals the overall attitude of the board of directors and top management concerning ethics and the significance of proper controls. Anyone searching for fraud could use these control elements to narrow the search area; for example, if a department had a poor attitude toward controls, then an auditor might consider that department to be a high-risk area.

Controllers should understand how these various factors actually operate in their areas of responsibility; that is to say, it is one thing to have written policies and procedures, but another to know that they are followed. Management may give lip service to certain policies but act in ways that condone departures from the standard. In the control environment, the controller's attention should be on the same matters that would warrant examination by an independent auditor.

As the internal control structure becomes more widely discussed among management members, many operating managers regard the matter as primarily a financial or accounting concern and not theirs. Because many evaluations have been made by either internal auditors or independent accountants, managers sense no direct tie-in to corporate governance and the achievement of the corporate objectives, such as profitability, growth, and adherence to ethical standards. What is needed, and what is occurring in many companies, is the education of operating management about their role in the control system.

One company, in an effort to educate all department managers, held a series of one-day seminars for the professional and management staff of the organization. In these meetings, the business objectives for each department were stated by the departmental vice president and supplemented by group discussion. The "control mechanisms," or actions required to accomplish each department's objectives, were reviewed for their effectiveness. The relationship of the elements of internal control to the attainment of departmental objectives was appraised.

Although the elements may differ by organization, the example company covered these control segments as meaningful to its operating management:[1]

- Organization controls: Personnel standards, a plan of organization, and the corporate culture

- System development and change controls
- Authorization and reporting controls; planning and budgeting; accountability
- Accounting system controls
- Safeguarding controls: Protection of assets and avoidance of unintentional risks
- Management supervisory controls: Supervision and management information
- Documentation controls: Formal policies and procedures; systems documentation

The objective of the approach was to involve all of management in the educational process and make use of the company's control system to attain departmental objectives.

Accounting System

Another element of the internal control structure is the accounting system. The proper direction of the accounting system is one of the principal responsibilities of the controller. An effective accounting system encompasses those principles, methods, and procedures, as well as those records that will:

- Identify properly and record all valid transactions
- Describe the transactions on a timely basis and in sufficient detail to permit proper classification of transactions for financial reporting
- Determine the time period in which the transactions occurred so as to permit recording in the proper accounting period
- Measure the value of the transaction in a manner that permits recording of the proper monetary value in the financial statements
- Permit proper presentation of the transactions and related required disclosures in the financial statements

Appraising the Control System

Given the inappropriate activity by some businesspeople, such as the issuance of fraudulent financial statements, kickbacks, and bribery, the adequacy of the control systems takes on increased importance. Yet such a determination usually cannot be done quickly or easily. An analytical and detailed approach probably is desirable. Some representative actions in the area of procedure, some essential elements in the control system, and a suggested assignment of responsibility for different phases of control are discussed in the next few sections.

There are two fundamental steps to be taken by management in evaluating internal controls. First, management must identify the principal activities, risks, and exposures in each operating component of the business and define the control objectives related to those activities. Second, management must describe, perhaps by flowcharts, and understand the various systems used to process transactions, safeguard assets, and prepare the financial reports. Management then uses this information to evaluate the system, giving particular attention to possible significant weaknesses, in order to ascertain that the system provides reasonable assurance that the control objective can be achieved.

Identifying the Activities, Risks, and Control Objectives

One way to identify a company's principal activities and control objectives is to separate the typical company into four basic operating components and define the control objectives of the various activities in each component. Suggested components are sales, production or service, finance, and administration. Examples of control objectives are:

- *Sales control objectives.* That correct billings are produced for shipped products or services rendered, customer credit is checked prior to approving orders, and customer returns are approved.
- *Production or service control objectives.* That minimal scrap occurs as products are created, the correct quantities of products are produced, and pilferage is kept to a minimum.
- *Finance control objectives.* That cash receipts are deposited on the day of receipt, petty cash is issued only with proper authorization, and bad debts are properly authorized before being removed from the receivables ledger.
- *Administration control objectives.* That office equipment is purchased only with the proper authorization, vacations are taken only with previous authorization, and hiring occurs only after proper authorization.

Another approach is to identify types of transactions common to most businesses. Each transaction flow is a grouping of related events, and the focus is on whether appropriate control exists over each step in the transaction through the processing system. Some suggested transaction cycles are the revenue cycle, production cycle, payments cycle, and time cycle (economic events caused by time, such as an interest accrual). In any event, whatever approach is used results in the identification of major functions and the control objectives for each.

In reviewing operations, transactions, or cycles, the possibility of loss or risk (or error in the financial statements) should be considered in an effort to minimize theft, for example, and to provide early warning of other potential loss, including:

▪ Loss or destruction of assets
▪ Fraud or embezzlement
▪ Statutory sanctions or violations
▪ Excessive costs or insufficient revenues
▪ Unacceptable accounting
▪ Erroneous recording
▪ Expropriation

Understanding Control Systems

Accounting transactions should be clearly flowcharted, so that they can be studied for possible weaknesses by the controller's staff. This review involves a businessperson's perspective of what should be done, a consideration of things that can go wrong, and a recognition of the accounts that would be affected. Any issues concerning the control of those transactions should be documented.

When reviewing the flowcharts for control weaknesses, five general control objectives should be kept in mind:

1. *Authorization.* Was the transaction authorized by management? This could be evidenced in a general way by establishing related policies, contract authorization limits, investment limits, standard price lists, and so on. Or, in a given situation, a specific authorization may be needed.
2. *Recording.* Transactions should be recorded in the proper account, at the proper time (proper cutoff), with the proper description. No fictitious transactions should be recorded, and erroneous material or incomplete descriptions should be avoided.
3. *Safeguarding.* Physical assets should not be under the physical custody of those responsible for related record-keeping functions. Access to the assets should be restricted to certain designated individuals.
4. *Reconciliation.* Periodic reconciliations of physical assets to records, or control accounts, should be made. Some examples are bank reconciliations,

securities inventories and physical inventories of raw material, and work in process and finished goods to control accounts.

5. *Valuation.* Provision should be made for assurances that the assets are properly valued in accordance with generally accepted accounting principles—and that the adjustments are made.

CONTROLS TO USE IN YOUR BUSINESS

This section describes over 140 controls that can be used throughout a company's accounting systems. They are organized first by their appearance on the balance sheet (e.g., cash controls first, investments controls second, etc.), followed by controls for revenue and then for a number of miscellaneous topics, including foreign exchange, hedges, and leases. Not all are recommended for installation; on the contrary, the controller should pick and choose from this list based on the corporate requirements, keeping in mind the cost-effectiveness of each control. The controls list follows.

Cash²

1. *Control check stock.* This is a key control. All check stock must be locked up when not in use. Otherwise, it is a simple matter for someone to take a check from the bottom of a check stack (where its loss will not be noticed for some time), forge a signature on it, and cash it. The key or combination to the lock must be kept in a safe place, or else this control will be worthless.

2. *Control signature plates.* This is a key control. Many companies use either signature plates or stamps to imprint an authorized signature on a check, thereby saving the time otherwise required of a manager to sign checks. If someone obtains access to a signature plate and some check stock, he or she can easily pay him- or herself the contents of the entire corporate bank account. The best control is to lock up signature plates in a different storage location from the check stock, so a perpetrator would be required to break into two separate locations in order to carry out a really thorough check fraud.

3. *Separate responsibility for the cash receipt and bank reconciliation functions.* If a person has access to both the cash receipt and bank reconciliation functions, it is much easier to commit fraud by altering the amount of incoming receipts, and then pocketing the difference. To avoid this, each function should be handled by different people within the organization.

4. *Perform bank reconciliations.* Although widely practiced and certainly necessary, bank reconciliations are not preventive controls, and so this step should be implemented *after* the control of check stock and signature plates. Bank reconciliations are most effective when completed each day; this can be done by accessing the daily log of cash transactions through the company's bank's Internet site. By staying up-to-date on reconciliations, evidence of fraudulent check activity can be discovered more quickly, allowing for faster remedial action.

5. *Reconcile petty cash.* There tends to be a high incidence of fraud related to petty cash boxes since money can be removed from them more easily. To reduce the incidence of these occurrences, unscheduled petty cash box reconciliations can be initiated, which may catch perpetrators before they have covered their actions with a false paper trail. This control can be strengthened by targeting those petty cash boxes that have experienced unusually high levels of cash replenishment requests.

6. *Require that bank reconciliations be completed by people independent of the cash receipts and disbursement functions.* The bank reconciliation is intended to be a check on the activities of those accounting personnel handling incoming and outgoing cash, so it makes little sense to have the same people review their own activities by completing the reconciliation. Instead, it should be done by someone in an entirely different part of the department, and preferably by a senior person with a proven record of reliability.

7. *Require that petty cash vouchers be filled out in ink.* Anyone maintaining a petty cash box can easily alter a voucher previously submitted as part of a legitimate transaction and remove cash from the petty cash box to match the altered voucher. To avoid this, all vouchers should be completed in ink. To be extra careful, users should be required to write the amount of any cash transactions on vouchers in words instead of numbers (e.g., "fifty-two dollars" instead of "52.00") since numbers can be modified more easily than words.

8. *Compare the check register to the actual check number sequence.* With pre-numbered checks, the check numbers listed in the computer's check register should be compared to those on the checks. If a check were to be removed from the check stock, then this action would become apparent when the check number on the check stock no longer matches the check number in the computer system.

   If the check stock is on a continuous sheet, as is used for sheet-fed dot-matrix printers, then the more likely way for a perpetrator to steal checks would be to detach them from the top or bottom of the stack of check stock. In this case, the problem can be detected by keeping separate track of the last check number used, as well as of the last check number on the bottom of the stack. Unfortunately, many accounting clerks keep such a list of check numbers used with the check stock, so a perpetrator can easily alter the last number listed on the sheet while stealing checks at the same time. For this reason, the list of check numbers used should be kept in a separate location.

9. *Review uncashed checks.* All checks that have not been cashed within 90 days of their check dates should be reviewed. In a few cases, it may be possible to cancel the checks, thereby increasing the available cash balance. This review can also highlight checks that have gone astray. By placing stop payment orders on these checks, the company can keep them from being cashed by other parties, while new checks can be issued to the proper recipients.

10. *Route incoming cash payments through a lockbox.* Having customers send payments directly to a bank lockbox eliminates a number of control points within a company since it no longer has to physically handle any forms of cash. Some payments will inevitably still be mailed directly to the company, but the proportion of these payments will drop if customers are promptly asked to send future payments to the lockbox address.

11. *Verify amount of cash discounts taken.* A cash receipts person can falsely report that customers are taking the maximum amount of early payment discounts when they have not actually done so and can pocket the amount of the false discount. This can be detected by requiring that photocopies of all incoming checks be made and then tracing payments on which discounts have been taken back to the copies of the checks. This is a less common problem area, because it requires a perpetrator to have access to both the receipts and payments aspects of the accounting operation, and so is a less necessary control point.

Investments

Transfers between Available-for-Sale and Trading Investments

1. *Require board approval of substantial changes in investment account designations.* Management can modify the amount of reported gains or losses on investments by shifting investment designations from the "available-for-sale" investment portfolio to the "trading" portfolio. If the gain or loss on

such a change in designation is significant, the board of directors should be notified in advance of the reason for the change and its impact on the level of earnings.

Investments: Transfers of Debt Securities among Portfolios

1. *Impose investment limits.* When investing its excess funds, a company should have a policy that requires it to invest only certain amounts in particular investment categories or vehicles. For example, only the first $100,000 of funds are insured through a bank account, so excess funding beyond this amount can be shifted elsewhere. As another example, the board of directors may feel that there is too much risk in junk bond investments and so will place a general prohibition on this type of investment. These sorts of policies can be programmed into a treasury workstation, so that the system will automatically flag investments that fall outside a company's preset investment parameters.

2. *Require authorizations to shift funds among accounts.* A person who is attempting to fraudulently shift funds out of a company's accounts must have approval authorization on file with one of the company's investment banks to transfer money out to a noncompany account. This type of authorization can be strictly controlled through signatory agreements with the banks. It is also possible to impose strict controls over the transfer of funds *between* company accounts since a fraudulent person may uncover a loophole in the control system whereby a particular bank has not been warned *not* to allow fund transfers outside of a preset range of company accounts, and then shift all funds to that account and thence to an outside account.

Prepaid Expenses

1. *Reconcile all prepaid expense accounts as part of the month-end closing process.* By conducting a careful review of all prepaid accounts once a month, it becomes readily apparent which prepaid items should be converted to an expense. The result of this review should be a spreadsheet that itemizes the nature of each prepaid item in each account. Since this can be a time-consuming process involving some investigative work, it is best to review prepaid expense accounts shortly before the end of the month, so that a thorough review can be conducted without being cut short by the time pressures imposed by the usual closing process.

2. *Review all employee advances with the payroll and payables staffs at least once a month.* A common occurrence is for an employee to claim hardship prior to a company-required trip and request a travel advance. Alternatively, an advance may be paid when an employee claims that he or she cannot make it to the next payroll check. Whatever the reason for these advances, they will be recorded in an employee advances account, where they can sometimes be forgotten. The best way to ensure repayment is a continual periodic review, either with the accounts payable staff who process employee expense reports (against which travel advances should be netted) or the payroll staff (who deduct pay advances from future paychecks).

3. *Require approval of all advance payments to employees.* The simplest way to reduce the burden of tracking employee advances is not to make them in the first place. The best approach is to require management approval of any advances, no matter how small they may be.

Receivables

1. *Confirm payment terms with customers.* Receivable collections can be particularly difficult when the sales staff has established side agreements with customers that alter payment terms—especially when the sales staff does not communicate these new terms to the collections department. The existence of these deals can be discovered by confirming payment terms at the time of invoice creation with selected customers and then working with the sales manager to reprimand those sales staff members who have authorized special terms without notifying anyone else in the company.

2. *Require approval of bad debt write-offs.* A common form of fraud is for a collections person to write off an invoice as a bad debt and then pocket the customer payment when it arrives. Companies can avoid this situation by requiring management approval of all bad debt write-offs (although staff members usually are allowed to write off small balances as an efficiency measure). Management should be particularly wary when a large proportion of bad debt requests come from the same collections person, indicating a possible fraud pattern.

3. *Require approval of credits.* Credits against invoices can be required for other reasons than bad debts—incorrect pricing or quantities delivered, incorrect payment terms, and so on. In these cases, management approval should be required not only to detect the presence of false credit claims, but also to spot patterns indicating some underlying problem requiring correction, such as inaccurate order picking in the warehouse.

4. *Match invoiced quantities to the shipping log.* It is useful to spot-check the quantities invoiced to the quantities listed on the shipping log. Doing so allows for the detection of fraud in the billing department caused by invoicing for too many units, with accounting staff members pocketing the difference when it arrives. This is a rare form of fraud since it generally requires collaboration between billing and cash receipts staff members, and so the control is needed only where the fraud risk clearly exists.

5. *Verify invoice pricing.* The billing department can commit fraud by issuing fake invoices to customers at improperly high prices and then pocketing the difference between the regular and inflated prices when the customer check arrives. Having someone compare the pricing on invoices to a standard price list before invoices are mailed can spot this issue. As was the case for the last control, this form of fraud is possible only when there is a risk of collaboration between billing and cash receipts staff members, so the control is needed only when the fraud risk is present.

Inventory in Transit

1. *Audit shipment terms.* Certain types of shipment terms will require that a company shipping goods must retain inventory on its books for some period of time after the goods have physically left the company or that a receiving company record inventory on its books prior to its arrival at the receiving dock. Although in practice most companies will record inventory only when it is physically present, this is technically incorrect under certain shipment terms. Consequently, a company should perform a periodic audit of shipment terms used to see if there are any deliveries requiring different inventory treatment. The simplest approach is to mandate no delivery terms under which a company is financially responsible for transportation costs.

2. *Audit the receiving dock.* A significant problem from a record-keeping perspective is that the receiving staff may not have time to enter a newly received delivery into the corporate computer system, so the accounting and purchasing staffs have no idea that the items have been received. Accordingly, items sitting in the receiving area should be compared regularly to the inventory database to see if they have been recorded. Supplier billings also can be compared to the inventory database to see if items billed by suppliers are not listed as having been received.

3. *Reject all purchases that are not preapproved.* A major flaw in the purchasing systems of many companies is that all supplier deliveries are accepted at the

receiving dock, irrespective of the presence of authorizing paperwork. Many of these deliveries are verbally authorized orders from employees throughout the company, and often these employees are not authorized to make such purchases or are not aware that they are buying items at high prices. This problem can be eliminated by enforcing a rule that all items received must have a corresponding purchase order on file that has been authorized by the purchasing department. By doing so, the purchasing staff can verify that there is a need for each item requisitioned and that it is bought at a reasonable price from a certified supplier.

Inventory Accounting

1. *Conduct inventory audits.* If no one ever checks the accuracy of the inventory, it will gradually vary from the book inventory, as an accumulation of errors builds up over time. To counteract this problem, schedule a complete recount of the inventory from time to time or an ongoing cycle count of small portions of the inventory each day. Whichever method is used, it is important to conduct research in regard to why errors are occurring, and attempt to fix the underlying problems.

2. *Control access to bill of material and inventory records.* The files containing bills of material and inventory records should be accessible to only a very small number of well-trained employees. By limiting access in this way, the risk of inadvertent or deliberate changes to these valuable records will be minimized. The security system should also store the keystrokes and user access codes for anyone who has accessed these records, in case evidence is needed to prove that fraudulent activities have occurred.

3. *Keep bill of material accuracy levels at a minimum of 98 percent.* The bills of material are critical for determining the value of inventory as it moves through the work-in-process stages of production and eventually arrives in the finished goods area since they itemize every possible component that comprises each product. These records should be regularly compared to actual product components to verify that they are correct, and their accuracy should be tracked.

4. *Pick from stock based on bills of material.* An excellent control over material costs is to require the use of bills of material for each item manufactured and then require that parts be picked from the raw materials stock for the production of these items based on the quantities listed in the bills of material. By doing so, a reviewer can hone in on those warehouse

issuances that were *not* authorized through a bill of material since there is no objective reason why these issuances should have taken place.

5. *Require approval to sign out inventory beyond amounts on pick list.* If a standard pick list is used to take raw materials from the warehouse for production purposes, then this should be the standard authorization for inventory removal. If production staff members require any additional inventory, they should go to the warehouse gate and request it, and the resulting distribution should be logged out of the warehouse. Furthermore, any inventory that is left over after production is completed should be sent back to the warehouse and logged in. By using this approach, the cost accountant can tell if there are errors in the bills of material that are used to create pick lists since any extra inventory requisitions or warehouse returns probably represent errors in the bills.

6. *Require transaction forms for scrap and rework transactions.* A startling amount of materials and associated direct labor can be lost through the scrapping of production or its occasional rework. This tends to be a difficult item to control since scrap and rework can occur at many points in the production process. Nonetheless, the manufacturing staff should be well trained in the use of transaction forms that record these actions, so that the inventory records will remain accurate.

7. *Restrict warehouse access to designated personnel.* Without access restrictions, the company warehouse is like a large store with no prices—just take all you want. This does not necessarily mean that employees are taking items from stock for personal use, but they may be removing excessive inventory quantities for production purposes, which leads to a cluttered production floor. Also, this leaves the purchasing staff with the almost impossible chore of trying to determine what is in stock and what needs to be bought for immediate manufacturing needs. Consequently, a mandatory control over inventory is to fence it in and closely restrict access to it.

8. *Segregate customer-owned inventory.* If customers supply a company with some parts that are used when constructing products for them, it becomes very easy for this inventory to be mingled with the company's own inventory, resulting in a false increase in its inventory valuation. Although it is certainly possible to assign customer-specific inventory codes to these inventory items in order to clearly identify them, a more easily discernible control is to physically segregate these goods in a different part of the warehouse.

Inventory Valuation

1. *Audit inventory material costs.* Inventory costs are usually either assigned through a standard costing procedure or as part of some inventory layering concept, such as LIFO (last in, first out) or FIFO (first in, first out). In the case of standard costs, assigned costs should be compared regularly to the actual cost of materials purchased to see if any standard costs should be updated to bring them more in line with actual costs incurred. If it is company policy to update standard costs only at lengthy intervals, then it should be verified that the variance between actual and standard costs is being written off to the cost of goods sold.

   If inventory layering is used to store inventory costs, then the costs in the most recently used layers should be periodically audited, tracing inventory costs back to specific supplier invoices.

2. *Audit production setup cost calculations.* If production setup costs are included in inventory unit costs, there is a possibility of substantial costing errors if the assumed number of units produced in a production run is incorrect. For example, if the cost of a production setup is $1,000 and the production run is 1,000 units, then the setup cost should be $1 per unit. However, if someone wanted to artificially increase the cost of inventory in order to create a jump in profits, the assumed production run size could be reduced. In the example, if the production run assumption were dropped to 100 units, the cost per unit would increase tenfold to $10. A reasonable control over this problem is to regularly review setup cost calculations. An early warning indicator of this problem is to run a report comparing setup costs over time for each product to see if there are any sudden changes in costs. Also, access to the computer file storing this information should be strictly limited.

3. *Compare unextended product costs to those for prior periods.* Product costs of all types can change for a variety of reasons. An easy way to spot these changes is to create and regularly review a report that compares the unextended cost of each product to its cost in a prior period. Any significant changes can then be traced back to the underlying costing information to see exactly what caused each change. The main problem with this control is that many less expensive accounting systems do not retain historical inventory records. If so, the information should be exported to an electronic spreadsheet or separate database once a month, where historical records can then be kept.

4. *Review sorted list of extended product costs in declining dollar order.* This report is more commonly available than the historical tracking report noted in the

last numbered point, but contains less information. The report lists the extended cost of all inventory on hand for each inventory item, sorted in declining order of cost. By scanning the report, items that have unusually large or small valuations can be spotted readily. However, finding these items requires some knowledge of what costs were in previous periods. Also, a lengthy inventory list makes the efficient location of costing problems difficult. Thus, from a control perspective, this report is inferior to the unextended historical cost comparison report.

5. *Control updates to bill of material and labor routing costs.* The key sources of costing information are the bill of materials and labor routing records for each product. It is easy to make a few modifications to these records in order to substantially alter inventory costs. To prevent such changes from occurring, impose strict security access to these records. If the accounting software has a change tracking feature that stores data about who made changes and what changes were made, then be sure to use this feature. If used, periodically print a report (if available) detailing all changes made to the records and scan it for evidence of unauthorized access.

6. *Review inventory for obsolete items.* The single largest cause of inventory valuation errors is the presence of large amounts of obsolete inventory. To avoid this problem, periodically print a report that lists which inventory items have *not* been used recently, including the extended cost of these items. A more accurate variation is to print a report itemizing all inventory items for which there are no current production requirements (possible only if a material requirements planning system is in place). Alternatively, a report that compares the amount of inventory on hand to annual historical usage of each item can be used. With this information, schedule regular meetings with the materials manager to determine what inventory items should be scrapped, sold off, or returned to suppliers.

7. *Verify the calculation and allocation of overhead cost pools.* Overhead costs are usually assigned to inventory as the result of a manually derived summarization and allocation of overhead costs. This can be a lengthy calculation, subject to error. The best control over this process is a standard procedure that clearly defines which costs to include in the pools and precisely how these costs are to be allocated. In addition, regularly review the types of costs included in the calculations, verify that the correct proportions of these costs are included, and ensure that the costs are being correctly allocated to inventory. A further control is to track the total amount of overhead accumulated in each reporting period; any sudden change in the amount may indicate an error in the overhead cost summarization.

Fixed Assets

1. *Ensure that fixed asset purchases have appropriate prior authorization.* A company with a capital-intensive infrastructure may find that its most important controls are over the authorization of funds for new or replacement capital projects. Depending on the potential amount of funding involved, these controls may include a complete net present value (NPV) review of the cash flows associated with each prospective investment, as well as multilayered approvals that reach all the way up to the board of directors. A truly comprehensive control system will also include a postcompletion review that compares the original cash flow estimates to those actually achieved, not only to see if a better estimation process can be used in the future, but also to see if any deliberate misrepresentation of estimates was initially made.

2. *Compare capital investment projections to actual results.* Managers have been known to make overly optimistic projections in order to make favorable cases for asset acquisitions. This issue can be mitigated by conducting regular reviews of the results of asset acquisitions in comparison to initial predictions and then tracing these findings back to the initiating managers. This approach can also be used at various milestones during the asset construction to ensure that costs incurred match original projections.

3. *Verify that correct depreciation calculations are being made.* Incorrect depreciation calculations do not pose any potential loss of assets, but erroneous calculations can result in an embarrassing adjustment to the previously reported financial results at some point in the future. This control should include a comparison of capitalized items to the official corporate capitalization limit, in order to ensure that items are not being inappropriately capitalized and depreciated. The control should also include a review of the asset categories in which each individual asset has been recorded, in order to ensure that an asset has not been misclassified and therefore incorrectly depreciated.

4. *Verify the fair value assumptions on dissimilar asset exchanges.* Accounting rules allow for the recording of a gain or loss on the exchange of dissimilar assets. Because this calculation is based on the fair value of the assets involved (which is not already clearly stated in the accounting records), the possibility exists for someone to artificially create an asset fair value that will result in a gain or loss. This situation can be avoided by having an outside appraiser review the fair value assumptions used in this type of transaction.

5. *Ensure that capital construction projects are not delayed for accounting reasons.* Accounting rules require the capitalization of the interest expense associated with the construction of certain types of assets. By artificially delaying the completion date of an asset, or by delaying the official completion date for accounting purposes, the time period over which interest expense can be ascribed to a project and capitalized as part of its cost can be extended improperly, thereby reducing the overall corporate interest expense and increasing profits. This problem can be avoided by personally reviewing the physical status of construction projects in relation to planning documents, such as Gantt charts, and determining the validity of reasons for delays in completion.

6. *Verify that fixed asset disposals are properly authorized.* A company does not want to have a fire sale of its assets taking place without any member of the management team knowing about it. Consequently, the sale of assets should be properly authorized prior to any sale transaction being initiated, if only to ensure that the eventual price paid by the buyer is a reasonable one.

7. *Verify that cash receipts from asset sales are properly handled.* Employees may sell a company's assets, pocket the proceeds, and report to the company that the asset was actually scrapped. This control issue can be reduced by requiring that a bill of sale or receipt from a scrapping company accompany the file for every asset that has been disposed of.

8. *Verify that fixed assets are being utilized.* Many fixed assets are parked in a corner and neglected, with no thought to their being profitably sold off. To see if this problem is occurring, the accounting staff should conduct a periodic review of all fixed assets, which should include a visual inspection and discussion with employees to see if assets are no longer in use.

9. *Test for asset impairment.* In a variety of circumstances, the net book value of an asset should be reduced to its fair value, which can result in significant reductions in the recorded value of an asset. This test requires a significant knowledge of the types of markets in which a company operates, the regulations to which it is subject, and the need for its products within those markets. Consequently, only a knowledgeable person who is at least at the level of a controller should be relied on to detect the presence of assets whose values are likely to have been impaired.

Current Liabilities

1. *Include an accrual review in the closing procedure for bonuses, commissions, property taxes, royalties, sick time, vacation time, unpaid wages, and warranty*

claims. There are many possible expenses for which an accrual is needed, given the size and repetitive nature of some expenses. This control is designed to force a continual review of every possible current liability as part of the standard monthly closing procedure, so that no key accruals are missed.

2. *Review accrual accounts for unreversed entries.* Some accruals, such as unpaid wage accruals and commission accruals, are supposed to be reversed in the following period, when the actual expense is incurred. However, if an accountant forgets to properly set up a journal entry for automatic reversal in the next period, a company will find itself having recorded too large an expense. A simple control point is to include in the period-end closing procedure a review of all accounts in which accrual entries are made, to ensure that all reversals have been completed.

3. *Create standard entries for reversing journal entries.* As a continuation of the last control point, an easy way to avoid problems with accrual journal entries that are supposed to be reversed is to create boilerplate journal entry formats in the accounting system that are preconfigured to be reversed automatically in the next period. As long as these standard formats are used, there will never be an unreversed journal entry.

4. *Include a standard review of customer advances in the closing procedure.* If a company regularly deals with a large number of customer deposits, there is a significant risk that the deposits will not be recognized as revenue in conjunction with the completion of any related services or product sales. This problem can be avoided by requiring a periodic review of the status of each deposit as part of the period-end closing procedure.

5. *Include an accrual review in the closing procedure for income taxes payable.* A common practice is to accrue for income taxes only on a quarterly basis, when estimated taxes are due. The trouble is that this process results in the exclusion of a substantial expense from all monthly financial statements that do not fall at the end of each reporting quarter and so tends to skew the reported results of those months. By including in the closing procedure a line item requiring the accrual of an income tax liability, the accounting staff is forced to address this issue every time financial statements are issued.

6. *Maintain historical expense information about warranty claims both for ongoing product sales and new product introductions.* If a company creates a warranty expense accrual for a new product based on its standard claim rate for existing products, the warranty expense will probably be underaccrued for the initial introductory period of the product since more product problems

will arise early in a product launch that are corrected in later models. A good control over this underreporting is to track warranty expenses separately for new model introductions and ongoing sales, so a reasonable basis of information can be used for each type of accrual.

7. *Match the final monthly payroll pay date to the last day of the month.* The unpaid wage accrual can be significant when employee pay dates differ substantially from the last day of the reporting period. This problem can be partially resolved by setting the last (or only) pay date of the month on the last day of the month and by paying employees through that date, which eliminates the need for any wage accrual. This control is most effective for salaried employees, who are typically paid through the pay date. There is usually a cutoff for hourly employees that is several days prior to the pay date, so some wage accrual would still be necessary for these employees.

8. *Automate the period-end cutoff.* A common closing activity is to compare the receiving department's receiving log for the few days near period-end to the supplier invoices logged in during that period, to see if there are any receipts for which there are no supplier invoices. This is a slow and error-prone activity. A good alternative is to use the computer system to locate missing invoices automatically. The key requirements are a purchase order system covering all significant purchases, as well as rapid updating of the inventory database by the warehouse staff when items are received. If these features exist, a batch program can be written linking the purchase order, inventory, and accounting databases and comparing inventory receipts to received invoices. If no invoice exists, the program calculates the price of the missing invoice based on the purchase order. It then creates a report for the accounting staff itemizing all receipts for which there are no invoices and calculating the price of the missing invoices. This report can be used as the basis for a journal entry at month-end to record missing invoices.

9. *Create a standard checklist of recurring supplier invoices to include in the month-end cutoff.* A number of invoices arrive after month-end that are related to services and for which an accrual should be made. The easiest way to be assured of making these accruals is to create a list of recurring invoices, with their approximate amounts, and use it as a check-off list during the closing process. If the invoice has not yet arrived, then accrue for the standard amount shown on the list.

10. *Automate or sidestep the matching process.* The most common way to establish the need for a payment to a supplier is to compare an incoming supplier invoice to the authorizing purchase order and to receiving

documentation to ensure that the item billed has been accepted. If both these sources of information agree with the invoice, then the accounts payable staff can proceed with payment. The trouble is that this process is terribly inefficient and highly error-prone. There are three ways to improve this critical control point:

- *Use matching automation software.* Most high-end accounting software packages offer an automated matching system that automatically compares all three documents and highlights mismatches for further review. The trouble is that this software is expensive; requires linked computer databases for accounting, purchasing, and the warehouse; and also still requires manual labor to reconcile any mismatches it locates.

- *Authorize payments at the receiving point.* This advanced concept requires the presence of a computer terminal at the receiving dock. Upon receipt of a shipment, the receiving staff authorizes payment by accessing the purchase order in the computer system that relates to the receipt and checking off those items received. The computer system then schedules a payment without any supplier invoice. This approach is theoretically the most efficient way to control the payables process, but requires considerable custom programming, as well as training of the receiving staff.

- *Shift payments to procurement cards.* A large proportion of all purchases are too small to require any matching process since the labor expended exceeds the value of the control. Instead, create a procurement card system and encourage employees to make purchases with the cards, up to a maximum limit. This program greatly reduces the number of transactions requiring matching, thereby focusing the attention of the accounts payable staff on just those transactions most likely to contain errors of a significant dollar value.

Contingencies

1. *Include an assessment of contingent debt guarantees in the closing procedure.* Companies tend not to review debt guarantees on a regular basis, so the sudden failure of the obligor to pay can come as a considerable surprise, resulting in the recognition of a large debt obligation. This control is designed to force a regular review of any debt guarantees as part of the regular monthly closing schedule.

2. *Include an assessment of debt covenant violations in the closing procedure.* It is not at all uncommon for a company to be unaware of debt covenant

violations until informed of them by the lender, resulting in the immediate acceleration of debt into the short-term debt category. This problem can be avoided by including a covenant review in the regular monthly closing schedule.

3. *Include an assessment of debt covenant violations in the budgeting process and interim financial planning.* Debt covenant violations are sometimes inadvertently caused by specific finance-related activities that could have been avoided if management had been aware of the impact of their actions. These problems can sometimes be avoided by including a covenant violation review in the budgeting procedure.

4. *Include an assessment of all contingency reserves in the monthly closing procedure.* Contingency reserves tend to be set up once and forgotten, although the underlying contingencies may change in size over time. A reasonable control is to require a periodic review of the size of all reserves in the monthly closing procedure as a standard line item, thereby repeatedly bringing the issue to management's attention.

Debt: General

1. *Require evidence of intent and ability to recategorize debt from short term to long term.* If a company shifts the classification of its short-term debt to the long-term debt category, this can mislead investors and creditors in regard to the company's short-term obligations. A good control is to require evidence supporting the reporting shift, such as a board motion to take on replacement long-term debt, plus a signed long-term loan to pay off the short-term debt. This documentation should be attached to the journal entry that shifts short-term debt into the long-term debt category.

2. *Require approval of the terms of all new borrowing agreements.* A senior corporate manager should be assigned the task of reviewing all prospective debt instruments to verify that their interest rate, collateral, and other requirements are not excessively onerous or conflict with the terms of existing debt agreements. It may also be useful from time to time to see if a lending institution has inappropriate ties to the company, such as partial or full ownership in its stock by the person responsible for obtaining debt agreements.

3. *Require supervisory approval of all borrowings and repayments.* As was the case with the preceding control point, high-level supervisory approval is required for all debt instruments—except this time it is for final approval of each debt commitment. If the debt to be acquired is extremely large, it may

be useful to have a policy requiring approval by the board of directors, just to be sure that there is full agreement at all levels of the organization regarding the nature of the debt commitment. To be a more useful control, this signing requirement should be communicated to the lender, so that it does not inadvertently accept a debt agreement that has not been signed by the proper person.

Debt: Extinguishment

1. *Include in the debt procedure a line item to charge unamortized discounts or premiums to expense proportionate to the amount of any extinguished debt.* The general ledger accountant may not remember to write off any unamortized discount or premium when debt is extinguished, so the debt extinguishment procedure should include a line item requiring that this task be addressed. Otherwise, expense recognition potentially could be delayed until the original payment date of the debt, which may be many years in the future.

2. *Report to the board of directors the repayment status of all debt. GAAP requires that all unamortized discounts and premiums be recognized in the current period if there is no reasonable chance that the debt will be repaid.* Since this acceleration has a significant impact on reported earnings in the current period, there may be some unwillingness to classify debt as unable to be paid. By requiring a standard report to the board of directors regarding the status of debt repayments at each of its meetings, the board can decide on its own when amortization must be accelerated and can force management to do so.

Convertible Equity

1. *Verify the market value of equity on conversion dates when the market value method is used.* If a company uses the market value method to record the conversion of debt to equity, it is possible to influence the gain or loss recorded, depending on fluctuations in the stock price from day to day. Accordingly, the market price of the stock should be independently matched to the date on which the conversion took place. Also, it is possible to include in the conversion procedure a fill-in blank where the stock price can be noted, dated, and initialed. This approach makes it much easier to trace transactions, and also holds accountants responsible for their entries.

2. *Verify the market value of equity on debt retirement dates when offsetting equity entries are being reversed.* When a convertible bond is issued with its equity

conversion feature already in the money, the intrinsic value of the equity portion of the bond must be credited to the additional paid-in capital account. If the bond is later retired, the equity portion of the bond must then be removed from the additional paid-in capital account its intrinsic value on the date of the retirement. Any difference between the original and final intrinsic values is charged to either a gain or loss on the extinguishment of debt. The presence of a potential gain or loss on extinguishment makes it more likely for manipulation to occur in both the timing and the calculation of the extinguishment transaction. To ensure that the proper equity value is used, match the date of the debt retirement to the equity valuation on that date. Also, include the correct retirement calculation in the corporate accounting procedures manual to ensure that it is handled properly.

3. *Include a review of accrued interest expense on all recently converted debt.* If the terms of a company's bond agreements state that bond holders must forfeit accrued interest on converted debt, then there will be a temptation to also avoid recording this accrual on the books as an expense, as is required by GAAP. Consequently, the formal procedure used to convert debt to equity should include a line item for the general ledger accountant to record this accrued interest expense and also require a signature on the procedure to ensure its completion.

4. *Verify expense calculations associated with any sweetened conversion offers.* GAAP requires the recognition of a debt conversion expense associated with any completed conversion from bonds to equity, in the incremental amount of the net increase in fair value of stock obtained through a sweetened conversion offer. Since this results in an added expense, there will be a tendency simply to process the total conversion and not recognize the incremental expense, which could be substantial. Accordingly, a copy of the relevant portions of the original bond agreement should be attached to any journal entry that records a conversion to equity, which provides documentation of the initial conversion price. When the calculation is verified by an internal auditor or senior accounting person, this provides documentation of the initial baseline conversion price.

Legal Capital and Capital Stock

1. *Independent substantiation must be obtained to verify the valuation of stock issued in exchange for goods and services received.* When stock is swapped for goods or services, the stock is valued at the fair value of the goods or

services. Since the offsetting debit is to an expense, the amount of this valuation can have a major impact on reported profit levels. This control is designed to force the accounting staff to go through the steps of obtaining outside verification of the fair value at which they have chosen to record the transaction.

Treasury Stock

1. *Require the use of a separate additional paid-in capital account for treasury stock transactions.* If treasury stock is resold to investors at a loss, the loss is first charged to any remaining gains from previous treasury stock sales, with remaining losses being offset against the retained earnings account. Since a reduction in the retained earnings balance can be construed as a reduced level of financial performance, there is an incentive to charge these losses elsewhere. A typical ploy is to charge the losses to the general additional paid-in capital account, which usually contains a much larger balance than the additional paid-in capital account for treasury stock. By creating the separate additional paid-in capital account for treasury stock and requiring its use in all treasury stock procedures, it is much less likely that treasury stock losses will be diverted away from the retained earnings account.

2. *Require board approval of all stock repurchases conducted under greenmail situations.* A normal treasury stock transaction has no impact on expenses, but a greenmail situation does since the difference between the market price and usually much higher price paid must be charged to expense. It is clearly in the interests of a company not to record this incremental expense since it can result in a massive reduction in profits during the period when the payment is made. Consequently, the board should be made aware of the expense consequences when it approves a greenmail stock repurchase.

Stock Appreciation Rights (SAR)

1. *Include SAR compensation expense accruals in the standard closing procedure.* A company could delay or ignore any changes in the value of SAR grants to its employees, thereby avoiding the recognition of any associated compensation expense. This problem can be avoided by including the accrual as a standard action item in the monthly closing procedure. The issue can also be highlighted by including it as a footnote attached to the financial statements, thereby requiring periodic updating of the footnote information.

2. *Use a standard stock valuation form when calculating SAR compensation expense.* A company can use a variety of methods for determining the market value of company stock as part of its recognition of compensation expense, especially when the shares are not publicly traded. This can give rise to different methods being used over time, depending on which one results in the smallest compensation expense recognition. The best way to avoid this problem is to create a standard calculation form, which forces the use of a single calculation format for all SAR-related compensation expense calculations.

Revenue Recognition

1. *Compare the shipping log and shipping documents to invoices issued at period-end.* This control is designed to spot billings on transactions not completed until after the reporting period had closed. An invoice dated within a reporting period whose associated shipping documentation shows the transaction as having occurred later is clear evidence of improper revenue reporting. If invoices are based on services instead of goods provided, then invoices can be matched to service reports or time sheets instead.

2. *Issue financial statements within one day of the period-end.* By eliminating the gap between the end of the reporting period and the issuance of financial statements, it is impossible for anyone to create additional invoices for goods shipping subsequent to the period-end, thereby automatically eliminating any cutoff problems.

3. *Compare customer-requested delivery dates to actual shipment dates.* If customer order information is loaded into the accounting computer system, run a comparison of the dates on which customers have requested delivery to the dates on which orders were actually shipped. If there is an ongoing tendency to make shipments substantially early, there may be a problem with trying to create revenue by making early shipments. Of particular interest is when there is a surge of early shipments in months when revenues would otherwise have been low, indicating a clear intention to increase revenues by avoiding customer-mandated shipment dates. It may be possible to program the computer system to not allow the recording of deliveries if the entered delivery date is prior to the customer-requested delivery date, thereby effectively blocking early revenue recognition.

4. *Compare invoice dates to the recurring revenue database.* In cases where a company obtains a recurring revenue stream by billing customers periodically for maintenance or subscription services, there can be a temptation to

create early billings in order to record revenue somewhat sooner. For example, a billing on a 12-month subscription could be issued after 11 months, thereby accelerating revenue recognition by 1 month. This issue can be spotted by comparing the total of recurring billings in a month to the total amount of recurring revenue for that period as compiled from the corporate database of customers with recurring revenue. Alternatively, the recurring billing dates for a small sample of customers can be compared to the dates on which invoices were actually issued.

5. *Identify shipments of product samples in the shipping log.* A product that is shipped with no intention of being billed is probably a product sample being sent to a prospective customer, marketing agency, and so on. These should be noted as product samples in the shipping log, and the internal audit staff should verify that each of them was properly authorized, preferably with a signed document.

6. *Verify that a signed acknowledgment of bill and hold transaction has been received for every related transaction.* If a company uses bill and hold transactions, then this control is absolutely mandatory. By ensuring that customers have agreed in advance to be billed for items to be kept in the company's warehouse, the controller can be assured of being in compliance with the strict GAAP rules applying to these transactions. Also, a continual verification of this paperwork will keep managers from incorrectly inflating revenues by issuing false bill and hold transactions.

7. *Confirm signed acknowledgment of bill and hold transactions with customers.* If a company begins to match bill and hold acknowledgment letters to invoices issued to customers (see last control), the logical reaction of any person who wants to fraudulently continue issuing bill and hold invoices is to create dummy acknowledgments. Consequently, it is useful to contact the persons who allegedly signed the acknowledgements to verify that they actually did so.

8. *Do not accept any product returns without an authorization number.* Customers will sometimes try to return products if there is no justification required, thereby clearing out their inventories at the expense of the company. This can be avoided by requiring a return authorization number, which must be provided by the company in advance and prominently noted on any returned goods. If the number is not shown, the receiving department is required to reject the shipment.

9. *Compare related company addresses and names to customer list.* Comparing the list of company subsidiaries to the customer list enables the determination of whether any intercompany sales have occurred and if these

transactions have all been appropriately backed out of the financial statements. Because employees at one subsidiary may conceal this relationship by using a false company name or address, the same information at all the other subsidiaries must be verified by matching subsidiary names and addresses to their supplier lists, as it is possible that the receiving companies are *not* trying to hide the intercompany sales information.

Revenue: Barter

1. *Require a written business case for all barter transactions.* Require the creation of a business case detailing why a barter transaction is required and what type of accounting should be used for it. The case should be approved by a senior-level manager before any associated entry is made in the general ledger. The case should be attached to the associated journal entry and filed. This approach makes it less likely that sham barter swap transactions will be created.

Revenue: Cash Payments to Customers

1. *Verify that cash-back payments to customers are charged to sales.* Compare the customer list to the cash disbursements register to highlight all cash payments made to customers. Investigate each one and verify that the revenue account was debited in those instances where cash-back payments were made. This should not apply to the return of overpayments made by customers to the company.

Revenue: Recording Transactions at Gross or Net

1. *Create a revenue accounting procedure to specify the treatment of gross or net transactions.* When a company deals with both gross and net revenue transactions on a regular basis, there should be a procedure that clearly defines for the accounting staff the situations under which revenues shall be treated on a gross or net basis. This reduces the need for internal audit reviews (see next control) to detect revenue accounting problems after the fact.
2. *Review the revenue accounting for potential pass-through transactions.* In situations where there is either an extremely high cost of goods sold (indicating a possible pass-through transaction) or where there is no clear evidence of the company acting as principal, taking title to goods, or accepting risk of ownership, the internal audit staff should review the appropriateness of the transaction.

3. *Trace commission payments back to underlying sale transactions.* Keep a list of all business partners who pay the company commissions, and run a periodic search on all payments made by them to the company. The internal audit staff can then trace these payments back to the underlying sales made by the company and verify that they were recorded at net, rather than at gross.

Revenue: Long-Term Construction Contracts

1. *Compare declared percentage of completion to estimated work required to complete projects.* A very common way to record excessive revenue on a construction project is to falsely state that the percentage of completion is greater than the actual figure, thereby allowing the company to record a greater proportion of revenues in the current period. Although difficult to verify with any precision, a reasonable control is to match the declared percentage of completion to a percentage of the actual hours worked, divided by the total estimated number of hours worked. The two percentages should match.

2. *Ensure that project expenses are charged to the correct account.* A common problem with revenue recognition under the percentage of completion method is that extra expenses may be erroneously or falsely loaded into a project's general ledger account, which can then be used as the justification for the recognition of additional revenue related to that project. Auditing expenses in active project accounts can spot these problems.

3. *Promptly close project accounts once projects are completed.* It is not a difficult matter to store project-related expenses incorrectly in the wrong accounts, and may be done fraudulently in order to avoid recognizing losses related to excessive amounts of expenses being incurred on specific projects. This problem can be resolved by promptly closing general ledger project accounts once the related projects are complete. Closing project accounts can be included in the month-end closing procedure, thereby ensuring that this problem will be addressed on a regular basis.

4. *Control access to general ledger accounts.* Employees are less likely to shift expenses between general ledger construction accounts if they are unable to access the accounts, or if they have no way of reopening closed accounts. This can be achieved by tightly restricting account access and especially access to the closed or open status flag for each account.

5. *Compare the dates on supplier invoices in the construction-in-progress account to the project start date.* Since precontract costs must be charged to expense,

there is a temptation to hold these supplier invoices until after the project contract has been signed, so they can be stored in the construction-in-progress account instead as an asset. To detect this problem, examine a selection of invoiced expenses in the account to see if any are dated prior to the project's contract date.

6. *Review journal entries shifting expenses into construction-in-progress accounts.* Since precontract costs must be charged to expense, there is a temptation to increase short-term profits by shifting these expenses into the construction-in-progress account with a journal entry. To spot this problem, review all journal entries adding expenses to the construction-in-progress account.

7. *Consistently aggregate expenses into overhead accounts and charge them to individual projects.* Different overhead expenses could be charged to various projects or the same pool of overhead costs could be applied inconsistently to the accounts, thereby effectively shifting expenses to those projects that would result in the greatest revenue increase under the percentage of completion revenue recognition method. To avoid this problem, periodically verify that the same expenses are being consistently charged to overhead cost pools over time and that the same allocation method is used to shift these expenses from the overhead cost pools to project accounts.

8. *Exclude the cost of unused materials from cost-to-cost percentage of completion calculations.* Typically, at the beginning of a project, more materials than are initially needed are purchased. This increases the amount of recognizable revenue early in a project when the cost-to-cost percentage of completion method is used. To avoid this problem, remove all unused materials from the calculation.

9. *Compare the percentage of revenues recognized to expenses recognized.* When revenues associated with a project are recognized, a second entry must be made to shift costs from the construction-in-progress account to the cost of goods sold. If this second entry is missed for any reason, profits will be unusually high. To spot this problem, compare the amount of recognized revenue to recognized expenses for each project and verify that it matches the most recent gross profit estimate for the project. If the percentage is higher, some expenses probably have not been recognized.

10. *Review prospective project issues with the construction manager.* A common fraud involving project accounting is to shift the timing and amount of recognized losses on projects. These losses can be delayed in order to make the current period's results look better or can be made excessively large or small in order to meet reporting targets. Although it is quite difficult to ascertain if the size of a loss is correct, it is possible to guess *when* a loss

should be recognized. By having regular discussions with a project's construction manager regarding ongoing and upcoming project-related issues, it is possible to see when significant unbudgeted costs are to be incurred, thereby giving some insight into the need for loss recognition.

11. *Watch for expense loading on cost-plus contracts.* When a company is guaranteed by the customer to pay for all expenses incurred, there exists a temptation to load extra expenses into an account. These expense additions can be spotted by looking for charges from suppliers whose costs are not normally charged to a specific type of contract, as well as by looking for expense types that increase significantly over expenses incurred in previous periods, and by investigating any journal entries that increase expense levels.

Revenue: Service Activities

1. *Review underlying contract terms for all proportional performance revenue calculations.* The proportional performance method is the most aggressive service revenue calculation method, in that revenues can be recognized earlier than with most other revenue recognition methods. For this control, trace each revenue-creation journal entry back to the related service contract and verify that collection is reasonably assured and that billings are not tied to specific actions. If either of these cases holds true, other more conservative revenue recognition methods must be used that may reduce the amount of revenue recognized.

2. *Regularly review service contracts for potential losses.* Losses on service contracts must be recognized as expenses immediately, even if the losses are only estimated. Since there is a natural reluctance to recognize losses in advance of the actual event, a good control is to include a standard review of estimated losses on service contracts as part of the monthly closing process.

Revenue Recognition When Collection Is Uncertain

1. *Verify that the correct gross margin percentage is used for the recognition of gross margins upon the receipt of cash.* The gross margins associated with installment sales should be deferred until the related cash payments are received from customers. This margin typically is aggregated for all sales within a specific time period and used for all receipts related to that time period. If the gross margin percentage for a different period were to be incorrectly used to recognize gross margin dollars, there would be an impact on the reported level of profitability. The best control over this issue

is a procedure clearly stating how to calculate, track, and apply gross margins when cash is received. A secondary control is a regular review of all calculations made to recognized gross margins.

Revenue Recognition When Right of Return Exists

1. *Include a sales return allowance calculation in the standard closing procedure.* By requiring someone to address the issue of return allowances as part of every period-end close, there is a much greater chance that the allowance amount will be verified against actual returns, resulting in an accurate return allowance.
2. *Verify the amount of the return allowance against actual experience.* Examine the basis for a specific returns allowance amount being recorded, comparing it to actual experience with the same or similar products in the recent past. However, this is an after-the-fact control that must be repeated regularly to ensure that allowance levels are reasonable.
3. *Review the condition of returned inventory.* Sales returns tend not to be in pristine condition, so a company must record a write-down to their fair value at the time of the return. However, the warehouse staff tends to place them back in stock without any consideration of condition, resulting in the overstatement of finished goods inventory. A good control is to have all sales returns set to one side for review, after which they are either shifted back to stock at full value, thrown away, donated, or reclassified as used stock and assigned a reduced inventory value.

Accounting for Leases: Lessee

1. *Verify existence of leased assets.* A leasing agency could continue to charge a company for lease payments even after the underlying asset has been returned or a fraudulent employee could sell off or take custody of an asset, leaving the company to continue making the lease payments. In either case, the assets listed on lease invoices should be traced periodically to the actual assets.
2. *Verify correct depreciation period for assets acquired under a capital lease.* Under a capital lease, the lessee must depreciate the assets acquired under the terms of the lease. If the asset were to be recorded in the fixed assets tracking module of the accounting system in the normal manner, this is likely to result in a system-designated depreciation period. Such a depreciation period is acceptable if the capital lease involves a transfer of ownership. However, if the lessor retains ownership at the end of the lease, the depreciation period must be limited to the lease term. Using a

shorter depreciation period will increase the periodic depreciation expense, so this issue has an impact on earnings. Consequently, verification of the depreciation period should be a standard review item in the month-end closing procedure.

3. *Ensure that the financial analysis staff is aware of all scheduled lease payments.* If a company uses leases for a large part of its financing needs, lease payments may comprise a significant part of its cash flow planning. If so, the person responsible for the cash forecast should be kept aware of the stream of required lease payments for all leases, as well as any changes in those payments, and any guaranteed residual values that must be paid to the lessor at the end of a lease. This can be accomplished most easily by requiring the legal department to send a copy of each signed lease document to the accounting department, where the leases can be summarized for cash planning purposes.

Accounting for Leases: Lessor

1. *Include in the annual accounting activity calendar a review of residual asset values.* The lessor is required by GAAP to conduct at least an annual review of the residual value of all leased assets and to adjust those valuations downward if there appear to be permanent valuation reductions. Any such adjustment will result in the recognition of a loss, so there is a natural tendency to avoid or delay this step. By including it in the standard schedule of activities, the accounting staff is more likely to conduct it.

Lease Terminations

1. *Match the date of the lease termination notification to the recognition of any losses associated with the termination.* Management can alter the timing of losses related to lease terminations by recognizing the losses later than the date of the termination notification. This control requires that the losses be recognized in the period of notification. The control is best included in a standard review procedure, to ensure that it is consistently followed and enforced.

Translation of Foreign Currency: Financial Statements

1. *Gain external auditor approval of any changes in translation method.* A key difference between the current rate and remeasurement methods of translation is that translation adjustments under the current rate method are placed in the balance sheet, whereas adjustments under

the remeasurement method are recognized on the income statement as gains or losses. The accounting staff could be tempted to shift between the two methods in order to show specific financial results on the corporate income statement. For example, if there were a translation gain, the remeasurement method likely would be used in order to recognize it on the income statement. This problem is especially likely when the criteria for using one method over the other could be construed either way. The best way to avoid this problem is to have a disinterested third party (i.e., the auditors) approve any change in method over what was used in the preceding year.

2. *Require management approval of calculations for the status of inflationary economies.* It is possible to alter the translation method based on the inflationary status of a foreign economy, possibly resulting in the recognition (or not) of translation gains or losses on the income statement. If an accountant were inclined to shift the translation method, a defensible basis for doing so is the inflationary status of the economy in which a foreign entity does business. The inflationary status could be altered either by using incorrect inflation data or shifting the beginning and ending dates of the calculation to correspond to inflation data more in line with the required result. This issue can be resolved by requiring management or internal audit reviews of these calculations, especially when a change in inflationary status has occurred recently.

Translation of Foreign Currency: Transactions

1. *Verify that all gains and losses on incomplete currency transactions are updated in the periodic financial statements.* If there have been unusually large fluctuations in the exchange rates of those currencies in which a company has outstanding transactions, there may be a temptation to avoid recording any interim gains or losses prior to settlement of the transactions, on the grounds that the temporary fluctuations will even out prior to settlement. However, this ongoing delay in recognition of gains and losses not only misstates financial statements, but also can build over time into much larger gains or losses, which can come as quite a shock to the users of the financial statements when the changes are eventually recognized. Accordingly, the standard checklist for completing financial statements should itemize the recognition of interim gains and losses on incomplete foreign exchange transactions.

ELEMENTS OF INTERNAL ACCOUNTING CONTROL

Seven basic elements are necessary to meet the broad objectives of good internal accounting control—objectives that include safeguarding the assets against loss arising from intentional (fraud) or unintentional errors and producing reliable financial records for internal use and for external reporting purposes. These elements are:

1. *Competent and trustworthy personnel, with clearly defined lines of authority and responsibility.* People are the most important ingredient in a control system. If employees are competent and trustworthy, then reliable financial statements can result even though other control elements are missing. Incompetent and dishonest personnel, even given a theoretically good system of controls, will produce worthless statements. Thus, a proper evaluation of employees is paramount.

2. *Adequate separation of duties.* To prevent intentional or unintentional errors, several separations are desirable:
   - *Separation of operating responsibility from financial record keeping.* In those instances where an operating department maintains its own records and prepares its own financial reports, there is a temptation to bias data to report improved performance. Grouping of the financial records under a controller is desirable.
   - *Separation of custody of the assets.* Separation of accounting from custody is done to protect the company against defalcation. Thus the separation of custody of cash from maintenance of the accounts receivable is desirable to reduce the possibility of converting cash to personal use and adjusting the customer account by a fictitious credit.
   - *Separation of the authorization of transactions from the custody of any related assets.* For example, the person authorizing the payment of an invoice should not sign the check that pays the bill.
   - *Separation of duties within the accounting function.* Those maintaining the general ledger should be separated from those handling the subsidiary ledger, or those handling cash journals should be separated from those handling sales journals.

3. *Proper procedures for authorization of transactions.* Authorizations may be general or specific, depending on management desires. Management may give general approval for sales to customers, given a certain credit approval. Or management may desire to approve each contract above a given amount, say $10 million.

4. *Adequate records and documents.* The documents must provide reasonable assurance that the transaction is properly recorded and that the asset is controlled. Thus purchase orders, receiving reports, and vendor invoices should exist.

5. *Proper physical control over both assets and records.* Properly controlled warehouses, safety deposit vaults, and fireproof safes are examples of physical control. Proper safeguard of records against destruction or other loss is necessary.

6. *Proper procedures for adequate record keeping.* Procedures to assure the proper recording of all transactions—such as procedure manuals—may be desirable.

7. *A staff that can provide independent verifications.* The existence of an internal audit staff, or other means of checking, may be helpful.

 ## LEVELS OF CONTROLS

In reviewing internal controls, the greatest amount of time usually is spent in analyzing and evaluating the very detailed controls that exist. And perhaps this is the way it should be. However, given the responsibilities of the board of directors and top management, the ultimate purpose of the system is to aid in meeting the business goals and objectives. Hence the control system to be reviewed should include all levels of planning and related control. All these levels can be included in three groups:

1. *Strategic. Board of directors and top management, who plan and control:*
   ▪ Organizational structure
   ▪ Corporate goals and objectives
   ▪ Long-range planning procedures
   ▪ Marketing policy decision making
   ▪ Management policy decision making
   ▪ Financial policy decision making

2. *Tactical. Board of directors and senior management, who plan and control:*
   ▪ Annual profit plans
   ▪ Executive–personnel policies (inventories, replacement)
   ▪ Capital expenditures
   ▪ Annual research and development plan

3. *Operational, where planning and control involves:*
   ▪ Credit approval practices
   ▪ Treatment of uncollectible accounts

- Billing procedure
- Purchasing procedure
- Salary and wage authorization
- Pension plan performance

Consideration has to be given to which of the controls in a company should be handled at each level and, further, which should require corporate-level (as opposed to divisional) review and approval.

 FRAUD

Fraud is an *intentional financial misstatement or the misappropriation of funds.* Fraud is not an unintentional mistake, such as an incorrect accounting estimate, the application of a cost to an incorrect account, or a lost inventory tag during a physical count.

Common Types

Fraud is a complex subject. Different types of individuals and different activities may be involved. Some of the types of fraud are management fraud, employee fraud, computer fraud, and financial reporting fraud. The controller may be curious about commonly occurring kinds of fraud. A few of the more common kinds are listed next. This list should not be considered complete because the types of fraud are limited only by the imagination of the perpetrator:

- *Generate bills from nonexistent companies.* Employees can bill the company for services from a nonexistent company. This is easy if the accounts payable staff does not review services for completion or materials for receipt. The fraud is detected by auditing billing approvals. Also, the auditor can review the numerical sequence of invoices received from the supplier to see if most of the supplier's invoices are going to the company.
- *Pay personal bills.* Employees can have the company pay their own bills for them, or have the company pay for items that were ordered for employees through the company. The fraud is detected by auditing bills received and can be prevented only by rigorous approvals of all expenses.
- *Alter approved expense amounts.* Employees can alter expense reports after supervisors have approved the reports. The fraud is difficult to detect, but auditors may be able to find altered or erased numbers on those reports.

This type of fraud can be prevented by routing expense reports directly to the accounts payable department after the supervisors approve them, so that the employees who originally submitted the reports do not have further access to the documents.

▪ *Rig bids between purchasers and suppliers.* Buyers can be influenced to accept high bids in exchange for kickbacks from suppliers. The fraud is detected by comparing winning bid amounts to market rates, and by reviewing the number of bids rejected due to spurious causes. For example, cheaper bids can be thrown out by marking the bid receipt date as being later than the posted due date (and can be audited by comparing the bidder sign-in date in the visitor log to the date posted on the bid by the purchasing department).

▪ *Submit multiple expense receipts.* Employees can submit credit card receipts in one month for reimbursement and then submit the actual receipt for reimbursement in a different month. The fraud is detected by comparing expense reports that were submitted over a period of several months.

▪ *Cancel reimbursed education.* Employees can cancel classes that have been paid for by the company and pocket the proceeds (or have the classes paid for by a second party, such as the Veteran's Administration, and keep the overpayment). The fraud is detected by getting permission to review the college's financial records for each employee. The fraud still can occur if the company only pays on proof of completion of a class because a second party can pay for the class.

▪ *Sell company assets.* Employees can sell company assets right off the company premises and have the check made out and delivered to them. The fraud is detected by frequent reviews of fixed assets records to actual assets. Prevention can be difficult if a high-level person is the perpetrator.

While the controller has an interest in preventing any type of fraud, this chapter discusses the two kinds with which he or she should be especially concerned: management fraud and financial reporting fraud.

Some Causes

If a controller is aware of the circumstances that encourage fraud, he or she may be more sensitive to signs that it has occurred. In most circumstances, and certainly when collusion is involved, there is no way to guarantee the absence of fraud. But there is reason to conclude that fraud results from a combination of pressures on the individual officer or employee and the circumstances that allow the act to occur. The conditions that lay the foundations for fraud include:

- *Poor internal controls or a poor internal control environment*
  - Management does not punish or prosecute offenders.
  - Management does not set an example of high ethical standards.
  - Management does not stress the need for strong controls.
  - Management has not published rules governing ethical conduct.
  - Highly placed executives are seen as lavish spenders on business trips.
  - The CEO approves heavy business expenditures by his or her staff despite restrictive policies and procedures.
- *Existence of heavy financial pressures on individuals*
  - Heavy personal indebtedness
  - Socially unacceptable behavior (e.g., gambling, use of drugs or alcohol)
  - Extravagant means of living
  - High inflation rates not accompanied by adequate adjustment in compensation
- *Other sources of pressure*
  - Unreasonable profit goals for the company, or for a division or subsidiary
  - High rate of management personnel turnover
  - Management operating and financial decisions dominated by a very aggressive individual
  - The company is part of a declining industry
- *Contributing conditions*
  - Inadequate hiring practices (e.g., lack of reference checks)
  - Deteriorating living environment
  - Undesirable personal traits
  - Unsatisfactory home life

Note that some of the above signs are difficult to detect.

Management Override

The responsibility for an effective internal control system rests with management. Yet some of the most widely publicized cases of improper activity are those that were carried on by a limited number of business managers themselves. These are the cases that are among the most difficult to detect.

Quite often fraud committed by senior management is more subtle than the "ordinary ways," for it involves management override. This condition occurs when executives with sufficient real or apparent authority cause subordinates to conceal or record transactions improperly, or cause documents to be processed outside of the established procedure. These executives are in a position to override the controls. Such actions may result in a material misstatement of financial results or condition and/or a defrauding of the company. The controller, along with the independent accountants and internal auditors, should be alert to, or assess the risks of, such a possibility. Management override probably would not occur under normal circumstances, but these conditions might tempt some managers:

- Management compensation is directly and substantially affected by operating results, and those results tend to be erratic.
- The management of the business unit is under extreme pressure to achieve specified earnings.
- The operating unit is in an industry experiencing a large number of business failures.
- The organization has been sold and the management will benefit from the price, which is related to operating results and financial condition.

Some of the areas where management override is more common include:

- *Reserve estimates.* Inventory reserves, reserves for doubtful accounts, tax accruals, and litigation reserves, among others, may be understated in order to increase profits.
- *Depreciation allowances.* Depreciation rates on machinery and equipment might be changed.
- *Sales.* Advance sales may be billed, or shipments may be made ahead of schedule.
- *Cost of sales.* Cost of sales may be understated, thus providing higher margins (and possibly later inventory losses).
- *Deferring expenses.* Current expenses may be capitalized on one pretext or another, to be written off over a period of time.

AUDITING FOR FRAUD

Auditing for fraud, especially for small-scale fraud, is like looking for the proverbial needle in the haystack. There are several reasons why it is so difficult to find:

- *Too many transactions.* The auditor typically reviews only a small number of transactions. If fraud is only being committed with one transaction out of many, the odds of finding the fraud are slim.
- *Ineffective use of audit time.* Looking for fraud is very time-consuming. There are hundreds, if not thousands, of ways to remove company assets illegally, and tracking down all possibilities will fill the work schedule of any internal audit staff.
- *Audits have time limits.* Like all well-run projects, fraud audits have specific time boundaries; once the completion date is reached, the audit team moves on to another audit. Since fraud audits can take considerable periods of time to uncover issues, there may not be time available to detect a suspected fraud situation.
- *Trend analysis is not sufficient.* Smaller cases of fraud will not be highlighted by analyzing expense levels over time because the small surges in expense levels will not appear significant.
- *Perpetrators know the procedures.* Those who are committing frauds may not only know the procedures being circumvented, but also may be in charge of the procedures. If so, the frauds may be cleverly concealed because the criminal parties are experts in the control procedures. The auditor, on the other hand, is not trained primarily in fraud detection, but in evaluating overall systems of controls and reporting. Thus, in terms of training or ability, the perpetrator may outclass the auditor.
- *Fraud is hard to recognize.* Fraud is difficult to detect even when looking at it. The perpetrator probably has taken a great deal of time to carry out the fraud and has either eliminated or reduced all traces of the crime. For example, when conducting an audit, how many auditors will follow up on missing documentation? The reason for the missing documentation may be simple misfiling, but it may also be deliberate misplacement to cover a fraud situation.

These points are not designed to make the auditor despair of ever uncovering a fraud; doing so is difficult, but not impossible. The question is:

What tools can be used to hone in quickly on likely fraud situations? These suggestions may help:

- *Watch the environment.* As stated several times in this chapter, the environment is a key factor. If management has a low regard for controls, that attitude may rub off on employees. If management uses the company for personal gain, then other employees may feel that it is acceptable for them to do so as well. Of course, the environment may be worse in one area; if so, then the auditor's fraud search should narrow to that area.
- *Watch the controls.* If control over an area is concentrated in one person's job, then the opportunity for fraud has been presented to that employee. The auditor should not only review such situations, but also recommend splitting responsibilities in order to remove any temptation from the employee.
- *Watch employee lifestyles.* Some perpetrators flaunt their wealth and bring their gains back to the workplace in the form of fancy automobiles or new clothes. We are not suggesting that the auditor review the parking lot each day, but an inquiring person might want to know why an accounting clerk is driving an expensive sports car.
- *Be available.* Fraud can be surprisingly well-known among employees. For the auditor to be told about such situations by employees, availability is crucial. Consequently, the successful fraud auditor is the one who talks to auditees frequently, is available at audit sites, and is known for protecting sources.

 NOTES

1. Paul G. Makosz and Bruce W. McCuaig, Gulf Canada Resources, "Is Everything under Control? A New Approach to Corporate Governance," *Financial Executive* (6, no. 1 January–February 1990): 26.
2. Adapted with permission from the Controls sections of all chapters in Bragg, *GAAP Policies and Procedures* (John Wiley & Sons, 2007).

CHAPTER THREE

Planning and the Strategic Plan

THIS CHAPTER DISCUSSES THE various elements of the strategic plan and provides an overview of the planning process. It reviews some of the basic questions raised in the planning process and considers the elements of strategic planning, for example, constructing a mission statement, factors to consider when picking objectives and strategies, and possible ways to manage the planning process. The next two chapters examine the strategic plan by looking at the qualified long-range plan and the annual plan.

STRATEGIC PLAN OVERVIEW

Strategic planning begins with the present and extends as far into the future as useful for planning purposes. The purpose of strategic planning is to set the company guidelines and policies that serve as the basis for the next echelon of plans, which are the development plan and the operations plan. The strategic plan focuses on the needs, dangers, and opportunities facing the company. It identifies the key decisions that must be made and usually sets guidelines and deadlines for making them. The process guides the company in decisions about the current generation of products as well as the next and succeeding generations of products and markets. This thinking and communicating process helps ensure that the plans and decisions of the various units are moving the company to the same agreed-on objectives.

The plan must contain these six elements:

1. *A statement of purpose.* Identifying the purpose of the plan gives the reader the reason for the action required. It sets forth the objective. The purpose of the strategic plan may be broad, but as the plans become more detailed, so also must the reasons for proposed action become more specific.
2. *Actions to take.* The purpose of formulating a plan is to take action, and the plan must stipulate what kind of action need be taken. Again, the more detailed the purpose, the more specific must be the action—from general terms in the strategic plan to minute details in a segment of an operating plan.
3. *Resources to use.* The basic task of management is to use all resources wisely. A firm's resources include not only funds but also people, plant and equipment, technical know-how, and other proprietary knowledge. Plans must indicate which resources are needed and whether they are on hand or must be acquired, to avoid a conflicting assignment or a less than optimal use of these resources.
4. *Goals to meet.* The goals define the level of accomplishment expected from the action taken. Goals answer the question: What is to result from the activity?
5. *Time schedules to follow.* Progress toward goals must be measured not only in degree of achievement but also in time.
6. *Assumptions made.* The important underlying conditions on which the plan depends must be made known to those who approve the recommendations. If these conditions do not come to pass, then the responsible executive must be made aware of this situation at planned checkpoints so that corrective action, including changes in plans, may be made.

Most companies prepare just a single budget scenario, which is their best guess regarding how the next year will turn out. This scenario is based upon a range of supporting assumptions, any one of which can lead to diverging results—and usually does. So, though the controller may spend a considerable amount of time on that "mainstream" budget scenario, just that one version will not be enough to prepare for what may—and probably will—happen.

It makes sense to add two more scenarios, one for the absolute worst case, where bankruptcy is looming, and one for the most phenomenal sales success. It is unlikely that either one will ever happen, but if a management team does not plan for success, it never *will* happen, and bankruptcy scenarios are far more frequent than one might think. Consequently, it is useful to know what resources a company will need for a phenomenally successful year, and how deeply it will have to cut expenses to avoid bankruptcy. Is that enough scenarios? No.

There are gaping holes between the two opposite-extreme scenarios and the mainstream version. Realistically, actual results will fall into either of those two holes, so the controller should spend some time figuring out what to do for situations that are somewhat above and below the mainstream scenario.

This multitude of models does not mean that a controller should spend an equal amount of time on each one. The mainstream scenario requires the most work because it is (presumably) the most likely, with less work needed for the less likely ones. Nonetheless, spend at least some time determining financial results at a high level for each scenario, and conceptualize what those situations will do to a company's operations.

The strategic plan is usually communicated to the board of directors in summary form, and typically includes these areas:

- Comparison to the prior year plan
- The major planning assumptions
- The growth strategy
- Business goals
- Perceived strengths, weaknesses, opportunities, problems, and threats
- Profit plans for the existing business
- Programs and strategies for new business development
- Financial summaries of major factors, trends, and return on assets

Remember to keep in mind, while reading about the nuts and bolts of the planning process, that it is difficult to encourage long-term thinking and planning because most companies reward their employees based on short-term results. Thus, long-term planning will not work without long-term incentive plans. Also, strategic planning still involves largely unquantifiable factors such as experience, instinct, guesswork, and luck. Finally, beware that most long-range plans involve too much quantification of rough guesses and estimates. A good plan does not require detail down to the nth degree!

SYSTEM OF PLANS

This section discusses how the various types of plans work together. But first some planning terminology is defined. A *plan* is a predetermined course of action. A *strategic plan* is the company's formal plan for achieving its objectives with policies, strategies, and detailed actions. The process of thinking ahead, of making a judgment on a course of action for which consideration has been given to the feasible alternatives, is the planning process.

An integrated planning structure has three components:

1. At the summit, or vertex, is the *strategic plan.* It seeks to outline in general terms the characteristics and objectives of the firm. As detailed later in this chapter, the plan should include a clear statement of the company's basic purpose ("Business Mission"), a set of objectives to accomplish this purpose ("Developing Long-Range Objectives"), and a detailed list of strategies needed to meet the objectives ("Developing Long-Range Strategies"). The plan should also include a statement of assumptions needed to match the goals, such as an assumed continuing increase in the national gross national product or inflation rate throughout the planning period.

2. Stemming from the strategic plan is the *development plan,* which concerns itself with the development of new products, services, and markets. It works toward:
   - Establishing those conditions that foster the creation of new products and markets
   - Gathering pertinent data to identify those fields with the highest potential return on the corporate resources. This effort also involves establishing the procedures needed to identify areas of less desirable growth
   - Determining resource requirements and the scheduling needed to implement the program as it passes into normal operations
   - The development plan includes a divestment plan for selling, merging, or shutting down parts of the business. It also includes a diversification plan for developing new products for new markets by internal development, merger, or acquisition.

3. Also proceeding from the strategic plan is the *operations plan,* which focuses largely on the existing generation of products and existing markets. It is detailed in nature and specifies plans by individual function, which in essence becomes the annual plan.

PLANNING CYCLE

A company's planning cycle is typically an iterative process and roughly follows this path:

- Set tentative goals and objectives
- Analyze expected internal and external environments in which it expects to operate for the planning period
- Make assumptions about this environment and the company's current posture
- Conduct a market analysis to determine or confirm the most effective marketing method
- Devise a marketing plan (taking into account the new products and markets, and the status of existing markets and products) for each year of the planning cycle
- Create a market support plan by year (sales strategy, required staff, advertising and sales promotion, etc.)
- Develop sales estimates by year, product, territory, and salesperson, based on the market support plan
- Complete the related organization and manpower needs throughout the rest of the company, based on the sales estimate, and itemize the costs by monthly planning period
- Develop fixed assets (facilities) plans by year of need and amount of expenditure
- Develop the financial plan (cash, cash generation, income and financial condition, time-phased)
- Reach conclusions as to whether the plan is satisfactory. If not, the iterative process may begin again until an acceptable plan is developed.
- Approve the strategic plan. Once done, the appropriate sections serve as the basis for developing a detailed annual plan.

An important part of the planning cycle is the *environmental analysis* since it is the foundation of the company's strategic direction. The company's environment has two aspects:

1. *The external environment.* The external environment consists of influences outside the company that are or will be dominant factors in its activities. The factors can include:

- *Economic.* The stage of the business cycle, level of general business activity, entrance of new competitors, stage in the industry cycle, and foreign exchange rates.
- *Technical.* New products of the same type or of a different kind that serve the same need, new processes, and new capital equipment.
- *Political.* Legislation affecting the product/activity, court decisions relating to interpretation of the laws, and administrative actions affecting the enforcement of the law.
- *Social.* Social mores change, and what may be acceptable in one country may be unacceptable in another.

2. *The internal environment.* The internal environment consists of those forces inside the company that will be significant forces in just how it will function. These factors should be considered:
   - *Company strengths and weaknesses.* This involves: (a) knowing the functions and areas in which the company performs well, (b) understanding how its strengths compare with those of competitors, and (c) reaching conclusions on whether its strong points may be improved and its weaknesses overcome. Some of the indicators to examine are:

   Bottleneck Operations or Personnel
   Product acceptability
   Share of the market
   Marketing posture
   Proprietary product status
   Manufacturing costs
   Quality control
   Product deliverability
   Patent status
   Research and development success
   Raw material sources
   Foreign market status
   Plant capacity
   Financial strength
   Judgment and skill of the management team
   Flexibility and capacity to change
   - *The success factors.* It is vital to know what particular attributes are responsible for the company's success. It may be such characteristics as

good quality control, quick response time to sales orders, personality of the representatives, solid engineering, and so on.

▪ *Status of each product in each market segment.* Included in this grouping might be:

   ▪ Understanding the life-cycle stage of each product (embryonic, growth, mature, declining)

   ▪ Understanding each business segment as to market share and growth rate, according to the Boston Consulting Group matrix, as either:

      * A *star:* high market share, high growth rate
      * A *cash cow:* high market share, low growth rate, significant generator of cash
      * A *wildcat:* low market share, high growth rate; probably a cash user until the product is more developed
      * A *dog:* low market share, low growth; a candidate for divestment

Those who know the market and the product must be able to reach objective decisions about each. Knowledge of these internal and external factors is important in deciding on the corporate mission and the strategy needed to reach the corporate objectives.

 ## PLANNING ROLES

The CEO is responsible to the board of directors for the strategic plans of the company; therefore, the CEO is the chief long-range planner. However, the long-range planning process must involve most members of management. Accordingly, *who* does the planning will depend on the company's circumstances. The planning could involve only the CEO; or the chief executive and his or her staff; or a committee composed of representatives of each major discipline or each major operating group; or even a separate permanent planning department that would provide leadership and coordination of the process, with adequate support from the chief line and staff officers.

Which of these options it will be hinges on several factors, including:

▪ *The stage of evolution of planning in the company.* If the planning is informal and sporadic, the chances are that the chief executive will be the chief planner, with limited assistance from others.

- *The attitude of the CEO.* This may determine the breadth or depth of the planning activity. Support from this source is a must for effective planning.
- *The size of the company.* Generally, the larger the company, the more likely it is to make formal long-range plans.
- *The nature of the company's markets.* Military suppliers, for example, often do more planning than consumer goods manufacturers.

In general, a balanced planning group containing several disciplines is desirable; these disciplines should include marketing, engineering, finance, human resources, and research.

The controller's role is obvious in the later stages of converting strategies into financial terms for the planning period. However, there is also work to be done in the earlier phases of strategic planning in these areas:

- *The corporate mission.* The mission is determined based on a thorough knowledge of the company's strengths and weaknesses and a host of subjective opinions. If erroneous financial or economic assumptions are used, then the controller should disclose them and provide alternative suggestions.
- *The corporate long-range objectives.* The controller should make any analysis for long-range objectives based on financial facts or calculations.
- *Developing strategies.* The controller should conduct the financial analysis related to some of the strategies. Areas to analyze would include the profit impact of alternative choices or relative to cost effectiveness, unrealistic earnings estimates of proposed acquisitions, unduly optimistic economic assumptions, an excessive inflation rate, excessive use of bottleneck operations, or cost estimates that are too low.

PLANNING TIMING AND THE PLANNING PERIOD

To achieve a sound strategic or short-term plan on a reasonably timely basis, it is desirable to prepare a calendar of events. With respect to the strategic plan, this may be issued at the time of the chief executive's announcement of the annual strategic planning effort. A sample calendar of events is outlined below. In this instance, the cycle for the strategic plan is separated from the short-range planning cycle, in order to distribute more evenly the time spent in the planning effort. The key plan dates are:

May 31	Issuance of general guidelines by the CEO to division heads and other interested parties
July 31	Receipt of division plans by chief planning officer
September 30	Completion of review and analysis of division plans by corporate staff
October 31	Preparation of consolidated and corporate position
November 30	Review with top management and board of directors

Although the dates cited indicate the latest acceptable time for completion of the activity, there is in fact continuous communication between the corporate and division planners, and often the financial officer will devise alternative scenarios that are needed for the long-term financial plans.

Strategic planning is sometimes referred to as long-range planning. But just how far ahead should a company plan? What are some of the factors to be considered in selecting the proper period for which to plan? Each business has characteristics that must be identified in determining the time period of planning. Obviously, a company should plan ahead only so far as is useful. Surveys on this subject indicate that among companies that do long-range planning, the most common period is five years, although the trend is toward a greater distance into the future.

Some of the factors that serve as a guide in selecting the proper planning time span are:

■ *Lead time for product development.* This includes the length of time from the data for a new product until the design, manufacture, and distribution are completed. One company may take three months, whereas another may require several years.

■ *Life span of the product.* The probable period before a product is considered obsolete will be a factor.

■ *Market development time.* This period will vary tremendously, from several years for a complicated industrial product to perhaps only several weeks for women's fashions.

■ *Development time for raw materials and components.* Some extractive industries, such as iron ore mining and oil drilling, may require a decade of advance planning. Wood products companies may consider a period beyond the life expectancy of their current management.

■ *Time for construction of physical facilities.* For many plants, a minimum of two years for design and construction of a plant and its equipment is needed.

- *Payout period for capital investment.* The period over which the investment in capital equipment will be recovered must be weighed. Payoff may vary from several months in a highly speculative and profitable field (i.e., certain chemicals) to perhaps more than a decade (for some utilities). Consider the conditions that will prevail during this payout period to focus on the probability of recovering the investment and earning an adequate return on it.

Many companies find it practical to update the strategic plan on an annual basis. In effect, one year is dropped and a new one is added. Each year, as new perceptions of the business or new opportunities or threats emerge, the new factors are studied and incorporated into the planning process and resultant plan. However, changes in the conditions should not be the excuse for revision of the plan when, over and above those changes, the operating group is not achieving its goals. The impact of the deviation and expected year-end (or other period) result can be identified and reported to management without changing the plan.

 ## BUSINESS MISSION

One of the principal tasks of top management is to formulate the basic purposes of the company. Doing this requires a great deal of thinking as to what the business is all about. It is this mission statement that serves as the guideline for strategic planning.

How should the mission statement be formulated? In smaller companies it tends to depend largely on the thinking and values of the CEO. But in larger companies it is done more effectively by consultation and exchange of ideas among the management (although the CEO still has an important voice). Why? Because any basic change in the nature of the business can have ramifications for the operating methods, the interrelationship of people, and the use of skills.

There is no uniform content in mission statements, which vary from lofty statements of principle, representing the values of the CEO, to very detailed and concrete guidelines. Excess detail may be counterproductive, and vague statements may not be useful in formulating objectives and strategies. A middle ground best serves the purpose.

What factors are important to the survival and growth of the company? The next subjects, which can be identified and/or refined by the planning meetings, should be considered when creating a mission statement:

- Product or product line
- Market and market share
- Profitability on sales, assets, and/or shareholders' equity
- Growth in sales, market share, specific product lines, earnings, earnings per share, jobs, and/or markets served
- Research and development (R&D)
- Productivity or efficiency
- Flexibility in R&D methods, meeting customer delivery needs, and/or responding to competitive actions
- Company image
- Observance of a code of conduct
- Development of the managerial pool, staff training and retention

Based on a consideration of these factors, here are three examples of company mission statements:

1. To be the predominant supplier of electronics countermeasures to the U.S. Air Force
2. To assist our clients in achieving cost-effective employee benefit plans through the effective marketing of innovative and specially designed concepts intended to reflect the strengths of the client company
3. To maintain a viable, growing business by designing, developing, manufacturing, and marketing custom-engineered products and services to meet the needs of selected utility and construction companies

Keep in mind that the principal application of a mission statement is to serve as a guide to policy decisions, to provide direction. Accordingly, it should be quite specific, not a lofty statement of admirable purpose. Also, careful designation may be important; that is, whether the product/service is defined in broad terms or more narrowly described. The wording of the statement can be significant. Thus, a statement that company Y is in the communications business might have quite a different impact from a statement that it is in a narrower business line, such as newspapers, television, and/or radio. And the mission generally should include the scope of operations. Although the mission will identify the line of business, the scope will delineate the market (e.g., the United States rather than worldwide).

A realistic statement of purpose probably will be influenced by these three factors:

1. The basic competence and characteristics of the company (e.g., skill of the management, capital resources, operational capabilities, physical assets, geographical locations, availability of skilled personnel, bottlenecks, raw material sources, etc.).
2. The expectations of those who have something at stake in the firm: management, shareholders, creditors, employees, suppliers, and customers. The relative weight of each group's influence will help shape the relative importance of different elements of the mission.
3. The expected future external environment (e.g., regulation, social trends, inflation rates, and the stage of the business cycle).

 ## DEVELOPING LONG-RANGE OBJECTIVES

Once the business mission has been determined, the long-term objectives must be established. The establishment of objectives is an interactive process, closely coupled with the determination of strategies. One influences the other. In any event, experience shows that satisfactory long-term objectives must be:

- *Suitable.* An objective should support the basic purposes and missions of the company. Achieving the objective should move the enterprise in the direction of meeting its purpose.
- *Feasible.* Objectives should be achievable. Setting an unrealistic goal serves no useful purpose. Any objective should be established giving recognition to the expected environment: competitive actions, technical achievements, political feasibility, and so on.
- *Compatible.* Each objective should be compatible with the other objectives. For example, the objective for product A or strategic business unit X should be in harmony with the objectives for the overall organization.
- *Measurable.* Actual results should be measurable against planned results over a specified time span. Thus, if the objective is "to attain a sales level of $100 million by the year 2013," then attainment is readily identifiable. Objectives may be quantified in dollars, units, cost, rate, or percentage. Only when the objective is stated in concrete terms and for specified periods of time can its attainment be measured objectively.
- *Flexible.* Objectives should not be easily changed; nor should they be immovable. When major unforeseen contingencies occur, objectives should be changed to more realistic ones.

▪ *Motivating.* Another important characteristic of a proper objective is its motivating power. An objective should not be so easily achieved that it is certain of attainment. Nor should it be too difficult to accomplish. It should be set at such a level that those to be judged by it generally agree it can be reached. Thus, those who are to meet an objective should have a voice in setting it. The management members involved should regard it as a commitment to be met with adequate effort.

In practice, most companies have only a few long-term planning objectives. In theory, however, goals or objectives could be set for every function and every department in the business. Typically, many of the objectives are financially expressed and relate to sales volume, profitability, and market share. But measures may be developed for any number of factors that need change: labor content, share of minorities in the workforce, skill diversification in the engineering or research staff, labor turnover rates, productivity, R&D expenditures, and so on. Exhibit 3.1 provides some illustrative long-term objectives for the company as a whole.

Those involved in setting company objectives should realize that major objectives are closely related to subobjectives. Thus, the return on shareholders' equity must be supported by a proper gross margin objective and asset turnover objective and a satisfactory leverage factor. The margin objective in

EXHIBIT 3.1 Sample Company Long-Term Objectives

	Achieve by Year	
Objective	20X0	20X5
Aggregate sales volume (millions)	$560	$1,200
Percent of non-U.S. sales	20%	25%
Percent of new products	15%	30%
Operating profit (% of sales)	17%	22%
Rate of return:		
On total assets	10%	12%
On net worth	19%	25%
Earnings per share	$2.50	$4.25
Price/earnings ratio	11x	15x
Labor content in products	25%	22%
Minorities as percentage of workforce	10%	12%

turn should allow for a product mix objective, a sales volume objective, and, perhaps, a productivity increase goal.

Setting realistic long-term objectives is not as simple as having one executive, the CEO, or a group dictate a figure or goal. To be sure, the process might commence with suggestions from those sources; but it is more satisfactory to have some identifiable points of reference recognizable by those who must meet the objective. What are these? How can they be determined? Some of the ways to make that determination are:

- *Use past performance, with trend exploration.* In some instances, use last year's performance and adjust for experienced improvement. This method must be used with caution since previous performance levels may be quite poor in relation to the rest of the industry; using such previous performance as a future goal may set the company at a competitive disadvantage.
- *Adjust past performance for the impact of expected forces.* Recognition is given to the result of expected changes, both internal and external, such as product obsolescence, government regulations, new product developments, competitive actions, industry sales forecasts, and so on.
- *Analyze competitors.* Using 10K reports from those publicly held competitors who file reports with the Securities and Exchange Commission, analyses can be made of competitive performance. Return on assets, gross margin percentage, sales volume trends, funds spent on R&D, selling expenses, individual competitor data, and group data can be used as a basis for calculating desired performance on some measurable item.
- *Employ environmental, situational, and strategic analyses.* In the analytical study of operations, certain comparative relationships will become evident. The impact of expanding the more productive or effective ones can be judged or calculated on such matters as sales volume (e.g., the impact of advertising, or the use of a certain channel of distribution, changing prices). The best methods used in one area might be applied to other areas. In turn, these actions could affect the objective.

DEVELOPING LONG-RANGE STRATEGIES

After the basic mission and long-range planning objectives have been determined, the next step is to search out those strategies best able to achieve the objectives. As used herein, the word "strategy" means the way, or means, by which the company deploys its human and financial resources and its physical assets to achieve the business purpose.

A great deal has been written about identifying and evaluating strategies. However, the process is largely an art, and developing a successful strategy often involves a great deal of luck. In strategic planning the emphasis usually is on products, markets, and marketing. In developing successful strategies, the company's creative talents should be enlisted to suggest the most ingenious and comprehensive strategies possible. This development task may be assigned to gifted individuals or groups in marketing, planning, or other departments who have a reasonable knowledge of the operations. Sources that may provide clues for potential alternative strategies include:

- A review of company reports and records
- Observation and discussion of the company's operations, including its known or alleged strengths and weaknesses
- A review of competitive or comparable businesses
- Discussion of the situation and alternatives with people who are familiar with the industry and the company or who have encountered similar problems, such as consultants, educators, members of boards of directors, and think tanks

After the list of alternative strategies has been developed, it should be screened by knowledgeable people (perhaps the CEO and other members of top management) to eliminate the impractical strategies. Then the remaining strategies should be evaluated on both a qualitative and quantitative basis. Qualitative factors include the impact on other product lines or organizational units or on the corporate image. Quantitative measures may include contribution margin, cost effectiveness, return on assets, market share, and operating profit.

This art of determining the strategy requires a good insight into the company's strengths and weaknesses, good judgment and intuition, and a willingness to examine some new ideas.

Specifically, strategy development demands:

- Comprehending the current status of the business and where continuance of the same policies and strategies will take it. This involves identifying such factors as:
  - Major products
  - Major markets

- Important strengths and weaknesses of the company as compared to the competition
- Current major strategies
- Knowing the economic contribution (e.g., cash flow and operating profit) of the various segments by product, market, and profit center
- Understanding the company objectives and how they may differ from results of continuing the present activity
- Recognizing some of the strategies that may or could be involved in the strategic planning, and selecting the practical ones for study
  - *Product strategies.* Product design, new product development, adding new products by purchase or acquisition, product obsolescence, life cycle of products
  - *Market strategies.* Adding or dropping markets, changing distribution channels, methods of sales, prices, terms of sale, delivery methods, advertising media, promotional methods
  - *Manufacturing strategies.* Plant locations, subcontracting, foreign sources, manufacturing techniques, material content, quality control
  - *R&D strategies.* University affiliations, joint ventures, licensing, purchase of rights, patents
  - *Financial strategies.* Inventory financing, credit terms, debt structure, employee stock option plans, stock issues, control systems, the planning system, inflation hedging, foreign exchange practices, leasing instead of purchasing fixed assets
  - *Human resource strategies.* Organization structure, style of management, decentralization, downsizing, recruitment policies, training programs, wage and salary levels, executive replacement
- Evaluating the proposed individual strategies and judging how they will assist in meeting the business objective

Some alternative strategies may be deduced from the list of the basic types of strategies. The next list provides a few specific illustrations of strategies undertaken. What strategies must be employed or changed obviously depends on the problems to be overcome. The strategies appear in typical groupings of product strategies, market strategies, and operating efficiency.

Products

- Change the style of packaging to appeal to middle-age customers.
- Change packaging to smaller quantities to attract elderly singles.

- Add a related product that would use the same distribution channel and methods as the other products.
- Drop line Y, which provides no contribution margin.
- Modify the product so it will serve a function not now recognized.
- Consider private brands in the Southeast.

Markets and Marketing

- Enter the Eurozone market through a joint venture.
- Change prices to meet the competition of the R chain.
- Increase local advertising to cover TV in markets W, X, and Y.
- Change from sales representatives to agents in the Northwest territory.
- Reduce the promotional effort on product T in the marketplace because of its declining stage in the life cycle.

Operating Efficiency

- Switch to the just-in-time inventory control method in Los Angeles and San Francisco.
- Establish a warehouse in Denver.
- Enforce terms of sale in order to increase receivables turnover.
- Dispose of the Kansas City subsidiary because of losses and the lack of growth prospects.
- Sell the Chicago office building. Reduce space requirements, and move to a less expensive location.

CHAPTER FOUR

Long-Range Financial Plan

C HAPTER 3 PROVIDED AN overview of strategic planning. In this chapter, the strategic plan becomes more specific through numerical examples as the next topics, which are segments of the long-range plan, are examined:

- Trend of revenues and profits
- Capital investments
- Cash flows and financing requirements
- Key statistics
- Risk analysis
- Breakdown by business unit/product line/geography
- Financial position

 ## LAYOUT AND PURPOSE

The elements of the business plan that were described in Chapter 3 did not address the means by which the plan could be achieved. Targets were set, but there was no discussion of how the company would get from its current situation to the new targets. The long-range plan shows anticipated growth rates from the present to the targets, as well as the capital expenditures and capital requirements needed. The plan is backed up by a set of key statistics that indicate changes in such areas as coverage of loan covenants and liquidity.

The long-range plan also includes an in-depth risk analysis. The risk of significant revenue and profit changes are listed, along with probabilities of the changes occurring. From this analysis it is possible to infer the risk of the corporation's not meeting its goals and to gain a general idea of the risk of financial loss that the company is willing to undertake to achieve its goals.

Finally, the plan should include subsidiary plans that categorize projected sales and profits by strategic business units, product lines, and geographical regions, helping to determine where the greatest risks and opportunities lie in the plan.

The long-range plan differs significantly from the annual plan (as described in Chapter 5). The differences are noted in Exhibit 4.1.

After examining the exhibit, the reader may conclude that the long-range plan is not as large or detailed as the annual plan; that is a correct assessment. The long-range plan deals with long-term needs and key statistics and does not concern itself with low-level detailed costs. The plan is meant to be easily modified for what-if analysis, and a relatively small model with linked graphics is best for that purpose.

The *purpose* of the long-range plan is to give management a rough-cut analysis of whether its business plan is achievable and of the risks and funding involved. Also, the long-range plan is used to assist lenders in determining the risk involved in lending to the company.

In the absence of a chief financial officer (CFO), the controller is responsible for the long-range plan. The plan quantifies the goals and strategies enumerated in the business plan, and numerical analysis logically falls into the realm

EXHIBIT 4.1   Differences between the Annual and Long-Range Plans

Task	Long-Range Plan	Annual Plan
Lists costs by individual account	No	Yes
Includes subsidiary budgets (purchasing, labor, etc.)	No	Yes
Used for monthly comparison to actual results	No	Yes
Has cash budget	Yes	Yes
Has P&L and balance sheet budgets	Yes	Yes

of the controller. However, input into the long-range plan must come from all departments. For example, all departments must submit capital requests. The sales department must contribute minimum/maximum expected revenue figures by product. The engineering department must contribute estimated margin information by product.

 ## TRENDS OF REVENUES AND PROFITS

The business plan will itemize a target sales level to be reached by a specified date, or an average growth rate. The long-range plan must specify the anticipated growth by individual year. This growth does not have to be a steady trend line from year to year. Instead, the plan should tie revenue levels to new products coming onto the market, new business units being created, or new geographical areas being reached.

Similarly, the trend of profits should be tied to the anticipated costs of creating new products, capital expenditures, marketing campaigns, or other growth-related costs.

The format of this section of the plan should be graphical, with numerical backup if needed. Exhibits 4.2 and 4.3 show examples of such graphs. Each

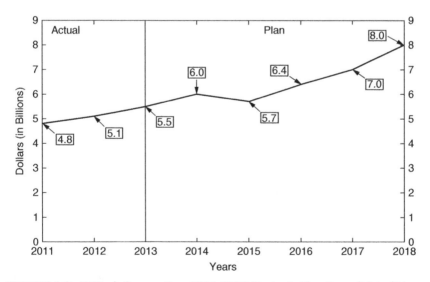

EXHIBIT 4.2 Hi-Tech Corporation, 2011–2018 Strategic Plan Consolidated Net Sales (Dollars in Billions)

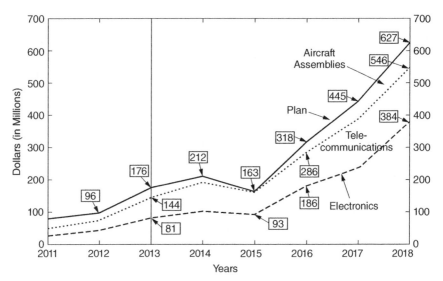

EXHIBIT 4.3   Hi-Tech Corporation Consolidated Net Income by Strategic Business Unit, 2011–2018 Strategic Plan (Dollars in Millions)

example shows both actual revenues and profits for the last few years of operations as well as projections through the period of the business plan.

 CAPITAL INVESTMENTS

The long-range plan should include a listing of capital investments required to attain the revenue and profit objectives. The investment amount should also include working capital requirements (cash invested in receivables and inventories, less the amount of accounts payable). There is a growing trend in industry toward eliminating working capital by shrinking inventories and receivables. If the company plans to pursue such a strategy, that goal should be built into the business plan since it will have a significant impact on capital requirements.

Capital requirements should be listed by product, business unit, or geographical area, so that management can easily determine the costs associated with launching a new product or business unit or selling into a new geographical area. Exhibit 4.4 presents a typical capital plan.

EXHIBIT 4.4 Capital Requirements (Dollars in Millions)

	New Technology Company 20XX–20YB Strategic Plan
Aircraft Product A	
Assembly Line	$34.1
Assembly Building	17.2
Working Capital	43.0
Total	94.3
Communications Product B	
Assembly Line	11.0
Assembly Building	14.1
Working Capital	29.3
Total	$54.4

Capital requirements are especially useful when determining returns on investment and strategy risks, as discussed in the "Risk Analysis" section of this chapter.

 ## CASH FLOWS AND FINANCING REQUIREMENTS

The long-range plan should include cash requirements for each year of the plan. This is one of the most crucial parts of the long-range plan because management must know about the risk of future indebtedness as well as the need to issue stock or bonds. If stock is issued, then management must be aware of the projected impact on earnings per share (an increased number of shares outstanding will water down the earnings per share in the absence of additional earnings). In addition, management must be aware of the company's projected debt/equity mix because this will affect the cost of capital.

If future indebtedness is more than management is comfortable with, then the capital requirements part of the long-range plan can be reviewed to determine where the requirements are coming from. For example, if $150 million of additional debt or equity is required over the course of the long-range plan and capital requirements are as shown in Exhibit 4.4, then management may want to review the benefits of Aircraft Product A in great detail since that product is responsible for the majority of capital requirements.

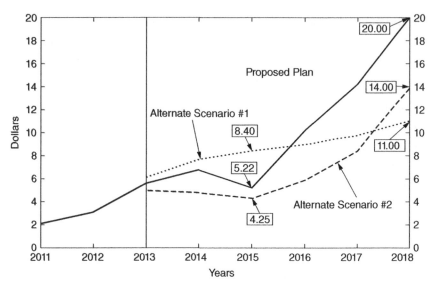

EXHIBIT 4.5   Hi-Tech Corporation Earnings per Share: Three Scenarios, 2011–2018 Strategic Plan (Dollars in Millions)

Product profitability assumptions are a key component of projected cash flows; the strategic plan should contain assumptions regarding expected competition that may reduce margins and internal quality, target costing, or other initiatives that may increase margins. Exhibit 4.5 shows earnings per share under several scenarios. This kind of chart is very useful to management because decisions regarding addition or elimination of products will directly affect earnings per share. Exhibit 4.6 shows a simple calculation of cash flows for a long-range plan.

RISK ANALYSIS

The long-range plan should include an in-depth assessment of the risks that will occur as a result of the business plan. The commentary should include some or all of these topics:

- *Competitive response.* Competitors will have a response to any new product introduction or expansion into a new geographical area. The response may be price cuts, lawsuits, or lobbying for government regulation.

EXHIBIT 4.6 Hi-Tech Corporation Statement of Consolidated Cash Flows, 2011–2015 Strategic Plan (Dollars in Millions)

	Present Year (Indicated Final)	Plan Year				
		2007	2008	2009	2010	2011
Cash Flows for Operating Activities						
Net earnings	$176	212	163	318	445	$627
Depreciation and amortization	174	214	244	240	250	200
Deferred taxes, etc.	4	4	—	—	—	—
Working capital provided by operations	354	430	407	558	695	827
Increase (decrease) in operating-related working capital items	255	149	(221)	(7)	(55)	(45)
Net cash flows from operating activities	99	281	628	551	640	872
Cash Flows from (Used by) Investing Activities						
Equity interest (Corp. X)	—	—	—	—	—	(800)
Capital expenditures	(118)	(420)	(100)	(50)	(50)	(50)
Proceeds from asset sales and retirements	1	—	20	—	—	—
Net cash flows used in investing activities	(117)	(420)	(80)	(50)	(50)	(850)
Cash Flows from (Used by) Financing Activities						
Dividends to shareholders	(52)	(53)	(53)	(58)	(58)	(63)
Changed (reduction) in short-term bank debt	116	(135)	(200)	(150)	—	—
Additions to long-term debt	—	500	—	—	—	—
Reduction in long-term debt	(21)	(42)	(50)	(250)	(240)	(350)
Net cash flows from (used by) financing activities	43	270	(303)	(458)	(298)	(413)
Increase (decrease) in cash and cash equivalents	25	131	245	43	292	(391)
Cash and equivalents at beginning of year	172	197	328	573	616	908
Cash and equivalents at end of year	$197	328	573	616	908	$517

79

- *Capital cost overruns.* Construction projects have been known to exceed their budgets. A worst-case scenario could help management anticipate funding requirements.
- *Step cost trigger points.* A step cost is an expense that increases substantially when a specific activity level is reached, such as when the capacity of a manufacturing facility is reached and an entirely new facility must be constructed to handle the next increment of production volume. Management should be aware of the most significant step cost trigger points and the costs required to increase capacity beyond those points.
- *Nationalization of facilities.* Some countries have a history of nationalizing certain industries with little or no compensation to the previous owners of expropriated facilities. If management becomes aware of such a problem, then it may wish to relocate its new facilities.
- *Ecological costs.* Some companies, notably in the asbestos and tobacco industries, have been targets of lawsuits due to products that were later found to be unsafe. In addition, any product or process that has significant chemical waste by-products should be brought to the attention of management since resulting lawsuits or government fines could destroy any profits from sale of the product.
- *Sales fluctuations.* Sales projections are sometimes inaccurate. Management should be aware of the worst- and best-case scenarios. The worst case may result in significant losses to the company, and the best case may require construction of additional production facilities.
- *Raw material scarcity.* Some raw materials are in short supply or are tightly controlled by the producer. If so, sales projections may fall short due to the company's inability to produce enough product to meet demand.
- *Deterioration of margins.* Competing products may come onto the market that will cause margins to deteriorate due to price cuts. The company should make some attempt to identify this risk from both national and international competitors and derive a likely range of margin percentage reductions to factor into the long-range plan.
- *Technological advances.* Advances in technology may make a product obsolete (e.g., as slide rules were made obsolete by calculators). Although these advances may be hard to predict, trade literature presents news of experimental technology that may allow the company to forecast a decline in its market. For example, the movie video rental market is projected to decline as on-demand movie rentals become available through cable television companies.

The risk assessment section is among the most crucial parts of the long-range plan. Some of this information can be researched during the construction of the business plan (see Chapter 3), but the long-range plan attempts to quantify the cost associated with each of the factors just noted. Armed with this information, management can then alter the business plan as necessary both to reduce the company's risk to an acceptable level and to maximize its profits.

 ## BREAKDOWN BY BUSINESS UNIT/PRODUCT LINE/GEOGRAPHY

The long-range plan should include capital expenditure, revenue, margin, and profit breakdowns so that management can determine where it can expect its greatest returns as well as its greatest risk of loss. Typical detailed breakdowns include these areas:

■ *Business unit.* The business plan frequently categorizes sales and profits by business unit. A breakdown of this kind may highlight projected problems in specific business units that management can correct.
■ *Product line.* The business plan may include the rollout of a new product. If so, a summary of the costs associated with the new product (e.g., marketing, advertising, R&D, and capital costs) should be listed. An attached commentary should include an assessment of minimum/maximum/expected sales levels, probability of capital cost overruns, and possible competitive responses to introduction of the new product.
■ *Geography.* The business plan may include expansion into geographical areas. If so, the cost of advertising and marketing campaigns should be itemized. If the areas are in other countries, the company may have to build production facilities in those locations; if so, the capital cost should also be included. Finally, the working capital cost of the expansion should be included. The breakdown should utilize all of these "hard" numbers in a summary that includes risk assessments of such factors as nationalization of facilities, minimum/maximum/expected sales levels, and possible capital cost overruns.

 ## FINANCIAL POSITION

The long-range plan should include a profit and loss statement as well as a balance sheet for each year of the long-range plan. This information is not just

EXHIBIT 4.7 Hi-Tech Corporation Statement of Consolidated Financial
Position at Year-End, 2011–2015 Strategic Plan (Dollars in Millions)

	Actual		At Plan Year-End				
	12/31/09	12/31/10 (Indicated Final)	2011	2012	2013	2014	2015
Assets							
Current Assets							
Cash and equivalents	$172	197	328	573	616	908	$517
Receivables	576	614	640	510	550	650	600
Inventories	1,037	1,320	1,400	1,200	1,300	1,200	1,200
Prepaid items	46	44	40	40	40	40	40
Total	1,831	2,175	2,408	2,323	2,506	2,798	2,357
Long-term Assets							
Minority interests (Corp. X)	—	—	—	—	—	—	800
Property, plant and equipment	2,407	2,522	2,942	3,022	3,072	3,122	3,172
Less: accumulated depreciation and amortization	792	966	1,180	1,404	1,644	1,894	2,094
Net	1,615	1,556	1,762	1,618	1,428	1,228	1,878
Other assets	75	80	80	80	80	80	80
Total	1,690	1,636	1,842	1,698	1,508	1,308	1,958
Total Assets	$3,521	3,811	4,250	4,021	4,014	4,106	$4,315

for internal use. Lenders want this information to determine corporate risk when approving loans; investors want this information to determine their investment positions with the company.

The long-range plan should simply extend the typical income statement and balance sheet through the number of years covered by the plan. Exhibits 4.7 through 4.9 provide examples of those statements.

Some companies include a statement of financial highlights with their standard financial statements. The highlights usually include estimates of projected backlogs, sales, earnings, a few key expenses, and the return on assets or equity. Exhibit 4.10 shows an example of a financial highlights

EXHIBIT 4.8 Hi-Tech Corporation Statement of Consolidated Financial Position at Year-End, 2011–2015 Strategic Plan (Dollars in Millions)

	Actual		At Plan Year-End				
	12/31/09	12/31/10 (Indicated Final)	2011	2012	2013	2014	2015
Liabilities and Equity							
Current Liabilities							
Notes payable to banks	$ 319	$ 435	$ 300	$100	—	—	$ —
Current portion of long-term debt	21	21	—	50	50	50	50
Accounts payable	563	590	610	540	590	500	500
Accrued items	187	212	200	160	170	190	170
Income tax payable	17	34	43	37	65	90	100
Other current liabilities	26	27	28	15	20	20	25
Total	$ 1,133	1,319	1,181	902	895	850	$ 845
Long-term Obligations							
Senior debt—existing	$ 863	842	800	750	500	300	$ —
Senior debt—new	—	—	500	500	500	450	400
Other long-term obligations	142	140	110	110	110	120	120
Total	$ 1,005	982	1,410	1,360	1,110	870	$ 520
Deferred Income Taxes							
Shareholders' equity	$ 47	50	40	30	20	10	$ 10
Paid-in capital	$ 310	310	310	310	310	310	310
Retained earnings	1,026	1,150	1,309	1,419	1,679	2,066	2,630
Total equity	$ 1,336	1,460	1,619	1,729	1,989	2,376	$2,940
Total Liabilities and Equity	$ 3,521	3,811	4,250	4,021	4,014	4,106	$4,315

statement. Finally, the projected earnings per share and the projected net earnings are the items of most concern to investors. As such, they are commonly graphed to draw the attention of investors to them. Exhibits 4.11 and 4.12 provide examples of graphed earnings per share and projected net earnings.

EXHIBIT 4.9 Hi-Tech Corporation Statement of Consolidated Earnings, 2011–2015 Strategic Plan (Dollars in Millions)

Item	Actual		Plan Year				
	Past Year	This Year (Indicated Final)	2011	2012	2013	2014	2015
Net sales	$5,052	5,500	6,000	5,700	6,400	7,000	$8,000
Operating costs							
Manufacturing	$4,461	4,815	5,204	4,995	5,420	5,791	$6,544
Marketing	40	41	39	40	42	46	52
Research and development	50	55	120	114	128	140	160
General and administrative	41	39	37	38	42	43	44
Total	$4,592	4,950	5,400	5,187	5,632	6,020	$6,800
Operating margin	$ 460	550	600	513	768	980	$1,200
Other expenses							
Interest expense	$ 181	223	200	190	180	100	$ 50
Other (net)	111	15	15	(10)	10	10	10
Total	$ 292	238	215	180	190	110	$ 60
Earnings before income taxes	$ 168	312	385	333	578	870	$1,140
Income taxes	72	136	173	170	260	425	513
Net earnings	$ 96	176	212	163	318	445	$ 627

EXHIBIT 4.10 Hi-Tech Corporation Financial Highlights, 2011–2015 Strategic Plan (Dollars in Millions Except per Share)

Item	Actual		Plan Year				
	Past Year	This Year (Indicated Final)	2011	2012	2013	2014	2015
New orders	$3,800	3,600	2,500	8,470	6,400	7,500	$8,200
Sales backlog (year-end)	5,650	3,750	250	3,020	3,020	3,520	3,720
Net sales (consolidated)	5,052	5,500	6,000	5,700	6,400	7,000	8,000
Net earnings							

EXHIBIT 4.10 (Continued)

Item	Actual Past Year	This Year (Indicated Final)	Plan Year 2011	2012	2013	2014	2015
Amount	96	176	212	163	318	445	627
Percentage of sales	1.9%	3.2%	3.5%	2.9%	5.0%	6.4%	7.8%
Per share	3.09	5.66	6.79	5.22	10.16	14.22	20.00
Capital expenditures	115	115	420	100	50	50	50
Research and development expense	50	55	60	57	64	69	70
Book value per share (year-end)	$43.03	46.93	51.87	55.38	63.57	75.91	$93.78
Return on average equity—(%)	7.45%	12.59%	13.78%	9.74%	17.11%	20.39%	23.59%
No common shares outstanding (thousands)—year-end	31,050	31,110	31,210	31,220	31,290	31,300	31,350

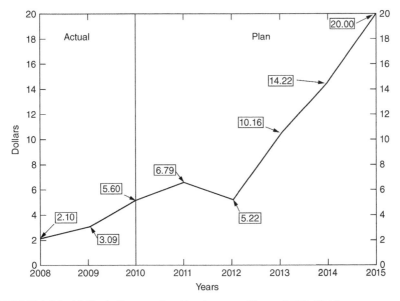

EXHIBIT 4.11 Hi-Tech Corporation Earnings per Share, 2008–2015 Strategic Plan

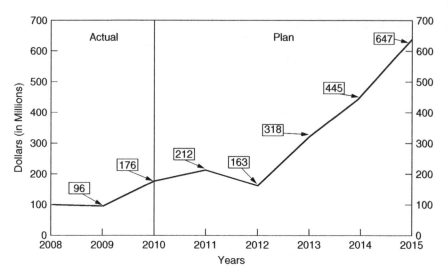

EXHIBIT 4.12   Hi-Tech Corporation Consolidated Net Earnings, 2008–2015
Strategic Plan (Dollars in Millions)

CHAPTER FIVE

Annual Plan

THE PURPOSE OF THIS chapter is to explain the budgeting procedure and how the many subsidiary plans interlock to form the complete budget. Because the capital budgeting process is a complex part of the overall budget, it is discussed in Chapter 14. After an overview of the planning process, we give special emphasis to the sales planning process, since the accuracy of that budget determines the accuracy of the rest of a company's final budget. There is also a discussion of a variety of special budgeting topics, including the flex budget, attrition budgeting, and the most appropriate number of budgeting scenarios to prepare.

SYSTEM OF PLANS

At the highest level, the annual budget is the method by which the company implements its long-range plan. The goals set forth in the long-range plan are used as the basis for the annual budget, given such restrictions as funding limitations, legal issues, and general economic conditions. In the budgeting process, revenues, costs, levels of operations, facilities, financial resources, and personnel are all considered and interrelated. The appropriateness of levels and

EXHIBIT 5.1 Sales Budget

Product	No. of Units	Unit Selling Price	Total Sales
R	20,000	$33.00	$ 660,000
S	30,000	54.50	1,635,000
T	50,000	21.25	1,062,500
U	5,000	78.50	392,500
Total	105,000		$3,750,000

types of costs and expenses are analyzed and interrelated, and modeling is used to predict the financial impact of alternative operating decisions. Thus budgeting is an iterative process that aids the manager in revising plans until an acceptable one is reached.

The budget contains these subsidiary budgets:

- *Sales budget.* The sales forecast is the starting point in budget preparation. Exhibit 5.1 shows an abbreviated sales budget.
- *Production budget.* Once the tentative estimate of sales has been agreed on, the next step is a determination of the quantities of finished goods that must be produced to meet both the sales and inventory requirements. Exhibit 5.2 illustrates this calculation of units to be produced.
- *Purchases budget.* After the levels of production have been set, the next job to be undertaken is the sometimes laborious task of determining the quantities of raw material needed to meet the production and inventory requirements. This function is, first, a matter of extending the units of production times the units of each raw material needed, as shown in Exhibit 5.3.

EXHIBIT 5.2 Production Budget

Description	Product R	Product S	Product T	Product U
Quantity required for sale	20,000	30,000	50,000	5,000
Desired ending inventory	5,000	5,000	10,000	500
Total requirements	25,000	35,000	60,000	5,500
Less:				
Beginning inventory	3,000	2,000	8,000	1,000
Required production	22,000	33,000	52,000	4,500

EXHIBIT 5.3 Unit Purchasing Requirements Based on Production Budget

| Raw Material | Finished Product | | | | Total Unit Requirements |
	R	S	T	U	
AA	11,000	33,000	—	9,000	53,000
BB	22,000	—	52,000	9,000	83,000
CC	11,000	66,000	104,000	4,500	185,500

Then, after usage has been calculated, the value of needed purchases, in light of existing inventories, can be set. The dollar value is determined on the basis of expected unit cost prices that may be furnished by the purchasing department. The purchases budget is constructed basically in the format shown in Exhibit 5.4.

Very often it is necessary to group purchases by class of material rather than to enumerate each individual type of material. In particular, this practice is used where unit prices are small.

- *Labor budget.* Another budget dependent on the production budget is that of direct labor. The accuracy of this budget is highly dependent on the accuracy of the labor routings (detailed analyses of the labor needed to build a product) for each product. Also, if a product's bill of materials is not accurate, then more labor is required to assemble the product, thereby affecting the labor budget. Finally, the labor content of the labor routing is strongly influenced by the assumed length of the production run, which in turn is dependent on the equipment setup time. Because the controller probably is not qualified to evaluate the accuracy of a labor routing, it would be wise to bring together a team of experienced engineers to

EXHIBIT 5.4 Purchases Budget

| Raw Material | Requirements | | | Less: Beginning Inventory | Quantity to Be Purchased | Unit Price | Purchases Budget |
	Production	Ending Inventory	Total				
AA	53,000	2,000	55,000	3,000	52,000	$4.00	$208,000
BB	83,000	5,000	88,000	10,000	78,000	2.00	156,000
CC	185,500	20,000	205,500	20,000	185,000	1.00	185,500
Total							$549,500

EXHIBIT 5.5 Labor Budget

Product	Quantity	Standard Labor Hours per Unit	Total Standard Labor Hours	Direct Labor Budget (at $6 per Standard Labor Hour)
R	22,000	1.0	22,000	$132,000
S	33,000	2.5	82,500	495,000
T	52,000	.5	26,000	156,000
U	4,500	2.5	11,250	67,500
Total			141,750	$850,500

regularly review the setup times and assumed length of production runs for accuracy. Another issue is that the production manager may staff the same number of direct labor employees, irrespective of short-term variations in production levels, in order to maintain a consistent long-term workforce. If so, labor routings, which *are* based on production levels, may not be an accurate source of information for the labor budget. The budget is computed as shown in Exhibit 5.5.

▪ *Manufacturing expense budget.* Total manufacturing expenses for the expected production level must be ascertained on the basis of the activity of each type of expense and/or each department or cost center. The final estimate, arbitrarily assumed to be 50 percent of direct labor for this overly simplified illustration, is summarized in Exhibit 5.6. A more accurate

EXHIBIT 5.6 Manufacturing Expense Budget

Description	Amount
Indirect labor	$125,000
Payroll taxes and insurance (40%)	50,000
Provision for vacation wages	43,250
Utilities	52,000
Supplies	25,000
Repairs and maintenance	67,000
Depreciation	47,000
Property taxes	10,000
Property insurance	6,000
Total	$425,250

EXHIBIT 5.7 Computation of Finished Goods Inventory

Product	Quantity	Unit Cost	Total Sales
R	5,000	$14.00	$ 70,000
S	5,000	28.50	142,500
T	10,000	8.50	85,000
U	500	35.50	17,750
Total			$315,250

budget would have elements that varied with production volume; for example, variable expenses such as supplies would have a different budget depending on the amount of product produced. Some companies also use a step-type budget in which new, predetermined budgets are used for different levels of production activity.

■ *Inventory budget.* All information necessary to calculate the investment in inventories is now available. The value of the finished inventory is computed as demonstrated in Exhibit 5.7. A similar procedure is followed with respect to raw materials, supplies, and work in process. The total value of inventories is then summarized as in Exhibit 5.8.

Seven steps should be taken in budgeting the major individual items of materials and supplies:

Step 1. Determine the physical units of material required for each item of goods to be produced during the budget period.

Step 2. Accumulate these into total physical units of each material item required for the entire production program.

EXHIBIT 5.8 Inventory Budget

Statement of Estimated Ending Inventories as of December 31, 20XX	
Raw materials	$ 38,000
Supplies and parts	4,000
Work in process	97,500
Finished goods	315,250
Total	$454,750

Step 3. Determine for each item of material the quantity that should be on hand periodically to enable the production program to run smoothly with a reasonable margin of safety. The calculation of the minimum quantity on hand should include the size of the most economic order quantity.

Step 4. Deduct material inventories that are expected to be on hand at the beginning of the budget period to ascertain the total quantities to be purchased.

Step 5. Develop a purchase program that will ensure that the quantities will be on hand at the time they are needed. The purchase program must pay attention to such factors as economical size of orders, economy of transportation, and margin of safety against delays.

Step 6. Test the resulting budget inventories by standard turnover rates.

Step 7. Translate the inventory and purchase requirements into dollars by applying the expected prices of materials to budgeted quantities.

The inventory of goods actually in the process of production between stocking points can be estimated best by applying standard turnover rates to budgeted production. Control over the work-in-process inventories can be exercised by a continuous check of turnover rates. Where the production capacity of individual processes, departments, or plants is found to be excessive, the processes, departments, or plants should be subjected to individual investigation.

The budget of finished goods inventory must be based on the sales budget. If, for example, it is expected that 500 units of item A will be sold during the budget period, it must be ascertained what number of units must be kept in stock to support such a sales program. When reviewing inventories for control purposes, it is not wise to control based on the total inventory amount since the inventory levels of individual stock items are bound to be either too high or too low. Each major inventory must be reviewed separately for reasonableness.

▪ *Selling, general, and administrative budget.* Through detailed budgeting and summary by individual departments, the other expenses of the business are estimated. They are summarized in Exhibit 5.9, which shows an administrative-type budget. This budget assumes relatively fixed costs and is useful when the expense level should not be influenced by day-to-day sales levels, but rather by long-term output (depending on the industry, some sales may take a year to close), and is composed primarily of personnel costs. General and administrative expenses can be judged based on either their comparison to the previous year's expenses, their relationship to sales as a percentage, or a comparison with the industry average.

EXHIBIT 5.9 Selling, General, and Administrative Budget

Items	Selling Expense	General and Administrative Expense	Financial Expense
Salaries—executives	$ 74,000	$ 90,000	$ —
Salaries—salespeople	198,000	—	—
Commissions—agents	17,500	—	—
Fringe benefits	108,800	36,000	—
Advertising space	50,000	—	—
Bad debts	—	10,000	—
Traveling expenses	220,000	9,500	—
Rent	12,000	3,000	—
Supplies	21,000	7,000	—
Interest expense	—	—	1,900
Discount on sales	—	—	18,000
Total	$701,300	$155,500	$19,900

- *Research and development budget.* The R&D budget differs from the other budgets because the amount of funds allocated to it can be a very subjective issue. Funding can be based on these criteria:
  - The amount of funds available
  - The budgets of current R&D projects
  - The R&D activities of competitors, and the company's need to match competitive R&D expenditures
  - The need for R&D in the strategic plan

  Once the total R&D amount has been allocated, the funds must be allocated to individual projects, and the controller should help create budgets for the individual projects.

- *Capital assets budget.* Exhibit 5.10 shows a budget for capital expenditures based on a detailed review of facility requirements and the availability of cash.

EXHIBIT 5.10 Capital Assets Budget

Capital Expenditures Budget for the Year Ending December 31, 20XX	
Buildings	$120,000
Machinery and equipment	132,500
Total	$252,500

EXHIBIT 5.11 Cost of Goods Sold Budget

Statement of Estimated Cost of Goods Sold	
Raw materials	
Inventory, January 1, 20X5	$ 52,000
Add: purchases (Exhibit 5.4)	549,500
Total available	601,500
Less: inventory, December 31, 20X5	38,000
Transfer to work in process	563,500
Direct labor (Exhibit 5.5)	850,500
Manufacturing expense (Exhibit 5.6)	425,250
Total charges to cost of production	1,839,250
Add: work in process, January 1, 20XX	97,500
Total	1,936,750
Less: work in process, December 31, 20XX	97,500
Transfer to finished goods	1,839,250
Add: finished goods inventory, January 1, 20XX	202,500
Total	2,041,740
Less: finished goods inventory, December 31, 20XX (Exhibit 5.8)	315,250
Estimated cost of goods sold	$1,726,500

- *Cost of goods sold budget.* The requisite information is now available to prepare a tentative statement of income and expense. First, of course, the statement of estimated cost of goods sold is computed, as shown in Exhibit 5.11.
- *Cash budget.* This is a projection of the anticipated cash receipts and disbursements and the resulting cash balance. A cash budget is used for a number of reasons:
  - To point out peaks or seasonal fluctuations in business activity that necessitate larger investments in inventories and receivables
  - To indicate the time and extent of funds needed to meet maturing obligations, tax payments, and dividend or interest payments
  - To assist in planning for growth, including the required funds for capital investments and working capital
  - To indicate well in advance of needs the extent and duration of funds required from outside sources and thus permit the securing of more advantageous loan terms

- To determine the extent and duration of funds available for investment
- To plan the reduction of bonded indebtedness or other loans
- To permit the company to take advantage of cash discounts, thereby increasing its earnings

The cash budget is created by projecting each cost element involving cash. It is very useful for controlling cash flow by comparing actual and forecasted performance. Exhibit 5.12 shows a cash budget.

The *sources of cash receipts* are collections on account, cash sales, royalties, rent, dividends, sale of assets, sale of investments, and new financing. These

EXHIBIT 5.12 Cash Budget

Item	Year Total
Cash and cash equivalents at beginning of period	$ 1,330,000
Cash receipts	
From operations:	
Collections on account	47,946,000
Cash sales	1,730,000
Interest receivable	205,000
Insurance proceeds	360,000
Miscellaneous	240,000
Total from operations	50,481,000
From other activities:	
Common stock issue	2,000,000
Short-term borrowings	4,725,000
Long-term debt issue	1,000,000
Total from other activities	7,725,000
Total cash receipts	58,206,000
Total cash available	59,536,000
Cash disbursements	
For operations:	
Accounts payable and accrued items	24,089,000
Payrolls	13,700,000
Interest	2,170,000
Federal and state income taxes	7,185,000
Total from operations	47,144,000
	(Continued)

EXHIBIT 5.12 (Continued)

Item	Year Total
For other activities:	
Repayment on long-term debt	3,496,000
Dividends	2,600,000
Capital expenditures	3,500,000
Total for other activities	9,596,000
Total cash disbursements	$56,740,000
Cash and cash equivalents at end of period	$ 2,796,000

items can be predicted with reasonable accuracy. Usually the most important recurring sources are collections on account and cash sales. Experience and knowledge of trends will indicate what share of total sales probably will be for cash. For example, assume that an analysis of collection experience for June sales reveals the collection data shown in Exhibit 5.13.

If next year's sales in June could be expected to fall into the same pattern, then application of the percentages to estimated June credit sales would determine the probable monthly distribution of collections. The same analysis applied to each month of the year would result in a reasonably reliable basis for collection forecasting. These experience factors must be modified not only by trends developed over time, but also by the estimate of general business conditions as reflected in collections, as well as contemplated changes in terms of sale or other credit policies.

If a complete operating budget is available, the controller should have little trouble in assembling the data into an estimate of *cash disbursements*. The usual

EXHIBIT 5.13 Distribution of Bad Debt Losses

Description	% of Total Credit Sales
Collected in June	2.1
July	85.3
August	8.9
September	2.8
October	.3
Cash discounts	.5
Bad debt losses	.1
Total	100.0

EXHIBIT 5.14 Statement of Planned Income and Expense

Net Sales (Exhibit 5.1)	$3,750,000
Cost of goods sold (Exhibit 5.11)	1,726,500
Gross profit	2,023,500
Operating expenses:	
Advertising and selling (Exhibit 5.9)	701,300
General and administrative (Exhibit 5.9)	155,500
Total operating expenses	856,800
Operating profit	1,166,700
Other income—discount on purchases	5,000
	1,171,700
Other expenses	
Interest expense (Exhibit 5.9)	1,900
Discount on sales (Exhibit 5.9)	18,000
	19,900
Profit before income taxes	1,151,800
Income taxes (40%)	460,720
Net income	$ 691,080

cash disbursements in a company consist of payroll, materials, taxes, dividends, traveling expenses, other operating expenses, interest, purchases of equipment, and retirement of stock.

The cash budget plays a vital role in the budgeting process because it is a check on the entire budgeting program. If the operating budget goals are achieved, the results will be reflected in the cash position. Failure to achieve budgeted performance may require the treasurer to seek additional sources of cash.

The subsidiary budgets converge, or roll up, into a set of planned financial statements, which are described next.

▪ *The statement of planned income and expense.* Exhibit 5.14 shows a sample statement of income and expense. In practice, this statement might be detailed by product lines, territories, or channels of distribution.
▪ *The statement of planned sources and uses of cash.* Exhibit 5.15 presents a sample statement of sources and uses of cash. This statement is extremely useful in determining the viability of a company. If the controller sees that more cash is required than is being generated by operations for several future periods, then the budget may need further enhancement to boost cash flow.

- *The statement of planned financial position.* The final effect of all the planning is reflected in the statement of planned financial position at the close of the budget period. Usually such a statement is prepared in comparative form with the actual or expected position at the beginning of the budget period as well as at the close. Exhibits 5.16 and 5.17 illustrate the statement and the related statement of retained earnings.

EXHIBIT 5.15 Statement of Planned Sources and Uses of Cash

Cash balance, December 31, 20XX		$ 460,000
Estimated cash receipts:		
Collections on accounts receivable	$3,672,500	
Proceeds from sale of common stock	500,000	
Proceeds from notes payable	50,000	
Total estimated receipts		4,222,500
Total cash available		$4,682,500
Estimated cash disbursements:		
Accounts payable—materials and supplies	$ 580,600	
Accounts payable—other	428,000	
Notes payable	300,000	
Salaries and wages	1,330,000	
Accrued income taxes	785,050	
Items—other	202,050	
Interest expense	1,900	
Dividends	210,000	
Capital assets	252,500	
Total estimated disbursements		4,090,100
Estimated cash balance, December 31, 20XX		$ 592,400

EXHIBIT 5.16 Statement of Planned Financial Position

	Assets			
	Actual December 31, 20XX		**Estimated** December 31, 20XX	
Current assets				
Cash		$ 460,000		$ 592,400
Accounts receivable	$ 250,000		$ 322,500	
Less: Reserve for doubtful accounts	15,000	235,000	20,000	302,500

EXHIBIT 5.16 (Continued)

Assets				
	Actual		**Estimated**	
	December 31, 20XX		**December 31, 20XX**	
Inventories:				
Raw material	$ 52,000		$38,000	
Supplies	4,000		4,000	
Work in process	97,500		97,500	
Finished goods	202,500	356,000	315,250	454,750
Prepaid items		3,000		3,000
Total current assets		$1,054,000		$1,352,650
Fixed assets				
Land	$ 25,000		$25,000	
Buildings	375,000		495,000	
Machinery & equipment	625,000		757,500	
Total	$1,025,000		$1,277,500	
Less: Reserve for depreciation	210,000	815,000	257,000	1,020,500
Total assets		$1,869,000		$2,373,150

Liabilities and Shareholders' Equity		
Current liabilities		
Accounts payable	$ 60,000	$ 80,400
Notes payable	300,000	50,000
Accrued salaries and wages	30,000	55,000
Accrued income taxes	370,400	46,070
Accrued items—other	28,000	80,000
Total current liabilities	$ 788,400	$ 311,470
Ownership equity		
Common stock	$ 250,000	$ 350,000
Capital contributed for common stock in excess of par value	500,000	900,000
Retained earnings	330,600	811,680
Total ownership equity	$1,080,600	$2,061,680
Total liabilities and shareholders' equity	$1,869,000	$2,373,150

EXHIBIT 5.17   Statement of Planned Retained Earnings

Balance, December 31, 20XX	$ 330,600
Add: Estimated net income for the year 20XX	691,080
Total	$1,021,680
Less: Dividends to be paid in 20XX	210,000
Estimated balance, December 31, 20XX	$ 811,680

 ADDITIONAL BUDGET MODELING TOPICS

This section addresses three additional topics related to the creation of a budget model: how to budget for the attrition of personnel during the budget period, how to install a flex budget, and whether additional versions of the annual budget should be prepared. The discussion follows:

- *Attrition budgeting.* One problem with budget models is trying to anticipate the number of employees who will leave the company during the budget year, which is expressed as a general reduction in the wage expense. One option is to budget for no departures, which results in the maximum possible wage expense, and one which the budget preparer knows in advance is unlikely to occur. Another possibility is to attempt to predict exactly who is leaving and when, which is subject to an extraordinary degree of error. An alternative approach is to incorporate into the budget an attrition percentage that is based on a company's historical experience. This is the only alternative that has some justifiable basis. It tends to be more accurate in larger companies since averages work better across several thousand employees than just a few dozen or hundred. To derive a reasonable attrition percentage, review the attrition for the past year and strip out those departures caused by one-time events, such as the closure of a facility. Also, if the job market is tightening and the company employs mostly skilled positions, then assume that the replacement interval for positions will be longer, which results in a higher attrition percentage. Since the timing of attrition is nearly impossible to predict, it is easier to apply the same percentage across the entire year. It may be more inaccurate earlier in the year, but the average level of attrition should move closer to the anticipated level by the end of the year.

■ *Flex budgeting.* Perhaps the single most tedious part of updating a budget is altering the myriad expense line items every time someone makes a change to the estimated revenue level. Revenue is far and away the most commonly tweaked number in a budget, so the underlying expenses have to be continually recast to be in proper proportion to the changed revenue levels. This is a major chore not only for the accounting staff maintaining the budget, but also for those managers who must be contacted about changes to the expense levels they had previously authorized. A recasting of the budget model will largely eliminate this problem. Instead of making changes to the expense line item for every expense in the budget, it is much easier to set up each one as either a flexible expense account or one that is fixed within a broad range of revenue levels. If it is fixed, there is no need for change, unless there is an enormous alteration in budgeted revenue levels. However, many other expenses will vary directly with revenue; in these cases, it is possible to revise the budget formulas so that they are listed as percentages of the monthly revenue level. By making these formula alterations, it becomes an easy matter to adjust revenue and see a swath of expense changes ripple through the budget model—with no manual intervention whatsoever. Though the flex budget discussion has centered on tying expenses to specific revenue levels, it is also possible, and probably more accurate, to tie some expenses to other levels of activity. For example, telephone usage or office expenses should be linked more properly to the number of budgeted employees, while utility costs can be tied either to square footage used or the number of machines in operation. Thus, it is possible to link expenses to a number of activity measurements in a flex budget.

■ *Budget versions.* Most companies prepare just a single budget scenario, which is their best guess regarding how the next year will turn out. This scenario is based upon a range of supporting assumptions, any one of which can lead to diverging results—and usually does. So, though you may spend a considerable amount of time on that "mainstream" budget scenario, just that one version will not be enough to prepare you for what may—and probably will—happen. It makes sense to add two more scenarios, one for the absolute worst case, where bankruptcy is looming, and one for the most phenomenal sales success. Sounds unlikely that either one will ever happen? If you don't plan for success, it never *will* happen, and bankruptcy scenarios are far more frequent than you might think. Consequently, it is useful to know what resources you'll need for a phenomenally successful year, and how deep you will have to cut to avoid bankruptcy. There are large gaps between the two opposite-extreme scenarios and the mainstream version. Realistically, actual results will fall into either of those two holes, so you should spend some time figuring out what you will do for situations that are somewhat above and below the mainstream scenario. Thus, five budget scenarios is a reasonable number to prepare. However, if some of the underlying assumptions are more likely than not to occur or to fail, then you may want to add some extra models just for those specific situations.

ANNUAL PLANNING CYCLE

This section provides an overview of the process of developing an annual planning cycle in a company with several operating divisions.

First, the company management issues specific guidelines concerning the plan to the operating divisions and the corporate executives involved. The guidelines are intended to ensure that:

■ Actions taken during the year will be consistent with corporate policy and strategy as decided in the strategic plan.
■ The financial assumptions will be consistent and realistic (e.g., tax rates, inflation rates, capital expenditure levels).

When received, the division plans are consolidated to form the total company picture. The division plans are prepared by function (i.e., sales, facilities, human resources, etc.). Then the consolidated plan, and that of each division, is evaluated in the corporate office. Some reiteration may be necessary to arrive at an acceptable plan. In fact, after each of the detailed budgets is prepared by the accounting staff, the figures are compared with past experience and tested by checking significant relationships. For example, the sales staff is usually only capable of selling a certain amount each year, so if the budgeted sales level increases, so too should the number of salespeople. Discussions are held with the functional supervisors or department heads to clarify any seemingly out-of-line condition.

When the overall picture is judged satisfactory at top management and board of director levels, the division is notified of the approved plan. However, when the plan is presented to the board of directors for approval, it should include summaries of key statistics, major assumptions, and risk assessments.

Once the budget is approved, the business enters a new phase. The budget must be attained, so the budget becomes a control tool. For this purpose, actual operating results of the period are compared with the budget. Variances are analyzed, and corrective action is taken wherever necessary. Quite often, economic and competitive pressures force the company's results away from its plan; if so, the budget must be revised.

 ## ROLE OF THE CONTROLLER

The controller plays a major role in assisting management in the plan development phases. He or she must:

- Provide the basic financial guidelines by which the plan should be constructed, including:
  - Allowable capital commitments
  - Tax rates, including those on income, sales, and property
  - Bases for estimating accounts payable, inventory levels, receivables, and so on
  - Interest expense rates
  - Guidance on accounting practices to be used
- Provide the format for all major financial statements, including supporting detail statements, so that appropriate analysis may be made. This is necessary to permit the analysis of data and consolidation of the financials.
- Analyze segments of the plan for reliability and reasonableness of information.
- Analyze areas that appear questionable, in a financial sense, so that suggestions can be made for improving profitability.
- Consolidate the financials to form the company's overall financial position.
- Evaluate the overall plan against targets or financial measures, and recommend changes where appropriate.
- Summarize all important aspects of the plan for presentation to top management for approval.

 ## SALES PLANNING: THE BASE OF ALL BUSINESS PLANS

The sales plan is the foundation of the entire system of plans: production plan, marketing plan, R&D plan, administrative expense plan, facilities plan, working capital plan, and financing plan. In order to create adequate subsidiary plans, companies must develop the best possible sales plan.

Sales managers often view the market as made up of three parts and estimate sales in accordance with this view:

1. Sales of existing products and/or services to existing customers
2. Sales of existing products and/or service to new customers
3. Sales of new products to existing as well as new customers

All of these sales may be necessary to avoid a natural decline in sales over a period of time and to reach the long-term corporate sales objective.

STEPS IN DEVELOPING THE NEAR-TERM SALES PLAN

The seven planning steps listed are typical when industry estimates of future sales levels are available or when some useful external data may be reliable and when the involved executives are accustomed to being provided with relevant sales and gross profit analyses.

Step 1. The sales manager requires the following starting information in order to develop the sales plan:
- Worksheets in the proper format for providing the sales estimate, by month and by product or salesperson, for the planning year
- Sales performance for the last year by salesperson in monetary and physical units
- Industry data on expected next-year total sales
- Any other analyses based on external information, developed by the market research, giving a clue to expected business conditions for the coming plan year
- Any other data the sales manager needs to help in developing sales estimates
- Analyses giving the estimated sales impact of planned sales promotions, and reasons for the cause or precise location of below-plan performance in the sales area

Step 2. The sales executive provides a detailed (e.g., by product, salesperson, or territory) estimate of sales for the planning year. Ideally, the sales manager will do this with the advice of the sales staff. When doing so, the sales manager will advise the sales staff on such issues as the percent sales

EXHIBIT 5.18 Sales Plan by Territory

Sales Territory	This Year	Total	Quarter 1	2	3	4
West	$212,400	$230,000	$ 46,000	$ 63,720	$ 79,040	$ 41,240
Rockies	75,000	78,750	15,750	23,620	31,500	7,880
Southwest	134,600	150,750	37,690	45,200	45,200	22,660
Central Plains	53,400	56,100	14,000	16,900	16,900	8,300
Middle West	171,300	186,700	33,600	65,300	50,000	37,800
Southeast	91,400	95,100	19,000	28,500	21,000	26,600
Total	$738,100	$797,400	$166,040	$243,240	$243,640	$144,480

increase expected, the estimated impact of promotional campaigns, and the actions of competitors.

Step 3. At the top executive level, the estimates are consolidated and company totals determined. Exhibit 5.18 shows a summarized sales plan.

Step 4. Executive management discusses the proposed sales level in terms of its reasonableness.

Step 5. When the sales budget is tentatively approved (an iterative process), the data are provided to other functional executives to develop their segments of the annual plan. Several iterations can take place, based on such issues as adjustments for capacity, competitive actions, and the possible lack of raw materials, until an operating plan is agreed on.

Step 6. The operating budget and capital budget, together with the related financial statements, are consolidated and tested for financial acceptability. Further iteration may be necessary if financial concerns arise.

Step 7. When the board of directors approves the plan, an executive is held responsible for each segment of the plan.

METHODS FOR DETERMINING THE SALES FORECAST

The methods used to arrive at the sales forecast in the sales plan will influence the quality of the information. Weight must be given to both internal and external factors. External factors, such as general economic conditions, industry trends, total market potential, and competitive reactions, are beyond the company's control, but may greatly affect the sales potential. Internal factors—conditions within the company—include production capacity, product quality, sales experience and history, special advertising programs, and pricing policy.

This section discusses some of the more common methods of estimating sales. What system is used may depend on several related factors:

- *Time.* The time span available and the frequency of the data
- *Resources needed or available.* Human resources, computers, financial sophistication, and cost
- *Data input.* What data are needed, and the consistency, availability, and variability of that data
- *Output.* Reliability, extent of detail, capability of the forecasting method for detecting trend changes, and capability of revealing direction changes that have taken place

The most commonly used forecasting techniques are described next.

Statistical Methods

Basically, a statistical technique is applied to a series of relevant numbers to arrive at a forecast of sales for the industry or company. Then this forecast is modified by the expected impact of sales efforts, promotional campaigns, and so on, to arrive at a sales plan for the company. Among these techniques are:

- *Time series analysis.* Using the least-squares method, an existing series of values is converted into a trend and extrapolated for a future time period. The analysis accounts for cyclical movements and seasonal patterns to arrive at the forecast.
- *Correlation.* A series is located with which the company's sales, or sales of a particular product line, seem to correlate or move sympathetically. The annual product sales are plotted against the index and, based on the leading factor, calculated for the planning period.

Judgmental Methods (Nonstatistical)

The judgmental method involves gathering estimates from several groups. Sometimes, for example, *estimates of salespeople* are used. The sales staff members are supplied with actual unit and dollar sales for the past few years and create estimates based on that information and their personal knowledge of their territories and customers. This method has the advantage of using knowledge-able people as well as letting them have a say in creating the forecast. Yet sales personnel tend to provide optimistic forecasts, they may not give weight to broad economic indicators, and their estimates may be deliberately reduced if compensation is based on the quotas that will be derived from the sales forecast.

Additionally, *customer surveys* may be made. Sales staff members can ask customers for purchase estimates for the upcoming year. Such surveys are used when other methods of forecasting are not reliable. They are useful when the number of customers is small, so that a few make up a large proportion of the company's business. However, the method is time consuming, and users may be uncooperative.

Finally, *executive opinion composites* can be developed. The executive staff is familiar with the industry and company sales picture. In this method, estimates are secured from a group of executives and then the opinions are combined. However, if the executives really do not know the market, then their opinions are just guesses, based on few facts.

Other Methods

For some types of products, the total market is well known. In addition to the industry total unit volume and/or dollar volume, the rate of growth has been calculated and often the estimated sales for the next year or two have been determined—perhaps by the industry association. In any event, the planner knows what *share of the market* the company has secured in the past. This market share is then adjusted for the estimated impact of special sales promotions, or estimated competitive activity is applied to the projected total market to arrive at the company portion of the estimated industry sales for the coming year.

The *end-use analysis* technique depends on having a sound estimate of the total end-use market for which products the company's articles serve as component parts or elements. To use the automotive industry as an example, if the expected unit sales of automobiles are known or have been estimated, then the supplier company can estimate its probable sales during the planning period for its product. This market, plus the estimated replacement business, can be combined to arrive at sales expectations. This method bears a close relationship to the customer survey procedure.

The *product-line analysis* makes use of the fact that often major products are sold through different channels of distribution or methods of sales than other products, and the sales and sales effort may be managed by product line. Under these circumstances, a company's internal sales analyses by product, subanalyzed by territory, may be the starting point of determining the sales estimate, supplemented by some other techniques to arrive at the sales plan.

The *market simulation* technique involves the use of a computer and the construction of a mathematical model of the market. Modifying input for the different factors that influence the market permits the calculation of various sales estimates.

These three groups of indicators are of practical value in creating market forecasts:

1. *Leading indicators.* These are series that usually reach peaks or troughs before general economic activity. Some leading indicators are:
   - *Length of the average workweek.* Employers find it more economical to increase the number of hours worked each week before hiring additional employees. These longer workweeks may lead to an upturn of one or more months, or they may coincide with the change.
   - *Number of unemployment claims.* The number of persons who sign up for jobless benefits reflects the change in present or anticipated business activity. The fewer who sign up, the better. This index usually turns up before a turning point in economic activity.
   - *Gain in new orders for consumer goods.* When new orders are received, materials and supplies are purchased, workers are hired, and output increases. Recoveries have occurred as much as four months after gains in new orders.
   - *Increase in stock prices.* A rise in the Standard & Poor's index of 500 companies usually indicates higher actual and expected profits. Advances in the stock market have preceded improvements in business activity by three to eight months.
   - *Number of new housing starts.* Several months pass from the time a building permit is issued until construction begins. Gains in building permits issued have led business upturns by 0 to 10 months.
   - *Number of new orders for plant and equipment.* When such orders are received, construction and manufacturing activity increases. These signals have preceded economic upturns by as much as six months, but also have trailed such change by up to nine months.
   - *Net change in inventories.* As companies expect an increase in sales, they tend to build their stocks of inventory on hand. This index has led business recoveries by zero to eight months.
2. *Coincident indicators.* These are series that tend to move with aggregate economic activity. Some coincident indicators are the number of

employees on the nonagricultural payroll, personal income, and manufacturing and trade sales.

3. *Lagging indicators.* These are series that reach turning points after the aggregate economic activity has already turned. Some lagging indicators are the ratio of consumer credit to personal income, the prime rate charged by banks, and the average duration of unemployment.

Many sales forecasting professionals do a good job of predicting domestic sales, but have difficulty with international projections. Some of the reasons for less than sensational sales results in the global marketplace include:

- ▪ *Inadequate market research.* Marketing executives sometimes think that the experience in one market is automatically transferable to others.
- ▪ *Tendency to overstandardization.* Instead of encouraging some local innovation, some salespeople think the same product or packaging applies to all markets.
- ▪ *Inflexibility in the entire marketing program.* The same programs are forced on every business unit. Yet experience has shown that some facets are unacceptable in local markets. Although some central guidance is desirable, forced adoption, without listening to local arguments, destroys local enthusiasm.
- ▪ *Lack of adequate follow-up.* Although there may be impressive kickoff programs, momentum is lost because local progress is not monitored.

If a company is alert to the advantages of globalization and is desirous of taking advantage of economies of scale in marketing, manufacturing, R&D, distribution, and purchasing, it needs to avoid the deficiencies mentioned above.

 ## CHANGES IN THE SALES MIXTURE

Most companies have a variety of product lines, each making a different contribution toward fixed expenses. Changes in the break-even point as well as the operating profit can result from shifts in the mixture of products sold, even though the sales prices are unchanged and the total dollar sales volume meets expectations. Such results can occur also from changes in distribution channels or sales to different classes of customers if the rearrangement affects the contribution of the product over and above variable costs. Actually, when a break-even chart is used, an underlying assumption is that the proportion of each

EXHIBIT 5.19 Impact of a Change in Sales Mix on Profits

	Sales		Variable	Marginal Income over Variable Costs	
Product	%	Amount	Costs	Amount	% of Net Sales
A	40.00	$ 4,000.00	$2,600.00	$1,400.00	35.00
B	50.00	5,000.00	4,000.00	1,000.00	20.00
C	10.00	1,000.00	875.00	125.00	12.50
Total	100.00	$10,000.00	$7,475.00	2,525.00	25.25
Fixed Costs				1,200.00	
Operating Profit				$1,325.00	

product sold, or sales through each channel of distribution, is unchanged. Very often this does not happen; the proportionate drop is not the same for all products. The higher-priced lines, for example, may decline much more rapidly than others. Such changes must be recognized in evaluating the data.

The effect of a change in sales mixture is illustrated in the calculations shown in Exhibit 5.19. Assume the following proportion of sales among three products, the indicated variable costs, fixed costs, and profit.

The break-even point can be calculated as:

$$\frac{\$1,200}{.2525} = \$4,752$$

If, however, sales increase on the higher-margin items, the break-even point would decrease. Such a change is illustrated in Exhibit 5.20.

EXHIBIT 5.20 Impact of Change in Sales Mix on Break-Even Point

	Sales			Marginal Income over Variable Costs	
Product	%	Amount	Variable Costs	Amount	% of Net Sales
A	60.00	$ 6,000.00	$3,900.00	$2,100.00	35.00
B	35.00	3,500.00	2,800.00	700.00	20.00
C	5.00	500.00	437.50	62.50	12.50
Total	100.00	$10,000.00	$7,137.50	2,862.00	28.625
Fixed Costs				1,200.00	
Operating Profit				$1,662.50	

The break-even point can be calculated in this way:

$$\frac{\$1,200}{.28625} = \$4,162$$

This break-even point has dropped by $560 as a result of the changes in sales mixture.

 ## CHANGES IN THE SALES PRICE

It should be clear that a change in selling price affects the break-even point and the relationship between income and variable costs. The controller should also be aware that a change in selling price may have an even greater effect on marginal income than a corresponding percentage increase in variable costs. For example, in Exhibit 5.21, a 10 percent drop in selling prices is equivalent to an 11.1 percent increase in variable costs in regard to the break-even point and marginal income.

Sales were reduced by 10 percent of $50,000 to a level of $45,000. As variable costs were not changed, these costs as a percent of sales are 44.44 percent, an increase of 11.1 percent. Computing the revised variable cost as a percent of net sales based on the original $50,000 of sales produces a variable cost of $22,222. This is 11.1 percent higher than the original variable cost.

EXHIBIT 5.21 Impact of Price Change on Break-Even Volume

	Present Selling Prices		With a 10% Reduction in Sales Price		Equivalent Increase in Variable Costs	
Sales	$50,000	100.00	$45,000	100.00	$50,000	100.00
Variable costs	20,000	40.00	20,000	44.44	22,222	44.44
Marginal income	30,000	60.00	25,000	55.56	27,778	55.56
Fixed costs	15,000	30.00	15,000	33.33	15,000	30.00
Operating profit	15,000	30.00	10,000	22.23	12,778	25.56
Break-even volume	$25,000		$27,000		$27,000	

CHANGES IN THE COST

An increase or decrease in the amount of fixed cost changes the operating profit by a like amount, while the break-even point is changed by a like percentage. To illustrate, assume a case where fixed costs are reduced by $10,000, or 33.3 percent. Exhibit 5.22 shows the operating profit and break-even points.

In the example, with a reduction of $10,000 in fixed costs, the operating profit naturally increased by a like amount.

Moreover, fixed costs were reduced by 33.3 percent, so the break-even point declined by 33.3 percent, from a $75,000 sales volume to $50,000.

This calculation assumes that no change would take place in variable costs, but in practice a change in fixed costs may be accompanied by a change in the variable. For example, installation of a labor-saving device may increase depreciation and maintenance charges and decrease direct labor costs and related payroll charges. If an increase in fixed costs is being discussed, the probability of an increased sales volume should be reviewed. Furthermore, alternatives should be examined, such as subcontracting or renting of space and equipment in lieu of purchasing. The acquisition of permanent assets will decrease the firm's ability to adjust its costs to lower levels should a reduced sales volume ever necessitate such action. Opportunities for the reduction of fixed expenses should not be overlooked in any attempt to reduce costs. A lowering of fixed costs increases the margin at any sales level, and, by reducing the break-even point, the company is able to withstand a greater drop in income before losses appear.

EXHIBIT 5.22 Impact of Cost Changes on Break-Even Sales

	Present		Fixed Costs Reduced by $10,000	
	Amount	% of Net Sales	Amount	% of Net Sales
Net sales	$200,000	100	$200,000	100
Variable costs	120,000	60	120,000	60
Marginal income	80,000	40	80,000	40
Fixed costs	30,000	15	20,000	10
Operating profit	50,000	25	60,000	30
Break-even sales	$ 75,000		$ 50,000	

Changes in unit variable costs or expenses also affect the break-even point. Most cost reduction programs center around this category because here a great many possibilities are open for cost reduction. For example, changes in the type of material used, the purchase price of material, or the amount of scrap or waste can affect variable costs. Changes in manufacturing processes, hourly labor rates, plant layout, or employee training methods, or the introduction of incentive payments can all affect labor costs. General economic conditions may influence the ability of a firm to reduce variable costs. Very often the reduced sales volume permits more effective maintenance of equipment during shutdown periods. Then, too, in such periods the labor turnover rate and material prices are usually reduced. Of course, such conditions may force sales price reductions, which negatively affect the company's profits.

CHAPTER SIX

Sales

S ALES MANAGEMENT IS A dynamic area, constantly facing new problems. The controller has a great impact on the resolution of these problems. An extensive review of sales and distribution costs can help sales executives make prudent decisions consistent with the company's goals.

This chapter discusses the controller's role in relation to the sales department, as well as typical kinds of analyses to apply to sales, the applicability of standards to the sales staff, issues regarding product pricing, and reports that are useful for describing the performance of sales revenue, margins, and costs.

 ROLE OF THE CONTROLLER

The controller's skills are useful in sales accounting and analysis to assist marketing executives in these areas:

- *Problems of product.* The initial selection of the product or consideration of changes in the line, sizes, and colors generally should be based on the collective judgment of the sales manager (for marketing considerations), the manufacturing executive (production problems), and the controller (cost considerations). The controller should be able to indicate the probable margin on the product, as well as the effect of volume on the margin or the effect of changes in quality, composition, and manufacturing processes on the cost to make or sell. In the continuing review of sales trends, the controller may be able to identify unfavorable trends that could require a redirection of the sales effort or a change in the product.

■ *Problems of price.* In many companies, pricing procedures are not reviewed on a periodic basis. Although cost is not the only determining factor, it must be considered in maximizing the return on investment. The controller must be able to provide all the available cost information. Total costs, marginal or differential costs, and out-of-pocket costs must be considered in developing the price structure. This is true for competitive bids or for establishing price lists for the usual type of sale.

An analysis of sales volume and related prices may reveal that unfavorable variances often result from salespeople having too much authority in setting prices. Obviously, as production costs change, the information should be communicated to the sales executives for consideration of appropriate price changes. Also, assistance should be provided in setting volume price breaks for different sizes of orders.

■ *Problems of distribution.* The controller creates and reviews statistics for unfavorable trends. The controller should also research differences in the selling cost through different channels of distribution, as well as in different customer accounts and sizes of orders. Controller input is needed on such issues as:

- The minimum order size to accept
- Restriction of the sales effort on large volume accounts that purchase only low-margin products
- Desirability of servicing particular types of accounts through jobbers, telephone solicitation, mail order, and so on
- Discontinuance of aggressive sales efforts on accounts where annual sales volume is too low
- The best location for branch warehouses

■ *Problems relating to the method of sale.* The controller can assist the sales manager by providing information on historical costs and preparing alternative cost scenarios for various selling methods. For example, such analyses can include the impact of distributing samples, using various advertising programs, and costs of market tests.

■ *Problems of organization.* Because the sales management function is dynamic, organizational changes are necessary to satisfy the new requirements. In making these changes, information related to potential sales by product or territory may assist in reassigning or hiring new salespeople.

▪ *Problems of planning and control.* The controller can be active in any of these areas:

  ▪ *Sales budgets and quotas.* Detailed records about the distribution of sales by territory, product, and customer, coupled with the sales manager's knowledge of product changes and trends, provide basic information necessary in an intelligent setting of sales budgets, quotas, and standards. The controller also may provide services in connection with forecasting and market studies.

  ▪ *Distribution expense budget and standards.* A history of past expenses as recorded in the accounting department provides much-needed data in setting budgets and standards for the measurement and control of the selling effort.

  ▪ *Periodic income and expense statements.* These can be by territory, commodity, method of sale, customer, salesperson, or operating division. Increasing levels of detail can spotlight specific levels of weakness.

  ▪ *Special analyses to reveal performance problems.* Typical special reports cover sales incentive plans (to see which plan will motivate the staff to sell the most profitable products), branch office and warehouse expenses, customer development expense, and salesperson's compensation in comparison with sales garnered and the industry pay structure. The controller also has the responsibility to see that adequate procedures are followed and that the sales planning and control is sound from a financial viewpoint.

SALES ANALYSIS

The evidence is unmistakably clear in any business that general information is of little value in making key marketing decisions and directing sales efforts. The data must be specific and directly related to the problem under examination.

Types of Sales Analyses Needed

There are many types of sales analysis. Some analyses chart past sales performance, while others involve determining trends in comparison with past periods and/or the relationship to budget, gross profit, selling expense, or net profit. Analyses may be expressed in physical units or dollar volume. Typical analyses are by product, territory, channel of distribution, method of sale, customer, size of order, terms of sale, organization, and salesperson. These analyses may be developed not merely with regard to sales, but from gross profit to profit after direct selling expense or ultimately to the net profit of the segment being measured. Other analyses related to unrealized sales may be useful, such as unfilled orders, cancellations, and lost sales.

The controller may find that the sales manager can use certain of these analyses monthly or periodically—for example, sales by territory, by product lines, or by salesperson. Other analyses may be made only for a special investigation, when it is expected that the tabulation will reveal out-of-line conditions. In any event, it is the controller's responsibility to design and install procedures and records in such a fashion (e.g., by reorganizing the chart of accounts) that the maximum information is made available with a minimum of effort.

Deductions from Sales

In any analysis of sales, the importance of sales deductions should not be overlooked. Although reviews may relate to net sales, the clue to substandard profits may lie in the deductions—high freight cost, special allowances, or discounts. These factors may reveal why unit prices appear too low. In particular, it may be helpful to prepare an analysis of deductions by responsibility: the manufacturing division, for defective products; the traffic department, for erroneous freight allowances; and the sales division, for allowances to retain customer goodwill.

Sales Department Bottlenecks

The basic concept of throughput management is to locate the bottleneck in an operation and implement a variety of techniques to eliminate or at least reduce the impact of that bottleneck, such as by having an adequate inventory buffer in front of it, supplementing it with similar work centers (even if less efficient), outsourcing work, or by shifting quality inspectors to a spot in front of the work center (which prevents flawed work-in-process from entering the bottleneck operation. What if the bottleneck is in the sales department?

Let's take a typical sales process as a example: the sales staff locates prospects, meets with them, issues a quote, conducts a product demonstration, negotiates the contract, and then passes the order to the rest of the company for delivery. If a company wants to increase sales, the usual response is to add more sales staff to drum up business—but what if they are drumming up plenty of initial leads, and yet sales are still not increasing? If so, compare the capacity of each step in the sales process just noted to the amount of actual sales activity for the same step. For example, there may be only a small group assigned the task of creating quotes, and they cannot keep up with inquiries brought to them by the sales staff. This leads to prospects becoming frustrated and taking their business elsewhere.

The controller's role in discovering these problems is to measure the capacity of each activity in the sales process and match it to the amount of actual activity. Every time the capacity and actual activity measures match, there is a bottleneck. It is also easy to spot bottlenecks by measuring the backlog in front of each process step—large backlogs indicate the presence of a bottleneck. Locating these problems is the crucial first step to increasing a company's sales.

Typical Conditions Found by Sales Analyses

Many businesses find that a large proportion of the sales volume arises from a small share of the product line. Likewise, a small proportion of customers provide the bulk of the business. Such conditions reflect the fact that only a small part of the selling effort is responsible for most of the business. This information may prove useful in permitting the concentration of sales effort and the consequent reduction in selling expenses or redeployment of the sales staff to different customers or territories. When product analysis reveals un-satisfactory conditions, a simplification of the product line may be indicated. Although the line may not be limited only to volume items, many sales managers are beginning to realize that not all varieties need be carried. Smart executives will let their competitors have the odd sizes or colors and concen-trate on the more profitable articles.

The controller can use the drill-down technique to pinpoint specific areas that cause problems. For example, the controller notes that sales are $20,000 lower than expected in the period. By drilling down to the next level of detail, the problem is more clearly defined as being caused by the Northeast region. By drilling down to the next level of detail, the controller finds that salesperson X in the Northeast region has fallen far short of the sales goal. Even further detail may show which specific items in the product line are not being sold by salesperson X. This kind of analysis allows the sales manager to correct the low sales problem with specific actions.

Other Uses of Sales Analysis

The controller can perform many simple sales analyses to guide the sales effort. Here are a few:

- *Sales planning and setting of quotas.* Past experience is a factor.
- *Inventory control.* To plan inventories properly, a business should be familiar with past sales and probable future trends in terms of seasonal fluctuations and type of product.
- *Setting sales standards.* Past experience is a factor.
- *Enhancing the distribution of sales effort.* The company may be concentrating its effort in too restrictive an area. Consideration of potential sales, competitive conditions, and cost factors may dictate a wider coverage. Alternatively, analysis might reveal that the territory is not being covered fully.
- *Enhancing the sales effort on products.* A study of sales and potential sales may reveal the restriction of sales effort to certain products, resulting in the neglect of other and more profitable ones. Also, a comparison of sales by product with previous periods will reveal trends.
- *Enhancing the sales effort in terms of customers.* Analysis of consumer buying trends should reveal information about the types of merchandise purchased by each customer. Also, comparison with the sales of a similar period for the previous year will reveal whether the company is making headway in securing the maximum amount of profitable business from each customer. Analysis by customer account, coupled with other information and discussions with the sales manager, will show certain accounts that cannot possibly provide a profitable volume, even if developed. Such analysis may permit greater utilization of the sales effort elsewhere.

Sales and Gross Profit Analysis

Sales efforts should be directed and focused on profitable volume. To accomplish this, sales executives must be provided with all the facts related to profit. Therefore, analyses of sales must include a detailed analysis of gross profit. For example, a salesperson's report should indicate the comparative gross profit by periods as well as sales. Although high gross profit does not necessarily signify a high net profit (because the selling costs may be excessive), it is an indicator.

Variations in gross profit may result from changes in the selling price, product sales mixture, returns, or volume, largely controlled by the sales executive, or from changes in manufacturing efficiency, controlled by the production executive. These facts should be recognized when reviewing changes in gross profit. The causes of variances should be divided into those that are the responsibility of the sales executive and of the production executive.

 ## SALES STANDARDS

A standard is a scientifically developed measure of performance. The most widely used sales standard is the quota, which is the amount of dollar or physical volume of sales assigned to a sales unit. The quota may involve other considerations, such as gross profit, new customers, collections, or traveling expenses, thereby representing a composite standard of performance. Often sales standards are not appreciated by sales managers, who are of the opinion that standards substitute impersonal statistics for sales leadership. However, sales standards reveal weaknesses in performance, are a basis for rewarding merit, and set a stimulating goal for each salesperson to achieve. There are three primary requirements in developing tools for the sales executive:

1. *Sales standards are the result of careful investigation and analysis of past performance, taking into consideration expected future conditions.* Sales standards represent the opinion of those best qualified to judge what constitutes satisfactory performance. Judgment about detailed operations must rest largely with the sales executives. Opinions about expected general business conditions should represent the combined judgment of the executive staff, including the chief executive, the sales manager, and the controller.
2. *Sales standards must be fair and reasonable measures of performance.* Nothing will be so destructive to morale as a sales quota that is set much too high. Experience shows that such standards will be ignored. The standards must be attainable by the caliber of salesperson the company expects to be representative of its sales staff.
3. *Sales standards will need revision from time to time.* Because sales conditions change frequently, the measuring stick must change to keep pace.

The sales representative should be thoroughly informed about the method of arriving at the quota and convinced that the amount of assigned sales is justified according to the existing conditions. Then, and only then, will the salesperson exert all efforts to meet the quota.

Sales representatives react to sales quotas, as with all standards, somewhat differently, particularly at first. Some are stimulated to their highest efficiency, whereas others are discouraged. Some sales executives place considerable emphasis on recognizing this human element in setting their quotas.

The objection sometimes raised—that efforts are lessened after quotas are reached—is seldom valid if performance is properly rewarded. The chief difficulty arises when quotas are exceeded as a result of some fortuitous circumstance in which the sales representative has had no part or for which the representative's share of the credit is uncertain. The solution here rests with extreme fairness in handling individual cases and with the development of confidence in the knowledge and integrity of sales executives.

Illustrations of Sales Standards

Sales standards may be expressed in terms of effort, results, or the relation of effort to result. For example, a salesperson may be required to make 3 calls a day or 15 calls a week. If the calls are made, the standard is met. Again, as a result of these calls, 10 orders must be received for every 15 calls made. Another standard is simply to secure a certain dollar volume from a given territory, regardless of the number of calls made or the percentage of orders per call.

Although the applicability of sales standards to various industries and types of trading concerns may differ, the controller may consider discussing the following standards with the sales manager:

- *Standards of effort*
  - Number of calls made per period
  - Number of calls made on prospective customers
  - Number of dealers and agencies to be established
  - Number of units of sales promotional effort to be used
- *Standards of results*
  - Percentage of prospects to whom sales are to be made
  - Number of customers to whom new articles are to be introduced or sold
  - Number of new customers to be secured
  - Amount of dollar volume to be secured
  - Number of physical units to be sold
  - High-throughput physical units to be sold
  - Amount of gross profit to be secured
  - Amount of profit to be secured

- Amount to be sold to individual customers
- Dollar or physical volume of individual products to be sold
- Percentage of gross profit to be returned
- Average size of order to be secured
- Relation of sales deductions to gross sales
- *Standards expressing relationship of effort and result*
  - Number of orders to be received per call made
  - Number of new customers to be secured per call made on prospects
  - Number of inquiries or orders to be received per unit or per dollar of sales promotional effort expended
  - Relation of individual direct selling expense items to volume or gross profit
  - Relation of sales administration or supervision costs to volume or gross profit

Revision of Sales Standards

Some standards of sales performance can be set with a high degree of exactness. The number of calls a salesperson should make, the percentage of prospects to whom sales should be made, and the physical units that should be sold to each customer are illustrative of performance measures that frequently lend themselves to accurate measurements. However, many factors in sales performance are so governed by conditions beyond the control of the salespeople that the standards must be revised promptly to meet important changes in such conditions. Where a salesperson is given some latitude in price setting, the gross profit may vary with competitive conditions beyond his or her control. Strikes, droughts, and floods may suddenly affect the sales possibilities in a particular territory. If the sales standards are to be effective measures of sales performance, they must be revised promptly as conditions change. Careless measurement of performance soon leads to discouragement, resentment, and disinterest in the task.

 SALES REPORTS

It is the function of the controller to furnish the sales executives with the sales facts. However, it is one thing to furnish the information and another to see that it is understood and acted on. To ensure the necessary understanding, the controller must adapt the report to the reader. Information for the needs of the chief executive will be different from that for the sales manager, and reports for subordinate sales executives will differ even more. The extent of the information required and the form of presentation will depend on the capabilities of the individual, the individual's responsibilities, the type of organization, and the philosophy of sales management.

Some sales managers can use vast amounts of statistical data effectively, whereas others prefer summaries. Accordingly, the controller should offer to develop reports to meet individual requirements. The use of charts, graphs, and summaries will greatly enhance the communication of the sales data to sales management. In many instances, a narrative report citing the significant issues or problems is the most effective tool. Depending on the seriousness of the problem, or where major actions are being recommended, a meeting may be in order.

The matters that may be included in a sales report may cover any of these items:

- Actual sales performance, with month or year-to-date figures
- Budgeted sales for both the period and year-to-date
- Comparison of actual sales by firm with industry figures, including percentages of the total
- Analysis of variances between budgeted and actual sales and reasons for differences
- Sale–cost relationships, such as cost per order received
- Sales standards—comparison of actual and quota sales by salesperson
- Unit sales price data
- Gross profit data

These data may be expressed in physical units or in dollars. Aside from actual or standard sales performance, some may relate to orders, cancellations, returns, or lost sales.

Top sales executives should receive information in summary fashion. For example, a comparison of actual and planned sales by product line or territory is appropriate information for the sales manager. Trend reports that show increasing or declining sales by major category are useful. Also, an orders-on-hand report gives the sales manager information about the likely short-term direction of sales. Exhibit 6.1 shows such a chart.

For control purposes, the performance of each segment of the sales organization should be made known to the supervisor responsible. It follows, therefore, that reporting must be available for each division, district, area, branch, and salesperson. As reports relate to increasingly lower levels of management, such information can become massive in extent. To avoid lengthy reports, the controller can use "exception" reports. This method eliminates data where performance was satisfactory and details only that which did not reach acceptable levels. Such a report could list, for example, only those salespeople who were 5% or more under budget, or only those customers on whom a loss was realized. These reports can use direct costs only or can also include allocated overhead costs. Exhibit 6.2 presents an exception report for salespeople.

EXHIBIT 6.1 Report on Sales Order Activity

		Orders on Hand				
Description	Order on Hand, 6/30/XX	Orders Received	Orders Canceled	Orders Delivered	Units	Sales Value in $
Vehicles						
Type A	50	25	5	10	60	120.0
Type B	100	—	5	20	75	262.5
Type C	150	50	—	5	195	838.5
Type D	60	10	—	5	65	97.5

EXHIBIT 6.2 Exception Report—Salesperson Performance

Description	Actual Sales	Under Budget Amount	%
Performance satisfactory	$ 827,432	$112,610	15.8
Under budget performance			
Abernathy	32,016	1,760	5.2
Bristol	17,433	1,390	7.4
Caldwell	19,811	1,320	6.2
Fischer	24,033	1,470	5.8
Gordon	8,995	480	5.1
Inch	27,666	1,820	6.2
Long	4,277	600	12.3
Mather	39,474	3,800	8.8
Owens	43,189	4,400	9.6
Subtotal	216,894	17,040	7.9
District total	$1,044,326	$ 95,570	9.2

PRODUCT PRICING

In the field of product pricing, the controller can exert some preventive accounting control by bringing facts to bear on the problem before unwise decisions are made. This control activity is closely related to profit planning: The influence of prices on company profits is obvious, and the best controls on costs and expenses will not succeed in producing a profit if selling prices are set incorrectly. The controller can perform these product pricing functions:

- Help establish a pricing policy that will be consistent with the corporate objectives.
- Provide unit cost analysis as one factor in price setting.
- Project the effect on earnings of proposed price changes and alternatives.
- Gather pertinent information on competitive price activity.
- Analyze the historical data on prices and volumes to substantiate probable trends as they may influence proposed price changes.
- Determine for management the influence on profits of changes in price, product mix, sales volume, and so on.

Cost Basis for Pricing

Over the long term, no company can sell all or most of its products at less than cost; therefore, adequate cost information is indispensable. In the short term, the role played by the cost factors depends on the circumstances. For example, if a product is built to order, then costs will be more important. Furthermore, if competition is weak or if a company is the price leader, then cost information will play a larger role than if the opposite situations exist.

The question then arises: What kinds of costs are required? For different purposes, different types of costs may be desirable. One type of cost may be suitable for a short-range decision and quite another type for long-term purposes. Moreover, for pricing, the usual historical cost approach may not meet the requirement. In short, the controller should be aware of the several costing methods and the limitations of each and select that concept most suited to the purpose at hand.

Before reviewing several alternative costing techniques, some general observations are useful. First, prices relate to the future. Therefore, costs to be used in determining prices must be prospective. Recognition should be given to cost levels expected to prevail in the period under review. Probable raw material and labor costs should be considered. Prospective changes in process ought to be reflected in cost estimates.

Obviously, inflation must be considered, and the best available information should be obtained to recognize what future rates of inflation can be expected. In this forecasting, the controller should utilize, to the extent practicable, the modern scientific tools of statistical sampling, simulation methods, decision analysis techniques, and price-level analysis. Consideration should also be given to the replacement cost of the productive capacity or capital assets. Prices must provide for the future replacement of these productive assets at the projected costs.

The controller should assist in determining the sales price that will produce the greatest net profit over a long period of time. Too high a profit over the short term may invite competition or governmental regulation. The basic procedure is for the controller to secure from the sales manager the probable number of units that can be sold at various price levels. Then the unit cost and total cost at the corresponding production levels are calculated. Then the volume at which the greatest total profit is secured can be determined.

Finally, all costs related to a product should be considered, not merely the cost to manufacture. It defeats the purpose of developing a comprehensive and detailed costing study if manufacturing costs are carefully calculated but selling or other expenses are applied as an overall percent without regard to the direct expense and effort specifically applicable to the product.

Although many costing methods are in use, four approaches warrant discussion:

1. *Total cost method.* Under this concept the cost of the product is determined, and to this figure is added the desired profit margin. Such a calculation is shown in Exhibit 6.3. The total cost method has the advantage of being easy to calculate and being able to recover all costs. However, it does not distinguish between direct costs and total costs (critical for short-term pricing decisions), and ignores the possibility of using even higher prices to achieve a greater return.

2. *Direct cost method.* This approach recognizes only the incremental costs of a product. These are the costs directly associated with the product that would not be incurred if the product were not manufactured or sold. Any selling price received above this floor represents a contribution to fixed expenses. Applying this principle to Product A described under the total cost method produces the information shown in Exhibit 6.4.

If the product must be sold for its incremental costs or less, then the company would not earn less profit, and might possibly earn a higher profit, by not manufacturing and selling the product. Full consideration must be given, however, to lost business if the withdrawal of the product would cause the loss of other business.

EXHIBIT 6.3 Total Cost Method

	Product A Unit Cost and Selling Price
Cost and expenses	
Raw material	$10.00
Direct labor	4.00
Manufacturing overhead	6.00
Total manufacturing cost	20.00
Research and development expense (10% of manufacturing cost)	2.00
Selling and advertising expense (20% of manufacturing cost)	4.00
General and administrative expense (10% of manufacturing overhead)	.60
Total cost	26.60
Desired profit margin (25% of total cost)	6.65
Proposed selling price	$33.25

EXHIBIT 6.4 Direct Cost Method

	Product A Unit Cost and Selling Price
Cost and expenses	
Raw material	$10.00
Direct labor	4.00
Variable manufacturing expense	1.50
Variable selling expense	1.50
Variable administrative expense	.30
Total variable or incremental cost	17.30
Fixed expense applicable to the product	2.50
Total direct costs	$19.80

This costing method is of most use when additional sales may be made at reduced prices (e.g., to private brand business), when idle plant capacity can be utilized only at reduced prices, and when these added sales do not create problems in the regular marketplace.

Marginal costs are used for short-term decisions only because they do not include long-term fixed costs that are an important factor in the viability of a product's long-term profitability. The great danger is the tendency to secure a larger and larger volume of sales on an incremental basis, with an ultimate deteriorating effect in the market and a large share of business that does not return its proper share of all costs. Furthermore, under such conditions there is no profit from the products that are priced only to cover their costs.

3. *Return on assets method.* This method maximizes the return on assets employed. It gives attention to the capital invested in manufacturing or sales facilities or working capital. This formula may be used to calculate the sales price required to produce a return on assets employed:

$$\text{Unit price} = \frac{\dfrac{\text{Cost} + (\text{Desired \% return} \times \text{Fixed assets})}{\text{Annual sales volume in units}}}{1 - (\text{Desired \% return})(\text{Variable assets as \% of sales volume})}$$

In the formula, cost represents the total cost of manufacturing, selling, administrative, and research expenses. The percent return represents that rate desired on assets employed. The fixed assets represent plant and equipment. The variable assets represent the current assets that are a function of volume and prices. Applying some assumptions, a unit price of Product A may be calculated in this manner:

$$= \frac{\dfrac{\$2,660,000 + (.20 \times \$300,000)}{100,000}}{1 - (.20 \times .30)}$$

$$= \frac{\$2,720,000/(100,000 \text{ units})}{1 - .06}$$

$$= \frac{27.20}{.94} = \$28.936$$

The proof is computed in this way:

Income and costs	
Sales (1,000,000 units at $28.936)	$ 2,893,600
Costs	2,660,000
Income before taxes	$ 233,600
Assets employed	
Variable (30% of $2,893,600)	$ 868,080
Fixed	300,000
Total assets employed	$ 1,168,080
20% return on assets employed of $1,168,080	$ 233,600

In a multiproduct company, there is a problem with allocating capital employed to the various product lines. This problem can be solved by allocating assets to the product lines. Exhibit 6.5 shows some methods of prorating assets to product lines.

4. *Target cost method.* This method is considerably different from the other costing methods. Target costing means that the new product design team determines the price at which the product must sell and then designs a product with a cost to fit that price level. The controller must be involved in the initial cost determination before the product is produced, to ensure that planned costs allow for an adequate profit margin. The controller will also be involved in later cost studies to see if actual costs match the planned costs.

EXHIBIT 6.5 Methods Used to Allocate Corporate Assets to Product Line

Item	Possible Bases
Cash	In ratio to total product cost
Accounts receivable	In ratio to sales, adjusted for significant differences in terms of sale
Raw material	In ratio to actual or expected usage
Work-in-process	In ratio to actual or expected usage
Finished goods	In ratio to cost of manufacture
Fixed assets	In ratio to conversion costs (labor and variable manufacturing overhead) or labor hours

The discussion on product pricing has to do principally with establishing prices for unrelated customers under competitive conditions. A special aspect of product pricing relates to international transfer prices—the value assigned to goods or services produced in one country for the use or benefit of a related company in another country.

Transfer prices, which should be reflected in the sales plans and planned net income of both the producing and receiving companies, probably should be established through the joint efforts of the sales executive and a member of the controller's department. This is the case due to complicated IRS regulations that relate to actual or expected costs, capital employed, functions performed by each party, and the risks involved.

The setting of product prices is complex and includes the evaluation of many variables. It is the task of the controller to provide all pertinent facts for management's judgment. The various costing methods must be considered and the most appropriate applied to each company's unique set of circumstances. In addition to the applicable costs, other factors in setting product prices should be summarized for management's review:

- Return on invested capital or assets employed
- Assets employed and turnover
- Percent of plant capacity utilized
- Percent of product line for each product
- Percent of market
- Competition pricing and percent of market

Throughput Basis for Pricing

Throughput analysis is helpful for determining prices. It focuses on management of the company bottleneck in order to maximize profits. The classic bottleneck is a work center somewhere in a company's production area that does not have sufficient capacity to meet all sales needs. The bottleneck operation is readily evident from the large queue of unfinished work located just upstream from it. To maximize profitability, a company should accept jobs that have a combination of the highest throughput margin (price minus the cost of direct materials) and the lowest use of the bottleneck operation. For example, a product with a throughput margin of $10 that uses one minute of the bottleneck operation has a throughput/minute of $10, and is superior to another product with a throughput margin of $20 but which uses 4 minutes of the bottleneck operation, which results in a throughput/minute of $5.

Consequently, price setting should be focused on wringing the highest possible throughput/minute from each product.

What if a company has more capacity than it can sell? Then the bottleneck is said to have shifted into the marketplace. When the potential exists to gain a sale, the only decision point is whether any additional operating expenses or investment required to obtain the order will be adequately offset by the increased throughput. However, there is a new constraint that now enters the picture, which is working capital.

When a company resells products acquired elsewhere, its primary limitation is likely to be the amount of cash available to support its working capital needs. If it sets prices too low, then its sales may skyrocket, but it won't have sufficient funding to support the receivables associated with the new sales. The solution is to focus intently on the working capital bottleneck. If a product sale has a combination of the shortest customer payment terms and the largest throughput margin, then it is using the minimum amount of the working capital constraint. Conversely, sales of low-margin products on long payment terms use the largest amount of the constraint, and are to be discouraged.

7

Distribution Expenses

T HE COSTS OF GETTING the manufactured products to the customer have become relatively more significant in recent years, as the cost of manufacturing products generally has declined. In fact, for some companies, the total costs of distribution of the products are in excess of the production or procurement costs.

Although in most companies more effort has been directed toward analysis and control of production costs, the costs of distribution have either not been available in usable form or not been communicated to marketing management for decision making. Executives responsible for distribution of the products must be made aware of the cost components to effectively plan and carry out a proper distribution system effort. The controller must develop the control mechanisms, secure the facts and interpret them, and communicate the information to the marketing executives. To be effective, the marketing executive must understand the accounting control information and use it to develop better marketing plans. The increasing costs of distribution can be controlled and even reduced if the controller works with the sales and marketing management to develop the necessary control techniques.

Any controller who tackles distribution cost control will find that the problems usually are much more complex than those relating to production costs. First, psychological factors require more consideration. In selling, the attitudes of the buyer and the salesperson are variable, and competitive reaction cannot be overlooked. This is in sharp contrast to production, where the worker is generally the only human element. Moreover, in marketing activities, the methods are more flexible and more numerous than in production, and several agencies or channels of distribution may be used. Such conditions make the activities more difficult to standardize than production activities. Also, the constant changes in method of sale or channel of distribution are factors that make it harder to secure basic information. Even when the information is secured, great care must be taken in its interpretation. Where indirect or allocated costs are significant, the analyses may require a more relative marginal or incremental cost approach.

The bulk of this chapter covers the detailed analysis and control of distribution costs.

 ## ROLE OF THE SALES MANAGER

The sales manager is responsible for the requisite sales volume of the right products and the planning and control of distribution costs. These may seem like two diametrically opposed objectives. However, the situation is a problem of balance; if more money is spent for the distribution effort, what does the business receive in return? Usually the sales manager is under pressure to increase sales while reducing selling expenses. Thus, he or she must know whether distribution costs are really too high, and if they are too high, just where: What salesperson? What territory? What expense? The sales effort must be guided carefully, and this can be done only if the correct accounting information comes from the controller. The sales manager must have an intelligent analysis of distribution costs as a basis from which to work.

 ## ANALYZING DISTRIBUTION COSTS

There are several ways to analyze distribution costs:

- *By the nature of the expense or object of expenditure.* This information is recorded in the general ledger and can easily be converted into trends in expense line items or expenses as a percentage of revenue. However, the controller must dig deeper in order to tell the sales manager why certain expenses are too high, who is responsible for the excess costs, and what can be done to improve the situation.

▪ *By contribution margin.* The contribution margin is calculated by deducting from sales those direct costs incurred in obtaining that segment of the sales being analyzed. The expenses not deducted from revenues in computing contribution margins are those not changed by the decision under review. The contribution margin is used for short-term tactical decisions, but it is not good for long-term decisions because it does not factor in the recovery of total costs, which includes overhead. This approach has several advantages:

- ▫ Measurement of the immediate gain to the company's overall profit by the transaction under review
- ▫ Facilitation of management's decision because those costs to be changed are already separated from costs not affected
- ▫ Avoidance of errors and controversy that arise due to cost allocations
- ▫ Simplicity of application since direct costs are identifiable more readily than total costs, including the necessary allocations
- ▫ Ease of data collection

▪ *By functions or functional operations performed.* This kind of analysis requires five steps:

- ▫ Establish the functional operations to be measured, such as sales calls, shipments from the warehouse, and circular mailings.
- ▫ Segregate the costs of the functions for measurement, either through specific accounts in the general ledger or through allocations.
- ▫ Establish units of measurement of functional service. For example, the pounds of shipments might be the measure of the shipping expense, or the number of the salespeople's calls might serve as one measurement of direct field selling expense.
- ▫ Calculate a unit cost of operation by dividing the total controllable functional cost by the number of units.
- ▫ Take corrective action if significant cost variances occur.

▪ *By matching revenues to functions.* This analysis matches expenses with related revenues, so the controller can demonstrate the results of a specific distribution effort. This kind of analysis requires cost distributions for direct and indirect costs. Direct costs are fairly obvious, but indirect costs are exceedingly difficult to spread among the various cost objects. The controller would be wise to spend a considerable amount of time subdividing the indirect costs into smaller pieces and using different allocation bases to apportion the costs in a logical manner among the cost objects. The degree of sophistication of the allocation may depend on whether the analysis is short range or long range. All costs must be included for long-range analysis, so all allocated costs must be identified. If decisions are of limited scope and for a short period, such as the sale to a private brand customer for the next year, then perhaps only direct expenses ought to be considered.

The sales manager can more effectively manage the sales function with this information.

ANALYZING BY APPLICATION

Years of experience with distribution cost analysis have proven its value. Although the degree of refinement may vary in different companies, the general approach can be described in this way:

- Determine which type of analysis is required for a particular situation, such as an analysis by method of delivery
- Classify distribution costs according to those that are direct and indirect
- Select and apply the allocation bases to the indirect expenses. This includes a segregation and proper treatment of variable, as opposed to fixed, costs
- Prepare the analysis and commentary for the appropriate executive. Four steps must be taken to arrive at significant cost and profit relationships:
  1. Determine the gross profit by segment
  2. Accumulate the direct expense by segment, and deduct this from gross profit to arrive at the profit after direct expense
  3. Prorate the indirect expense to arrive at the final net profit
  4. Prepare the necessary subanalyses to pinpoint the conditions needing correction

The next sections discuss the steps required to perform detailed analyses by territory, product, customer, and size of order.

Analysis by Territory

A territory is any geographical area used by a company for sales planning, direction, or analysis. Where goods are sold greatly affects net profit because there are striking differences between territories in terms of sales potential, gross margins, and net profit. If goods are sold free on board (FOB) at a central point and at the same price, then the gross profit is unchanged. However, if the product is sold on a delivered price basis, then the gross margin is different because of transportation charges. Also, the total distribution costs (including marketing and selling) are different in different territories. The cost to sell in densely populated New York is different from the cost to sell in western Texas. Because of these dissimilar conditions, executives must have an analysis of distribution costs by territory. Such information permits the sales manager to rearrange the sales effort where necessary and to direct the sales effort into the most profitable areas.

Analysis by territory applies when a large geographical area is covered. Thus, a manufacturer covering a national market would greatly benefit from such an analysis, whereas a retail store probably would not. Exactly what type of territorial analysis needs to be made depends on the problem and the type of organization. If a territorial sales executive is responsible for costs and results, then a complete analysis by this responsibility area is desirable. If the question is one of the cost to sell in a small town versus a city, such a segregation must be made.

Once the points of weakness are discovered through analysis, correction action must be taken. Some possibilities are:

- Reorganize territories to allow efforts to be more in line with potentials
- Rearrange territory boundaries to reduce selling expenses and secure better customer coverage
- Shift salespeople to different areas
- Increase emphasis on neglected lines or customers in the territory
- Change the method of sale or channel of distribution (e.g., switch from a salesperson to an agent)
- Change the warehouse locations in the territory
- Eliminate unprofitable territories
- Change the advertising policy or expenditure in the territory

Analysis by Product

In today's economy, the design, style, or type of product a firm sells may change constantly. Hence every company is sooner or later faced with the problem of what products it should sell. Will the firm sell the best or the cheapest line? Will it promote the use of a new plastic? Should it introduce a silent airplane motor? The answer to questions like these is twofold. First, through market analysis, a determination must be made about what the customers want and what price they will pay. Then, through cost analysis, it must be determined whether the company can make and sell the article at a profit. Therefore, an analysis by products is desirable.

Many firms, in order to increase sales volume, often add new products to the line. Sometimes these new products fit into the line and permit certain economies. Often, however, the different products require new services in varying degree. For this reason, too, an analysis by product is necessary to determine the cost to sell, as well as the net profit.

Generally speaking, the sales effort should be directed toward those products with the greatest net profit possibilities, and cost analysis is necessary to know just which products these are. This is not to say that a company should drop a low-margin item; it may be contributing more than out-of-pocket costs, or it may be necessary for customer convenience. Furthermore, there may be little possibility of selling a high-margin item to a customer. For example, there may be no chance of selling any quantity of a high-profit glue instead of a low-margin paint product to a paint manufacturer. There are more factors in selling than merely cost considerations, but such conditions must be watched and held within reasonable limits. Distribution cost analyses by commodity, then, are of use in the direction of the sales effort.

In making product cost analyses, many controllers may find that the net profit on an entire line of products is not great enough, or even that losses are being sustained. When such conditions are revealed, usually steps are taken to increase that margin because the firm may not be in a position to drop an entire product line. This is but another way of saying that analysis is a means of controlling costs because the manufacturing or distribution costs may be too high.

Finally, product cost analyses help to set selling prices when the company is in a position to use cost as a major price-setting guide. Such analyses are desirable in conjunction with determining maximum price differentials to particular customers.

It is self-evident to most controllers that a product analysis of distribution costs should be made when the characteristics of the commodity or the methods of distribution are such that a uniform basis of allocation is not indicative of the effort or cost to sell. In this case, pounds or units of sale or sales dollars may be a fair measure of selling expense. However, such an apportionment is inaccurate or misleading in a number of circumstances:

- *If there are differences in the time or amount of sales effort required.* Product A, which sells for $0.60 each, may require about three times the effort of product V, which sells at $0.30 each. Neither sales dollars nor units would be a fair basis. Perhaps one product would require a higher degree of technical assistance and more frequent callbacks when compared with another. Again, specialty salespeople may merchandise one product, and general-line salespeople may handle another. All such circumstances result in different costs to sell, and should be so reflected in the analyses.

▪ *If there are differences in the method of sale.* Obviously, if one product is sold exclusively by mail order and another by salespeople, the selling cost cannot be prorated on a sales dollar or unit basis.

▪ *If there are differences in the size of the order.* When one product is sold in 10-pound lots and another is sold in tank cars, many of the distribution costs will differ.

▪ *If there are differences in channels of distribution.* One product may be sold directly to retailers, whereas another is distributed through wholesalers. Here, also, there is a difference in distribution costs.

The analysis by product ordinarily reveals areas of weakness where some corrective action can be taken, such as:

▪ Shifting the emphasis of the sales effort to more profitable lines or bringing effort in line with sales potential
▪ Adjusting sales prices
▪ Eliminating certain unprofitable lines, package sizes, colors, and so on
▪ Adding new product lines related to the family, with consequent sharing of the fixed distribution expense
▪ Changing the method of sale or channel of distribution
▪ Changing the type, amount, and emphasis of advertising
▪ Revising packaging, design, quality, and so on

Analysis by Customer

It costs more to sell to some types of customers than to others and more to one customer within a type than to another. Some customers require more services, such as warehousing, delivery, or financing. Some customers insist on different pricing, particularly when different size orders or annual purchases are factors. Again, the types of products sold to some classes of customers differ from others. All these are reasons why analyses by customers are necessary to measure the difference in net profit. Aside from use in the direction of sales effort, these analyses serve in setting prices and controlling distribution costs.

In most firms the analyses by customers will not be continuous. The sales manager may be interested in whether money is being made on a particular account, or changes may be contemplated only on certain groups of accounts. On these occasions, special analyses can be made.

Although analyses may be made by individual customers, particularly when there are a few high-volume accounts, by and large the analyses will relate to certain groups or categories. The two basic factors in selecting the classification to be used are the amount of distribution services required (the primary reason for differences in distribution costs) and the practicality of segregating the distribution costs. Classifications that have proved useful include:

- Amount of annual purchases
- Size of orders
- Location
- Frequency of salespeople's calls
- Type of agent (retailer, wholesaler, or Internet retailer)
- Credit rating of customers

In making an analysis by classification of customer, one approach is to gather all customers in the applicable group and determine total costs for that group. This approach may be time-consuming. Another method involves a sampling procedure, wherein representative customers in each category are selected and the cost of servicing them is determined. A modification of this approach is to make a thoroughly detailed analysis in some areas and a sample run in other areas.

Because relatively few distribution cost items can be charged directly to customers, allocations must be made. Statistical data from various reports will be necessary, such as the number of calls made to customers, the time spent with customers, or the number of orders.

Occasionally a decision must be made about whether business with a specific customer should be continued or whether the method of sale to the customer ought to be changed. For example, changing the selling method from field calls to a phone basis may result in retaining valuable business while securing a contribution margin in line with normal operating requirements.

An analysis by customer provides information of great value to the sales manager. It gives a clear view of the number of accounts in various volume brackets and the average value of orders. In using this information for corrective action, consideration must be given to the production volume needed to cover fixed production costs. The information will furnish facts for executive discussion regarding these issues:

- Discontinuance of certain customer groups
- Price adjustments

Need for Higher Margins for Certain Groups

- Changes in the method of sale

Analysis by Size of Order

Another analysis is by size of order. One of the causes of high distribution costs and unprofitable sales is the small order—not because it is small but because the revenue is not high enough to cover all the related transaction costs and still make a profit. There are many instances when small orders cannot be discontinued; however, corrective action can be taken to bring the problem under control. The controller's first step is to get the facts through an analysis of distribution costs by size of order.

The problem is naturally more important in some companies than in others, especially when the order-handling costs are relatively large or fixed.

The procedure for analyzing distribution costs by size or order is similar to that for other analyses. It involves segregating order-handling costs into fixed costs and variable costs. In this case, certain costs will be recognized as fixed for all sizes of orders, others will vary with the money volume, and still others will vary with physical volume. Five steps must be followed:

1. Determine the size of the order groups to be studied (e.g., below $25, $26 to $50, etc.).
2. Classify the costs according to those that vary with the size of the order (e.g., packing), those that are uniform for orders of all sizes (e.g., accounts receivable bookkeeping), and those that must be considered as general overhead (e.g., advertising and supervision costs).
3. Identify the factors that govern the amount of the variable expense applicable to orders of different sizes (e.g., dollar value, weight, or handling size).
4. Apply the factors of variability to the variable expenses and add the uniform costs, thereby arriving at a direct cost of orders by sizes.
5. Apply the overhead costs by some suitable factor, such as hundredweight or dollar value, to arrive at the total order cost.

Other Analysis Issues

Other analyses may also prove useful:

- *By channel of distribution.* This analysis is useful where a choice in channel of distribution may be made in order to direct sales into the most profitable channel. The analysis needs to be made from time to time as cost trends change.

- *By method of sale.* The same comments as in the case of analysis by channels of distribution are applicable.
- *By salesperson.* Such analysis measures the salesperson's performance in terms of profit and to better direct salespeople in their activities.
- *By organization or operating division.* This analysis is useful when there are separate selling divisions. It is used to measure performance of the divisional executive. Examples are analyses by departments in a department store, by stores in a retail chain store company, and by branches in a manufacturing organization.

In making recommendations based on the distribution cost analysis, before the decision is reached, every possible effect on every activity of the business must be considered. When deciding whether a certain territory must be dropped, the net effect on profit, the change in factory volume with the same fixed expense, and the resulting differences in unit cost must be considered. Also, dropping a territory may mean that any warehousing infrastructure servicing that territory must also be closed.

 ## SETTING THE DISTRIBUTION BUDGET

The advertising and sales promotion expense often is planned and controlled on a project basis. Some boards of directors prefer to approve these projects in a manner similar to capital budget requests. The reasons for this kind of approval are varied. For many companies—retail stores or consumer goods producers like Procter & Gamble or Coca-Cola Inc., for example—advertising and promotion is a major expenditure. Moreover, it is difficult to measure the effectiveness of advertising or sales promotion programs, and the results of the program may be less immediate and less direct than other types of marketing effort, such as direct selling. Finally, unlike other selling efforts, advertising sales promotion is usually organized as a separate department or as an outside agency.

The purpose of advertising varies in different circumstances. Although the general purpose is to support the broad marketing objectives, more specific goals include:

- Educating consumers in the use of the product or service
- Reducing the cost of other selling efforts
- Increasing sales
- Establishing or maintaining trademarks or brand names

- Developing new markets
- Meeting or outdoing competition
- Maintaining prices
- Introducing new products or services
- Creating favorable public opinion
- Avoiding unfavorable legislation

Two methods are used to establish an advertising sales promotion budget.

1. *The lump-sum appropriation method.* This method entails authorizing the expenditure for advertising and sales promotions related to some factor. Its advantage is simplicity. Although it lacks a scientific basis, there may be a perceived long-term relationship between advertising expenditures and the sales level. Under this plan the total amount to be spent could be based on:
   - A percentage of planned or budgeted sales
   - A percentage of the prior year sales or perhaps an average of several past years
   - A fixed amount per unit of product expected to be sold
   - An arbitrary percentage increase over the prior year's expenditure
   - A percentage of gross profit on the product for the prior year or the planning year
   - A percentage of net income of the prior year or planning year
2. *The estimated amount required to attain certain objectives.* Under this method, strategies and tactics are determined so that the relevant costs for each tactic can be estimated to derive a total cost for the year. In some cases the marginal or gross profit from the additional units estimated to be sold can be compared with the advertising expense to determine if the project seems to make financial sense. This can be done on an incremental advertising expense and quantity basis to ascertain at which point, if any, the incremental unit advertising cost exceeds the incremental marginal profit after all direct costs. Exhibit 7.1 shows such an analysis.

The controller must know that the business is being operated efficiently, and this requires measuring sticks: *standards.* A complete analysis of past operations must be the starting point. By this analysis it may be determined that 1,000 calls have been made by salespeople in a given territory, at a cost of $5 per call, and with certain sales results. But the questions of how many calls should have been made by the sales staff and what the cost per call should have been are left unanswered. These answers must be ascertained if effective

EXHIBIT 7.1 Incremental Advertising Expense and Profit Margin

Incremental Block	Incremental Advertising Expense	Additional Units Estimated to Be Sold	Estimated Marginal Unit Income	Incremental Unit Advertising Cost	Unit Increment (Decrement) to Profit	Total Margin
1	$0	20,000	$1.00	$ —	$1.00	$20,000
2	25,000	30,000	1.20	.83	.37	11,100
3	25,000	70,000	1.30	.36	.94	65,800
4	25,000	50,000	.90	.50	.40	20,000
5	25,000	50,000	.80	.50	.30	15,000
6	25,000	30,000	.70	.83	−.13	−3,900
7	25,000	30,000	.60	.83	−.23	−6,900
8	25,000	20,000	.50	1.25	−.75	−15,000
9	25,000	10,000	.40	2.50	−2.10	−21,000

control of the sales effort is to be exercised. It may be known that 1,000 orders have been handled at a clerical cost of $0.50 per order, but what would the cost have been if the clerical work had been directed efficiently? In brief, standards by which to judge the distribution performance and signal its weaknesses are needed.

It would be foolish to contend that all distribution activities can be highly standardized. In fact, it is never possible to standardize production activities completely. However, it is possible to establish standards for a large number of distribution activities. After all, if no one is competent to judge what distribution effort is necessary to secure certain results and what it will cost to do it, then management is indeed in a helpless position.

If many cost and performance factors are not under constant control, the executive's profit goal is almost certain to be unmet. But such control implies standards. Warehouse labor hours never appear too high in the absolute; they become too high only when measured against what they should be under the circumstances—that is, only when a standard is applied.

Distribution cost standards may be either of a general nature or in units that measure individual performance. Cost standards that are of a general nature are:

■ Selling cost as a percentage of net sales
■ Cost per dollar of gross profit
■ Cost per unit sold

▪ Cost per sales transaction

▪ Cost per order received

▪ Cost per customer account

These standards are useful indicators of trends for the entire distribution effort and also can be applied to individual products, territories, branches, or departments.

However, these general standards do not necessarily indicate points of weakness in terms of individual responsibility. If costs are to be controlled, the performance of the individual must be measured. Consequently, the controller must set standards for controllable costs of individual cost items or functions. For example, standards in the warehouse could be the cost per item handled or cost per shipment. Standards for the direct sales force could be the cost per mile traveled or cost per day.

Five Steps to Set Distribution Standards

Step 1. Classify the costs according to functions and activities expressive of individual responsibility. The cost of such major functions as direct selling, advertising, transportation, warehousing, credit and collection, and financing can be separated in most businesses and subjected to individual study and control. The costs of the major functions should be further classified by individual activities that make up the functional service. For example, the credit and collection costs may be separated into credit approvals, posting charges, posting credits, and writing collection letters.

Step 2. Select units or bases of measurement through which the standards can be expressed. The measure may apply to the effort used, to cost, to results achieved, or to the relationship of these factors. For example, salespeople are each expected to make a certain number of sales calls per day. The sales call constitutes a measure of effort used. The cost of writing orders in the order department can be measured in terms of the number of orders or order lines written. Salespeople are expected to produce a certain number of orders or to secure a certain number of new accounts. This number is a measure of results, and the units of measurement are orders and new accounts. Finally, salespeople may be required to hold their direct costs to within (for example) 8% of their sales volume. Here the measurement is in terms of the relationship of particular costs to the results in sales volume, and the basis of measurement is the ratio of one to the other.

Although such specific units of measurement are not available for all distribution activities, some basis must be selected before the standards can be applied. Where specific units are not available, more inclusive or composite bases must be used. For example, the entire credit and collection cost may be measured by the number of accounts carried, or the entire advertising cost may be measured by its ratio to dollar sales volume.

Step 3. Analyze past experience relative to the cost of the functions and the specific activities involved with a view to selecting the best experience and the best procedure. Doing this may involve intensive study of individual methods of operation similar to that employed in the development of production standards.

Step 4. Consider the effect on costs of expected changes in external conditions and of the planned sales program. If increased sales resistance is expected, an estimate must be made about its effect on such costs as advertising and direct selling. If the program calls for a lengthening of the installment credit period, the effect on the financing cost must be estimated.

Step 5. Summarize the judgment of those executives whose experience and training qualify them to judge the measures of satisfactory performance.

The standards that are finally set will cover a variety of warehouse functions. Thus, a standard cost might be applied to the warehousing function as a whole. Within this general function many individual cost standards may be applied that relate to specific activities, such as clerical costs of order handling and physical assembling.

Keep in mind that different standards must be set for different territories, products, channels of distribution, classes of customers, departments, and so on, wherein different conditions prevail.

Additional Information Needed to Use Standards

To use standards effectively, a company must regularly record and store information about items quite dissimilar from the usual accounting information. These data are illustrative of the items to be recorded:

- Analyses of sales in physical units
- Number of sales transactions classified in terms of size, hour of day, and so on
- Number of quotations made
- Number of orders classified in terms of size, period in which received, and so on
- Number of order lines written

- Average number of salespeople (which may be subdivided by experience level)
- Number of salesperson-days
- Number of calls on old and new customers
- Number of days salespeople travel
- Number of miles salespeople travel
- Average number of customers classified with regard to location, annual volume, and so on
- Number of labor hours of salespeople, advertising and display people, warehouse workers, truck drivers, delivery personnel, maintenance workers, and clerical workers
- Number of returns and allowances classified in terms of cause
- Number of units of advertising space or time used in the various advertising media
- Number of advertising pieces mailed: letters, circulars, folders, calendars, and so on
- Number of pieces of advertising material distributed: window cards, store displays, inserts, and so on
- Number of samples distributed
- Number of demonstrations performed
- Number of inquiries received
- Number of new customers secured
- Number of shipments
- Analyses of shipments in physical units
- Dollar value of shipments
- Number of ton-miles units of shipping
- Number of deliveries
- Number of parcels delivered
- Number of miles of truck operation
- Number of shipping claims handled
- Physical volume of goods handled in warehouses
- Average size of physical inventory carried
- Rates of turnover in dollars and physical units
- Average number of accounts carried
- Number of invoices
- Number of invoice lines
- Number of remittances received
- Number of collection letters sent
- Average number of days accounts are outstanding
- Average amount of receivables carried

Many of these items must be further classified by territories, commodities, and departments to supply the full information needed.

Such information will be useful for many purposes in the direction of distribution activity, but it is essential to a program of standards. In the past, many firms have neglected to accumulate and use such information. It is not uncommon to find a company that has the most exacting records of a production machine, such as its purchase date, cost, working hours, idle hours, and maintenance cost. However, that same firm may have been employing a salesperson whose total cost has greatly exceeded the cost and maintenance of the machine, but about whom little detailed information has been kept. The salesperson's activity report can provide some of these data.

In many firms the distribution data are entirely too meager. More information must be collected if the distribution program is to be directed wisely.

8

Direct Materials and Labor

THE COST OF A product is split among direct materials and labor, overhead, distribution, and general and administrative costs. All of these costs can contribute a significant amount to the total cost of a product, but direct materials and labor traditionally have been the largest cost elements for most products. Thus, the controller should be mindful of any control systems that will allow tight monitoring of these costs.

Controlling direct materials and labor costs is the subject of this chapter. In addition, there are many references in the text to the impact of just-in-time (JIT) systems on cost controls, which call into question the need for some traditional (and extensive!) control systems, such as those used for direct labor tracking. This chapter also includes a discussion of the deleterious effects on production results of several traditional variance reports, and why these results occur.

 OBJECTIVES

A manufacturing cost accounting system is an integral part of the total management information system. In analyzing costing systems, the controller must recognize the purpose of the manufacturing cost accounting system and relate it to production or operating management problems. The objectives must be clearly defined if the system is to be utilized effectively. Fundamental purposes of a cost system may vary in importance from one organization to another; however, they may be summarized in this way:

- *For control of costs.* Control of costs is a primary use of manufacturing cost accounting and cost analysis. The major elements of costs—labor, material, and manufacturing expenses—must be segregated by product, by type of cost, and by responsibility. For example, the actual number of parts used in the assembly of an airplane section, such as a wing, may be compared to the bill for materials and corrective action taken when appropriate.
- *For planning and performance measurement.* Closely related to cost control is the use of cost data for effective planning and performance measurement. Some of the same information used for cost control purposes may be used for the planning of manufacturing operations. For example, the standards used for cost control of manufacturing expenses can be used to plan these expenses for future periods with due consideration to past experience relative to established standards. Cost analysis can be utilized, as part of the planning process, to determine the probable effect of different courses of action. Again, a comparison of manufacturing costs versus purchasing a particular part or component can be made to help with make-or-buy decisions. The use of cost analysis would extend to many facets of the total planning process.
- *For price setting.* A critical reason for supplying cost data is to establish selling prices. Materials and labor typically are large components of the cost of a product, and so form a bottom limit below which prices should not be dropped.
- *For inventory valuation.* One of the key objectives of a costing system is the determination of a product unit cost and the valuation of inventories. Inventory valuation is also a prerequisite to an accurate determination of the cost of goods sold in the statement of income and expense. The manufacturing cost system should recognize this fact and include sufficient cost details to accomplish this purpose.

ROLE OF THE CONTROLLER

A fundamental responsibility of the controller in the product cost area is to ensure that the manufacturing cost systems have been established to serve the needs and requirements of the production executives. The controller is the fact finder regarding costs and is responsible for seeing that factory management is furnished with sufficient cost information on a timely basis and in a proper format to effect control and planning. It is imperative that the cost data be accurate and that production management be provided with a clear interpretation of the facts. Merely presenting the facts is not enough; the cost information must be communicated in an understandable manner because many production executives are not fully aware of the ramifications. The controller should develop educational techniques to aid the factory management in the utilization of cost data for effective decision making. A sound cost philosophy must be adopted at all levels of responsibility. The controller's staff should have a thorough understanding of the factory operations and how the products are manufactured and should be able to relate the cost figures to various products. Doing this takes extra effort and cooperation between the controller's staff and the operating personnel.

To carry out this responsibility and serve production management properly, the controller must be assured that the right cost system has been designed and adequate implementing procedures have been developed to accumulate and record the cost information. The cost system must be flexible so that changes can be made as the needs of factory management vary. A common change to the costing system includes provision for additional cost information in special circumstances or during alternative cost analyses. As variances are analyzed and out-of-line conditions are reported, production managers can change methods or vary their cost information requirements. Emphasis should be placed on areas requiring improvement; less time should be devoted to on-standard operations.

Unfortunately, under a just-in-time system, manufacturing managers need feedback regarding costs far more frequently than on a monthly basis. JIT products are manufactured with little or no wait time, and consequently can be produced in periods much shorter than was the case under the line manufacturing concept. Therefore, if a cost problem occurred, such as too many direct labor hours required to finish a part, then the formal accounting system would not tell the line managers until well after the problem had happened.

Fortunately, JIT principles stress the need to shrink inventories and emphasize overall cleanliness, thereby making manufacturing problems highly visible *without* any product costing reports. A subset of JIT is cellular (group) manufacturing, in which equipment is generally arranged in a horseshoe shape, and one employee uses those machines to make one part, taking the piece from machine to machine. Consequently, there is little or no work-in-process (WIP) to track, and any scrapped parts are immediately visible to management because they cannot be hidden in piles of WIP. Based on manufacturing concept, line managers can do without reports, except for daily production reports concerning actual quantities versus budgeted quantities that meet quality standards.

Just-in-time manufacturing places the controller in the unique position of looking for something to report on. Because direct labor and materials costs are now largely fixed, the controller's emphasis should switch to planning the costs of new products and tracking planned costs versus actual costs. As the JIT manufacturing environment tends to have small cost variances, the controller should question the amount of effort to be invested in tracking direct labor and materials variances versus the benefit of collecting the data.

Another area in which the controller can profitably invest time-tracking information is the amount of time that a product uses at the bottleneck operation. Since bottleneck usage is the key driver of corporate profitability, it is extremely useful to place a continuing focus on reengineering or out-sourcing those products using large amounts of bottleneck time.

While much less important than bottleneck tracking, the controller can also investigate non–value-added production activities, such as:

- Number of material moves
- Number of part numbers used by the company
- Number of setups required to build a product
- Number of products sold by the company, including the number of options offered
- Number of product distribution locations used
- Number of engineering change notices
- Number of parts reworked

Under JIT, the controller should be careful *not* to report several traditional performance measures:

- *Machine efficiency.* If there is a report on machine efficiency, line managers will be encouraged to create an excessive amount of WIP in order to keep their machines running at maximum utilization.
- *Purchase price variances.* If there is a report on purchase price variances, the materials staff will be encouraged to purchase large quantities of raw materials in order to get volume discounts, thereby bloating inventory.
- *Head count.* If there is a report on head count, the manufacturing manager will be encouraged to hire untrained contract workers, who may produce more scrap than full-time, better-trained employees.

■ *Scrap factor.* If the firm includes a scrap factor into a product's standard cost, line managers will take no corrective action unless scrap exceeds the budgeted level, thereby incorporating scrap into the production process.

■ *Labor variances.* If there is a report on labor variances, accountants will expend considerable labor in an area that has relatively fixed costs and not put time into areas that require more analysis.

■ *Standard cost overhead absorption.* If there is a report on standard cost overhead absorption, management will be encouraged to overproduce to absorb more overhead than was actually expended, thereby increasing profits, increasing inventory, and reducing available cash.

TYPES OF COST SYSTEMS

Experience in determining costs in various industries has given rise to several types of cost systems that suit the various kinds of manufacturing activities. A traditional costing system known as a *job order system* normally is used for manufacturing products to a specific customer order or unique product. For example, the assembly or fabrication operations of a particular job or contract are collected in a separate job order number. Another widely used costing system is known as a *process cost system*. This system assigns costs to a cost center rather than to a particular job. All the production costs of a department are collected, and the departmental cost per unit is determined by dividing the total departmental costs by the number of units processed through the department. Process cost systems are used more commonly in food processing, oil refining, flour milling, paint manufacturing, and so on.

No two cost accounting systems are identical. Many factors determine the kind of system to use, such as product mix, plant location, product diversity, number of specific customer orders, and complexity of the manufacturing process. It may be advisable to combine certain characteristics of both types of systems in certain situations. For example, in a steel mill the primary system may be a process cost system; however, minor activities, such as maintenance, may be on a job cost basis. The controller should thoroughly analyze all operations to determine the system that best satisfies all needs.

The controller should be aware of two issues currently affecting the job order and process costing systems:

1. JIT manufacturing systems allow the controller to reduce or eliminate the record keeping needed for job cost reporting. Because JIT tends to eliminate

variances on the shop floor by eliminating the WIP that used to mask problems, there are few cost variances for the cost accountant to accumulate in a job cost report. Therefore, the time needed to accumulate information for job costing may no longer be worth the increase in accuracy derived from it, and the controller should consider using the initial planned job cost as the actual job cost.

2. One of the primary differences between process and job shop costing systems is the presence (job shop) or absence (process flow) of WIP. Since installing a JIT manufacturing system inherently implies reducing or eliminating WIP, a JIT job shop costing system may not vary that much from a process costing system.

 MEASURING DIRECT MATERIAL COSTS

The term "direct material" refers to material that can be definitely or specifically charged to a particular product, process, or job and that becomes a component part of the finished product. The definition must be applied in a practical way, for if the material cannot be conveniently charged as direct or if it is an insignificant item of cost, it probably would be classified as "indirect material" and allocated with other manufacturing expenses to the product on some logical basis. Direct material also should include the cost of packing supplies necessary to deliver the goods to the customer, as well as any normal losses due to scrap, evaporation, spoilage, or shrinkage. Excessive amounts of scrap should be expensed or charged to the overhead account.

In its broadest sense, material planning and control is providing the required quantity and quality of material at the required time and place in the manufacturing process. By implication, the material secured must not be excessive in amount, and it must be fully accounted for and used as intended. The extent of material planning and control is broad and should cover many areas, such as plans and specifications; purchasing; receiving and handling; inventories; usage; and scrap, waste, and salvage. In each of these phases, the controller has certain responsibilities and can make contributions toward an efficient operation.

Because material is such a large cost item in most manufacturing concerns, effective utilization is an important factor in the financial success or failure of the business. Proper planning and control of materials with the related adequate accounting has advantages in that it:

- Reduces inefficient use or waste of materials
- Reduces production delays by reason of lack of materials

- Reduces the risk from theft or fraud
- Reduces the investment in inventories
- Reduces the required investment in storage facilities
- Provides more accurate interim financial statements
- Assists buyers through a better-coordinated buying program
- Provides a basis for proper product pricing
- Provides more accurate inventory values

CONTROLLING DIRECT MATERIAL COSTS

Before describing direct material cost controls, those costs must be defined. Direct material costs include the invoice price for the direct material, the inbound freight cost, sales taxes and duties, and the cost of delivery pallets or other freight containers. Any discounts should be taken from the material cost, while licensing or royalty payments should be added to the cost.

With respect to materials, as with other costs, control in its simplest form involves the comparison of actual performance with a measuring stick—standard performance—and the prompt rectification of adverse trends. However, it is not simply a matter of saying "350 yards of material were used, and the standard quantity is only 325" or "The standard price is $10.25 but the actual cost to the company was $13.60 each." Many other refinements are involved: The standards must be reviewed and better methods found, or checks and controls must be exercised before the cost is incurred. The central theme, however, is still the use of a standard as a point of measurement.

Although the application of controls will vary in different firms, some of the considerations that must be handled by the controller are described in the next sections.

Purchasing and Receiving

- Establishment and maintenance of internal checks to ensure that materials paid for are received and used for the purposes intended. Since some purchases are now received on a just-in-time basis, the controller may find that materials are now paid for based on the amount of production manufactured by the company in a given period, instead of a large quantity of paperwork associated with a large number of small-quantity receipts.
- Audit of purchasing procedures to ascertain that bids are received where applicable. A JIT manufacturing system uses a small number of long-term

suppliers, however, so the controller may find that bids are restricted to providers of such services as janitorial duties and copier repairs.

▪ Comparative studies of prices paid for commodities with industry prices or indexes.

▪ Measurement of price trends on raw materials. Many JIT supplier contracts call for price decreases by suppliers at set intervals; the controller should be aware of the terms of these contracts and audit the timing and amount of the changes.

▪ Determination of price variances on current purchases through comparison of actual and standard costs. This determination may involve purchases at the time of ordering or at the time of receipt. The same approach may be used in a review of current purchase orders to advise management in advance about the effect on standard costs. In a JIT environment, most part costs would be contractually set with a small number of suppliers, so the controller would examine prices charged for any variations from the agreed-on rates.

Material Usage

▪ Comparison of actual and standard quantities used in production. A variance may indicate an incorrect quantity on the product's bill of materials, misplaced parts, pilferage, or incorrect part quantities recorded in inventory.

▪ Preparation of standard cost formulas, to emphasize major cost items and as a part of a cost reduction program.

▪ Preparation of reports on spoilage, scrap, and waste compared with standard. In a JIT environment, no scrap is allowed for and certainly none is included in the budget as a standard.

▪ Calculation of costs to make versus costs to buy.

This list suggests only some of the methods available to the controller in dealing with material cost control.

CONTROLLING DIRECT MATERIAL QUANTITIES

Standards of material usage may be established by at least three procedures:

1. By engineering studies to determine the best kind and quality of material, taking into account the product design requirements and production methods

2. By an analysis of past experience for the same or similar operations
3. By making test runs under controlled conditions

Although a combination of these methods may be used, best practice usually dictates that engineering studies should be made. To the theoretical loss must be added a provision for those other unavoidable losses that are impractical to eliminate. In this decision, past experience will play a part. Past performance alone, of course, is not desirable in that certain known wastes may be perpetuated. This engineering study, combined with a few test runs, should give fairly reliable standards.

Quantity standards are based on certain production methods and product specifications. It would be expected, therefore, that quantity standards should be modified as these other factors change, if such changes affect material usage. For the measuring stick to be an effective control tool, it must relate to the function being measured. However, the adjustment need not be carried through as a change in inventory value, unless it is significant.

In the best material quantity control scheme, the firm knows in advance how much material should be used on the job, frequently secures information about how actual performance compares with standard during the progress of the work, and takes corrective action where necessary. The supervisor responsible for the use of materials, as well as his or her superior, should be aware of these facts. At the lowest supervisory level, details of each operation and process should be in the hands of those who can control usage. At higher levels, of course, only overall results need to be known.

The method to be used in comparing the actual and the standard usage will differ in each company, depending on several conditions. Some of the more important factors that will influence the controller in applying control procedures to material usage are:

▪ The production method in use
▪ The type and value of the materials
▪ The degree to which cost reports are utilized by management for cost control purposes

One of the most important considerations is the nature of the production process. In a job order or lot system, such as an assembly operation in an aircraft plant, where a definite quantity is to be produced, the procedure is quite simple. A production order is issued, and a bill of material or "standard requisition" states the exact quantity of material needed to complete the order.

If parts are spoiled or lost, it then becomes necessary to secure replacements by means of a nonstandard or excess usage requisition. Usually the foreman must approve this request, and, consequently, the excess usage can be identified immediately.

If production is on a continuous process basis, then a periodic comparison can be made of material used in relation to the finished product. Corrective action may not be as quick here, but measures can be taken to avoid future losses.

Just as the production process is a vital factor in determining the cost accounting plan, so also it is a consideration in the method of detecting material losses. If losses are to be localized, then inspections must be made at selected points in the manufacturing process. At these various stations, the rejected material can be counted or weighed and costed if necessary. When there are several distinct steps in the manufacturing process, the controller may have to persuade the production group of the need and desirability to establish count stations for control purposes. Once these stations are established, the accountant's chief contribution is to summarize and report the losses over standard.

Another factor in the method of reporting material usage is the type and value of the item itself. A cardinal principal in cost control is to place primary emphasis on high-volume items. Hence valuable airplane motors, for example, would be identified by serial number and otherwise accurately accounted for. Items with less unit value, or not readily segregated, might be controlled through less accurate periodic reporting.

Management often is not directly interested in dollar cost for control purposes, but only in physical units. There are no differences in the principles involved, only in the applications. Under these conditions, the controller should see that management is informed of losses in terms of physical units. In this case, the cost report would be merely a summary of the losses. Experience shows, however, that as the controller gives an accounting in dollars, other members of management will become more cost conscious.

A variation on using quantity standards and materials variation reporting is JIT variance reporting. One of the cornerstones of the JIT concept is that only what is needed is ordered. What is used is not wasted, and there should be no materials variances. Of course, even at world-class JIT practitioners, there is scrap; however, there is much less than would be found at a non-JIT company. Consequently, the controller must examine the cost of collecting the variance information against its value in correcting a small number of scrap causes. The conclusion may be that JIT does not require much materials variance reporting, if any.

In comparing actual and standard material costs, the use of price standards permits the segregation of variances as a result of excess usage from those incurred by reason of price changes. By and large, however, the material price standards used for inventory valuation cannot be considered as a satisfactory guide in measuring the performance of the purchasing department. Prices of materials are affected by so many factors outside the business that the standards represent merely a measure of what prices are being paid compared with what was expected to be paid.

A review of price variances may, however, reveal some informative data. Exceedingly high prices may reveal special purchases for quick delivery because someone had not properly scheduled purchases. Or higher prices may reveal shipment via express when freight shipments would have been satisfactory. Again, the lowest-cost supplier may not be utilized because of the advantages of excellent quality control methods in place at a competing shop. The total cost of production and the impact on the marketplace need to be considered—not merely the purchase price of the specific item.

One negative result of recording a purchase price variance is that the purchasing department may forgo close supplier relationships in order to get the lowest part cost through the bidding process. Part bidding is the nemesis of close supplier parings (a cornerstone of JIT) because suppliers know they will be kicked off the supplier list, no matter how good their delivery or quality, unless they bid the lowest price.

In practice, the responsibility for setting price standards varies. Sometimes the cost department assumes this responsibility on the basis of a review of past prices. In other cases the purchasing staff gives an estimate of expected prices that is subject to a thorough and analytical check by the accounting staff. Probably the most satisfactory setup is through the combined effort of these two departments.

Where products are costly and relatively few in number, the controller may find it useful to provide management periodically with both the changes in standard prices and an indication about the effect of price changes on the standard cost of the product. Such statements may stimulate thinking about material substitutions in processes or specifications.

MEASURING DIRECT LABOR COSTS

Labor accounting and control are important. Also, those costs that are closely related to labor costs have grown by leaps and bounds: costs for longer vacations, more adequate health and welfare plans, pension plans, and increased Social Security taxes. These fringe benefit costs now approximate 30 percent to 40 percent of many payrolls. For all these reasons, the cost of labor is an important cost factor.

The objectives of labor accounting are twofold:

1. A prompt and accurate determination of the amount of wages due the employee
2. The analysis and determination of labor costs in such manner as may be needed by management (e.g., by product, operation, department, or category of labor) for planning and control purposes

The advent of JIT manufacturing systems has called into question the need for reporting the direct labor utilization variance. This variance revolves around the amount of a product that is produced with a given amount of labor; thus, a positive labor utilization variance can be achieved by producing more product than may be needed. An underlying principle of JIT is that only as much as is needed is produced, so JIT and labor utilization variance reporting are inherently at odds with each other. If JIT has been installed, then the controller should consider eliminating this type of variance reporting.

CONTROLLING DIRECT LABOR COSTS

As with direct materials cost controls, direct labor costs must be defined before considering controls. Direct labor is that labor which can be specifically identified with providing a service, completing a project, or building a product. Such costs include assembly, inspection, processing, and packaging. When accounting for a large project, direct labor typically will include many types of labor that fall into the overhead classification in other forms of production; this is because nearly all positions, such as janitorial and maintenance, can be directly associated with the project. Nonproductive time that cannot be associated with a specific service, product, or project will become part of overhead. For example, break time for an employee who is working on one product can logically be assigned to that product; however, cleanup time for a factory that produced multiple products should be assigned to overhead.

The cost of labor has a number of components, and these are assigned to either direct labor cost or overhead cost. The governing criteria in assigning a cost to either direct labor or overhead is that a labor cost component should be assigned to direct labor if the cost is incurred because the company uses direct labor to produce a service, product, or project. In other words, most employee benefits will not be incurred unless direct labor is performed and, therefore, those costs must fall into direct labor. Typical employee benefit costs that fall into this category are:

- Cost of living allowances
- Group life insurance
- Health insurance
- Holiday pay
- Pension costs
- Productivity bonuses (both individual and group)
- Social Security
- Unemployment insurance compensation (state and federal)
- Vacation pay
- Worker's compensation insurance costs

The assignment of these costs to direct labor or overhead will vary depending on the situations of individual firms, so the controller should consult with the company's external auditors for an opinion on this matter.

In controlling direct labor costs, as with most manufacturing costs, the ultimate responsibility must rest with the line supervision. Yet line supervisors must be given assistance in measuring performance, and certain other policing or restraining functions must be exercised. Herein lie the primary duties of the controller's organization. Among the means at the disposal of the chief accounting executive in labor control are:

- Institute procedures to limit the number of employees placed on the payroll to that called for by the production plan
- Provide preplanning information for use in determining standard labor crews by calculating required standard person-hours for the production program
- Report hourly, daily, or weekly standard and actual labor performance. This reporting would not be necessary in a JIT environment
- Institute procedures for accurate distribution of actual labor costs, including significant labor classifications to provide informative labor cost analyses. This reporting would not be necessary in a JIT environment
- Provide data on past experience with respect to the establishment of standards. This reporting would not be necessary in a JIT environment
- Keep adequate records on labor standards and be on the alert for necessary revisions

- Furnish other supplementary labor reports, such as:
  - Hours and cost of overtime premium, for control of overtime
  - Cost of call-in pay for time not worked to measure efficiency of those responsible for call-in by union seniority
  - Comparative contract costs (old vs. new union contracts)
  - Average hours worked per week, average take-home pay, and similar data for labor negotiations
  - Detailed analysis of labor costs over or under standard. This reporting would not be necessary in a JIT environment
  - Statistical data on labor turnover, length of service, and training costs
  - Union time—cost of time spent on union business

A JIT manufacturing environment creates significant changes in direct labor costs that the controller should be aware of. When a manufacturing facility changes from an assembly line to manufacturing cells, the labor efficiency level drops because machine setups become more frequent. A major JIT technique is to reduce setup time to minimal levels, but even the small setup times required for cellular manufacturing require more labor time than the zero setup times used in long assembly-line production runs. Consequently, if management is contemplating switching to cellular manufacturing, the controller should expect an increase in the labor hours budget. Also, if the labor cost does not increase, the controller should see if the engineering staff has changed the labor routings (standard hours required to produce a product itemized by skills required and department) to increase the number of expected setup times.

The following discussion on labor standards does not apply to a JIT manufacturing environment, especially one that uses cellular (i.e., "group") manufacturing layouts. Labor utilization standards can be improved by increasing the amount of production for a set level of labor, and this is considered to be good in an assembly line environment. Under JIT, however, producing large quantities of parts is not considered acceptable; under JIT, good performance is producing the exact quantity of parts that are needed, and doing so with quality that is within present tolerance levels. Once the correct quantity of parts is produced, the direct labor staff stops production; this creates unfavorable labor utilization variances. Therefore, measuring a JIT production facility with a labor utilization variance would work against the intent of JIT since the production manager would be encouraged to produce more parts than needed and would not be mindful of the part quality.

The improvement of labor performance and the parallel reduction and control of costs require labor standards—operating time standards and the related cost standards. Setting labor performance standards is a highly analytical job that requires a technical background of production processes as well as a knowledge of time study methods. This may be the responsibility of a standards department, industrial engineering department, or cost control department. Occasionally it is under the jurisdiction of the controller. Establishment of the standard operation time requires a determination of the time needed to complete each operation when working under standard conditions. Hence this study embodies working conditions, including the material control plan, the production planning and scheduling procedure, and layout of equipment and facilities. After all these factors are considered, a standard can be set by the engineers.

In using time standards for measuring labor performance, the accounting staff must work closely with the industrial engineers or those responsible for setting the standards. The related cost standards must be consistent; the accumulation of cost information must consider how the standards were set and how the variances are analyzed.

Generally, performance standards are not revised until a change of method or process occurs. Because standards serve as the basis of control, the accounting staff should be on the alert for changes put into effect in the factory but not reported for standard revision. If the revised process requires more time, the production staff usually will make quite certain that their measuring stick is modified. However, if the new process requires less time, it is understandable that the change might not be reported promptly. Each supervisor naturally desires to make the best possible showing. The prompt reporting of time reductions might be stimulated through a periodic review of changes in standard labor hours or costs. In other words, the current labor performance of actual hours compared with a standard should be but one measure of performance; another measure is standard time reductions, also compared with a goal for the year.

It should be the responsibility of the controller to see that the standards are changed as the process changes to report true performance. If a wage incentive system is related to these standards, the need for adjusting process changes is emphasized. An analysis of variances, whether favorable or unfavorable, will often serve to indicate revisions not yet reported.

Effective labor control through the use of standards requires frequent reporting of actual and standard performance. Furthermore, the variance report must be by responsibility. For this reason the report on performance is prepared for each foreman as well as for the plant superintendent. The report may or may not be expressed in terms of dollars. It may compare person-hours or units of production instead of monetary units, but it always does compare actual and standard performance.

In a JIT environment, the manufacturing departments are tightly interlocked with minimal WIP between each department to hide problems caused by reduced manpower. In other words, if an area is understaffed, then downstream workstations will quickly run short of work. Consequently, the most critical direct labor measure in a JIT environment is a report of absent personnel, delivered promptly to the production managers at the start of the workday, so they can reshuffle staff members to cover all departments and contact the missing personnel.

Generally speaking, labor rates paid by a company are determined by external factors. The rate standard used is usually that normally paid for the job or classification as set by collective bargaining. If standards are set under this policy, no significant variances should develop because of base rates paid. Some rate variances, however, may be created and are controllable by management. Some of these reasons, which should be set out for corrective action, include:

- Overtime in excess of that provided in the standard
- Use of higher-rated classifications on the job
- Failure to place staff members on incentive pay, such as additional payments when objectives are achieved
- Use of a crew mixture that is different from the standard (more higher classifications and fewer of the lower, or vice versa)

The application of the standard labor rate to the job poses no great problem. Usually the accounting department applies the labor rate after securing the rates from the personnel department. Where overtime is contemplated in the standard, it is necessary, of course, to consult with production to determine the probable extent of overtime for the capacity at which the standard is set.

Labor requirements can be preplanned in some firms. The degree to which this preplanning takes place depends on the industry and particular conditions within the individual firm. Are business conditions sufficiently stable so that some reasonably accurate planning can be done? Can the sales department indicate with reasonable accuracy what the requirements will be over the short run? A useful preplanning application might be a machine shop where thousands of parts are made. If production requirements are known, the standard hours worked necessary can be calculated and converted to manpower. The standard hours worked may be stored in a computer by skills required and by department (i.e., a labor routing). After evaluating the particular production job, an experienced efficiency factor may be determined. Thus if 12,320 standard hours worked are needed for the planned production but an efficiency rate of only 80 percent is expected, then 15,400 actual hours worked must be scheduled. This requires a crew of 385 employees (at 40 hours per week for one week). This can be further refined by skills, or an analysis can be made of the economics of authorizing overtime. Steps should be taken to ensure that only the required number is authorized on the payroll for this production. As the requirements change, the standard person-hours should be reevaluated.

In a material requirements planning (MRP) environment, labor routings must be at least 95 percent accurate, and the firm must adhere strictly to a master production schedule. If the controller works in such an environment, then labor requirements can easily be predicted by multiplying the related labor routings by the unit types and quantities shown on the master schedule.

Wage Incentive Plans

In an effort to increase efficiency, a number of companies have introduced wage incentive plans, with good results. The controller is involved through the payroll department, which must calculate the monetary effect of such a plan. One facet of an incentive plan is germane to the costing process. When an incentive wage plan is introduced into an operation already on a standard cost basis, a problem arises about the relationship between the standard performance level at which incentive earnings commence and the standard performance level used for costing purposes. Moreover, what effect should the wage incentive plan have on the standard labor cost and standard manufacturing expense of the product? To cite a specific situation, a company may be willing to pay an incentive to labor for performance that is lower than that assumed in the cost standard (but much higher than actual experience). If such a bonus is excluded from the cost standard, the labor cost at the cost standard level will be understated. Further, there may be no offsetting savings in manufacturing expenses since the costs are incurred to secure performance at a lower level than the cost standard. These statements assume, of course, that the existing cost standard represents efficient performance even under incentive conditions. If, however, the effect of the incentive plan is to increase sustained production levels well above those contemplated in the cost standards, it may be that the product will be overcosted by using current cost standards and that these standards are no longer applicable. How should the cost standards be set in relation to the incentive plan?

In reviewing the plan, several generalizations may be made. First, there is no necessary relationship between standards for incentive purposes and standards for costing purposes. The former are intended to stimulate effort, whereas the latter are used to determine what the labor cost of the product should be. One is a problem in personnel management, whereas the other is strictly an accounting problem. With such dissimilar objectives, the levels of performance could logically be quite different.

Then, too, the matter of labor costing for statement purposes should be differentiated from labor control. As we have seen, labor control may involve nonfinancial terms—pieces per hour, pounds per hours worked, and so on. Labor control can be accomplished through the use of quantitative standards. Even if costs are used, the measuring stick for control need not be the same as for product costing. Control is centered on variations from performance standards and not on product cost variations.

A thorough consideration of the problem results in the conclusion that labor standards for costing purposes should be based on normal expectations from the operation of a wage incentive system under standard operation conditions. The expected earnings under the bonus plan should be reflected in the standard unit cost of the product. It does not necessarily follow that the product standard cost will be higher than that used before introduction of the incentive plan. It may mean, however, that the direct labor cost will be higher by reason of bonus payments. Yet because of increased production and material savings, the total unit standard manufacturing cost should be lower.

TARGET COSTING

The main point of this chapter has been to control production costs *after* a product design reaches the factory floor. However, by this time the components being used in the product have already been fixed and the design is one that must be produced using specific manufacturing methods. By the time a product reaches production, there really is not a great deal that the controller (or anyone else) can do to reduce product costs beyond a few percentage points that can be garnered from the extra efficiencies already noted in this chapter. A better approach that attacks costs before the design is finished is called target costing.

In essence, target costing requires many departments to become involved in the design stage, where they work together to create products that meet specific target costs that will create tolerable margins at predetermined product price points. If a product design cannot attain its target cost, then it is shelved. The methodology starts with a review of the market to see what prices are being charged by competing products, or what prices customers think they would pay if a new product design were to be sold. Then the accounting staff backs out a company-standard profit margin from the sale price, which leaves the target cost. This cost actually may be a range of costs since the sales and marketing staff may conclude that the product price will drop over time as competition increases, which will require a matching drop in costs if margins are to be maintained.

The target cost then goes to the design group, which includes not just the usual engineers but also a cost accountant and representatives from the production, marketing, and purchasing staffs. This group then breaks down the target cost further and assigns a target cost to subcomponents of the product; each of these costs is then worked on by a subgroup of the design team. All members of the groups pitch in to determine new ways to meet their cost targets, such as new production methods or the use of a small number of parts that can be purchased in sufficiently high volume to result in lower per-unit part prices from suppliers. The design team will go through a number of milestone reviews to see if it is coming close to its target cost. The team must prove in each succeeding review that it is coming closer to the target, or else the project will be canceled. For example, if the team can come within 12 percent of its target cost during the first milestone review, then the project is allowed to continue to the next milestone, where the team must be within 9 percent of its goal, and so on. This rigorous approach keeps the project on track and avoids any sudden surprises.

The role of the cost accountant is to continually recompile the cost of the product as it passes through its various design milestones (which may be a great deal of work if the product has a large number of component parts) and to feed this information back to the design team, which uses it to spot high-cost parts that will be subject to further design work. In addition, the cost accountant must continue to review product costs after the completed design is released to production, so that management can see if the designed cost is the same as the manufactured cost. This subsequent analysis should not just be a simple variance that gives management no clue regarding why costs have changed; instead, it should specifically note what internal processes or external part prices are causing the variances. Finally, there may be plans to continually reduce product costs over time, in which case the cost accountant will be responsible for tracking the progress of cost reductions and notifying management of specific problems in achieving these goals.

CHAPTER NINE

9

Overhead

T
HE INDIRECT MANUFACTURING EXPENSES, or overhead costs, of a manufacturing operation have increased significantly as business has become more complex and as the utilization of more sophisticated machinery and equipment has become more prevalent. As the investment in computer-controlled machinery has increased, improving productivity and reducing direct labor hours, the control of depreciation expense, power costs, machine repairs and maintenance, and similar items has received a greater emphasis by management.

Manufacturing overhead has several distinguishing characteristics compared with the direct manufacturing costs of material and labor. It includes a wide variety of expenses, such as depreciation, property taxes, insurance, fringe benefit costs, indirect labor, supplies, power and other utilities, clerical costs, maintenance and repairs, and other costs that cannot be associated directly with a process or job. These types of costs behave differently from direct costs, as the volume of production varies. Some will fluctuate proportionately as production increases or decreases, and some will remain constant or fixed and will not be sensitive to the change in the number of units produced. Some costs may be semivariable and fixed for a particular volume level; however, they may vary with volume, but not absolutely proportionately with volume, and probably can be segregated into their fixed and variable components.

In the midst of this plethora of fixed, variable, and semivariable costs, the controller must control costs as well as account for costs by process or job. This chapter provides an overview of how the controller can manage these tasks.

 ## NEED FOR OVERHEAD CONTROLS

The diverse types of expenses in overhead and divided responsibility concerning their management may contribute to the incurrence of excessive costs. Furthermore, the fact that many cost elements seem to be quite small in terms of consumption or cost per unit often encourages neglect of proper control. For example, it is natural to increase clerical help as required when volume increases to higher levels, but there is a reluctance and usually a delay in eliminating such help when no longer needed. The reduced requirement must be forecasted and anticipated and appropriate actions taken in a timely manner. Numerous expenses of small-unit-cost items in the aggregate can make the company less competitive: excessive hours worked for maintenance, use of special forms or supplies when standard items would be sufficient, personal use of supplies, or indiscriminate use of communications and reproduction facilities. All types of overhead expenses must be evaluated and controls established to achieve cost reduction wherever possible.

Although these factors may complicate the control of manufacturing overhead, the basic approach to this control is fundamentally the same as that applying to direct costs: the setting of budgets or standards, the measurement of actual performance against those standards, and the taking of corrective action when those responsible for meeting budgets or standards repeatedly fail to reach the goal.

Standards may change at different volume levels; in other words, they must have sufficient flexibility to adjust to the level of operations under which the supervisor is working. To this extent the setting and application of overhead standards may differ from the procedure used in the control of direct material and direct labor. Also, the controller can use activity-based costing (ABC) to assign costs to products (or other cost elements, i.e., production departments or customers). Activity-based costing is a process that summarizes costs, allocates those costs to activities, and then charges the fully costed activities to those products or processes that use the activities. This approach is better than the traditional method of assigning a uniform overhead rate to all production because using ABC results in more accurate product costing.

 ## RESPONSIBILITIES OF THE CONTROLLER

In formulating and reporting on overhead information, the controller should heed these suggestions to make the information more useful to the manufacturing executive:

▪ Base the budget (or other standard) on technical data that are sound from a manufacturing viewpoint and should be agreed to in advance by the manufacturing manager. As manufacturing processes change, the standards must change. Adoption of just-in-time (JIT) techniques may require, for example, a different alignment of cost centers. Further, for companies using a high proportion of mechanization, direct labor plays a less important role, while manufacturing expense (through higher depreciation charged, perhaps more indirect labor, higher repairs and maintenance, and power) becomes relatively more significant.

▪ Give manufacturing department supervisors, who will do the actual planning and control of expenses, the opportunity to fully understand the system, including the manner in which the budget expense structure is developed, and to generally concur in the fairness of the system.

▪ The account classifications must be practical, the cost departments should follow the manufacturing organization structure, and the allocation methods must permit the proper valuation of inventories as well as proper control of expense.

▪ Allocate the manufacturing costs as accurately as possible, so that the manufacturing executive can determine the expense of various products and processes. This topic is covered in more detail later in the "Activity-Based Costing: An Introduction" section.

▪ Where a budgeting process is operational, procedures must be in place that facilitate the preparation of the planning budget in an effective and timely manner (by provision of adequate forms, instructions, schedules, etc.).

▪ Where flexible budgets are in use, either identify or assist in the identification of the fixed and variable portions of costs.

▪ Determine that the costing methods provide reliable and acceptable accumulation and allocation by cost object and that variances are properly analyzed.

- Work with industrial engineers who will provide the technical data required for the development of standards, such as manpower needs, power requirements, expected downtime, and maintenance requirements.
- Work with the manufacturing executive to develop information collection procedures for assigning costs to activities and tracking product usage of those activities if an activity-based costing system is in place.

 ## ACCOUNT CLASSIFICATIONS

One requirement for adequate cost control or accurate cost determination is the proper classification of accounts. Control must be exercised at the source, and as costs are controlled by individuals, the primary classification of accounts must be by individual responsibility. Determining responsibility generally requires a breakdown of expenses by factory departments: either productive departments or service departments, such as maintenance, power, or the tool crib. Sometimes, however, it becomes necessary to divide the expense classification more finely to secure a proper control or costing of products—to determine actual expenses and expense standards by cost center. This decision about the degree of refinement will depend largely on whether improved product costs result or whether better expense control can be achieved.

A cost center, which is ordinarily the most minute division of costs, is determined on one of two bases:

1. One or more similar or identical machines
2. The performance of a single operation or group of similar or related operations in the manufacturing process

The separation of operations or functions is essential because a foreman may have more than one type of machine or operation in his or her department—all of which affect costs. One product may require the use of expensive machinery, and another may need only some simple hand operations. The segregation by cost center will reveal this cost difference. Different overhead rates are needed to reflect differences in services or machines required.

If the controller chooses to install an ABC system, then a very different kind of cost breakdown will be required. The ABC method collects costs by activities rather than by department. For example, under ABC, information might be collected about the costs associated with engineering change orders rather than the cost of the entire engineering department. If management decides that

EXHIBIT 9.1   Allocation of Costs to Expenses or Capital Accounts

Description	Capitalize	Expense
Advertising expenses		XXX
Costs of strikes		XXX
Depreciation and cost depletion	XXX	
Factory administration expenses	XXX	
General & administrative expenses related to overall operations		XXX
Income taxes		XXX
Indirect labor and production supervisory wages	XXX	
Indirect materials and supplies	XXX	
Interest		XXX
Maintenance	XXX	
Marketing expenses		XXX
Officers' salaries related to production services	XXX	
Other distribution expenses		XXX
Pension contribution related to past service costs		XXX
Production employee's benefits	XXX	
Quality control and inspection	XXX	
Rent	XXX	
Repair expenses	XXX	
Research and experimental expenses		XXX
Rework labor, scrap, and spoilage	XXX	XXX
Salaries of officers related to overall operations		XXX
Selling expenses		XXX
Taxes other than income taxes related to production assets	XXX	
Tools and equipment not capitalized	XXX	
Utilities	XXX	

Source: Adapted from Coopers & Lybrand LLP, *Analysis: Tax Reform Act of 1986,* New York: 1986, p. 176.

it wants both ABC and departmental cost information, then the controller must record the information twice—once by department and again by activity.

The accounts that are capitalized into the overhead account are well defined by generally accepted accounting principles (GAAP) and are presented in Exhibit 9.1.

Most of the debate surrounding the content of the overhead cost pool is about the segments of inventory to which the overhead should be applied. Overhead is not normally applied to raw materials, but arguments have been presented in favor of these two issues:

1. *Inbound transportation costs.* Where the cost of getting the goods to the factory site is identifiable with particular material or lots, the cost may properly be added to the raw material. If such allocation is impractical, it may be considered part of the manufacturing overhead.
2. *Purchasing department expense.* The cost of this department generally would continue at the same level from period to period regardless of receipts, so allocating the cost to raw materials would not be a proper matching of expenses with effort expended. The cost may be more properly treated as manufacturing overhead.

The overall discussion of overhead issues will become less important as more companies adopt just-in-time inventory systems. As inventories shrink, there will be only small quantities of work-in-process or finished goods on hand, so most overhead costs will flow directly to the income statement.

 ## FIXED AND VARIABLE COSTS

Another step in controlling manufacturing overhead is the segregation of costs into two groups: fixed or variable. Variable costs increase or decrease in direct proportion to the volume of work. Control is exercised by keeping the expense within the limits determined for the particular level of activity. Fixed costs do not vary with activity but remain much the same over a relatively short period of time. Control over this kind of expense rests with the executives who determine policy with respect to plant investment, inventory level, and size of organization. Failure to distinguish between these two types of expenses can result in failure to control overhead. This is because the controller cannot tell whether increased costs result from higher unit fixed costs as a result of lower volume or from failure to keep variable costs within proper bounds.

The segregation of fixed and variable expenses permits the adoption of the *flexible budget,* which is a budget that allows expenses to vary with the activity level of the department involved. The opposite kind of budget is the *fixed budget,* which is planned for a fixed activity level. Activity rarely stays at one level in practice, so fixed budgets are of little use if the volume level changes.

Another classification of manufacturing expenses is the semivariable expense. This expense varies with the volume of production, but not in direct proportion to that volume. Two techniques are available to control these expenses. One method is to determine for each semivariable expense in each department just what the costs should be at various operating levels. For example, if the expected range is between 60 percent and 90 percent of capacity, costs should be budgeted at every 5 percent level (i.e., 65 percent, 70 percent, 75 percent). The budget applicable to the actual volume level would be selected and interpolated between the 5 percent ranges if necessary. Then actual costs would be compared to the budget and corrective action taken.

Another method of applying budgetary control to semivariable expenses is to resolve them into their fixed and variable portions and treat each accordingly. The fixed portion could be considered the necessary expense at the lower level of the expected volume, and the difference between this and the higher level could be treated as variable.

A good starting point in determining the fixed and variable components of costs is past experience. This review should encompass not only total costs but also various measures of activity. It is necessary to determine how much costs vary, as well as the best tool or factor for measuring activity. For example, past activity may be related to standard direct labor hours, actual direct labor hours, or units of production. Review of past experience must be supplemented by good judgment in applying the data to future periods. Changes in wage rates, material costs, or supervisory staff, for example, must be considered in modifying the data for standard purposes.

Examples of fixed costs include:

- *Costs fixed by general management decisions*
  - Depreciation on buildings and machinery
  - Real and personal property taxes
  - Insurance (property and liability)
  - Salaries of production executives
  - Patent amortization
- *Costs fixed by production executive decisions*
  - Salaries of factory supervisory staff
  - Factory administrative expense
  - Safety expenses

Examples of variable costs include:

▪ Royalties on units produced
▪ Small tool expense
▪ Supplies
▪ Testing expense
▪ Salvage expense

Examples of semivariable costs (i.e., those costs that contain both fixed and variable elements) include:

▪ Repairs and maintenance
▪ Factory office salaries and expense
▪ Payroll taxes and insurance
▪ Utilities

Using the High–Low Method

The illustrative separation of the fixed and variable elements of a manufacturing expense by a simple method is shown next. Three assumptions for the example are:

1. At a level of 50 percent of normal capacity, the maintenance department expense is $80,000 per month, whereas experience shows that at a level of 80 percent of capacity, the cost is $128,000.
2. The variable factor, or measuring stick, is standard hours of production worked.
3. At an 80 percent capacity, the standard hours worked are 160,000.

The variable costs are $48,000, and the variable budget allowance is $0.80 per standard hour worked, calculated as follows:

	Capacity	
% Normal Activity	**Standard Hours Worked**	**Cost**
80%	160,000	$128,000
50%	100,000	80,000
Variable	60,000	$ 48,000
Unit variable cost		$ 0.80
($48,000/60,000)		

On such a budget structure, the maintenance department allowance for a month of 120,000 standard hours of production worked will be:

Fixed portion	$80,000
Variable ($0.80 × 120,000 − 100,000)	16,000
Total	$96,000

Note that the variable allowance is granted only for standard hours worked in excess of what was considered the lowest probable level of activity. However, the entire cost might be treated as variable within the same budget (120,000 × $0.80 = $96,000).

Graphic Determination of Fixed and Variable Costs

The use of only a few points to determine the variable expense is of limited value because only a few levels are considered. If more accuracy is desired, another convenient approach is to use a scatter chart. For example, assume that the data in Exhibit 9.2 on personnel department costs are available.

These numbers are then plotted on a chart as in Exhibit 9.3. The vertical axis represents the dollar costs, and the horizontal axis represents the factor of variability—standard hours worked in the illustration. After the points are

EXHIBIT 9.2 Comparison of Costs to Standard Hours Worked Activity Measure

Month	Factory Standard Hours Worked	Total Departmental Costs
January	20,000	12,200
February	16,000	10,600
March	13,000	9,400
April	14,000	9,800
May	17,000	10,400
June	19,000	12,000
July	21,000	12,400
August	23,000	12,600
September	25,000	13,600
October	22,000	12,200
November	18,000	11,800
December	19,000	11,600

EXHIBIT 9.3 Graphic Determination of Fixed and Variable Costs

plotted, a line of best fit may be drawn by inspection, in such a manner that half of the points are above it and half of the points are below it. Any highly variant items should be disregarded. For a higher degree of refinement, the method of least squares may be used. The least-squares method is a mathematical technique that derives a line of best fit with more precision than can be achieved by visually plotting the line.

The point at which the line of best fit intersects the vertical axis indicates the fixed cost that might be expected if the plant were in an operating condition but producing nothing. The total cost of any level of activity is determined by reading the chart. For example, at a level of 25,000 standard hours worked, the budget expense would be $13,400. This cost is made up of $5,500 fixed and $7,900 variable elements. The variable rate is $0.316 per standard hour worked.

The slope of the line on the chart indicates the degree of variability. Thus, a horizontal line represents a fixed cost, whereas a line that goes through the point of origin indicates a completely variable cost. Sometimes, in constructing a chart, the points show no tendency to arrange themselves along a line. If this situation exists, either cost control has been absent or a poor choice has been made about the factor of variability. Another factor should be tested to ascertain the cause.

A significant consideration in the control of manufacturing overhead expense through the analysis of variances is the level of activity selected in setting the standard costs. Although it has no direct bearing on the planning and control of the manufacturing expenses of each individual department, it does have an impact on the statement of income and expenses, as well as on the statement of financial position. As for the income statement, it is desirable to identify the amount of manufacturing expense absorbed by or allocated to the manufactured product, with the excess expense identified as variance from the standard cost. This variance or excess cost ordinarily should be classified as to cause. As for the statement of financial position, the normal activity level has a direct impact on inventory valuation and, consequently, on the cost-of-goods-sold element of the income statement, in that it helps to determine the standard product cost. It should be obvious that the fixed element of unit product costs is greatly influenced by the total quantity of production assumed. Management must clearly understand the significance of the level selected because in large part it determines the volume variance.

Generally speaking, there are three levels on which fixed standard manufacturing overhead may be set:

1. *The expected sales volume for the year, or other period, when the standards are to be applied.* All costs are adjusted from year to year. Consequently, certain cost comparisons are difficult to make. Furthermore, the resulting statements fail to give management what may be considered the most useful information about volume costs. Standard costs would be higher in low-volume years, when lower prices might be needed to get more business, and lower in high-volume years, when the increased demand presumably would tend toward higher prices. Another weakness is that the estimate of sales used as a basis would not be accurate in many cases.

2. *Practical plant capacity, representing the volume at which a plant could produce if there were no lack of orders.* Practical plant capacity as a basis tends to give the lowest cost. This capacity level can be misleading because sales volume will not average this level. Generally there are always large unfavorable variances, the unabsorbed expense.

3. *The normal or average sales volume, herein defined as normal capacity.* This capacity is the utilization of the plant that is necessary to meet the average sales demand over the period of a business cycle or at least long enough to level out cyclical and seasonal influences. This basis permits stabilization of costs and the recognition of long-term trends in sales. Each basis has advantages and disadvantages, but normal capacity seems to be the most desirable under ordinary circumstances.

Where one unit is manufactured, normal capacity can be stated in the quantity of this unit. In those cases where many products are available, it is usually necessary to select a common unit for the denominator. Productive hours are a practical measure. If the normal productive hours for all departments or cost centers are known, the sum of these will represent the total for the plan. The total fixed costs divided by the productive hours at normal capacity results in the standard fixed cost per productive hour.

Volume variances can also cause costing problems in an ABC environment. Activity costs are derived by dividing estimated volumes of activity drivers into activity cost pools to derive costs for individual activities. If the estimated volume of an activity driver deviates excessively from the actual amount, then the activity cost applied to a product may significantly alter the product's ABC cost. For example, there are estimated to be 1,000 material moves associated with a product in a month, and the total cost of those moves in a month is $10,000, which is $10 per move. If the actual number of moves associated with the product is 2,000, then the cost per move that is applied to product costs is off by $5 per move. However, if the ABC system collects actual activity driver volume information for every accounting period, then the volume variance will not occur.

 ## COST ALLOCATION

This section discusses traditional cost allocation systems, the need for activity-based costing, problems with the ABC model, and ways to report ABC information to management. Also, an ABC installation, ABC software models, analyzing non–value-added processes, and converting indirect costs to direct costs are briefly outlined. The ABC topic is much larger than this abbreviated discussion, so readers who wish to implement such a system should consult one of the many books available on the subject.

Traditional Cost Allocation

A traditional cost allocation system seeks to assign all indirect production costs to cost objects. Where possible, the indirect costs are assigned based on the use of those costs by the cost objects. If no usage relationship can be established, then the indirect costs will be assigned based on some broad allocation measure.

A cost is considered *indirect* if it cannot be directly assigned to a cost object with minimal effort. For example, one firm may consider an engineer's salary to be indirect if she works on numerous projects at once. However, another firm might expand additional effort to track that engineer's time, so that the salary cost can be directly assigned to cost objects. In the first case, the salary is considered an indirect cost. In the second case, the salary is considered a direct cost. Examples of costs that are generally considered to be indirect are repairs and maintenance, utilities, and depreciation.

A *cost object* is the item being measured. For example, the controller may wish to find the cost of a product, a department, or a geographical sales region. Each can be a cost object because the controller must accumulate a different, discrete set of cost information about each item.

The method for allocating costs is the *overhead rate*. This is a constant rate per unit of the application base. For example, the total amount to be allocated is $100,000, and the allocation base is units of production. If 10,000 units are expected to be produced, then $10 will be allocated for each unit produced. These overhead rates are usually determined at the beginning of the year in order to avoid seasonal fluctuations in the rate and to avoid the extra work needed to recalculate the rate for each accounting period. The overhead rate estimate is based on the projected amount of indirect cost divided by the expected volume of the allocation base. Since the rate is based on two estimates, it is obvious that incorrect overhead rates are fairly common. If the controller deems the overhead rate to be materially incorrect, then a midyear correction is appropriate. For lesser cases of under- or overabsorbed overhead, the variance should be factored into the current period's financial statements.

The base selected should be the one that best allocates costs. However, the "best" method is a matter of opinion in many cases, so that indirect labor is frequently misapplied. For those organizations with a large amount of indirect costs, an incorrect allocation base can have serious repercussions on product costing. For example, a cost that is reported too low may cause management to take steps to increase sales of that item, when it should be emphasizing the sales of other, more profitable products.

A typical allocation process follows:

- *Accumulate costs for all production cost centers and service cost centers.* An example of a product cost center is a sheet metal bending department. An example of a service cost center is a maintenance department.
- *Assign the cost of all service cost centers to the production cost centers.* For example, the maintenance department fills out time sheets that indicate that 30 percent of its labor and parts costs were used in maintaining the sheet metal bending department. If the maintenance department's total

assigned cost is $100,000, then $30,000 of the $100,000 will be charged to the sheet metal bending department.

▪ *Assign the total cost of the production cost centers to the cost objects produced in those centers.* For example, if half of the sheet metal bending department's time is spent producing bird feeders, then half of that department's total cost is assigned to the total production of bird feeders.

Sometimes service centers perform work for other service centers. When this happens, costs may be assigned from one service center to another. The reader should consult a cost accounting textbook for examples of the step-down allocation method. Service centers invariably have "leftover" costs that cannot be directly assigned elsewhere. An example of this is the salary of the supervisor, who is not directly involved in providing a service to a cost object. In such cases, the controller can use many bases to allocate the costs-to-cost objects. For example, common allocation bases are the number of people, labor hours, labor dollars, machine hours, square footage, volume of transactions (e.g., number of material moves, parts ordered, engineering change orders), and total revenues/costs (e.g., based on total revenue or expenses dollars).

Activity-Based Costing: An Introduction

Traditional cost accounting systems apply overhead to products based on the amount of direct labor they use. When direct labor was a significant proportion of the value being added to a product, this did not skew product costs significantly. However, as direct labor was gradually replaced by automation, the direct labor component dropped while overhead costs increased. As a result, many businesses find that their overhead rates are at 300 percent or more of their direct labor costs. Consequently, a slight change in a product's direct labor charge yields a significant product cost variation as the applied overhead amount swings dramatically up or down.

To combat this overhead application problem, several companies began to apply overhead based on other, more relevant, factors than direct labor. This resulted in multiple overhead rates being used at one time and required additional data collection for the different overhead application bases. Eventually, activity-based costing was invented. ABC is not a direct offshoot of the multiple overhead rate system. Instead, it assumes that costs are assigned based on resources consumed, so that resource costs are identified and then assigned to products based on their use of those resources. The ABC information is then accumulated into reports by product, customer, geographic region, or other reporting entities.

An ABC system requires a large amount of data collection. Cost data must be accumulated in ways that usually are not the same as the traditional by-department chart of accounts system. The controller must therefore recombine costs into "cost pools." In addition, the ABC system must derive a cost for various activities, and then the use of those activities by the reporting entity (products, customers, geographic regions, etc.) must be measured. This data collection either is handled on a project basis, so that ABC costs are derived only once, or built into a new costing system that either supersedes or exists beside the traditional costing system. Also, the ABC system must be designed carefully so that the data collection is not too burdensome. The ABC team should keep the number of cost pools and activity measures to a minimum. Once an ABC system is operational, the ABC team can analyze the model's accuracy and selectively add or delete items requiring data collection.

The information derived from an ABC model can be used to provide product cost information and inventory valuations, and control non–value-added costs. One of its greatest benefits is to assist management in determining the true costs of products that are otherwise buried in overhead and misapplied elsewhere. As a result, management has better gross margin information and can use that information to add or delete products or options more intelligently. If the ABC information is not presented to management, then its benefits will not be significant.

The information provided by the traditional costing system may conflict with the information provided by the ABC system. If, for example, management bonuses are calculated based on the results of the traditional system, then the ABC results may be ignored. Also, if a company has several divisions and ABC is not implemented in all of them, then the corporate controller will have incomplete comparative costing information. As a result, management action based on cost comparisons would not be possible.

Developing an ABC Model

For the purposes of this discussion, assume that costs are being accumulated only to report on product costs. To develop an ABC model, these eight steps must be completed:

1. *Identify activities.* This step has the following components:
   - ▪ *Define the boundaries of the project.* An ABC analysis can involve all aspects of the company, but completing such a project may take too

long to retain management's interest. Instead, the ABC project leader should consider a small, important target area for the initial ABC analysis and then expand the process at a later date. For example, the initial project could include the engineering and materials departments, but exclude marketing.

▫ *Document process flows.* List all activities within each target area. This information is usually recorded on a flowchart. Activities may cross over department boundaries. For example, the materials ordering process begins with the bill of materials in the engineering department before it moves to the materials department, where the actual ordering occurs. The flowcharts should be reviewed with key personnel from the areas being studied, so that flaws in the model can be corrected.

2. *Identify all direct costs.* Traditional costing methods already track direct costs in some detail, so this is an easy step if there are existing costing systems in place. If not, then identify the direct labor and materials costs that are associated with individual products. Accurate labor routings and bills of material are needed for proper direct cost identification. If there is an existing material requirements planning (MRP) system in place, then routings and bills of material should already be available.

3. *Assign indirect costs to cost pools.* Use the flowcharts developed during the first step to identify logical clusters of costs. This can be a very time-consuming step, for the costs in the general ledger are organized to support a traditional costing system, not an activity-based system that requires a different chart of accounts. As a result, many general ledger accounts will have to be subdivided into smaller pieces that are then summarized into cost pools. A sample list of cost pools that a manufacturing company might use includes:

▫ Accounts payable
▫ Depreciation
▫ Maintenance labor
▫ Material movement
▫ Plant management
▫ Production control
▫ Purchasing
▫ Quality control
▫ Receiving
▫ Rework
▫ Scrap
▫ Utilities

4. *Identify output measures.* Use the flowcharts developed during the first step to identify activities that consume costs. These activities measure the frequency and volume of demand placed on an activity by the product or service being produced. For example, every time a product is moved, costs are incurred for the labor of the forklift driver and depreciation expense for the forklift. Other examples of output measures are:
   - Number of parts
   - Number of suppliers
   - Number of units reworked
   - Number of material moves
   - Number of purchase orders
   - Number of customer orders
   - Number of engineering change requests
5. *Collect output measures.* Most companies use ABC on a project basis, so that output measures are collected only once. Such companies assume that output measures do not vary significantly in the short term and thus rely on ABC information for which the foundation data was collected only once. The alternative, and more accurate, approach is to collect the output measure information for each reporting period. Doing so requires information collection systems for items that were not previously tracked. Some output measures are difficult to track, so management must commit in advance to the extra time and cost of doing so.
6. *Calculate activity costs.* Divide the output measures into the cost pools to derive activity costs. For example, an output measure may be that 210 invoices were paid by accounts payable in a period. The cost of the accounts payable labor for that period was $1,672, so the cost per accounts payable activity (paying the invoice) was $7.96.
7. *Calculate product costs.* There are several layers of costs to add to a product under the ABC model:
   - *Add direct costs.* These are the direct labor and material costs that are directly attributable to a product, and usually are derived from labor routings and bills of material.
   - *Add activity costs.* Add the costs of all costed activities to the product cost. For example, if 32 invoices were paid in order to produce a product, then the cost of the payables activity for that product (using the $7.96 amount from the previous example) would be $7.96 multiplied 32 times, or $254.72.
   - *Add other cost pools.* Other costs can be added from cost pools for areas such as marketing and general and administrative expenses. For

example, if costs by geographic region are desired, then advertising costs can be subdivided by region and added to the total cost of products sold in each region.

8. *Use the information.* Review product costs based on the traditional costing system versus the new costing system. An ABC review will highlight costs that would otherwise have been lost in the total overhead cost. Typical management actions to reduce the overhead cost include:

■ *Reduce the number of product options.* The cost of designing, scheduling, and building product options is located in overhead and can be reduced by cutting the number of product options.

■ *Reduce the number of parts used.* The cost of designing, "sourcing" (the process of identifying and obtaining parts from a source or supplier), and purchasing parts is located in overhead and can be reduced by cutting the number of product options.

■ *Reduce the number of material moves.* The cost of moving parts is located in the materials department part of the overhead cost and can be reduced by cutting the number of material moves (which also cuts the cycle time!).

■ *Reduce the number of engineering change requests.* The cost of redesigning parts, sourcing new suppliers, and expediting purchases is located in the overhead cost and can be reduced by cutting the number of engineering change requests.

■ *Reduce the number of suppliers.* The cost of sourcing and qualifying new suppliers is located in the materials department portion of the overhead cost and can be reduced by cutting the number of suppliers.

Note that the list of possible management actions is identical to the activities used in the ABC model. The ABC model is designed in this manner to focus attention on activities in the production cycle. If management reduces the number of activities, then not only is the "traditional" overhead cost reduced, but also the production cycle time is slashed.

Special issues may arise when developing an ABC model, or the controller may decide to extend an existing ABC model to cover additional activities. Examples of these special situations are the use of ABC in the budgeting process, converting indirect costs to direct costs, and implementing a bill of activities. The next list may help the controller to deal with special ABC problems as well as to enhance existing ABC applications.

1. *Convert indirect costs to direct costs.* If indirect costs can be converted to direct costs, then product costs will be more accurate. One area for such

improvement is converting to a cellular manufacturing arrangement from an assembly-line arrangement. Product costing for an assembly line can be inaccurate because many product types may pass through specific work-stations or departments. As a result, costs are accumulated by workstation or department and then assigned to products based on labor hours or machine hours. In a cellular manufacturing environment, a small number of products are built by a small number of workers using a cluster of workstations that are reserved for producing that set of products. Conse-quently, costs are more easily assigned to products, and the costs of those grouped workstations can be considered direct instead of indirect.

2. *Purchase an ABC software package.* Many companies build ABC systems that are separate from their traditional accounting systems. Another approach to building ABC systems is to use the alphanumeric fields sometimes provided with general ledger packages to store output measures for each reporting period.

3. *Review non–value-added processes.* The controller can add a function to the process review phase of ABC, and review the process flowcharts for value-added versus non–value-added activities. A value-added activity converts resources into products or services. A non–value-added activity can be eliminated with no reduction in a product's or service's functionality or quality. This added step allows the controller to target non–value-added processes for elimination. The non–value-added processes can be ranked in importance by the time or cost required for each one. Armed with that information, management can then prioritize the processes for elimination or reduction. Examples of non–value-added activities are:

▪ Inspection
▪ Rework
▪ Moving
▪ Storage
▪ Queue time

A value-added analysis also notes the company's value-added activities. The controller can highlight this information and encourage an engineering team to reduce or eliminate any bottlenecks in those operations. This action increases the company's production capacity.

▪ *Implement a bill of activities.* To create an online ABC system, the company should create a bill of activities (BOA) that is similar to the bill of materials (BOM) already used for its products. The BOA lists the types and quantities of activities used during the production of a product. Management can focus on the BOA to discern the primary sources of activity-based costs and act to reduce those costs. Also, the BOA is needed to roll up activity costs for each period's cost reports, just as the BOM is used to roll up direct costs for each product.

▪ *Using ABC for budgeting.* Activity-based costing is rarely used for budgeting, but if the controller wishes to use it, then BOAs and BOMs should be used as the foundation data for standard costs. Multiplying the planned production quantities by the activity costs found in the bills of activity and direct costs found in the bills of lading will yield the bulk of all anticipated manufacturing costs for the budget period. The appropriate management use of budgeted activity costs is to target reductions in the use of activities by various products, as well as to reduce the cost of those activities. For example, the cost of paying a supplier invoice for a part used by the company's product can be reduced by either (1) automating the activity to reduce its cost, or (2) reducing the product's use of the activity, such as by reducing the number of suppliers, reducing the number of parts used in the product, or grouping invoices and only paying the supplier on a monthly basis.

 CONTROLLING OVERHEAD

The basic approach in controlling overhead is to set standards of performance and operate within the limits of these standards. Two avenues may be followed to accomplish this objective: One involves the preplanning or preventive approach; the other, the after-the-fact approach of reporting unfavorable trends and performance.

Preplanning can be accomplished on many items of manufacturing overhead expense in somewhat the same fashion as discussed in connection with direct labor. For example, the crews for indirect labor can be planned just as well as the crews for direct labor. The preplanning approach will be useful where a substantial dollar cost is involved for purchase of supplies or repair materials. It may be desirable to maintain a record of purchase commitments, by responsibility, for these accounts. Each purchase requisition, for example, might require the approval of the budget department. When the budget limit is reached, then no further purchases would be permitted except with the approval of much higher authority. Again, where stores or stock requisitions are the source of charges, the department manager may be kept informed periodically of the cumulative monthly cost, and steps may be taken to stop further issues, except in emergencies, as the budget limit is approached. By providing this kind of information, the controller will be able to find ways and means of assisting the department operating executives to keep within budget limits.

The other policing function of control is the reporting of unfavorable trends and performance. Doing this involves an analysis of expense variances. Here the problem is somewhat different from direct labor or material because of the different levels of activity. Thus, the variance due to business volume must be isolated from that controllable by the departmental supervisors.

Volume variance, regardless of cause, must be segregated from the controllable variances. Volume variance is defined as the difference between budgeted expense for current activity and the standard cost for the same level. It arises because production is above or below normal activity and affects primarily the fixed costs of the business. The variance can be caused by seasonal or calendar factors, such as the varying numbers of days in each month.

The controllable variances may be defined as the difference between the budget at the current activity level and actual expenses. They must be set out for each cost center and analyzed in such detail that the supervisor knows exactly what caused the condition. At least two general categories can be recognized. The first is the rate of *spending variance;* this variance arises because more or less than standard was spent for each machine hour, operating hour, or standard labor hour. This variance must be isolated for each cost element of production expense. An analysis of the variance on indirect labor, for example, may indicate what share of the excess cost is due to (1) overtime, (2) an excess number of workers, or (3) use of higher-rated workers than standard. The analysis may be detailed to show the excess by craft and by shift. As another example, suppliers may be analyzed to show the cause of variance as (1) too large a quantity of certain items, (2) a different material or quality being used, or (3) higher prices than anticipated.

Another general type of controllable variance is the *efficiency variance.* This variance represents the difference between actual hours used in production and the standard hours allowed for the same volume. Such a loss involves all elements of overhead. The controller should analyze the causes, usually with the assistance of production personnel. The lost production might be due to mechanical failure, poor or insufficient material, or inefficient labor. Such an analysis points out weaknesses and paves the way for corrective action by the line executives.

The accounting staff must be prepared to analyze overhead variances quickly and accurately to keep the manufacturing supervision and management informed. The variance analysis should focus on overhead losses or gains for which unit supervision is responsible and include such features as:

- The expenditure or rate variance for each cost element as an over- or under-the-budget condition for the reporting period and year to date. The budgeted amount for controllable expenses may be calculated by multiplying the operating hours by the standard rate per cost element and compared to the actual.
- The departmental variance related to the level of production.
- The amount of fixed costs, even though the particular supervisor may not be responsible for the incurrence.
- Interpretative comments about areas for corrective action, trends, and reasons for any negative variances.

It is not sufficient merely to render a budget report to the manufacturing supervisors; this group must be informed about the reasons for the variances. A continuous follow-up must also be undertaken to see that any unfavorable conditions are corrected. This follow-up may take the form of reviewing and analyzing weekly or even daily reports. Abnormal conditions such as excess training, overtime, absenteeism, and excessive usage of supplies must be isolated and brought to the attention of the responsible individuals who can take remedial action. Other data available, such as repair records, material and supplies usage reports, and personnel statistics records (e.g., turnover and attendance), also may be useful in determining variances.

One of the purposes of budgetary control is to maintain expenses within the limits of income. To this end, common factors of variability are standard labor hours or standard machine hours—bases affected by the quantity of approved production. If manufacturing difficulties are encountered, the budget allowance of all departments on such a basis would be reduced. The maintenance foreman, for example, may tell the controller that he should not be penalized in his budget because production was inefficient or that plans once set cannot be changed constantly because production does not come up to expectations. Such a situation may be resolved in one of at least two ways: (1) The forecast standard hours could be used as the basis for the variable allowance, or (2) the maintenance foreman could be informed regularly if production, and therefore the standard budget allowance, will be lower than anticipated. The first suggestion departs somewhat from the income-producing sources but does permit a budget allowance within the limits of income and does not require constant changes of labor force over a very short period. The second suggestion allows for more coordination between departments.

An important consideration is not *how* flexibility is introduced into the standard or budget but rather that it *is* introduced. Whether charts or tables are used to determine the allowable budget on a more or less automatic basis or whether the budget is adjusted monthly or quarterly on the basis of special review in relation to business volume is not essential. Either method can be employed successfully. The goal is to secure an adequate measuring stick that also keeps expenses at the proper level in relation to activity or income.

Many manufacturing executives in particular industries know from observation that certain expense relationships are the key to a profitable operation. Their experience has led to the use of a number of standards or standard relationships for manufactured expenses. These ratios usually are collected and distributed by industry trade associations or magazines devoted to the affairs of specific industries. Exhibit 9.4 presents some comparisons often used.

Treatment of Bottleneck Overhead

The preceding discussion of overhead controls implies that the controller should diligently shrink overhead costs wherever they are found. This is not the case if overhead costs relate to the company's bottleneck operation.

EXHIBIT 9.4 Operational Standards Used to Track Expenses

Item	As Related to
Total manufacturing expenses	Total direct labor costs
	Total direct costs
Indirect labor expense	Total standard direct labor
	Per direct labor hour
	Per actual direct labor hour
	Per machine hour
	Total manufacturing expense
Repair and maintenance expense	Per machine hour
Power	Per operating hour
Supplies	Per hour worked
Shipping and receiving	Per ton handled
Downtime expense	Per operating hour

In a bottleneck operation, the total profits of the company suffer if the bottleneck is not being fully utilized at all times. Given the goal of full utilization, the bottleneck operation tends to require significantly more support than other operations, which gives it the appearance of requiring an excessive amount of overhead costs. For example, it may be necessary to have maintenance staff assigned solely to the bottleneck operation, to ensure that it is made operational again as soon as possible in the event of a breakdown, even if they are not fully utilized.

Given the decisive negative impact on profits if the bottleneck is not operational, it is rarely a good idea to reduce expenditures for overhead costs that are used to support the bottleneck. To continue with the example, the controller may reduce labor costs by $50,000 per year by eliminating a maintenance position that is solely assigned to the bottleneck, but the company as a whole then loses $250,000 in lost profits because the bottleneck is now operational for a reduced period of time, due to maintenance delays.

 ## PRODUCTION REPORTS

The supervisory staff of the production organization extends over several levels of authority and responsibility from the assistant foreman, foreman, general foreman, division head, plant superintendent, and so on, up to the vice president of manufacturing. Likewise, the matters the supervisory staff controls involve materials, labor, and overhead, and each of these subjects has special aspects to be reported on. It is obvious, then, that production reports must cover a wide field of subject matter. Effective production control is possible only when the production executives are aware of the necessary facts related to plant operations, and the further the executive is from the actual production, the more he or she must rely on reports. As a result, a system of reports has been developed in most organizations for presenting the pertinent facts on the production activities.

Because reports will differ by industry and company, no standardized reports can be used for business in general. However, they may be divided into two general categories according to their purpose: (1) control reports and (2) summary reports. As the name implies, control reports are issued primarily to highlight substandard performance so that corrective action may be taken promptly. These reports deal with performance at the occurrence level and are usually detailed in nature and frequent in issuance. Summary reports show the results of performance over a longer period of time, such as a month, and are an overall recapitulation of performance. They serve to keep corporate executives aware of factory performance and are, in effect, a summary of the control reports.

The reports may cover these subjects, among others:

- *Material.* Inventories, spoilage and waste, unit standard costs, material consumed, and actual versus standard usage
- *Labor.* Total payroll, unit output per hour worked, total production in units, average hourly labor rates, overtime hours and costs, bonus costs, and turnover
- *Overhead.* Actual versus budgeted costs, idle facilities, maintenance costs, supplies used, the cost of union business, and subcontracted repairs

In a production environment that has adopted just-in-time manufacturing systems, reports will no longer include standards because JIT assumes that most cost improvements can be managed in the design phase, not in the production phase, and that collecting variance information costs more in effort than is gained in tangible results. Thus, a set of JIT reports would include these items not related to standards:

- Inventory turnover
- Unit output per hour worked
- Total production in units
- Staff turnover
- Actual purchased costs versus planned costs
- Inventory accuracy
- Bill of material accuracy
- Bill of activities accuracy

Production executives will make good use of data bearing on their operations provided three fundamental rules are followed:

1. Reports should be expressed in the language of the executive who is to use them and in the form preferred by him or her (e.g., charts, graphs, or commentary).
2. Reports should be submitted promptly enough to serve the purpose intended. Control reports are of little value if issued too late to take corrective action.
3. The form and content of the reports should be in keeping with the responsibility of the executive receiving them. Midlevel executives are

interested in details, whereas higher executives are interested in departmental summaries, trends, and relationships.

The number of variance reports that are used by manufacturing management will decline as cellular manufacturing becomes the standard form of production. Since cellular manufacturing uses minimal work-in-process (WIP), month-end variance reports from the accounting department will arrive far too late for the information to be useful. For example, if a machine produces a part out of specification, then a production worker operating in a cellular layout will immediately detect the problem because the part will not be hidden in a pile of WIP. Consequently, management can detect and correct the problem immediately without the need for a report.

CHAPTER TEN

General and Administrative Expenses

T HE CATEGORY OF EXPENSES known as general and administrative (G&A) expense relates primarily to the costs of the various top management functions at the headquarters level having to do with overall policy determination and direction of the business. This chapter discusses the accounts included in the G&A category, allocation of cost, and G&A cost control.

FUNCTIONS INVOLVED

The typical medium- to large-size company would include the cost of these departments in the G&A expense category:

- Office of the chairman of the board
- Office of the president
- Financial organization:
  - Office of the chief financial officer
  - Investor relations department
  - Office of the controller

> Accounting department
> Tax department
> Financial planning and control department
> Financial information systems
> ▣ Office of the treasurer
> ▣ Cash administration
> Risk management
> Retirement plan investments
> ▣ Office of the chief internal auditor
> Financial auditing
> Systems auditing
> Special reviews

- Legal department:
  - ▣ Office of the vice president—legal
  - Office of the corporate secretary
  - Litigation
  - SEC relations
  - Patents and trademarks
- Corporate offices for the direction and control of these major functions:
  - ▣ Marketing
  - ▣ Manufacturing
  - ▣ Research and development
  - ▣ Human resources
  - ▣ Management information systems
  - ▣ Public relations
  - ▣ Strategic planning

To the extent that the purpose of these departments or organizational units have to do with overall policy determination, planning, direction, and control, they probably would be classified as G&A in the annual report to shareholders. Comparable expenses at the division or subsidiary level might or might not be so classified (although the methods of planning and control would be similar to those for the corporate activity).

ACCOUNTING FOR AND ALLOCATING ADMINISTRATIVE EXPENSES

The controller is responsible for developing and maintaining an accounting system that serves, among others, these purposes:

- Permits the reporting of expenses for external purposes in accordance with generally accepted accounting principles
- Allows the accumulation of costs by natural category to facilitate planning and control
- Accumulates costs on a "responsibility" basis so that a specific individual may be assigned responsibility for the planning and control of the costs
- Where appropriate, permits the allocation of expenses on some acceptable basis, such as benefits received, to cost objects—which might include divisions or cost centers or products that use the service
- Gives due weight to internal control concerns

Methods of allocation, and when costs should be allocated, are of special concern in the planning and control of assets. A basic tenet for responsibility accounting is that expenses should not be allocated to a department unless the supervisor can exercise control over such costs. If such control is present, then these allocation methods are possible:

- Allocate costs based on the amount of the resource consumed by the cost center receiving the service. For example, if a division uses a financial analyst's time to evaluate a prospective acquisition, then that analyst's time should be charged to the applicable division.
- Allocate costs using a common activity base, but only if the direct charge method is not feasible. Costs can be charged based on many activity bases, such as sales, assets employed, payroll, the number of new hires, square feet used, and the number of purchase orders issued. It is desirable to have a number of cost pools that are allocated using a number of different activity bases, *as long as costing accuracy is materially improved* by expending the extra effort on record keeping.
- Allocate variances between standard and actual costs to the same cost centers using the same allocation bases that were used for the initial allocation. The variances can be allocated in proportion to the costs allocated previously using standard rates.

Allocations should not be performed based on ability to bear the cost (e.g., the most profitable division is charged with most of the expenses) since excessive charges to profitable divisions can hide their true financial condition and can have a counterproductive effect on management behavior.

If supervisors have no control over the costs that are allocated to them, then the allocated costs should be separated from the revenues and costs for which they are responsible, especially if profit goals and bonuses are involved. Otherwise, managers will have no incentive to achieve their targeted goals when imposed allocated costs cuts into their targets.

 ## RESPONSIBILITY ACCOUNTING

Responsibility accounting is based on the assumption that every cost incurred must be the responsibility of one person somewhere in the company. For example, the cost of rent can be assigned to the person who negotiates and signs the lease, while the cost of an employee's salary is the responsibility of that person's direct manager. This concept also applies to the cost of products because each component part has a standard cost (as listed in the item master and bill of materials), which it is the responsibility of the purchasing manager to obtain at the correct price. Similarly, scrap costs incurred at a machine are the responsibility of the shift manager.

By using this approach, cost reports can be tailored for each recipient. For example, the manager of a work cell will receive a financial statement that only itemizes the costs incurred by that specific cell, whereas the production manager will receive a different one that itemizes the costs of the entire production department, and the president will receive one that summarizes the results of the entire organization.

As you move upward through the organizational structure, it is common to find fewer responsibility reports being used. For example, each person in a department may be placed in charge of a separate cost, and so each one receives a report that itemizes his or her performance in controlling that cost. However, when the more complex profit center approach is used, these costs are typically clumped together into the group of costs that can be directly associated with revenues from a specific product or product line, which therefore results in fewer profit centers than cost centers. Then, at the highest level of responsibility center, that of the investment center, a manager makes investments that may cut across entire product lines, so that the investment center tends to be reported at a minimal level of an entire production facility. Thus, there is a natural consolidation in the number of responsibility reports generated by the accounting department as more complex forms of responsibility reporting are used.

"UNIQUE" EXPENSES

This section examines those expenses that are in some ways unique to headquarters or central unit activities and that are not found charged to most departments.

Charitable contributions. In most companies, charitable contributions are approved by the board of directors or senior management as a separate budget item. Therefore, this approved list, sometimes plus an approval allowance for contingencies, is the basis for planning and control. It presents no special problem. There will be instances where a specific contribution is for the benefit of a division or subsidiary, and may be charged to it.

Incentive pay. Many companies have established incentive pay systems for the officers and top management, accruing the estimated expense in the G&A category (office of the chairman). Since the formula is known, the anticipated expenses can be planned and accrued on the basis of the expected relevant factors.

Audit fees. The cost of the annual audit by the independent accountants can be estimated, included in the planned expenses, and accrued. In many instances, the share attributable to the separate subordinate units of the entity can be charged to them and included in their budgets.

Legal fees. If certain litigation is under way or imminent, the cost can be estimated and accrued. Based on past history, if other litigation is likely, a contingency provision might be made. Again, if the legal costs relate to a particular organizational unit (and not the corporate entity as a whole), then the provision for the accrual and budget may be made in that unit.

Directors and officers insurance. This expense is incurred on behalf of the board of directors and senior managers of a company, and so should be absorbed at the corporate level.

Interest expense. Interest expense, being directly related to borrowed funds, is kept within limits through the control of business indebtedness. Control of interest-bearing obligations affects control of interest expense. When the financial budget of the company has been established, the amount of interest expense can be calculated on the basis of predicted borrowings, payments, and similar facts.

Income taxes. There are very few control problems in connection with income taxes. The first requirement is to establish a proper tax plan to minimize tax payments, to estimate monthly the amount due, and to make the proper accruals. Another function of the controller is to review carefully methods and transactions, securing tax counsel where necessary, to comply with all technicalities and thus secure the greatest tax advantage. Other than this, the controller's responsibilities relate to keeping the required records and substantiating data to support tax claims, advising on capital gain and loss transactions, and arranging the capital structure, as well as the investments, to secure the maximum benefits under the tax laws.

Corporate expenses. Numerous corporate expenses can be assigned to particular executives for control purposes—for example, state and federal capital stock taxes, franchise taxes, fees of fiscal agents, stock transfer taxes, and fidelity bonds and insurance.

Excess facility costs. Occasionally some companies find themselves in possession of distribution or production facilities that are too large for their production or storage needs. Usually the facilities were built or acquired without a sound analysis of the potential demand for the company's products or because of other errors in executive judgment. Whatever the reason, it is unwise to burden the current manufacturing or distribution operations with the charge. The costs often are carried as a separate administrative expense until the property can be disposed of. The continuing expenses usually consist of depreciation, taxes, insurance, and a certain amount of maintenance. It is a relatively simple matter to estimate the cost and establish a budget to cover it. Management generally should be alert either to dispose of the property on favorable terms or to rent it.

Bad debt losses. Another item of expense peculiar to the financial group is bad debt loss. Obviously this loss is not the sole criterion of the efficiency of the credit department. Any bad debt losses could be eliminated either by making only cash sales or by restricting credit sales only to the financially strongest firms. Such a policy would drive business to competitors who are willing to take reasonable credit risks. Any discussion of bad debt losses must therefore assume that a company is competitive from the standpoint of extending credit.

Control of the expense, of course, rests on effectively policing accounts receivable to discover evidence of slow payments.

Other income and expense. Most business firms have various items of income and expense that are of a nonoperating nature. The income may include interest income, royalties, rental income, dividends received, and income from sales of scrap. The expenses include loss on the sale of fixed assets and sales discounts. Based on past experience and knowledge about projected changes, reasonable estimates of these elements of income and expense can be made.

CONTROLLING COSTS

Accounting costs also can be controlled through standards of performance and cost. These standards can be applied to many office functions, just as they have been applied to manufacturing and sales functions. They are not applicable to all accounting activities and do not give the same degree of accuracy as in the factory. But in many offices, the possible cost savings for certain clerical activities are sufficient to justify the effort of establishing the standards. The application of setting standards to the measurement of clerical work is a six-step process.

1. *Preliminary observation and analysis.* This step is fundamental in securing the necessary overall understanding of the problem and in selecting those areas of activity that may lend themselves to standardization. Also, it assists in eliminating any obvious weakness in routine.
2. *Selection of functions on which standards are to be set.* Standards should be set only on those activities sufficient in volume to justify standards.
3. *Determination of the unit of work.* A unit must be selected in which the standard may be expressed. This unit will depend on the degree of specialization and the volume of work.
4. *Determination of the best method and setting of the standard.* Time and motion studies can be applied to office work, with sufficient allowance being given for fatigue and personal needs.
5. *Testing of the standard.* After the standard has been set, it should be tested to see that it is practical.
6. *Final application.* Application involves using the standard and preparing simple reports that the supervisor and the individual worker can see. It also requires a full explanation to the employee.

Exhibit 10.1 shows some accounting and clerical functions that lend themselves to standardization and the units of work that may be used to measure performance.

In addition to performance standards, unit cost activities can be applied to measure an individual function or overall activity. Thus, applying cost standards to credit and collection functions may involve various functions and units of measurement depending on the extent of mechanization, as shown in Exhibit 10.2.

The potential savings that may be realized throughout a company via the reduction of G&A expenses are usually not as great as those in the factory or

EXHIBIT 10.1 Accounting and Clerical Functions Subject to Measurement

Function	Unit of Standard Measurement
Order handling	Number of orders handled
Mail handling	Number of pieces handled
Billing	Number of invoice lines
Check writing	Number of checks written
Posting	Number of postings
Filing	Number of pieces filed
Typing	Number of lines typed
Customer statements	Number of statements
Order writing	Number of order lines

EXHIBIT 10.2 Accounting Activities and Related Cost Standards

Functional Activity	Unit Cost Standard
Credit investigation and approval	Cost per sales order
	Cost per account sold
	Cost per credit sales transaction
Credit correspondence records and files	Cost per sales order
	Cost per letter
	Cost per account sold
Preparing invoices	Cost per invoice line
	Cost per item
	Cost per invoice
	Cost per order line
	Cost per order
Entire accounts receivable records, including posting of charges and credits and preparation of customers' statements	Cost per account
	Cost per sales order
	Cost per sales transaction
Posting charges	Cost per invoice
	Cost per shipment

EXHIBIT 10.2 (Continued)

Functional Activity	Unit Cost Standard
Preparing customers' statements	Cost per statement
	Cost per account sold
Posting credits	Cost per remittance
	Cost per account sold
Calculating commissions on cash collected	Cost per remittance
Making street collections	Cost per customer
	Cost per dollar collected
Window collections	Cost per collection

EXHIBIT 10.3 Revenues Needed to Support Specific Costs

Salary Level	Gross Margin	Revenue Required
$40,000	90%	$ 44,444
$40,000	80%	$ 50,000
$40,000	70%	$ 57,143
$40,000	60%	$ 66,667
$40,000	50%	$ 80,000
$40,000	40%	$100,000
$40,000	30%	$133,333
$40,000	20%	$200,000
$40,000	10%	$400,000

sales operations. This is natural because the major expenses of a business are concentrated in the two functions of production and distribution. However, depending on the size of the gross margin percentage, it is far more effective to reduce costs to increase profits than to increase revenues to increase profits.

Exhibit 10.3 shows the revenues required to cover the cost of a person with a $40,000 salary. The exhibit shows that it is very much in the interest of a low-margin company to work hard to reduce G&A expenses to a bare minimum in order to enhance its net profits.

CHAPTER ELEVEN

Cash and Investments

S OUND CASH MANAGEMENT IS a basic financial function. Although it is usually the responsibility of the senior financial officer, the controller has an important role to play. This chapter reviews phases of cash management that the controller either handles or has a direct interest in.

OBJECTIVES OF CASH MANAGEMENT

Cash is a particularly vulnerable asset because, without proper controls, it is easily concealed and readily negotiable. Cash management has these objectives:

- Provide adequate cash for both short- and long-term operations
- Utilize company funds effectively at all times
- Establish accountability for cash receipts and provide adequate safeguards until the funds are placed in the company depository
- Establish controls to ensure that disbursements are made only for approved and legitimate purposes

- Maintain adequate bank balances to support proper commercial bank relations
- Maintain adequate cash records

 ## ROLE OF THE CONTROLLER

With respect to cash management, a cooperative relationship should exist between the controller and the treasurer. Duties and responsibilities will vary, depending on the type and size of the company. The treasury staff has custody of cash funds and administers the bank accounts. The treasurer is responsible for maintaining good relations with banks and other investors, providing the timely interest and principal payments on debt, and investing the excess cash. In addition, the treasurer usually has responsibility for cash receipts and disbursement procedures. In a smaller organization, the controller may take on the responsibilities of the treasurer.

The controller may have four responsibilities related to cash in companies large enough for separate treasury and controllership functions:

1. Develop the cash forecasts
2. Review the internal controls system with respect to both receipts and disbursements to assure its adequacy and effectiveness
3. Reconcile all bank accounts
4. Prepare periodic cash reports

The controller often performs these investment functions:

- Ascertains that the proper accounting principles are applied in valuing and recording investments
- Ensures that the proper detail records are maintained to provide proper accountability for investments
- Determines that the proper reports are issued to measure performance and otherwise provide the accounting information needed to properly oversee the management of investments
- Performs such reviews as are required to ascertain that an adequate internal control system exists for the protection of investments
- Periodically ensures the existence of investments by taking a physical inventory of evidence of their ownership

CASH COLLECTIONS

One of the primary objectives of financial management is the conservation and effective utilization of cash. From the cash collection viewpoint, there are three phases of control: the acceleration of collections, value dating, and proper internal control of collections.

Acceleration of Cash Receipts

Two methods are commonly used to speed up the collection of receivables: the lockbox and remote deposit capture.

A company can have its bank receive and process checks on its behalf, which is termed a *lockbox* service. The bank assigns a mailbox address to the company, which forwards this information to its customers. The customers mail their checks to the lockbox, where the bank opens the envelopes, scans all checks and accompanying documents, deposits the checks, and makes the scans available to the company through a web site. By using a lockbox, a company can eliminate some of the float involved in check processing, and eliminate some check processing labor. This also means that checks are no longer processed through the company's location, which greatly reduces the amount of cash controls that it needs.

How many lockboxes are needed? It depends on where customers are and the speed of the mail service from those locations. If customers are evenly distributed throughout the country and it is economically feasible to install multiple lockboxes, then the bank that will provide the lockbox can likely conduct an analysis of possible locations, based on sales by zip code.

Alternatively, if it appears that only a single lockbox is needed, then it is generally best to set up the lockbox in a large city that is roughly centrally located. For example, Chicago is an excellent location for checks being received within the United States.

Also, it is entirely possible that the company's current mail-to location yields acceptable results already. To see if this is the case, model results for the proposed lockboxes versus the current situation.

Remote deposit capture allows a company to avoid the physical movement of received checks to its bank. Instead, one can use a special scanner and scanning software to create an electronic image of each check, which it then transmits to the bank. The bank accepts the online image, posts it to the company's account, and assigns funds availability based on a predetermined schedule.

EXAMPLE

The controller of Portland Cement wants to know if it would be cost-effective to open a lockbox for the collection of receivables from customers. He gathers the following information for the group of states where customers would be asked to send their payments to a lockbox:

Average number of daily payments to lockbox	165
Average size of payment	$1,450
Rate of interest per day	0.02%
Mail time savings	1.0 days
Processing time savings	0.8 days

Based on this information, the controller calculates the collected balance at the lockbox as follows:

$$165 \text{ items per day} \times \$1,450 \text{ each}$$
$$\times (1.0 + 0.8) \text{ days saved} = \underline{\$430,650}$$

When invested at 0.02 per day, the $430,650 increase in the collected balance yields interest income of:

$$0.0002 \times \$430,650 = \underline{\$86} \text{ daily interest income}$$

The bank's lockbox fee is $0.25 per check processed, for which the daily cost calculation is:

$$165 \text{ checks} \times \$0.25 \text{ fee per check} = \underline{\$41} \text{ daily lockbox fee}$$

The controller finds that Portland will have a net daily gain of $45, or $11,700 over the standard number of 260 business days per year, and decides to implement the lockbox solution.

Additional factors in this calculation are the initial cost of contacting customers to have them route their payments to the new lockbox address, and the reduced cost of directly handling the checks that are now routed through the lockbox.

The key benefit of remote deposit capture is the complete elimination of the transportation float that arises when shifting checks from the company to the bank—which can be a considerable delay. If the delivery person misses the bank's cutoff time, then an entire extra day is added to this float. However, since remote deposit capture typically has extended processing hours, there is far less risk of incurring this extra delay.

Another benefit is that a company no longer needs a bank that is physically located near the company location. Instead, it can consolidate its banking relationships and use just a single provider who may be located anywhere in the country.

The system does not yet allow for the capture of non–U.S. dollar checks, so they must still be deposited at a local banking institution. However, for most companies, the volume of these checks is so low that they can be mailed to a bank with minimal additional contribution to float.

Finally, the company using this system should be aware that it is financially liable for the accuracy of the information they enter into the system. This is only a factor when the system cannot correctly scan the correct dollar amount, and the operator must manually enter the information instead. If the operator enters an incorrect check total, then the company will be liable for the variance.

Value Dating

When a bank receives a deposit of checks from a payee, it will credit the payee's account with the funds represented by the checks. However, the bank has not really received the cash yet since it must still collect the funds from the bank of the paying party. Until the bank collects the funds, it is at risk of having a negative cash flow situation if the payee uses the cash it has just received.

To avoid this risk, the bank posts the amount of the deposit with a *value date* that is one or more days later than the book date. This value date is the presumed date of receipt of the cash by the bank. Once the value date is reached, the payee has use of the funds. The value date may also be categorized by a bank as 1-day float, 2+ day float, so some similar term.

Value dating is not noticed by many controllers since it may not be mentioned at all in a monthly bank statement, and it can only be evaluated through a close examination of online records. Because of this obscurity, some banks take advantage of their customers and extend the value dating out beyond the point when they have actually received the cash. This gives a bank use of the funds for an additional period of time, at the expense of its customers. If an enterprising controller spots this problem, it is possible to negotiate with the bank to implement shorter-duration value dating.

CASH DISBURSEMENTS

The controller should maintain careful control over the timing of disbursements to ensure that bills are paid only as they are due and not before. In such a manner, cash can be conserved for temporary investment.

Another consideration in payment scheduling is the conscious use of the cash float. By recognizing in-transit items and the fact that ordinarily bank balances are greater than book balances because of checks not cleared, book balances of cash may be planned at lower levels. The incoming float may be balanced against the outgoing payments.

The relationship between the time a check is released to the payee and the time it clears the bank (i.e., the disbursement float) contains three elements:

1. The time needed for the check to travel by mail or other delivery from the issuer to the payee
2. The time required by the payee to process the check
3. The period required by the banking system to clear the check (i.e., the time from the deposit by the payee to the time the item is charged to the issuer's account)

In controlling this float, it is often helpful to trace the time interval of large checks to estimate the proper allowance for the time period required for checks to clear. Many banks now offer online access to their databases of cleared check information, so the controller knows the exact amount of cleared checks.

The controller can also maintain a zero balance account. With this system, the clearing account is kept at a zero balance. When checks are presented for payment, the bank is authorized to transfer funds from the corporate general account to cover the items. Payment may be made by draft. Comparable arrangements can be made for the treasurer to make wire transfers to the zero bank account on notification of the items being presented for payment. Zero bank balance arrangements can facilitate control of payments through one or a limited number of accounts. Such a system may facilitate a quick check of the corporate cash position.

Automatic balance accounts use the same account for receipts and disbursements. When the account is above a specified maximum level, the excess funds are transferred to the central bank account; conversely, when the balance drops below a minimum level, the bank may call for replenishment.

INVESTMENT OF SHORT-TERM FUNDS

In most companies, surplus or excess funds not needed for operating purposes or for compensating bank balances are available for investment. Prudent use of these funds can add to income. Although the financial officer will direct the investment of those funds, the controller should be concerned with adequate investment reporting and control.

Criteria for Selecting Investments

When considering various forms of cash investment, the controller should first consider the *safety of the principal* being invested. It would not do to invest company funds in a risky investment in order to earn extraordinarily high returns if there is a chance that any portion of the principal will be lost. Accordingly, a company policy should limit investments to a specific set of low-risk investment types. Also, some consideration should be given to the *maturity* and *marketability* of an investment. For example, if an investment in a block of apartment houses appears to generate a reasonably risk-free return and a good rate of return, it is still a poor investment from a cash management perspective because the investment probably cannot be converted to cash on short notice. Accordingly, it is best to only make investments where there is a robust market available for their immediate resale. The final consideration when making an investment is its *yield*—and this is truly the last consideration after the previous items have already been reviewed. Within the boundaries of appropriate levels of risk, maturity, and marketability, the treasurer can then pick the investment with the highest yield. Since these criteria tend to limit one to very low-risk investments, the yield will also likely be quite low.

The investment criteria for a company that finds itself in a rapid growth situation are more circumscribed. It typically burns through its cash reserves quite rapidly, so the liquidity of its investments must be extremely high in order to allow rapid access to it. Unfortunately, high liquidity is commonly associated with low investment returns, so the controller is forced to invest in low-yield investments. In addition, the company cannot run the risk of loss on its investments because it is critically important to keep cash available to feed the company's growth engine. Since risk is also associated with return, the treasurer must, once again, favor low-yield investments for minimal risk.

Investment Options

Within the investment boundaries just noted, there are a number of investment options available. Here are the most common ones that have low risk levels, short maturity dates, and high levels of marketability:

■ *Bankers' acceptances.* Banks sometimes guarantee (or *accept*) corporate debt, usually when they issue a loan to a corporate customer, and then sell the debt to investors. Because of the bank guarantee, they are viewed as obligations of the bank.

■ *Bonds near maturity dates.* A corporate bond may not mature for many years, but one can always purchase a bond that is close to its maturity date. There tends to be a minimal risk of loss (or gain) on the principal amount of this investment since there is a low risk that interest rates will change so much in the short time period left before the maturity date of the bond that it will impact its value. A variation on this type of investment is the municipal bond, for which there is no tax on the interest income; however, in consideration of this reduced liability, its yield also tends to be somewhat lower than on other types of bonds.

■ *Certificate of deposit.* These certificates are essentially term bank deposits, typically having durations of up to two years. They usually pay a fixed interest rate upon maturity, though some variable rate CDs are available. There is a perception that they are more secure than commercial paper since CDs are issued by banks, which are more closely regulated than companies. There is up to $100,000 of FDIC insurance coverage of this investment. The secondary market for CDs can vary, and calls for some review prior to making an investment. A more restrictive CD may require an early-withdrawal penalty.

■ *Commercial paper.* Larger corporations issue short-term notes that carry higher yields than on government debt issuances. There is also an active secondary market for them, so there is usually no problem with liquidity. Commercial paper is generally not secured; however, staying with the commercial paper issued by "blue chip" organizations minimizes the risk of default. Most commercial paper matures in 30 days or less, and rarely matures in greater than 270 days, in order to avoid the registration requirements of the Securities and Exchange Commission. Commercial paper is issued at a discount, with the face value being paid at maturity.

■ *Money market fund.* This is a package of government instruments, usually comprised of Treasury bills, notes, and bonds, that is assembled by a fund management company. The investment is highly liquid, with many investors putting in funds for as little as a day. There are varying levels of risk between different money market funds since some funds are more active in trying to outperform the market (with an attendant increase in risk).

- *Repurchase agreement.* This is a package of securities (frequently government debt) that an investor buys from a financial institution, under the agreement that the institution will buy it back at a specific price on a specific date. It is most commonly used for the overnight investment of excess cash from a company's cash concentration account, which can be automatically handled by the company's primary bank. The typical interest rate earned on this investment is equal to or less than the money market rate since the financial institution takes a transaction fee that cuts into the rate earned.
- *U.S. Treasury issuances.* The United States government issues a variety of notes with maturity dates that range from less than a year (U.S. Treasury certificates) through several years (notes) to more than five years (bonds). The wide range of maturity dates gives one a broad range of investment options. Also, there is a strong secondary market for these issuances, so they can be liquidated in short order. U.S. government debts of all types are considered to be risk-free, and so have lower yields than other forms of investment. At times, the demand for these issuances have been so strong that yields have been essentially zero.

The summary table in Exhibit 11.1 shows the key features of each of the above types of investments.

When any of the above investments are initially issued to an investor or dealer, this is considered a *primary market transaction*. It is quite likely that many of these investments will be subsequently resold to a series of investors, depending on the duration of the investment. These subsequent transactions are considered to be trading in the *secondary market*.

 ## ACCOUNTING FOR RECORDS OF INVESTMENT

A systematic manner of recording information relative to the purchase or sale of investments is required. In addition to the data required for lower of cost or market valuations, detailed records are necessary to provide the information needed to manage the portfolio, as well as to establish and support gains or losses for tax purposes.

EXHIBIT 11.1 Investment Comparison

Investment Type	Maturity	Issued by	Interest Rate	Interest Paid	Secured	Capital Access Prior to Maturity
Bankers' acceptances	Less than one year	Banks	Fixed	Discount to face value	Yes	Secondary market available
Bonds near maturity date	Multi-year	Corporations and governments	Fixed	Coupon	No	Secondary market available
Certificates of deposit	1 day to 2 years	Banks	Mostly fixed, variable available	On maturity	FDIC only	Secondary market available
Commercial paper	Overnight to 270 days	Corporations	Fixed	Discount to face value	No	Secondary market available
Money market fund	Weighted average of 90 days or less	Assemblage of federal government issuances	Variable	Periodic	No	Secondary market available
Repurchase agreement	Negotiable	Corporations and banks	Negotiable	On maturity	Yes	Negotiable
U.S. Treasury issuances	Varies	Federal government	Fixed	On maturity	No	Secondary market available

In some cases the file of invoices or statements from the broker may be sufficient. Indeed, these documents are the source of much information. Generally, however, the controller should establish a control account for investments in securities and support it with a securities ledger. This ledger should contain certain information:

- Stock ledger information:
  - Description of the issue: name, type, par value, certificate numbers
  - Dividend dates
  - Record of purchase: date, number of shares, price, commission, tax, total cost, broker

- ▪ Date and amount of dividends received
- ▪ Record of sale or disposition: date, broker, number of shares, sale or call price, commission, and net proceeds
- ▪ Dividends in arrears
- ▪ Loss or gain
- ▪ Bonded ledger information:
  - ▪ Description of issue: name, interest rate, maturity date, interest dates, serial numbers, tax position
  - ▪ Record of purchase: date, broker, price, accrued interest, commission, tax, total cost, maturity value
  - ▪ Date and amount of interest received
  - ▪ Amortization of premium or discount
  - ▪ Record of disposition: date, broker, redemption or sale price, accrued interest, commission, net proceeds
  - ▪ Loss or gain

Reports on Cash and Investments

In some companies a simple daily cash report is prepared for the CEO and treasurer. It summarizes the cash receipts and cash disbursements, as well as balances of major banks. Exhibit 11.2 provides an example. From the control

EXHIBIT 11.2 Daily Cash Report

Daily Cash Report as of the Close of Business, June 16, 20XX	
Balance, June 15, 20XX	$135,300
Receipts	10,200
Total	145,500
Disbursements	15,300
Balance, June 16, 20XX	$130,200
Bank Balances, etc.	
National City Bank	$65,900
Commerce National Bank	22,100
Ohio Trust Company	30,500
Total	118,500
Petty Cash and Payroll Funds	11,700
Total	$130,200

EXHIBIT 11.3 Comparison of Actual and Estimated Cash Activity

Weekly Cash Report
for the Week Ended November 16, 20XX

Description	Month to Date	
	Actual	Estimated
Beginning cash balance	$32,511	$32,510
Cash Receipts		
Government	18,310	18,000
Wholesale	67,730	65,500
Retail	21,100	23,400
Total	107,410	106,900
Cash Disbursements		
Accounts payable—expenses	12,860	12,300
Payrolls	37,010	36,900
Material purchases	19,340	14,300
Federal taxes	8,640	8,920
Capital expenditures	39,990	40,190
Other	2,030	2,000
Total	119,870	114,610
Ending cash balance	$19,781	$24,800
Estimated month-end balance		$30,000

viewpoint, it is desirable to know how collections and disbursements compare with estimates. Exhibit 11.3 shows such information. In addition to comparing actual and forecasted cash activity, it is also useful periodically to compare book balances with those required to meet the service charges or compensating balance requirements of the company's banks. Such a report compares the "object" balance with actual book and actual bank balances. This type of report provides effective cash utilization by recording the absence of excessive balances and by keeping bank balances adequate to fairly compensate the financial institution. Exhibit 11.4 shows such a report.

The activity in investments for most industrial firms normally will be quite limited, and few reports need be prepared. Periodic reports to management should include the name of each security, cost, current market value, effective yield, and any dividends received. For the overall portfolio, the controller

EXHIBIT 11.4　Actual and Objective Bank Balances

Bank	Actual per Book	Objective	(Over) Under Objective	Balances per Bank Statement
	Quarterly Report on Bank Balances			
Wells Fargo	$17,440	$17,800	$ 360	$19,120
JPMorgan Chase	16,850	16,500	(350)	17,180
Bank of America	14,310	15,700	1,390	15,810
Citibank	2,890	3,000	110	3,020
Other local	490	—	(490)	520
Total cash in banks—U.S.	51,980	53,000	1,020	55,650
Subsidiaries—foreign	8,190	7,000	(1,190)	8,600
Cash funds	760	750	(10)	—
Total cash	$60,930	$60,750	$ (180)	$64,250

should report on the overall cost, market value, and rate of return. Exhibit 11.5 shows a typical report on investment position.

CASH AND INVESTMENT CONTROLS

Cash enters a firm through these sources: mail receipts, over-the-counter cash sales, sales or collections made by salespeople or solicitors, and over-the-counter collections on account. Naturally, all businesses have other cash

EXHIBIT 11.5　Report on Investment Position

Security	Number of Shares	Market Value	Purchase Price	Rate of Return	Total Dividends for YTD
ABC Corporation	500	$ 37,000	$ 31,000	5.2%	$ 800
Atlas Construction	100	2,400	2,400	6.3	75
National Co.	1,000	30,000	31,000	6.5	1,000
USA Corporation	1,000	65,500	64,000	7.8	2,000
JPC Corporation	100	1,900	1,875	7.5	70
Security Co.	500	42,000	38,000	5.3	1,000
Total or average		$178,800	$168,275	6.5%	$4,945

transactions of a less routine nature, such as from the sale of fixed assets, that may be handled by the officers or require special procedures. Most of the cash problems center on the transactions listed in Exhibit 11.3 because the more unusual or less voluminous cash receipts are readily susceptible to a simple check.

Regardless of the source of cash, the principle of segregation of duties forms the basis for the prevention of errors or fraud. Such a system involves the separation of the actual handling of cash from the records relating to cash. It requires that the work of one employee be supplemented by the work of another. Certain results must always agree. For example, the daily cash deposit must be the same as the charge to the cash control account. This automatic checking of the work of one employee by another clearly discourages fraud and locates errors. Under such conditions, any peculations generally are restricted to cases of carelessness or collusion.

The system of internal control must be designed for each organization. However, some general suggestions will be helpful to the controller in reviewing the situation in his or her own company:

- All receipts of cash through the mails should be recorded in advance of transfer to the cashier. Periodically these records should be traced to the deposit slip.
- All receipts should be deposited intact daily. This procedure might also require a duplicate deposit slip to be sent by the bank or person making the deposit (other than the cashier) to an independent department, for use in subsequent audits.
- Responsibility for the handling of cash should be clearly defined.
- The functions of receiving cash and disbursing cash should be separate.
- The handling of cash should be separate from cash record maintenance. Cashiers should not have access to these records.
- Tellers, agents, and field representatives should be required to give receipts, while retaining a duplicate.
- Bank reconciliations should not be made by those handling cash or keeping the records. Similarly, a third party should mail statements to customers, including the check-off against the ledger accounts. A third party may also summarize cash records.
- All employees handling cash or cash records should be required to take a periodic vacation, and someone else should handle the job during such absence. Also, at unannounced times, employees should be shifted to other jobs to detect or prevent collusion.

- All employees handling cash or cash records should be adequately bonded.
- Where practical, cash sales should be verified by means of inventory records and periodic physical inventories.

Common Methods of Misappropriating Cash

These common methods of misappropriating cash can be a guide to the controller in designing control systems.

- *Mail receipts:*
  - Lapping, diverting cash, and reporting it some time after it has been collected; usually funds received from one account are credited against another account from which cash has been diverted earlier
  - Borrowing funds temporarily, without falsifying any records, or simply not recording all cash received
  - Overstating discounts and allowances
  - Charging off a customer's account as a bad debt and pocketing the cash
  - Withholding miscellaneous income, such as insurance refunds
- *Over-the-counter sales:*
  - Failing to report all sales and pocketing the cash
  - Under adding the sales slip and pocketing the difference
  - Falsely representing the refunds or expenditures
  - Registering a smaller amount than the true amount of the sale
  - Pocketing cash overages
- *Collections by salespeople:*
  - Conversion of checks made to cash
  - Failure to report sales
  - Overstating amounts of trade-ins
- *Disbursements:*
  - Preparing false vouchers or presenting vouchers for payment twice
  - Raising the amount on checks after they have been signed
  - Cashing unclaimed payroll or dividend checks
  - Altering petty cash vouchers
  - Forging checks and destroying them when received from the bank— substituting other canceled checks or charge slips

Where adequate internal control is used, most of these practices cannot be carried on without collusion.

In addition to the segregation of duties that has been described, certain other practices may be adopted to further deter any would-be embezzler. One of these tools is the surprise audit by the internal auditor and by public accountants. Another is the prompt follow-up of past-due accounts. Proper instructions to customers about where checks should be mailed, and a specific request that they be made payable to the company, and not to any individual, also will help. Bonding of all employees, with a detailed check of references, is a measure of protection. Special checking of unusual receipts of a miscellaneous nature will tend to discourage irregularities.

Controlling Disbursements

Once the cash has been deposited in the bank, it would seem that the major problem of safeguarding the cash has been solved. Indeed, it is quite true that control of cash disbursements is a relatively simple matter, if a few rules are followed. After the supplier's invoice has been approved for payment, the next step usually is the preparation of the check for executive signature. If all disbursements are subject to this top review, how can any problem exist? Yet it is at this point that the greatest danger is met. Any controller who has had to sign numerous checks knows that it is an irksome task—the review to ascertain that receiving reports are attached, the checking of payee against the invoice, and the comparison of amounts. Because it is such a monotonous chore, it is often done in a perfunctory manner. Yet this operation is essential to the control of disbursements. There are too many instances where false documents and vouchers used a second time have been the means of securing executive signatures. Prevention of this practice demands careful review before signing checks, as well as other safeguards. Those who sign the checks must adopt a questioning attitude on every transaction that appears doubtful or is not fully understood. Indeed, the review of documents attached to checks often will bring to light foolish expenditures and weaknesses in other procedures.

The opportunities for improper or incorrect use of funds are so great that the need for proper safeguards in the cash disbursement function cannot be overemphasized. These suggestions may be of use in determining safeguards:

- Except for minor petty cash transactions, do not settle payables in cash.

- All checks should be prenumbered, and all numbers accounted for as either used or void. Use of preprinted check stock can be avoided completely by using unnumbered check stock that is numbered during printing by the computer system. The computer printer can even print the authorized signature onto the check (although this raises concerns about access to the computer system instead of the check stock).
- All general disbursement checks for amounts higher than a predetermined amount should require two signatures. Signature cards should be updated regularly, so that people who leave the firm or move on to other positions in the company are not authorized to sign checks.
- Responsibility for cash receipts should be divorced from responsibility for cash disbursements. The cash functions should be split among several staff members. For example, the person who opens the mail should not be the person who applies payments against receivables records. Also, the person who approves payables for payment should not be the person who creates checks. The person who performs the bank reconciliation should not be involved with other cash activities.
- All persons signing checks or approving disbursements should be adequately bonded.
- Bank reconciliations should be made by those who do not sign checks or approve payments.
- The keeping of cash records should be entirely separate from the handling of cash disbursements.
- Properly approved invoices and other required supporting documents should be a prerequisite to making every disbursement.
- After payment has been made, all supporting documents should be perforated or otherwise mutilated or marked "paid" to prevent reuse.
- Annual vacations or shifts in jobs should be enforced for those handling disbursements.
- Approval of vouchers for payment usually should be done by those not responsible for disbursing.
- Special authorizations for interbank transfers should be required
- All petty cash vouchers should be written in ink.
- It may be desirable to periodically and independently verify the bona fide existence of the regularly used suppliers of recurring services, such as janitorial services, lawyers, and consultants.
- Have the company create a file of all checks created, and send it (preferably daily) to its bank under a positive pay system. The bank then matches presented checks against the check file to see if any checks are unauthorized.

The bank can also reverse the process by making available a list of each day's cleared checks, which the company can then reconcile to its list of printed checks.

▪ Secure the check stock and review it regularly. Anyone can create a check to him- or herself with stolen check stock.

▪ Purchase check stock that has been treated with special chemicals that deface checks if they are chemically tampered with or photocopied.

Bank Reconciliations

An important phase of internal control is the reconciling of the balance on the bank statement with the balance recorded on the company's books. If properly done, the task is much more than a listing of outstanding checks, deposits in transit, and unrecorded bank charges. For example, the deposits and disbursements as shown on the bank statement should be reconciled with those on the books. Also, endorsements should be compared with the payee and the payee should be checked against the record. Bank reconciliations should be handled by someone independent of any cash receipts or disbursements activities. Particular attention should be paid to outstanding checks of the preceding printing and to deposits at the end of the month to detect kiting—issued without a corresponding decrease in the company's cash balance.

Petty Cash Funds

Most businesses must make some small disbursements. To meet these needs, petty cash funds are established that operate on an imprest fund basis, so that balances are fixed. At any time the cash plus the unreimbursed vouchers should equal the amount of the fund. Numerous funds of this type may be necessary in branch offices or at each plant. A procedure should be provided to include limits on individual disbursements through this channel, proper approvals, and so on. If it is practicable, the person handling cash receipts or disbursements should not handle petty cash. Other safeguards would include surprise cash counts, immediate cancellation of all petty cash slips after payment, and careful scrutiny of reimbursements. Although the fund may be small, very considerable sums can be expended.

Investments

Many corporations contract with a major bank to serve as custodian of the securities, to make payment on incoming delivery, and to receive funds on outgoing delivery. The form of contract should provide maximum safeguards to the company.

Because opportunities for fraud exist, given the availability of telephonic transactions and the wire transfer of funds, care must be exercised in the form and nature of confirmation secured and the internal controls used in authorizing payment.

CHAPTER TWELVE

Receivables

A CCOUNTS RECEIVABLE ARE AN important item in the balance
sheets of most business concerns and must be carefully controlled to
avoid excessive working capital requirements. Proper procedures and
adequate safeguards on these accounts are essential not only to the continued
success of the enterprise but also to satisfactory customer relationships. Control
of accounts receivable begins before the agreement to ship the merchandise,
continues through the preparation and issuance of the billing, and ends with
the collection of all sums due. The procedure is closely related to cash receipts
control and inventory control, acting as the link between the two. This chapter
introduces ways to measure, manage, and control the receivables function.

 ## FUNCTIONS OF THE CREDIT DEPARTMENT

The credit manager should assist in stimulating business through a wise
extension of credit and also keep bad debt losses at a reasonably low level.
The credit manager is also responsible for collecting receivables. In detail, the
credit department's tasks are to:

▪ *Establish credit policies.* This involves such questions as the class of risk to accept, rigidity of credit term enforcement, and adjustment policies to be followed. These policies require constant adjustment, to reflect the impact of changing economic conditions on customers.

▪ *Investigate credit.* This requires a continuous procedure for securing and analyzing information concerning the responsibility of present and prospective customers. Information about customers can be collected from:
  ▪ Commercial credit reporting agencies, such as Dun & Bradstreet
  ▪ Trade references supplied by the customer
  ▪ Banks that hold a customer's loans, investments, and checking accounts
  ▪ Collection agencies
  ▪ Reports filed with the SEC by any companies that issue stock or bonds to the public

▪ *Approve credit.* This requires a procedure by which the credit department definitely approves new customers and regularly reviews the credit of old ones. A credit review for existing customers should be triggered by a request for more credit, recent late payments, an increase in claimed deductions, or skipped payments.

▪ *Establish credit limits.* Usually approval is limited to a certain amount, and a plan must be designed to check the extension of credit at this point or at least to notify the proper authority when the limit is reached. In addition, there will be situations when credit terms should not be granted, but the sale can still be made. In these cases, the company can either sell for cash or have backup guarantees by an individual, a second corporation, or a standby letter of credit.

▪ *Enforce discount terms.* Customers frequently take discounts offered for prompt payment after the time allowed. A policy must be established and a procedure designed for the enforcement of the discount terms.

▪ *Collect receivables.* Definite collection steps must be arranged for slow and delinquent accounts. This involves schedules of collection letters, follow-up procedures, and suspension of accounts from approved lists. In addition, the collections staff should be updated regularly on special collection techniques and sent to trade association meetings to swap information with collection personnel from other companies.

▪ *Adjust credit.* This involves settlement of accounts, participation in creditors' committees, and representation in receivership and bankruptcy proceedings. Also, responsibility for writing off bad accounts must begin with the credit department, although final approval may be required from the treasurer or controller, in the interest of sound internal accounting control.

▪ *Maintain credit records.* Files, reports, and ratings must be maintained as part of the credit analysis and collection effort.

▪ *Manage the collection process.* These items contribute to a tightly managed collections process:

  ▪ *Rapid billings.* Quick billings lead to shorter days' receivables outstanding, whereas extremely delayed billings may be difficult to collect.

  ▪ *Rapid cash application.* The job of the collections clerk is greatly facilitated when cash receipt information is quickly updated and forwarded to the collections staff. This avoids unnecessary calls on supposedly delinquent accounts that have actually already been paid.

  ▪ *Tickler file.* This file informs the collections clerk of the need to call customers on specific dates. A more advanced system is integrated with the accounting software to prompt the collections staff regarding whom to contact and the best times for doing so, as well as providing backup materials for each overdue invoice.

  ▪ *Confirmation letters.* When a collection agreement is complicated, it is best to summarize the agreement terms in a letter or e-mail and send it to the customer immediately, so there will be no confusion regarding payment.

▪ *Measure the collection process.* Understanding of the collection department's performance must be gained not only through quantitative measures, such as days' sales outstanding (DSO) and the percentage of overdue invoices. A review of bad-debt write-offs will indicate other problems, such as the reasons why credit was granted to customers who later defaulted. If these problems are tracked and corrected, then the volume of collection items will decline, thereby enhancing the quantitative performance measures.

An in-depth knowledge of the business may reveal reasons for large receivable balances that have nothing to do with high-risk customer accounts. For example, the DSO can be skewed by one very large invoice or by a large cluster of billings that occur at one time, such as at month-end. Also, a factoring arrangement may cause an abnormally low DSO.

The credit analyst typically makes credit decisions with the assistance of customer financial statements. When doing so, these are the items to look for:

▪ *Ratios.* These ratios show where cash is being tied up in a customer's organization, thereby not allowing cash availability for debt payments:

- *Days' sales outstanding.* If the customer's DSO is greater than its days of selling terms plus a third, then too much cash is tied up in receivables.
- *Quick ratio.* If the customer's quick ratio falls below 2 to 1, then the ability to pay may be hindered.
- *Inventory turnover.* If the customer's inventory turns are worse than the industry norm, then too much cash is being tied up in inventory. The presence of obsolete inventory is sometimes indicated by low inventory turns accompanied by a good current ratio (since the excessive inventory appears in the numerator of the current ratio calculation). Alternatively, if a company has good inventory turns but a poor current ratio, it may have too little working capital to support the level of business being transacted (called *overtrading*); if so, look for high debt levels or call the customer's bank for information. This type of company is a dangerous trading partner because its heavy debt load may cause it to crash quickly if its level of business drops.
- *Debt ratio.* If the customer's total liabilities are greater than 100 percent of equity, then the equity cushion available for payments to creditors is too small.
- *Seasonality.* Typically a company's books are closed during the slowest time of the year, when inventories are at their lowest, receivables have been collected, and debt has been paid down. If a company chooses to have its year-end in a different month from other companies in its industry, its key ratios may vary dramatically from industry norms, even though it may operate in a similar manner.
- *Trends.* If possible, the credit analyst should obtain the last three annual financial statements from key customers, and look for these danger signs that indicate where cash is being used and is therefore not available for payments:
  - *Decrease in inventory turnover.* This can indicate an increase in obsolete inventory, which the customer will probably not be able to convert to cash in the short term.
  - *Increase in the collection period.* This is a clear indicator of cash flow difficulties, except when the customer has a policy of paying its suppliers only after it has been paid by its customers.
  - *Increase in the ratio of total liabilities to equity.* This is a sign of excessive leverage, which can accelerate a company's financial problems and rapidly lead to bankruptcy if its cash flow falters.
  - *Increase in the rate of working capital turnover.* This is when sales increase, but the amount of working capital remains the same. Debt

is usually substituted for the needed working capital, which increases fixed costs and therefore the risk to the creditor.

 ## SHORTENING THE RECEIVABLES CYCLE

The cash manager is interested in getting cash payments into the company bank accounts as quickly as possible. The credit manager and the accounting department require transaction data that permit application of the payment to the proper account and invoice. Hence, cash acceleration procedures must address both of these concerns. These methods are used to accelerate collections.

- *Lockbox.* A lockbox is a post office box opened in the name of the seller but accessed and serviced by a remittance processor. Banks and others who process the remittances usually do so in a manner and at the time of day that allows funds to be more readily available to the depositor. Lockboxes offer these advantages over processing deposits at the premises of the seller:
  - Faster availability of the funds
  - Greater security over the remittance
  - Reduced processing costs
  - Greater reliability in deposit processing
  - Greater reliability in capturing necessary remittance data. Image processing involves capturing the image of the check and temporarily storing it in digital form. This enables the bank to immediately dispatch the check for clearing, while it uses the image to complete its work.
- *Wire transfer.* This is a series of telegraphic messages between two banks, usually through a Federal Reserve bank, wherein the sending bank instructs the Federal Reserve bank to charge the account of the receiving bank and advises the receiving bank of the transfer. Funds can clear within a few hours.
- *ACH (automatic clearinghouse) transfer.* This system, operating under the auspices of the National Automatic Clearing House Association, is a method for the commercial banks to exchange electronic payments without the high cost of Federal Reserve wires. In most instances, the payroll initiates a payment for credit to the bank account of the payee. Funds typically clear within one to two days.
- *Remote deposit capture.* This is the use of a special check scanner and scanning software to create an electronic image of each check that it wishes to deposit. The company then transmits the scanned check

information to its bank instead of making a physical deposit. The bank accepts the electronic information, posts funds to the company's account, and assigns funds availability based on a predetermined schedule. Remote deposit capture is useful for eliminating the physical delivery of checks to a bank, which accelerates cash flow.

▪ *Automatic cash application.* Automatic cash application involves the use of specialized software that requires an electronic feed of the magnetic ink character recognition (MICR) number on a check to determine each customer's bank account number, which it then uses to match each payment to outstanding balances. The software then uses a series of rules to search for invoices coming due for payment, and match them against the submitted payment. A properly configured system may be able to automatically apply as much as 90 percent of all cash receipts.

Accelerating cash collections is one means of reducing the amount receivables. In fact, if sales personnel are involved in collections, an incentive based on customer payment habits might be considered. However, the amount of funds tied up in receivables may result in part from antiquated or slow procedures in the order and billing process and not in the collection cycle. A detailed review of the procedures from receipt of the customer order, through shipment, to cash collection might be helpful in spotting areas for improvement. For example, in a typical manufacturing company, each step in the procedures from receipt of the customer order until final collection should be studied for means of expediting. Thus, these events ought to be analyzed for means of speeding up the process:

▪ Order receipt steps, such as processing the customer order from receipt in the mailroom or order department to the sales department
▪ Order processing steps in the sales department, such as separation of stock orders from custom orders
▪ Credit approval steps, such as the segregation of orders to be expedited and the acceleration of orders for known creditworthy customers
▪ Order shipping procedures, such as reviews by the shipper of a credit hold list prior to shipping product
▪ Order paperwork flow from the shipping department to the billing department
▪ Invoice preparation and mailing procedures
▪ Issuance of invoices by e-mail
▪ Prompt issuance of month-end statements

RESERVE FOR DOUBTFUL ACCOUNTS

The accounts receivable investment includes providing a reserve for estimated doubtful accounts. This may be accomplished in one of two ways when actual sales are made. First, a percentage of monthly sales (or credit sales) can be set aside based on past experience. Second, the accounts receivable aging and reserve should be reviewed for any probable uncollectible accounts. When dealing with the long-term business plan, the estimated percent of sales is the method most commonly employed.

 RECEIVABLES FRAUD AND CONTROL

The controller's first experience with fraud may be the review of "what went wrong" following the loss of assets. To avoid this problem, we provide a list of typical receivables frauds that the controller can prepare for through proper control systems, which are also mentioned. With proper controls, it should be much more difficult to perpetrate many of the frauds listed below.

Receivables Fraud

These examples should not be considered the only possible types of receivables fraud; dishonest people will continue to derive new methods of removing money from a company. Thus the controller must remain watchful.

- Ship materials to a false address and do not issue an invoice. Collusion is usually required, with one person in accounting and one person in the shipping department.
- Issue an invoice to a customer at a high price and record an invoice for the company's records at a lower price; when payment is received, the employee pockets the difference between the price paid and the price recorded. To do this, an employee must have control over the billing and cash receipts functions.
- Increase receivable balances with bogus transactions in order to procure loans secured against receivables. This can be accomplished by one billings person.
- Write off artificial discounts and adjustments; when full payment comes in, pocket the difference between the discounts and the full payment.

To do this, an employee must have control over the billing and cash receipts functions.

▪ Write off receivables as bad debts; when full payment comes in, pocket the written-off amount. To do this, an employee must have control over the billing and cash receipts functions.

Receivables Controls

There is a risk that some deliveries to customers will not be billed to them. Further, even though an invoice is prepared, the customer may be billed for an incorrect amount because of differences in the quantity shipped, price, or extensions. The controller must institute proper procedures to ensure that such risks are minimized. These procedures may be useful in controlling these receivables problems:

▪ *Compare source information.* Invoices to customers are compared to pre-numbered shipping memos by an independent party. This comparison includes both the quantity and the description of goods shipped, and all shipping memo numbers must be accounted for.

▪ *Audit prices and extensions.* Prices appearing on invoices are independently checked against established price lists, and all extensions and footings are checked.

▪ *Compare detail to summary records.* Periodically, the detail of the accounts receivable is checked against the general ledger total and reconciled, preferably by an internal auditor or other independent party.

▪ *Confirm balances.* Surprise mailings of monthly statements and confirmation requests should be made by third parties.

▪ *Segregate duties.* All handling of cash should be segregated from the maintenance of receivable records.

▪ *Review special adjustments.* All special adjustments for discounts, returns, or allowances should have special approval above a minimum amount.

▪ *Review bad debts.* A special record should be kept of all bad debts written off, and a follow-up should be made on those items to minimize the danger of collections being received and not recorded. Pay particular attention to whether a specific staff person initiates the bulk of the write offs since this is a fraud indicator.

▪ *Mail invoices separately.* Invoices may be mailed or e-mailed to customers by a separate unit.

CHAPTER THIRTEEN

Inventory

INVENTORY CAN BE ONE of the largest dollar items listed on the balance sheet. It can also be the cause of large and unexpected adjustments in the year-end financial statements, due to unexpected amounts of obsolete and missing stock. In fact, supporters of just-in-time (JIT) manufacturing systems consider inventory to be a liability since it is expensive in terms of insurance, storage space, moving costs, obsolescence, shrinkage, tracking costs, and working capital. Under the JIT system, minimal inventory reduces *all* of the above costs. Because minimal inventory and highly accurate inventory records are critical under *any* manufacturing system, this chapter focuses on installing inventory tracking systems, which can then be used to pinpoint inventory problems and lead to smaller inventories. In addition, this chapter discusses the valuation of inventories, the physical inventory procedure, and inventory fraud.

 ## INVENTORY MANAGEMENT SYSTEMS

Inventory management systems are a topic of considerable debate, as JIT systems gradually supplant material requirements planning (MRP) and various reorder point systems. This section examines:

■ The turnover statistic, which is the most universally used benchmark for analyzing the performance of an inventory management system
■ Overviews of each management system, as well as the advantages and disadvantages of each one
■ The cost of carrying inventories, as well as where responsibility for inventory systems should lie

Turnover

Turnover is the most universal measure of the manufacturing system's efficiency in using inventory. It is derived by dividing the usage factor by the average inventory. For example, the turnover of various inventories can be determined as follows:

■ *Finished goods.* Cost of goods sold/average inventory of finished goods
■ *Work-in-process.* Cost of goods completed/average inventory of work-in-process
■ *Raw materials.* Materials placed in process/average inventory of raw materials
■ *Supplies.* Cost of supplies used/average supply inventory

The result is the number of "turns," usually measured in turns per year. Turnover statistics must be analyzed with caution, for several factors can cause the same result. A slow turnover can indicate overinvestment in inventories, obsolete stock, or declining sales, but can also be caused by a commitment to fulfilling any order immediately. A very high turnover can indicate improved utilization through conversion to a JIT or MRP system, or it may be caused by keeping an excessively small amount of stock on hand, resulting in lost sales or increased costs due to fractional buying.

The purpose of business is turning a profit, not turning inventory. Evaluating a company's performance based on a turnover metric is not wise without more detailed information. If turnover is used to evaluate the performance of a new manufacturing system, such as MRP or JIT, then it is useful. If it is used to compare performance between accounting periods, it is useful as an indicator of underlying problems or improvements that must be researched further to determine the exact causes of any changes in the statistic.

Reorder Points

When there are known requirements, MRP and JIT systems will indicate when materials need to be ordered, and inventories can be planned accordingly.

When there is greater uncertainty, as in job-lot work, estimates of the volume level must be made, and a provision for error, through the use of safety stock, may be used. The reorder point is then calculated by multiplying the anticipated lead time in weeks by the estimated demand in units per week, plus a safety stock quantity. Reorder point systems tend to result in excess inventories and obsolete materials because parts will be ordered automatically even though the need for them may be declining. Typical turnover rates to be expected are three to six turns, although this statistic varies by industry.

At the time the stock level reaches the reorder point, a requisition is issued for additional inventory. Some of the more widely used means of signaling the time to reorder include:

- *Minimum–maximum system.* This method is used in connection with the inventory record. The minimum quantity level is the reorder point; the maximum level is the minimum quantity plus the economical order size.
- *Reserve stock method.* Under this system, the stock is divided into two parts: one for immediate use and one as a reserve. When use of the reserve is begun, additional stock is reordered. This system may involve two bins (one with the reserve stock) or one bin with the reserve stock identified (e.g., in a separate bay).
- *Visual check system.* When a manager with direct knowledge of the business activity checks the stock level, he or she can judge when to reorder.
- *Reservation method.* This method recognizes the available stock as well as the physical stock. Available stock is defined as stock on order, plus physical stock, less the unfilled requirement. The reorder point is based on the available stock rather than the physical stock.

Material Requirements Planning

Inventory is handled differently under the material requirements planning system. An MRP system schedules production through a master schedule. The system then multiplies the master schedule quantities by the bills of material for each item on the schedule to determine the gross part requirements for production needs. The gross requirements are then reduced by unallocated parts currently in stock to derive the list of parts to be ordered. The to-be-ordered list is grouped into convenient lot sizes, and the parts are ordered. Typical turnover rates to be expected are 6 to 15 turns, although this statistic varies by industry.

The MRP system improves inventory turns and brings order into unsystematic manufacturing systems by requiring high data accuracy levels. However, an MRP system is designed to work with long setup times, long production runs, long cycle times, and accepts scrapped parts; a JIT system, on the other hand, works toward short setups, short production runs, short cycle times, and zero scrapped parts. Thus, a JIT system inherently tends to create a leaner production system than does an MRP system. Finally, an MRP system results in excess inventory since orders are placed for standard lot sizes rather than for the exact amounts required.

Just-in-Time Systems

A just-in-time system involves many changes to a typical manufacturing system, which result in vastly reduced inventories. Turnover rates are typically 20 turns, though this metric varies considerably. Some of the changes are described here:

- *Purchasing.* A traditional system processes bids from many suppliers, takes the lowest bid, and orders in bulk, leaving leftover parts in the warehouse for future use. A JIT system uses a small number of long-term suppliers and orders only as much as is immediately needed, so that no extra parts are stored in the warehouse; suppliers deliver parts directly to the assembly area. There is no room for defective parts in a JIT system, so supplier quality systems are tested by company terms to ensure that parts will be delivered within specifications.
- *Delivery.* A traditional system builds to stock and releases finished goods as orders are received. A JIT system closely links its production schedule to suppliers' delivery schedules, thereby reducing its finished goods stocking requirements.
- *Manufacturing.* A traditional system produces long runs of one product before shutting down, reconfiguring the equipment for a different product, and producing another long run. A JIT system reduces setup times, so that (ultimately) it is economical to produce one item in a production run. Also, machines are rearranged into clusters called manufacturing cells, so that small jobs move rapidly through a common routing over several types of machines; this process reduces work-in-process (WIP) inventories. It also improves quality since one worker is responsible for a part through several production steps and can spot quality problems quickly, before many parts are produced. *Kanbans* are authorization cards that allow a worker to

produce a set amount of parts for an upstream workstation, thereby controlling the amount of WIP in the system.

▪ *Warehousing.* A traditional system receives supplier parts, stocks the parts, and issues them to the assembly floor based on a pick list. A JIT system avoids the warehouse entirely and sends the parts directly to the assembly floor.

▪ *Quality.* A traditional system accepts a set percentage of defective products and overproduces to allow for the variance. A JIT system uses statistical process control to identify upward or downward trends in variances, thereby predicting when a process will exceed its within-specification boundaries. In addition, supplier quality systems are closely tracked to ensure that received products are free of defects.

▪ *Inspection.* A traditional system inspects products after they have been produced and eliminates or reworks any defective products. A JIT system builds quality into the process, so that no inspection staff is needed and there are no products requiring rework.

▪ *Cycle time.* A traditional system has a long cycle time because parts sit in the warehouse before being kitted (removed from storage and clustered together for use in a production run), where they sit again, and between manufacturing workstations, where they sit in piles of WIP. A JIT system sends received parts directly from the receiving dock to the assembly area, where WIP is reduced by using manufacturing cells and kanbans.

▪ *Accounts payable.* A traditional system will not pay a supplier until an invoice is received and matched to receiving documentation from the receiving department. Under a JIT system, suppliers are paid based on how many units the manufacturer produces in each period; the number of parts that must have been received is calculated by multiplying the number of parts in the finished product by the quantity of the product that was produced. The traditional system would not work in a JIT environment since an immense amount of paperwork would be needed to process the increased number of small-volume receipts.

▪ *Working capital.* A traditional system requires working capital for inventories. Some JIT systems are now approaching negative working capital levels because their inventory requirements are very low and their payments terms with customers are shorter than their payment terms with suppliers. This situation allows a company to invest its cash flow more profitably in other activities.

▪ *Cost accounting.* A traditional system records variances on the shop floor, which are then summarized and reported back to the manufacturing managers by a cost accountant. A JIT system emphasizes cycle time, and recording cost information during production slows down cycle time. Also, JIT systems function with so little WIP that quality problems become obvious and can be corrected well before the cost accountant can summarize variance information and send it back to the manufacturing staff for corrective action. Thus, a JIT system uses minimal variance reporting.

■ *Product/Costs*. A traditional system measures variances caused by the manufacturing facility that affect the cost of a product. The JIT system has removed most variances from the manufacturing system, so the cost accountant's focus becomes setting a target cost during the design stage and assigning targeted subsidiary part costs to suppliers. The cost accountant then reports on variances caused by suppliers not meeting their cost targets.

A JIT system's biggest problem is replacing the existing system; it is so radically different that the existing system may come to a complete stop before the new system is properly implemented, thereby losing valuable production time. This problem is avoided by implementing the JIT system from the delivery end of the process and working backward toward the receiving function. Also, some JIT concepts, such as manufacturing cells, can be implemented and fitted into an existing system without unduly affecting production performance. As for its advantages, JIT systems require minimal computing power and working capital, and can create products with far less cycle time than any other system.

Cost of Carrying Inventories

The cost of carrying inventories is significant. First, working capital is required to pay for inventory; the interest cost of working capital is easily calculated when money is borrowed to obtain inventory or working capital. Interest may also be imputed by using a rate commensurate with the return on investment in other alternatives. Also, when funds are used to purchase inventory, the money is no longer available for other, possibly more worthwhile, projects. Other inventory costs also must be recognized, such as insurance, taxes, warehousing, storage and handling, pilferage, spoilage, and obsolescence. The total of these costs can easily range from 25 percent to 40 percent of the inventory value on an annual basis.

Inventory also causes a product's cycle time to increase. The total cycle time is the time required to build a product; reducing the cycle time increases the firm's speed to market, so that customer orders can be handled more rapidly. When parts must be received, moved into storage, kitted, and then moved to the assembly area for production, critical time is added to the production process. Just-in-time systems move the inventory straight from the receiving dock to the production floor, thereby reducing the cycle time drastically.

Responsibility for Inventory

The responsibility for inventory may generally be assigned as follows, with variations based on the company's organizational structure and products. *Manufacturing-related inventories*, such as raw materials, manufacturing supplies, and work-in-process, should be the responsibility of the chief manufacturing executive, so that the position has complete command over the materials needed to manufacture the finished product. *Sales-related inventories*, such as finished goods, can be the responsibility of either the chief manufacturing executive or the sales executive. A better job of estimating sales requirements will result from assigning these inventories to the sales executive. Moreover, the sales executive will pay greater attention to disposing of obsolete or slow-moving items, especially when the cost of obsolete inventory will be charged against his department.

Regardless of who is assigned the responsibility, the assignment must be clear, so that inventories are kept at manageable levels. There must also be full coordination among the purchasing, engineering, and production functions, so that parts are purchased only as needed and based on accurate bills of material. The controller is rarely responsible for the inventory but should be responsible for related internal control issues and inventory valuation methods.

 INVENTORY TRACKING

If perpetual inventory records are maintained with high accuracy, then no physical inventory need be conducted. An increasing number of companies are turning to the perpetual inventory method for these reasons:

- *Avoid wasted time.* Staff time is not utilized efficiently during the physical inventory process because staff members could be involved in other activities. Also, the production facility is shut down, allowing no revenue-generating products to be manufactured.

▪ *Improve product delivery performance and reduce freight costs.* High inventory record accuracy allows companies to promise shipments to customers with greater confidence because products can be built without delays due to missing parts. Also, rush charges for missing parts are avoided.

▪ *Achieve higher accuracy with ongoing counts.* Inventory counts should be done by the experts—the warehouse staff—and should be done at their leisure, which will ensure higher count accuracy. If a complete plant-wide physical inventory is performed, accuracy drops due to counts by less experienced nonwarehouse staff and the short time frame required to complete the count.

▪ *Avoid year-end surprises.* Many companies have been unpleasantly surprised by unexpected changes in inventory levels at year-end. These surprises can be avoided by constantly monitoring inventory levels with a perpetual inventory system.

▪ *Use data to reduce inventory and cut costs.* The transaction history that is a by-product of a perpetual inventory system allows the materials manager to make informed decisions regarding deletions of parts from stock. This is of value to the controller since cash requirements for additional inventory are reduced and can be enhanced as inventory is sold back to suppliers. As inventory is reduced, the staff needed to track it and the insurance needed to cover it can both be reduced, thereby improving the company's cash flow a second time.

A physical inventory can be eliminated if accurate perpetual inventory records are available. Many steps are required to implement a perpetual inventory system, requiring considerable effort. The controller should evaluate the company's resources prior to embarking on this process and adjust those resources accordingly in order to complete the project. In addition, the controller must realize that, once high accuracy levels are achieved, continued monitoring is needed to maintain those levels.

The 17 steps needed to implement an accurate perpetual inventory system are:

Step 1. *Select and install inventory tracking software.* The primary requirements for inventory tracking software are that it:
  ▪ *Track transactions.* One of the primary uses of a perpetual inventory system is the ability to list the frequency of product usage, which allows the materials manager to increase or reduce selected inventory quantities.

▪ *Update records immediately.* The perpetual inventory data must always be up-to-date because production planners must know what is in stock and because cycle counters must have access to accurate data. Batch updating of records is not acceptable.

▪ *Report inventory records by location.* Cycle counters need inventory records sorted by location in order to count the inventory most efficiently.

Step 2. *Test inventory tracking software.* The software installation team should create a set of typical records in the new software and perform a series of transactions to ensure that the software functions properly. In addition, create a large number of records and perform the transaction again, to see if the response time of the system drops significantly. If the software appears to function properly, continue to the next step. Otherwise, fix the problems with the software supplier's assistance, or acquire a different software package.

Step 3. *Train the warehouse staff.* The warehouse staff should receive software training immediately before using the system, so that they do not forget how to operate the software. Enter a set of test records into the software and have the staff simulate all common inventory transactions, such as receipts, picks, and cycle count adjustments.

Step 4. *Revise rack layout.* It is much easier to move racks prior to installing a perpetual inventory system because no inventory locations must be changed on the computer system. Create aisles that are wide enough for forklift operation, and cluster small parts racks together for easier parts picking.

Step 5. *Create rack locations.* A typical rack location is, for example, A-01–B-01. This location code means:

A = Aisle A

01 = Rack 1

B = Level B (numbered from the bottom to the top)

01 = Partition 1 (optional—subsection of a rack)

As you progress down an aisle, the rack numbers should progress in ascending sequence, with the odd rack numbers on the left and the even numbers on the right. This layout allows an inventory picker to move down the center of the aisle, efficiently pulling items based on sequential location codes.

Step 6. *Lock the warehouse.* One of the main causes of record inaccuracy is removal of items from the warehouse by outside staff. To stop such removal, lock all entrances to the warehouse. Only warehouse personnel should be allowed access to the warehouse. All other personnel entering the warehouse should be accompanied by a member of the warehouse staff to prevent the removal of inventory.

Step 7. *Consolidate parts.* To reduce the labor of counting the same item in multiple locations, group common parts in one location.

Step 8. *Assign part numbers.* Several experienced personnel should verify all part numbers. A mislabeled part is as useless as a missing part since the computer database will not show that it exists. Mislabeled parts also affect the inventory cost; for example, a mislabeled engine is more expensive than the item represented by its incorrect part number, which identifies it as, say, a spark plug.

Step 9. *Verify units of measure.* Several experienced personnel should verify all units of measure. Unless the software allows multiple units of measure, the entire organization must adhere to one unit of measure for each item. For example, the warehouse may desire tape to be counted in rolls, but the engineering department would rather create bills of material with tape measured in inches instead of fractions of rolls.

Step 10. *Pack the parts.* Parts should be packed into containers, then the containers should be sealed and labeled with the part number, unit of measure, and total quantity stored inside. A few parts should be left free for ready use. Containers should be opened only when additional stock is needed. This method allows cycle counters to verify inventory balances rapidly.

Step 11. *Count items.* Items should be counted when there is no significant activity in the warehouse, such as during a weekend. Elaborate cross-checking of the counts, as would be done during a year-end physical inventory, is not necessary. It is more important to have the perpetual inventory operational before warehouse activity increases again; any errors in the data will quickly be detected during cycle counts and flushed out of the database. The counts must include the part number, location, and quantity.

Step 12. *Enter data into computer.* An experienced data entry person should input the location, part number, and quantity into the computer. Once the data are input, another person should cross-check the entered data against the original data for errors.

Step 13. *Quick-check the data.* Have the data scanned for errors. If all part numbers have the same number of digits, then look for items that are too long or short. Review location codes to see if inventory is stored in nonexistent racks. Units of measure should match the part being described. For example, is it logical to have a pint of steel in stock? Also, if item costs are available, print a list of extended. Excessive costs typically point to incorrect units of measure. For example, a cost of $1 per box of nails will become $500 in the inventory report if nails are listed as individual units.

Step 14. *Initiate cycle counts.* Print out a portion of the inventory list, sorted by location. Using the report, have selected staff members count blocks of the inventory on a continuous basis. They should look for accurate part numbers, units of measure, locations, and quantities. The counts can concentrate on high-value or high-use items, but the entire stock should be reviewed regularly. The most important part of this step is to examine why mistakes occur. If a cycle counter finds an error, the cause of the error must be investigated and then corrected, so that the mistake will not occur again.

Step 15. *Initiate inventory audits.* The inventory should be audited frequently, perhaps as much as once a week. This allows the controller to track changes in the inventory accuracy level and initiate changes if the accuracy drops below acceptable levels. In addition, frequent audits are an indirect means of telling the staff that inventory accuracy is important and must be maintained. The minimum acceptable accuracy level is 95 percent, with an error being a mistaken part number, unit of measure, quantity, or location. This accuracy level is needed to ensure accurate inventory costing as well as to assist the materials department in planning future inventory purchases. In addition, establish a tolerance level when calculating the inventory accuracy. For example, if the computer record of a box of screws yields a quantity of 100 and the actual count reveals a quantity of 105, then the record is accurate if the tolerance is 5 percent but inaccurate if the tolerance is 1 percent. The maximum tolerance should be 5 percent, and this figure could be reduced for high-value or high-use items.

Step 16. *Post results.* Inventory accuracy is a team project, and the warehouse staff members feel more involved if the audit results are posted against the results of previous audits.

Step 17. *Reward staff members.* Accurate inventories save a company thousands of dollars in many ways. Therefore, it is cost-effective to encourage staff members to maintain and improve accuracy with periodic bonuses based on reaching higher levels of accuracy with tighter tolerances.

These are the basic steps needed to implement an accurate perpetual inventory system. However, several special cases require additional steps. Some of the more common cases are:

- *Customer-owned inventory.* Customer-owned inventory cannot be valued since the company does not own it. There are different solutions for different companies. For example, the company can avoid assigning a cost to the part, can assign different part numbers to a part based on who owns it, or can segregate the materials in an uncounted area. In these cases, be careful when assigning several part numbers to the same part, for engineering drawings and bills of material usually list only one part number for a part.

▪ *Consignment inventory.* One technique used by materials departments to improve the production process is to turn over some items to suppliers, who then have title to their own inventory in the production area. Because it is owned by suppliers, it should not be costed. To avoid incorrect costing, store this consignment inventory in clearly marked areas. It should not appear in the inventory database.

▪ *Materials at supplier locations.* Company-owned materials are sometimes kept at supplier or customer locations. These items can constitute a large unseen part of the inventory and can easily escape an otherwise rigorous inventory tracking system. It is the responsibility of the materials department to track this inventory, using a special location code for the off-site location and verifying the item quantities with the customer or supplier as part of the cycle count and periodic audit process.

▪ *Floor stock.* Floor stock is defined as the fasteners kept on the shop floor to assemble product. These items are typically kept in uncounted bins and replenished from the warehouse as the bins empty. The easiest way to deal with this material on the computer system is to avoid it. Floor stock is generally not expensive, and therefore has no significant impact on the accuracy of the financial statements if they are expensed instead of being capitalized into inventory. Also, the cost to count floor stock may not be worth the additional level of record accuracy in the perpetual inventory.

▪ Another approach to floor stock is to return as much of it as possible to the warehouse. A close review of floor stock turnover typically reveals that some of it turns slowly. If so, those items can be returned to stock and later requisitioned back to the shop floor as needed. This technique reduces the amount of uncounted floor stock.

▪ *Work-in-process.* Work-in-process (WIP) must be tracked in the perpetual inventory system because it can be large enough to have a significant impact on the financial statements. The easiest approach to this problem is to utilize cell manufacturing to reduce WIP in the manufacturing process—if it is not there, it does not have to be counted. However, because cell manufacturing is beyond the job scope of most controllers, encouraging data collection at each job station on the assembly floor may be more appropriate.

Data collection is difficult outside of the warehouse, where the staff is usually less well trained in data entry techniques. Several methods are possible, based on the controller's level of confidence in the staff's ability to enter data. One method is to have each manufacturing station log in those items entering its area and log out those items leaving its area. This is a time-consuming process that can move faster with bar coding or RFID tags.

A different method could work if bills of material are accurate. Then the progress of jobs through the shop can be tracked by simply logging in the stage of job completion. If the inventory tracking software is sophisticated enough, the WIP cost is calculated by comparing the job's reported stage of completion to the bill of materials.

 ## PHYSICAL INVENTORY PROCEDURE

The physical inventory is a manual count of all inventory on hand and is used to obtain an inventory valuation for the period-end financials. Many companies still use physical inventories; even those that have converted to perpetual systems may find that sections of the inventory located outside of the warehouse, such as WIP, require a periodic physical count. Companies using such advanced systems as manufacturing cells may still require a physical count of WIP, unless all production is allowed to flow through the manufacturing process and into finished goods prior to conducting the count.

Preplanning the inventory is critical. Follow these steps to ease the counting process:

1. *Use trained personnel.* The inventory counters should all be experienced warehouse personnel because they are familiar with the parts, as well as their related part numbers and units of measure. Front-office staff members have no place in the counting process because they do not know the parts, part numbers, or units of measure.
2. *Use "dead time."* It is difficult to count while production operations are occurring. Consequently, using weekend or evening time will hasten the counting process.
3. *Clean up in advance.* A messy counting area means that the counting team must find the stock before counting it; time can be saved by organizing the

inventory in advance, clearly labeling part numbers and units of measure, and cleaning the counting areas.

4. *Train the staff.* The physical inventory teams must be trained in counting procedures, as well as proper cutoff procedures and completion of forms. The training may require detailed written instructions.

5. *Cutoffs.* Items received after the cutoff period must be marked "do not count" and segregated. Items shipped must leave the dock by the cutoff period, or they will be included in inventory. No parts will move in or out of the warehouse while the count is being performed.

6. *Assign the staff.* Allocate inventory locations to specific counting teams.

7. *Organize.* The counting process involves the warehouse staff, the cost accountant(s), and the accounting staff. They must be tightly organized to achieve an accurate physical count. Because of the many departments involved, a person with significant experience and authority must lead the effort.

8. *Create an inventory tag form.* The tag is used to record the inventory count for each item and should include fields for the part number, description, location, unit of measure, counter's signature, and last job performed (if it is a WIP item). The tags must be *prenumbered.*

The counting process should include eight steps:

Step 1. *Notify the auditors.* If a company has its financial statements audited, then the auditors must be notified of the time and place of the physical inventory. An audit team will test counts, observe the procedure generally, and trace the counts to the inventory summary.

Step 2. *Assign counting teams to areas.* These areas should be counted:
  ▪ Central warehouse
  ▪ Receiving inspection
  ▪ Staging (kitting) areas
  ▪ Finished goods area
  ▪ Work-in-process areas
  ▪ Shipping area
  ▪ Outside storage (e.g., in trailer storage or company-owned inventory located at other companies)
  ▪ Rework areas
  ▪ Packaging materials

Equally important, the following items should *not* be counted:
  ▪ Tools and equipment

- Material handling containers
- Written-off inventory
- Maintenance equipment
- Office supplies
- Departmental expense items (e.g., glue, solder, and tape)
- Consignment inventory

Step 3. *Count all areas.* A prenumbered inventory tag should be attached to each area that has been counted, in order to prove that the count was completed. The tag should be a two-part form, so that one copy can be removed and used to summarize the inventory. The count is usually conducted by two-person teams, with one counting and the other recording the information.

Step 4. *Review counted areas.* The counted areas should be reviewed for missing or duplicate counts, and counts should be spot-checked for correct quantities, part numbers, and units of measure. High dollar-value items should be 100 percent checked.

Step 5. *Control tags.* All tags should be collected; missing or duplicate tag numbers should be looked for; any problems should be resolved before summarizing the information in the next step.

Step 6. *Summarize tags.* The tag information should be input into the computer or recorded manually on a summary sheet. The summary sheet should include all of the information contained on the tags. The summary report, whether automated or manual, should include space to mark down the market value of each item, so that the cost of each item can be marked to the lower of cost or market for financial statement reporting purposes.

Step 7. *Look for discrepancies.* Problems can be unearthed with any of these techniques:

- Compare the physical inventory records with perpetual records (if such records are kept).
- Review the extended costs for excessively large dollar values. Often, incorrect units of measure are the source of these errors.
- Review the unit counts for excessively high counts. Once again, incorrect units of measure may be the culprit.
- Compare expensive items in the inventory to the summary, to ensure that the correct quantities are recorded, and that their costs appear reasonable.

Step 8. *Review the cutoff.* Even with an excellent inventory count, the inventory can be severely misstated if inventory is included or excluded without a corresponding sale or liability entry in the accounting records. Receiving and shipping records for several days before and after the inventory count should be reviewed, and an accounting entry for each transaction should be verified.

 INVENTORY VALUATION

The selection of the method to value inventory has a significant impact on the reported earnings and financial condition of a company. Since the inventory is among the largest of the current assets, the method of valuing inventories is a very important factor in determining both the results from operations and the firm's financial condition.

The primary objective in choosing a cost basis for valuing inventories is to select the method that, under the circumstances, will most satisfactorily reflect the income of the period. In many instances, the units sold are not identifiable with the specific cost of the item, or such application is impractical. For this reason, a variety of cost applications have been developed that recognize differences in the relationship of costs to selling prices under various conditions. For example, the last in, first out (LIFO) method may be applicable where sales prices are promptly affected by changes in reproduction costs. Circumstances of the individual company or industry must govern, but uniform methods within the industry will permit useful comparisons.

Inventory Valuation Methods

The more common inventory valuation methods are:

- *Identified or specific costs.* Under this method, purchases are not commingled but are kept separate. The issue or sale is priced at the exact cost of the specific item. Such a system is not widely adopted because it requires too much physical attention and accounting detail. It is sometimes used in costing perishable stock or nonstandard units that have been purchased for a specific job.
- *First-in, first-out (FIFO).* This method assumes that items first received are first issued. To illustrate the operation, assume an opening inventory of 50 units at $10 each, receipts on January 11 of 10 units at a cost of $15, and issues on January 3 and 12 of 40 units each. The issue on January 3 would be costed at $10 per unit, leaving a balance of 10 units at $10 each. The issue of January 12 would be priced in this way:

10 units at $10 each	$100
30 units at $15 each	450
Total	$550

The requisition must be priced on two bases since two different acquisitions were issued.

▪ *Weighted average cost.* This procedure involves the determination after each receipt of the total quantity and value on hand. The total units are divided into the total value to secure an average unit cost. All issues are priced at this average cost until the next receipt, when the new average is computed. The unit price must be carried out to sufficient decimal places to retain accuracy.

Disadvantages of this method include the detailed calculations necessary and the length of time taken to reflect recent purchases in the average. It has the advantage of stabilizing costs when prices fluctuate.

▪ *Standard cost.* As the name implies, a predetermined or standard cost is used. The price variances on raw materials may be recognized when the material is received or when it is issued into production. Use of standard costs eliminates such clerical effort. No cost columns are needed on the ledger cards, and the repeated calculation of unit costs is avoided.

▪ *Last in, first-out cost (LIFO).* The use of this method assumes that the last unit purchased is the first to be requisitioned. The mechanics used are very similar to the FIFO method, except that requisitions are priced at the cost of the most recent purchase. For example, assume that 100 units are purchased at $4 each and that, later, 50 units are purchased at $6 each. A requisition for 75 units would be priced in this way:

50 units at $6	$300
25 units at $4	100
75 Total	$400

The purpose of the LIFO method is to state, as closely as possible, the cost of goods sold at the current market cost. This method reduces unrealized inventory profits to a minimum.

There are two problems with LIFO. First, record keeping is more extensive than that required for other valuation methods. If the oldest inventory is never used, then the company can have costing layers on that inventory that are many decades old. Second, if inventory levels drop to zero at period-end, the profit impact could be enormous, for the oldest cost layers may stretch back many years to times when product costs were significantly different. For example, Product A currently costs $10. If the oldest Product A cost layer is only $1 per unit and all of the inventory is used, then the cost of goods sold will be reduced to one-tenth of its current level, creating significant taxable income.

If a company is using the LIFO valuation method and is installing a just-in-time manufacturing system, then the controller should know that the cost of goods sold percentage may vary drastically while the inventory is being reduced and old inventory layers with different costs are being eliminated.

⬚ *Retail inventory method.* This method often is used by department stores, where inventory is marked item by item at selling price rather than cost. The average margin or markup is determined for the period, and this is applied against the ending inventory at retail to ascertain cost. It is a type of average costing.

In a stable price economy, fewer questions of inventory valuation policy normally arise. In periods of rapid price change, the valuation base selected may have a significant influence on income determination. Obviously, the effect of price changes is not uniform in every industry or in every company. Certain characteristics of the inventory determine the effect of price changes on a company. Among these are:

⬚ *Degree of selling price responsiveness to cost changes.* If prices bear little immediate relationship to costs, then the selling price to be realized on the disposition of the present inventory will not impair its value. There will be no cause for a write-down.

⬚ *Relative share of investment in inventories.* The larger the inventory, the greater the risk and the more significant the write-down if values decline substantially. A firm whose major investment is in inventory is more vulnerable to market changes than one that requires a heavy investment in plant and equipment to conduct business.

⬚ *Use of a price hedge.* Losses on the inventory are offset by gains on future sales in the commodities market.

- *Rate of inventory turnover.* If the turnover is rapid, then a shorter time will elapse between the sale of the goods and purchase of materials for additional sales. Thus, in periods of large market value changes, fluctuations in the inventory value will not be as marked.

Lower of Cost or Market, and Inventory Reserves

In some instances, a departure from the cost basis is justified. This occurs when the market value of the goods disposed of in the ordinary course of business is less than cost. Loss in value can occur by reason of damage, deterioration, obsolescence, changes in the price level, and other causes. Such loss should be recognized as a charge against the period in which it occurs. In these instances the goods should be valued at "market," which will be lower than cost. The market value of an item is the current cost of replacing it. One exception to this rule is when goods still can be sold at a fixed price, such as would be contained in the text of a long-term contract with a customer.

Most companies establish an inventory loss reserve in expectation of finding obsolete or damaged inventory over a period of time. The reserve is usually established as a percentage of the inventory and is based on historical or industry averages of actual losses. The reserve is deducted from the inventory on the balance sheet. As actual losses are uncovered, they are written off against the loss reserve. Since actual losses can be hidden on the balance sheet, each loss occurrence should be reported to management, in case any corrective action is necessary.

The controller must provide for a continuous review of procedures and transactions to ensure that inventories are being valued properly. This review will include procedures for notification when materials become unsalable, and should include creating a materials review board (MRB) that would periodically review the inventory. A typical MRB has representatives from the accounting, quality control, engineering, sales, and materials departments. The combined expertise of this group can be relied on to identify and properly disposition unsalable materials.

 ## INVENTORY FRAUD AND CONTROLS

As with other areas of a business, the controller should be aware of fraud schemes that are specific to the inventory area. This section covers the schemes and the most basic inventory controls.

Inventory Fraud

The year-end inventory count can be fraudulently increased in order to reduce the cost of goods sold and thereby create an artificially large profit. Also, company personnel may steal inventory and try to cover up the theft with artificially high inventory counts. Consequently, the counting team should look for these fraudulent schemes that may have occurred during or before the inventory count:

- Empty or mislabeled boxes
- Incorrect units of measure
- Diluted liquid inventory
- Excessively advanced sites of WIP completion
- Customer-owned stock included in the inventory count

In addition, the controller should watch for these fraudulent schemes that can occur when performing the inventory cutoff:

- Double-counting inventory that is in transit between two company-owned locations
- Counting inventory for which payables have not been recorded

An additional concern relates solely to JIT purchasing. Since JIT precludes competitive bidding, it may be possible for buyers to select suppliers who will kick back profits to them in exchange for the business. This problem is real, but is mitigated somewhat by the amount of interaction between company employees and the supplier. The product design function under JIT purchasing requires that the company's design engineers work closely with suppliers, and therefore they may be able to recognize a sham supplier.

Inventory Controls

Inventory controls should include physical control over the stock plus accuracy of the inventory information and of the bills of material that describe the inventory.

These controls can be used to *physically control* the inventory:

- Make the warehouse manager responsible for all inventory shortages
- Erect fencing around all inventory storage locations, and lock all entrances

- Permit only warehouse personnel into the warehouse, or require an escort for nonwarehouse personnel
- Record all transactions for items that enter or leave the warehouse, and require a signature from the receiving, kitting, or shipping person in the warehouse who handles each transaction

The controller should also institute reviews of the *inventory information* by someone who does not report to the inventory manager. The ideal person would be the internal auditor; in the absence of such a person, the cost accountant or a person similarly knowledgeable about inventory should conduct the reviews. If a perpetual inventory is available, then the review should be conducted weekly. The reviewer should take a random sample from the inventory report (sorted by location and including extended costs), and review that:

- Items physically in stock are listed on the report
- Items listed on the report are physically in stock
- Units of measure are correct
- High-dollar-value items are correct (sample 100 percent of these items)

The inventory report from the previous week should also be retained, so that these items can be reviewed:

- That the total number of part numbers in stock does not vary significantly from the previous week, or that such variances can be identified and explained
- That the total dollar value of inventory does not vary significantly from the previous week, or that such variances can be identified and explained

To control the *bill-of-material information,* it is important to cross-check additional items that are requested from stock during a job's production or returned to stock following a job's production. These transactions strongly indicate that a product's bill of materials is incorrect. Also, forms should be distributed to the production and kitting staffs, who can report on missing or duplicate parts. Finally, a review committee can systematically review all bills of material for inaccurate quantities, part numbers, and units of measure. Since the controller bases year-end inventory projections on product costs that in turn are based on bills of material, correcting the bills can eliminate the annoyance of larger year-end inventory variances.

Under a JIT manufacturing system, inventory is minimized, and, consequently, the risk of significant fraud is greatly reduced. However, to avoid collusion between buyers and suppliers (who no longer have to bid for work), the controller should periodically compare the company's supplier costs to a sample of costs from other suppliers. The controller should also review prices charged by suppliers versus prices contracted.

CHAPTER FOURTEEN

Property, Plant, and Equipment

C APITAL EXPENDITURE PLANNING AND control are critical to the long-term financial health of any company operating in the private enterprise system. Expenditures for fixed assets require significant financial resources, decisions are difficult to reverse, and the investment affects financial performance over a long period of time.

Investment in capital assets has other ramifications or possible consequences not found in the typical day-to-day expenditures of a business. Once funds have been used for the purchase of plant and equipment, it may be a long time before they are recovered. Unwise expenditures of this nature are difficult to retrieve without serious loss to the investor. Needless to say, imprudent long-term commitments can result in bankruptcy or other financial embarrassment.

Also, a substantial increase in capital investment is likely to cause a much higher break-even point for the business. Large outlays for plant, machinery, and equipment carry with them higher depreciation charges, heavier insurance costs, greater property taxes, and possibly an expanded maintenance expense. All these tend to raise the level of sales volume needed for the business to earn a profit.

In today's highly competitive environment, it is mandatory that companies make significant investments in fixed assets to improve productivity and take advantage of the technological gains being experienced in manufacturing equipment. The sophisticated manufacturing and processing techniques available make investment decisions more important; however, the sizable amounts invested allow for greater rewards in increased productivity and higher return on investment. This opportunity carries with it additional risks relative to the increasing costs of a plant and equipment.

These conditions make it imperative that wisdom and prudent judgment be exercised in making investments in capital assets. Management decisions must be made utilizing analytical approaches. Numerous mathematical techniques can assist in eliminating uneconomic investments and systematically establishing priorities.

ROLE OF THE CONTROLLER

The controller's financial knowledge is needed to evaluate the capital asset requirements that are generated by the first-level management. In many cases, heavy losses have been incurred because the acquisition decision was made with an optimistic outlook but without adequate financial analysis. The controller's staff must make an objective appraisal of the potential savings and return on investment.

After the chief executive officer (CEO) and board of directors have decided to make the investments, the controller must establish proper accountability, measure performance (procurement of the capital assets at the budgeted price), and institute recording and reporting procedures for control to ensure that the equipment has been received and installed and is fulfilling its intended use.

The controller's tasks in relation to property, plant, and equipment are to:

- Establish a procedure for the planning and control of fixed assets
- Establish hurdle rates on the types of fixed assets under consideration
- Review all requests for capital expenditures to verify the probable rate of return
- Ascertain that the plant and equipment expenditures required to meet the manufacturing and sales plans are included in the business plan and that funds are available to pay for the expenditures
- Establish controls to ensure that capital expenditures are kept within authorized limits
- Review economic alternatives to asset purchases, such as leasing or renting, or buying the manufactured item from other suppliers

- Establish a reporting system that informs managers about equipment's maintenance costs, idle time, productivity, and actual costs versus budget
- Maintain property records that identify all assets, describe their locations, track transfers and sales, and account for depreciation
- Maintain a depreciation policy for each type of equipment for book and tax purposes
- Ensure that proper insurance coverage is maintained for the fixed assets
- Ensure that proper internal control procedures apply to the machinery and equipment

 ## CAPITAL BUDGETING

The principal part of this chapter will and should be devoted to the capital budgeting process. Most of the accounting and reporting duties are known to the average controller, but more involvement in the budget procedure should be encouraged. Given the relative inflexibility that exists once capital commitments are made, it is desirable that the CEO and other senior executives be provided a suitable framework for selecting the essential or economically justified projects from among the many proposals, even though their intuitive judgment may be a key factor. When the undertaking begins, the expenditures must be held within the authorized limits. Moreover, for the larger projects at least, management is entitled, once the asset begins to operate, to be periodically informed how the actual economics compare with the anticipated earnings or savings.

The nine steps in a well-conceived capital budgeting process are outlined next. The appropriate line executive rather than the controller performs these steps.

Step 1. For the planning period of the short-term budget, determine a permissible range for capital commitments for the company as a whole and for each major division. This range tells management how much can be spent in the period.

Step 2. Encourage the presentation of worthy capital investment projects. For major projects, the target rate of return should be provided, and any other useful guidelines should be furnished, such as corporate objectives and plans for expansion.

Step 3. When the proposals are received, make a preliminary screening to eliminate those that do not support the strategic plan or that are obviously not economically or politically supported.

Step 4. After this preliminary screening:
  1. Classify all projects by urgency of need
  2. Calculate the economic benefits
Step 5. Review the project proposals for:
  1. Validity of nontechnical data
  2. Rate of return and any related calculations
  3. Compatibility with the financial resources available and any capital budget criteria
Step 6. Present the data to the board of directors and secure approval in principle.
Step 7. When the time approaches for starting a major project, the specific authorization should be reviewed and approved by the appropriate members of management. This process may require a review of the underlying data to be sure no fundamentals have changed.
Step 8. Prepare periodic reports to indicate costs incurred to date as well as the estimated cost to complete the project.
Step 9. Conduct a postcompletion audit to compare actual and estimated cash flow.

Establishing the Limit of the Capital Budget

The capital budgeting process begins with the setting of a maximum amount that may be spent on capital expenditures. The company's top management will set a capital budget amount, based on these factors:

- Estimated internal cash generation
- Availability and cost of external funds
- Current capital structure of the company (i.e., too much debt?)
- Strategic plans
- Stage of the business cycle
- Short- and medium-term growth prospects of the company and the industry
- Current and anticipated inflation rates
- Expected rate of return on capital projects compared with the cost of capital or other hurdle rates
- Age and condition of present plant and equipment
- New technological developments and the need to remain competitive
- Anticipated competitor actions
- Relative investment in plant and equipment compared with industry or selected competitors; this can be measured by comparing the ratio of fixed

assets to net worth, which indicates how much of the net worth is used to finance plant and equipment versus working capital

Supporting Information for Capital Expenditure Proposals

Every capital proposal must have sufficient supporting detail for top management to make an informed yes-or-no decision. The information that follows will be needed for these capital budgeting proposals:

For a *replacement* of existing equipment:

- The investment and installation cost of the new equipment
- The salvage value of the old equipment
- The impact on the company's bottleneck operation
- The economic life of the new equipment
- The operating cost of the new item over its life
- The reason for the expenditure

For an *expansion* of facilities, the preceding information about new equipment is needed, plus this information:

- The market potential for the new product
- The probable sales quantity and value of the output
- The marketing cost
- The new equipment's salvage value
- The change in productive capacity at the throughput operation
- The project's rate of return (several alternative methods are discussed in this chapter)

Method of Evaluating Projects

Because most companies do not have sufficient funds to undertake all projects, some means must be found to evaluate the alternative courses of action. The evaluation of quantitative information must be blended with good judgment, and perhaps good fortune, to select the most appropriate capital proposals for completion. For those companies using analytical tools, three elements are essential:

1. An estimate of the expected capital outlay, as well as the amount and timing of the estimated future cash flow

2. A technique for relating the expected future benefits to a measure of cost, such as the cost of capital
3. A means of evaluating the risk, which includes the probability of attaining the estimated rate of return

The more important valuation methods are the payback method and several rate-of-return analyses. These methods are reviewed in the next sections. Also, see the Throughput Analysis Method section later in this chapter, for an alternative view of how to evaluate a project.

Payback Method

The payback method calculates the time period needed to pay back a project's original investment from the project's cash flows. The payback method offers these advantages:

- It is useful when a business has minimal cash flow and must accept proposals that appear to promise a payback in a short time period.
- It is useful for appraising very risky investments where the threat of expropriation or capital wastage is high and difficult to predict.
- It is a simple computation and easy to understand.
- It is a rough indicator of profitability and, as such, allows the controller to reject obviously undesirable proposals.

However, the payback method also has these disadvantages:

- It does not consider earnings after the initial outlay is recouped, even though the cash flow after payback is the real factor in determining profitability. Essentially, the method confuses recovery of capital with profitability.
- It places undue emphasis on liquidity since the cash outflow must occur immediately after completion of the project in order to show a rapid payback. Thus, it has a tendency to reject highly profiled projects that do not have substantial cash flow in their early years.
- It does not recognize the gradual wastage of the asset. In other words, the time period over which the asset will be useful is of no importance, so assets that are discarded immediately after the payback has been achieved will be acceptable under this method.

Accountant's Method

This technique compares earnings to the average outstanding investment rather than the initial investment or assets employed. It is based on the underlying premise that capital recovered as depreciation is available for use in other projects and should not be considered a charge against the original project. The method may be varied to include the effect of income taxes and differing depreciation rates.

Exhibit 14.1 presents the accountant's method.

The accountant's method has two shortcomings. First, it is heavily influenced by the depreciation basis used. Double-declining balance depreciation will, of course, reduce the average investment outstanding and increase the rate of return. Second, it fails to reflect the time value of money. In the example, if the average investment was the same but income was accelerated in the early years and decelerated in later years, the rate of return would be identical. The major advantage of the accountant's method is that it is simpler to calculate than the discounted cash flow approach.

EXHIBIT 14.1 The Accountant's Method

Year	Net Earnings before Depreciation	Depreciation	Net Profit	Average Investment Outstanding
1	$ 300,000	$ 100,000	$ 200,000	$ 950,000
2	300,000	100,000	200,000	850,000
3	300,000	100,000	200,000	750,000
4	300,000	100,000	200,000	650,000
5	300,000	100,000	200,000	550,000
6	300,000	100,000	200,000	450,000
7	300,000	100,000	200,000	350,000
8	300,000	100,000	200,000	250,000
9	300,000	100,000	200,000	150,000
10	300,000	100,000	200,000	50,000
Total	$3,000,000	$1,000,000	$2,000,000	$5,000,000

$$\text{Rate of Return}: \frac{\text{Profit after Depreciation}}{\text{Average investment}} = \frac{\$2,000,000}{\$5,000,000} = 40\%$$

Discounted Cash Flow Methods

It is difficult to compare one project with another, particularly when the cash flow patterns vary. *When* cash is received becomes very important in that cash receipts may be invested and earn something. Because the discounted cash flow technique takes cash flow timing into account, it has been adopted as an effective tool in ranking and judging the profitability of the investments. The technique is used in either of two methods, the internal rate of return (IRR) method and the net present value (NPV) method.

The IRR method involves the determination of that rate of return at which the sum of the stream of after-tax cash earnings, discounted yearly according to current worth, equals the cost of the project. In other words, the IRR is the maximum constant rate of return that a project could earn throughout its life and just break even.

The method can be described in this way. Assume that an investment of $1,000 is made and, over a five-year period, an annual cash flow of $250 is secured. What is the rate of return? By using the present value calculation in Exhibit 14.2, we arrive at 8 percent. The application of the 8 percent factor to the cash flow results in a present value of approximately $1,000, as seen in Exhibit 14.2.

By trial and error, apply a range of discount factors until the proper one is found. Exhibit 14.3 uses a 10 percent discount factor and a 40 percent discount factor, $1 million investment, and $300,000 cash flow per year.

EXHIBIT 14.2 Derivation of the Present Value of a Predictable Cash Flow

Year	Annual Cash Flow (a)	Discount Factor (b)	Present Value (a) × (b)
1	$250	.926	$232
2	250	.857	214
3	250	.794	198
4	250	.735	184
5	250	.681	170
		Total present value	$998

Discounted Rate of Return:
10% + (30%(1,932 − 1,000)/(1,932) − 857)) = 36%

EXHIBIT 14.3 Computation of the Internal Rate of Return

Years from Start of Operation	(Expenditure) or Income	10% Discount Rate		40% Discount Rate	
		Discount Factor	Discounted Amount (000s)	Discount Factor	Discounted Amount (000s)
0	$(1,000,000)		$(1,000)		
0 to 1	300,000	.953	285.9	.844	253.2
2	300,000	.866	259.8	.603	180.9
3	300,000	.788	236.4	.431	129.3
4	300,000	.716	214.8	.308	92.4
5	300,000	.651	195.3	.220	66.0
6	300,000	.592	177.6	.157	47.1
7	300,000	.538	161.4	.112	33.6
8	300,000	.489	146.7	.080	24.0
9	300,000	.444	133.2	.060	18.0
10	300,000	.404	121.2	.041	12.3
Total Cash Flow	$ 3,000,000				
		Discounted Cash Flow	$1,932.3		$856.8

The four steps in applying the IRR method are:

1. Determine the amount and year of the investment.
2. Determine, by years, the cash flow after income taxes coming from the investment.
3. Extend the cash flow by two discount factors to arrive at present worth.
4. Apply various discount factors until the calculation of one comes close to the original investment and interpolate to arrive at a more accurate figure.

The disadvantages of the discounted cash flow method are:

- It is more complex than other methods.
- It requires more time for calculation.
- An inherent assumption is that reinvestment will be at the same rate as the calculated rate of return.

The advantages of the method are:

▪ It gives proper weighting to the time value of investments and cash flow.
▪ The use of cash flow minimizes the effect of arbitrary decisions about capital versus expenses, depreciation, and so on.
▪ It is comparable to the cost-of-capital concept.
▪ It allows the financial analyst to compare alternative projects.

The net present value method of evaluating capital expenditures also considers the time value of money. The difference between NPV and IRR is that a preselected rate is used with NPV—the rate that the company considers the minimum rate of return for taking the risk of the capital investment. If the sum of the present values of the stream of cash exceeds the cost of the proposed investment, then the rate of return exceeds the target and meets the earnings requirements. If the NPV is negative, then the proposal fails to meet the required earnings rate, and the project should be rejected. Exhibit 14.4 shows an NPV calculation.

When a discounted cash flow method is used to evaluate investments in another country, the significant test is the cash flow to the parent, not to the foreign subsidiary. Among the impediments to cash flow to the parent that must be considered in the decision are such items as currency restrictions, fluctuations in the foreign exchange rate, political risk, inflation, and withholding taxes.

EXHIBIT 14.4 Net Present Value Calculation

Year	Estimated Cash Flow	Discounting Factor at 22%	Present Worth
0	$800,000	1.000	$(800,000)
1	370,000	.820	303,400
2	350,000	.672	235,200
3	301,000	.551	165,851
4	215,000	.451	96,965
5	170,000	.370	62,900
6	110,000	.303	33,330
7	40,000	.249	9,960
8	10,000	.204	2,040
		Present value at 22% factor	$ 909,646

Hurdle Rates

A hurdle rate is the minimum rate of return that a capital project should earn if it is to be judged acceptable. It is not used for special projects, such as those required by law, no matter what the return on investment (if any) may be. Examples are pollution abatement or safety devices. Because of these special projects, a factor is commonly added to the hurdle rate, resulting in a slightly higher hurdle rate.

Some companies with multiple divisions use different hurdle rates for each line of business. This practice can be justified by the fact that among those businesses, different business risks exist (e.g., threat of expropriation), rates of return expectations are markedly different, and differing business strategies may apply and require different hurdle rates.

The basis of the hurdle rate is the cost of capital. This is the rate that long-term debt holders and shareholders require in order to be persuaded to furnish the required capital. Thus, assume that:

- A company capital structure target objective is $500,000 composed of 25 percent debt and 75 percent equity.
- In the current market environment, long-term bond holders require a 10 percent return (6 percent to the company after income taxes); a 17 percent return on equity is the going earnings rate.

The cost of capital would be calculated as shown in Exhibit 14.5.

Based on this analysis, if the company is to attract the capital required to stay in business, then, on average, all its capital investments should earn at least 14 percent after taxes. If this does not occur, then the shareholder return would be diluted.

EXHIBIT 14.5 Cost of Capital Calculation

Structure	Capitalization	Required Rate of Return after Taxes	Required Amount of Return
Senior debt	$125,000,000	6.0%	$ 7,500,000
Common stock	375,000,000	17.0%	63,750,000
Total	$500,000,000		$71,250,000

$$\text{Cost of capital} : \frac{\$71,250,000}{500,000,000} = 14\%$$

Project Risk Analysis

It would be helpful for the decision maker to know not only the expected rate of return, but also the probability of receiving that rate, as well as the range of returns possible, together with the probability of each occurring. If there is a strong probability of cash flows dropping below the expected rate, then the board of directors should be presented with this information along with the rest of the capital budget request.

Sensitivity analysis is a mathematical technique wherein changes may be made in any of the input factors and the consequent movement in the result observed. Those making estimates of return on investments know that the answers depend greatly on the assumptions. It is important to test how much an error in an assumption can sway the result. Such knowledge can permit analysts to concentrate their attention on the more important variables. The technique can provide considerable insight into a capital budget proposal.

Investments are made in capital assets with the expectation that the return will be sufficiently high not only to recoup the cost but also to pass the hurdle rate for such an expenditure. But the nature of investment is changing, as are the attendant risks, in the new manufacturing environment. This new environment has these characteristics:

- Although automation is viewed as a primary source of expense reduction, its installation often is preceded by redesigning and simplifying the manufacturing process. Many companies have achieved significant savings simply by rearranging the plant floor, establishing more streamlined procedures, and eliminating the non–value-added functions such as material storage and handling. After this rearrangement is accomplished, then automation might be considered.
- Investments are becoming more significant in themselves. While a stand-alone grinder may cost $1 million, an automated factory can cost $50 million or $100 million. Moreover, much of the cost may be in engineering, software development, and implementation.
- The equipment involved often is increasingly complex, and the benefits can be more indirect and perhaps more intangible. If there are basic improvements in quality, in delivery schedules, and in customer satisfaction, then methods can be found to measure these benefits.

Because of the high investment cost, the period required to earn the desired return on investment is longer. This longer-term horizon, together with the intangibles to be considered and the greater uncertainty, requires the controller to be more discerning in making the analysis. Usually the indirect savings and intangible benefits need to be recognized and included in the investment analysis.

Inflation

Those involved in analyzing capital investments may ponder how inflation should be handled. In the capital budgeting process, these questions should be considered:

- *Should adjustments be made for inflation in the cash flows?* Many companies do not adjust for inflation because it is difficult to get a reliable rate estimate. Also, for the same reason, only one inflation rate is used for the term of the analysis, rather than differing rates for different years.
- *Should specific inflation rates be used on different cost factors (e.g., labor and materials)?* Specific price indices exist for some materials, or groups of materials, and for wages in particular industries.
- *Should the hurdle rate be adjusted for inflation?* If the cash flows in the analysis are adjusted for inflation, then the hurdle rate should also be adjusted.

Ranking Capital Projects

When the reviews have been completed, the projects must be ranked in some order of priority because usually there are many more proposed capital expenditures than would normally be undertaken within the bounds of financial capability. A practical grouping that would be understood by management and operation executives alike follows:

- *Absolutely essential:*
  - Equipment that increases the capacity of the bottleneck operation
  - Government-required installations, such as safety or pollution abatement devices
  - Replacement of inoperable facilities without which the company could not remain in business
- *Highly necessary:*
  - Equipment that contributes to increased product quality
  - Equipment that reduces the cost of producing the product
- *Economically justified projects:*
  - New facilities, robotics, and equipment needed to produce new or additional products

▪ *All other:*
  ▪ Projects that cannot be justified with an economic analysis, such as donations, parking lot lighting, and cafeteria facilities

Projects based on economic return can be ranked by rate of return. The information is then presented to the board of directors for approval. When presented, the information should include the priority, rate of return, total cost, reasons for, benefits of, and risks attached to each project. The timing of all expenditures for all projects should be highlighted on a separate Gantt chart.

Throughput Analysis Method

The traditional capital budgeting approach involves having the management team review a series of unrelated requests from throughout the company, each one asking for funding for various projects. Management decides whether to fund each request based on the discounted cash flows projected for each one. If there are not sufficient funds available for all requests having positive discounted cash flows, then those with the largest cash flows or highest percentage returns are usually accepted first, until the funds run out.

There are several problems with this type of capital budgeting. First and most important, there is no consideration of how each requested project fits into the entire system of production—instead, most requests involve the local optimization of specific work centers that may not contribute to the total throughput (revenues minus totally variable expenses) of the company. Second, there is no consideration of the constrained resource (i.e., the bottleneck), so managers cannot tell which funding requests will result in an improvement to the efficiency of that operation. Third, managers tend to engage in a great deal of speculation regarding the budgeted cash flows resulting from their requests, resulting in inaccurate discounted cash flow projections. Since many requests involve unverifiable cash flow estimates, it is impossible to discern which projects are better than others.

A greater reliance on throughput accounting concepts eliminates most of these problems. First, the priority for funding should be placed squarely on any projects that can improve the capacity of the constrained resource, based on a comparison of the incremental additional throughput created to the incremental operating expenses and investment incurred.

Second, any investment requests not involving the constrained resource should be subject to an intensive critical review, likely resulting in their rejection. Since they do not impact the constrained resource, these investments cannot impact system throughput in any way, so their sole remaining justification must be the reduction of operating expenses or the mitigation of some type of risk.

The one exception to investing in nonconstraint resources is when there is so little excess capacity in a work center that it has difficulty recovering from downtime. This can be a major problem if the lack of capacity constantly causes holes in the inventory buffer and places the constrained resource in danger of running out of work. In this case, a good investment alternative is to invest in a sufficient amount of additional sprint capacity to ensure that the system can rapidly recover from a reasonable level of downtime. If a manager is applying for a capital investment based on this reasoning, he or she should attach to the proposal a chart showing the capacity level at which the targeted resource has been operating over the past few months, as well as the severity of holes in the buffer caused by that operation.

At what point should a company invest in more of the constrained resource? In many cases, the company has specifically designated a resource to be its constraint because it is so expensive to add additional capacity, so this decision is not to be taken lightly. The decision process is to review the impact on the incremental change in throughput caused by the added investment, less any changes in operating expenses. Because this type of investment represents a considerable step cost (where costs and/or the investment will jump considerably as a result of the decision), management must usually make its decision based on the perceived level of long-term throughput changes, rather than smaller expected short-term throughput increases.

The issues noted above have been addressed in the summary-level capital budgeting form shown in Exhibit 14.6. This form splits capital budgeting requests into three categories: (1) constraint-related, (2) risk-related, (3) non–constraint-related. The risk-related category covers all capital purchases for which the company must meet a legal requirement, or for which there is a perception that the company is subject to an undue amount of risk if it does *not* invest in an asset. All remaining requests that do not clearly call into the constraint-related or risk-related categories drop into a catch-all category at the bottom of the form. The intent of this format is to clearly differentiate between different types of approval requests, with each one requiring different types of analysis and management approval.

The approval levels vary significantly in the throughput-based capital request form. Approvals for constraint-related investments include a process analyst (who verifies that the request will actually impact the constraint), as well as generally higher-dollar approval levels for lower-level managers—the

Capital Request Form

Project name: _____

Name of project sponsor: _____

Submission date: _____ Project number: _____

☐ **Constraint-Related Project**		**Approvals**
Initial expenditure: $ _____	All	_____ Process Analyst
Additional annual expenditure: $ _____	$100,000	_____ Supervisor
Impact on throughput: $ _____		
Impact on operating expenses: $ _____	$100,001– $1,000,000	_____ President
Impact on ROI: $ _____		
(Attach calculations)	$1,000,000+	_____ Board of Directors

☐ **Risk-Related Project**		**Approvals**
Initial expenditure: $ _____		_____ Corporate Attorney
Additional annual expenditure: $ _____	<$50,000	
Description of legal requirement fulfilled or risk issue mitigated (attach description as needed):		_____ Chief Risk Officer
_____	$50,001+	_____ President
_____	$1,000,000+	_____ Board of Directors

☐ **Non-Constraint-Related Project**		**Approvals**
Initial expenditure: $ _____	All	_____ Process Analyst
Additional annual expenditure: $ _____	<$10,000	_____ Supervisor
☐ Improves sprint capacity? Attach Justification of sprint capacity increase	$10,001– $100,000	_____ President
☐ Other request Attach justification for other request type	$100,000+	_____ Board of Directors

---

EXHIBIT 14.6 Throughput-Based Capital Request Form

intent is to make it easier to approve capital requests that will improve the constrained resource. Approvals for risk-related projects first require the joint approval of the corporate attorney and chief risk officer, with added approvals for large expenditures. Finally, the approvals for non–constraint-related purchases involve lower-dollar approval levels, so the approval process is intentionally made more difficult.

POSTPROJECT APPRAISALS

In many companies, adequate analyses are made about the apparent economic desirability of a project, and acquisition costs are held within estimate, yet the project does not achieve the estimated rate of return. Some managements are unaware of such a condition because there is no follow-up on performance. For large projects, after a reasonable time period beyond completion, when all the bugs are worked out, a postaudit review should be made. The review might be taken by the internal audit group or perhaps by a management team consisting of line managers involved with the project and some members of the controller's staff. The objective is to compare actual earnings or savings with the plan, ascertain why the deviation occurred, and determine what steps should be taken to improve capital investment planning and control. The scope might range from the strategic planning aspects through the detailed control procedures.

An intelligently planned postaudit may provide these advantages:

- ■ It may detect weaknesses in strategic planning that lead to poor decisions, which in turn impact the capital budgeting procedures.
- ■ The postaudit might detect environmental factors that influence the business but were not recognized.
- ■ Experience can focus attention on basic weaknesses in overall plans, policies, or procedures as related to capital expenditures.
- ■ The postaudit can detect and correct strengths or weaknesses in individual performance—such as a tendency to have overly optimistic estimates.
- ■ It may enable corrections in other current projects prior to completion of commitments or expenditures.

The postaudit report commentary can focus on estimated cash flow through the date of the audit compared with actual cash flow, old versus new break-even points, and planned versus actual operating expenses.

OTHER ASPECTS OF FIXED ASSETS

The largest issue surrounding property, plant, and equipment, covered earlier in this chapter, is the set of policies and procedures used to acquire it (i.e., capital budgeting). However, a host of other smaller issues are involved as well.

- *Working capital.* In many instances, a capital expenditure also requires an increase in working capital to pay for additional inventories and accounts receivable. These amounts should always be factored into the capital budgeting investment amount as well as the rate of return calculation.
- *Lease versus buy.* The NPV method should be used to compare a lease acquisition against a buy acquisition. If the marginal (net of taxes) cost of funds to purchase the asset is known, the same discount rate can be applied to the stream of lease payments to arrive at the NPV. Usually the alternative with the lower NPV and the higher savings should be the one selected.
- *Idle equipment.* The controller should inform management about losses from idle equipment and place responsibility in an attempt to eliminate the avoidable and unnecessary costs. This reporting may encourage the disposal of any permanently excess equipment, giving consideration to the medium-term plans. Losses resulting from unused plant facilities can include depreciation, property taxes, insurance, and utilities. There are three causes of idle time:
  1. *Those controllable by the production staff.* Some causes are poor planning; lack of materials, tools, or power; machine breakdowns; or improper supervision.
  2. *Those resulting from administrative decisions.* Management may decide to build additional capacity, which may lead to idle facilities in the short term, until demand builds to match the capacity.
  3. *Those arising from economic causes.* These causes are beyond the control of the company, such as seasonal demand or excess capacity in the industry.

Internal Control Requirements

There are a small number of control issues surrounding equipment; the controller should implement this list:

- Identify all fixed assets, possibly by affixing a serial number to the item. Bar codes are sometimes used for easy scanning during fixed asset physical inventories.

- Transfer equipment between departments only with the written approval of the department head responsible for the physical security of the property. This is necessary in order to track locations for insurance purposes and to properly charge depreciation to the correct departments.
- Prevent equipment from leaving the plant without a property pass signed by the proper authority.
- Perform a physical inventory on all fixed assets.
- Maintain detailed records on each piece of equipment, as described below.
- Review purchase requisitions to ensure that piecemeal acquisitions are not made simply to avoid obtaining approval of higher authority.
- Review retirements of fixed assets to see if the equipment can be used by other departments before scrapping or selling.
- Secure bids on sizable transactions.
- Provide for proper insurance coverage during construction of equipment as well as when it is completed.
- Review expenses to ensure that capital expenditures are not treated as expenses, thereby avoiding budget overruns.
- Track the following items for capital projects:
  - Amount authorized
  - Actual commitments to date
  - Actual costs incurred to date
  - Estimated cost to complete
  - Indicated total cost
  - Indicated overrun or underrun compared to the project budget

Plant and Equipment Records

Adequate plant and equipment records are a necessary adjunct to effective control. They provide a convenient source of information for planning and control purposes as well as for insurance and tax (e.g., personal and real property tax) purposes.

Detailed records must be designed to suit the individual needs of the company. Property records should include this information:

- Name of the asset
- Type of equipment
- Control number
- Description
- Size

- Model
- Style
- Serial number
- Motor number
- Purchased new or used
- Date purchased
- Vendor name
- Invoice number
- Purchase order number
- Location (e.g., plant, building, floor, and department)
- Account number
- Transfer information
- Original cost information (e.g., purchase cost, freight, tax, installation, material, labor, and overhead)
- Additions to
- Date retired
- Sold to
- Scrapped
- Cost recovered
- Depreciation information (e.g., estimated life, annual depreciation, basis)

Plant and Equipment in Relation to Taxes

Many local communities and states levy real and personal property taxes or enforce payment of franchise taxes based on property values. Maintenance of adequate records can be a means of satisfying the taxing authorities on problems of valuation.

Plant and property values, through the resulting depreciation charges, are important from the federal income tax viewpoint. As mentioned, the depreciation allowance for tax purposes, if significantly different from depreciation for book purposes, can distort the profit before taxes and the tax charge. Where the estimate of useful life and the base for tax and book purposes are not significantly different, an effort should be made to bring the two in line, thereby saving the maintenance of a separate set of records. In any event, the burden of proof about the correctness of the depreciation claimed is placed on the taxpayer, who must keep the necessary records and other data to support the claim.

CHAPTER FIFTEEN

Liabilities

I T HAS BEEN SAID that the management, or planning and control, of a company's assets rests largely in the hands of the operating executives but that management of the liabilities and equity is primarily the responsibility of the financial executives. To an extent, this is true—the controller must closely plan and monitor liabilities to foresee changes in the company's liabilities.

This chapter discusses the practical considerations regarding liability planning, measurement, and control, as well as miscellaneous issues related to liabilities, such as bond ratings, debt capacity, and leverage.

OBJECTIVES

The purpose of liability management is to ensure that the company has enough cash to meet funding requirements for any purpose significant to its long-term financial health. Thus, it is not merely to avoid insolvency or bankruptcy. From the standpoint of the controller, the objectives of liability management are:

- Recording and disclosing the company's financial obligations in accordance with generally accepted accounting principles

- Reporting corporate liabilities in the proper form, as required by indentures and credit agreements
- Maintaining a sound financial structure of debt in proportion to equity through effective planning and control
- Securing necessary borrowed funds in a timely manner and at a cost that is competitive
- Creating and maintaining controls that restrict commitments within well-defined limits so that they do not result in excessive liabilities
- Permitting the company to maintain a prudent dividend policy

Many of the above objectives of liability management are interrelated.

 ## CONTROLS

Because of the differing nature of the various types of liabilities, it is practical in the accounting, planning, and control activities to treat each group separately. Here are some suggestions for what the controller can do to manage liabilities.

Current Liabilities

The controller can plan the liabilities by period. This is accomplished after the various asset levels (cash, receivables, inventories, plant, and equipment) are planned and when the operational plans (sales, manufacturing expenses, direct labor, direct material, selling expenses, and general and administrative [G&A]) are completed. It is helpful to group the current liabilities according to the categories to be identified in the statement of estimated financial position, such as accounts payable, accrued salaries and wages, accrued expenses, accrued income taxes, and notes payable.

The controller can also test the plan for compliance with credit agreements or other internally developed standards such as the current ratio, inventory turns, net working capital, and the industry average or competitor performance.

In addition, the controller can analyze each line item for ways to reduce the obligation. For example, he or she can use just-in-time (JIT) inventory methods to generate enough cash to reduce accounts payable or notes payable. Other ways to reduce inventory are to arrange with suppliers to receive goods on consignment or special payment terms. And the controller can monitor the period balances for any unfavorable developing trends, and take appropriate action. Finally, the controller can issue the appropriate control or informational reports, such as to the supervisor of accounts payable, the board of directors, or creditors. This might include updating the projected debt status to the year-end, summarizing contingent liabilities, or issuing information about payables aging, unfunded pension plan liabilities, foreign currency exposure, or outstanding obligations on leases.

Long-Term Liabilities

The controller can plan the long-term debt, by appropriate category, for the annual plan. He or she can test the plan against credit agreement requirements or standards for debt capacity, including that which might exist under the least favorable business conditions that are likely to prevail in the planning period. Moreover, he or she can monitor actual performance during the plan term for unfavorable developments, as well as report on the financial condition and outlook to the appropriate interests (e.g., bankers, bond holders, or the board of directors).

All Indebtedness Items

Here the controller can review the accounting to ascertain that generally accepted accounting principles (GAAP) are followed. He or she can also check the internal controls to ensure that the system is functioning properly. It would also be wise to keep reasonably informed about the status and probable trend of the debt market and any new debt instruments, both short and long term. If appropriate, this includes foreign markets.

Also, routines must be instituted to see that all liabilities are properly certified or approved by designated authority. The proper comparison of receiving reports, purchase orders, and invoices by those handling the detail disbursement procedure eliminates many duties by the officers; but the liabilities not covered by these channels must have the necessary review. The controller, for example, must approve the payrolls before payment. The chief purchasing agent must approve invoices for services because no receiving report is issued. Certain special transactions may require the approval of the president. Invoices for parts or services should be checked in the computer records for duplicate payments. In summary, the controller should consider the system of recording payables somewhat independently of the disbursements procedure to give added assurance that the necessary controls exist.

CREDIT AGREEMENT PROVISIONS

Indentures or credit agreements usually are tailored to fit the desires of both the lender and the borrower. However, a great many standard provisions apply to most loan agreements. The controller should be aware of the provisions that relate to indebtedness limits and certain uses of cash. This list of provisions includes examples of typical limitations:

- *Current ratio requirement.* The company covenants that it will not permit current assets at any time to be less than, for example, 150 percent of current liabilities.
- *Dividend limitation.* The company covenants that it will not pay or declare any dividends over a set amount. However, payments to preferred stockholders under existing agreements usually are allowed.
- *Debt.* The company and its subsidiaries will not incur or guarantee additional debt. Also, a ratio such as tangible assets to debt is used to establish a maximum allowable debt amount. This ratio is highly variable by situation, but a ratio of 2 to 1 is acceptable in most instances. The ratio should also be calculated on a consolidated basis, since companies may shift debt among subsidiaries in order to make some subsidiaries theoretically debt-free and therefore capable of acquiring more debt.
- *Guarantees.* The company will not guarantee the liabilities of a third party.
- *Subordinated debt.* The company covenants that it will not require additional debt that will act to lessen the claim of the current creditors on the company's existing assets.
- *Minimum working capital.* The company covenants that it will maintain a fixed amount of working capital to cover the firm's operating cash needs.
- *Negative covenants.* The company will not undertake to acquire additional debt without the permission of specific creditors or those creditors holding a minimum percentage of the company's debt.
- *Sale, lease.* The company will not sell or transfer any assets other than obsolete or worn-out property, provided the value of such transferred or sold items does not exceed a specific ratio, such as assets to equity. This clause is used to keep companies from liquidating those assets that are used as collateral on loans. Obviously, inventories are not included in this provision.

DEBT CAPACITY

The goal of the financial executive should be to arrange financing so that the owners of the business will receive the maximum economic benefit over the longer run, by increasing the share price and/or the level of dividends.

It can be demonstrated over a period of time, assuming normal profitability and the deductibility of interest expense for tax purposes, that prudent borrowing will increase the return to the shareholder. Given this potential for gain, there exists a powerful deterrent that discourages using long-term debt; that deterrent is the risk associated with servicing the debt. Debts and interest payments must be paid when due regardless of the company's financial condition, possibly resulting in unwelcome policy restraints or even the loss of the enterprise. These fixed payments also reduce a company's options to match the prices of competitors during price wars, resulting in reduced sales, lower margins, and possible losses.

With the deterrents to excessive debt loads being so severe, how is the controller to know what debt level is optimal? Some guidance in arriving at a decision may come from:

- *Institutional lenders.* Unlike financial officers of an industrial enterprise, bankers negotiate long-term loans at frequent intervals. Consequently, they are more familiar with the terms of recent agreements. Presumably they are also conservative and tend to err in the conservative direction. They should be able to judge if proposed standards will be acceptable in the marketplace. However, the acceptable amount of debt will vary based on market conditions and available interest rates.
- *Action of competitors.* The financial statements and loan agreements of public companies are available. The controller can derive ranges of debt levels for comparison purposes from such public information.
- *Analysis of past practice.* Historical analysis of debt and income behavior in the company in times of adversity and under normal conditions may provide some guidance.

Conventionally, there are two types of standards by which to judge long-term debt capacity: a capitalization standard and an earnings coverage standard. In arriving at a debt policy for a company, each should be considered and interrelated. In working with internally generated data, the controller can make refinements ordinarily not possible with the public data of other companies.

A widely used standard, often employed as a constraint in credit agreements, is the *long-term debt to equity ratio*. Thus long-term debt should not be more than, say, 25 percent of equity capital. It can also be expressed as a percent of total capitalization. In using such a standard, several determinations should be calculated, showing the impact, for example, of a 20 percent debt ratio versus a 25 percent debt ratio to judge the risk involved. Then, too, recognition must be given to the often wide variation between the principal of the debt and the annual debt service charge of interest and debt repayment. Although the ratio of debt to equity may be the same for many years, the debt repayment burden may be substantially different if it is paid off in 5 years instead of 30 years.

The *earnings coverage standard* measures the total annual amount required for debt service to the net earnings available for serving the debt. By relating the annual cash outflow for debt service to the net earnings available for this purpose, the standards seek to ensure that even in times of adversity there are sufficient funds to meet the obligation. Obviously, the greater the probability of change in cash flow, the higher the desired times–coverage ratio. The observed times coverages vary greatly by industry and by company. Typical well-financed companies may have a coverage of 15 times or more.

Debt coverage ratios should be calculated for a variety of economic circumstances, assuming both the worst possible cash flow and the most probable cash flow. The final analysis, debt policy, or appropriate capital structure can be determined only by an examination of the factors in the company and in the industry that influence the ability to repay debt; it is a matter of judgment and foresight regarding likely conditions.

BOND RATINGS

If a publicly held company issues debt, it can elect to have that debt rated by either Moody's, Standard & Poor's, or Fitch. These are the three top-tier credit rating agencies that the Securities and Exchange Commission (SEC) allows to issue debt ratings. A debt rating results in a credit score that indicates the perceived risk of default on the underlying debt, which in turn impacts the price of the debt on the open market. Having a credit score is essentially mandatory since most funds are prohibited by their internal investment rules from buying debt that does not have a specific level of credit rating assigned to it. The rating scores used by the three credit rating agencies are noted in Exhibit 15.1 and are in declining order of credit quality.

EXHIBIT 15.1 Credit Score Comparison

Definition	Fitch Rating	Moody's Rating	S&P Rating
Prime	AAA	Aaa	AAA
High grade	AA+	Aa1	AA+
	AA	Aa2	AA
	AA−	Aa3	AA−
Upper medium grade	A+	A1	A+
	A	A2	A
	A−	A3	A−
Lower medium grade	BBB+	Baa1	BBB+
	BBB	Baa2	BBB
	BBB−	Baa3	BBB−
Non-investment grade	BB+	Ba1	BB+
Speculative	BB	Ba2	BB
	BB−	Ba3	BB−
Highly speculative	B+	B1	B+
		B2	B
		B3	B−
Substantial risk	CCC	Caa1	CCC+

A company should expect to deal with a credit rating agency through a primary analyst who has considerable credit rating experience, and is usually ranked at the director level. The primary analyst is supported by a senior analyst having direct experience in the company's industry. The primary analyst is responsible for formulating a rating, and for the ongoing monitoring of that rating.

In order to develop a credit rating, the analyst team uses the financial statements that a company has previously filed with the SEC, but also needs detailed information about its budgets, internal operating reports, risk management strategies, and financial and operating policies. To this end, it will ask the management team to complete an initial questionnaire that usually requires five years of historical financial data, five years of forecasted financial results, a summary of the business and its objectives, a comparison of its market share and growth prospects to those of its peer companies, and the biographies of the senior management team. The focus of this analysis is forward-looking since the analyst team is most concerned with the company's future performance. Consequently, short-range and medium-range projections of a company's financial viability are considered more important than its historical performance.

A key part of the analysis will be a question and answer session with the management team. The controller will be expected to make a presentation about the company, after which the analysts will ask about any areas of weakness which could impact the nature of their eventual credit rating. The general thrust of their questioning is to compare the company's current financial situation to its strategic intentions, to see if its financial structure can support where management wants to take the company.

The analysts will use their agency's standardized rating methodology to assign a credit rating to the specific company debt for which they are being hired. It is difficult to estimate in advance what the rating may be since the relative weighting of factors in the methodology will vary based on individual circumstances. Generally speaking, the analysts will ascribe about 50 percent of the rating to the company's business profile and future prospects and 50 percent to its current financial profile.

If an agency issues a low credit rating, or downgrades an existing rating, the best reaction by the company is to not publicly challenge it. There is no upside to a company complaining bitterly about the perceived injustice of a low rating since it is very unlikely that the issuing agency will change its rating. The only result of such action is that the company has drawn attention to a negative opinion issued by a qualified third party, which may very well reduce investor confidence in the debt price. However, a company may certainly appeal the rating, usually by presenting new information to the agency. Appeals are very rare, comprising only about ½ percent of all ratings changes.

If a company wants to improve its credit rating, then it must take specific steps to make its financial structure more conservative, such as by issuing more stock and using the proceeds to pay down debt. This requires the development of a plan to achieve the higher credit rating, and communication of this information to the credit rating agency.

LEVERAGE

In considering capital structure, the controller must study the impact of leverage. Leverage involves financing an enterprise with senior obligations to increase the rate of return on the common equity. It is also known as trading on the equity. Exhibit 15.2 shows an application of leverage. Assume that the management has been earning, before income taxes, 37 percent on capitalization; that it believes it can continue to achieve this same return; and that the company can borrow at an 11 percent rate. If it borrows 20 percent of equity

EXHIBIT 15.2 Favorable Leverage

	100% Common Stock	Common Stock, plus Bond Capitalization
Capitalization		
Bonds (11%)		$ 20,000,000
Common stock	$100,000,000	$100,000,000
Total	$100,000,000	$120,000,000
Number of common shares	4,000,000	4,000,000
Income		
Income before taxes and interest	$ 37,000,000	$ 44,400,000
Bond interest	—	2,200,000
Income before taxes	$ 37,000,000	$ 42,200,000
Income taxes (46%)	7,020,000	19,412,000
Net income for common	$ 19,980,000	22,788,000
Return on equity	19.98%	22.79%
Earnings per common share	$ 5.00	$ 5.70
Dividend (40% payout)	$ 2.00	$ 2.28

EXHIBIT 15.3 Unfavorable Leverage

	100% Common Stock	Common Stock, plus Bond Capitalization
Capitalization		
Bonds (11%)		$ 20,000,000
Common stock	$100,000,000	$100,000,000
Total	$100,000,000	$120,000,000
Number of common shares	4,000,000	4,000,000
Income		
Income before interest and taxes	$ 10,000,000	$ 10,000,000
Bond interest	—	2,200,000
Income before taxes	$ 10,000,000	7,800,000
Income taxes (46%)	4,600,000	3,588,000
Net income for common	4,400,000	4,212,000
Return on equity	4.4%	4.21%
Earnings per common share	$ 1.10	$ 1.05
Dividend (40% payout)	$ .44	$ .42

and continues the rate of return on assets, the earnings per share, with favorable leverage, increases from $5.00 to $5.70 and the return on equity rises from 19.98 percent to 22.79 percent.

However, if under unfavorable leverage conditions management has been too optimistic and the earnings rate has been less than the bond interest rate, the results could be unsatisfactory—as illustrated in Exhibit 15.3. Here the rate of return on capitalization was less than the bond interest rate.

From an investor standpoint, in good times the leverage increases the earnings per share and the price of stock. However, in adverse times, the reverse condition exists, and the stock of a leveraged company becomes less attractive.

CHAPTER SIXTEEN

Equity

S HAREHOLDERS' EQUITY IS THE interest of the shareholders, or owners, in the assets of a company, and at any time is the cumulative net result of past transactions affecting this segment of the balance sheet. This equity is created initially by the owners' investment in the company, and may be increased from time to time by additional investments, as well as by net earnings. It can be reduced by distributions of the equity to the owners (usually as dividends). Further, it may also decrease if the enterprise is unprofitable. When all liabilities are satisfied, the remainder belongs to the owners.

Basic accounting concepts govern the accounting for shareholders' equity as a whole, for each class of shareholder, and for the various segments of the equity interest, such as capital stock, contributed capital, and earned capital. This chapter addresses such topics as the cost of capital, dividend policy, equity planning, and stock records.

ROLE OF THE CONTROLLER

The controller must properly account for the shareholders' equity, providing those analyses and recommending those actions that are consistent with enhancing shareholder value over the long term. Specifically, these tasks must be performed:

- Accounting for shareholders' equity in accordance with generally accepted accounting principles (GAAP). This includes the historical analysis of the source of the equity and the segregation of the cumulative equity by class of shareholder
- Preparing the appropriate reports on the status and changes in shareholders' equity as required by agencies of the U.S. government, management, credit agreements, and other contracts
- Making the necessary analyses to assist in planning the most appropriate source (e.g., debt or equity) of new funds, and the timing and amount required of each
- Maintaining in proper and economical form the capital stock records of the individual shareholders. In a larger firm, a separate department or outside stock transfer agent might perform these functions
- Making the required analysis periodically on such matters as:
    - Dividend policy
    - Dividend reinvestment plans
    - Stock splits/dividends
    - Stock repurchases
    - Capital structure
    - Trend and outlook for earnings per share
    - Cost of capital for the company and industry
    - Tax legislation as it affects shareholders
    - Price action of the market price of the stock, and influences on it

COST OF CAPITAL

Before determining the amount of a company's cost of capital, it is necessary to determine its components. This section describes in detail how to arrive at the cost of capital for these components, as well as the weighted average calculation that brings together all the elements of the cost of capital.

The first component of the cost of capital is *debt*. Debt is a company's commitment to return to a lender both the interest and principal on an initial or series of payments to the company by the lender. It can be short-term debt, which is typically paid back in full within one year, or long-term debt, which can be repaid over many years, with continual principal repayments, large repayments at set intervals, or a large payment when the entire debt is due, which is called a *balloon* payment. All these forms of repayment can be combined in an infinite number of ways to arrive at a repayment plan that is uniquely structured to fit the needs of the individual corporation.

The second component of the cost of capital is *preferred stock*. This is a form of equity that is issued to stockholders and that carries a specific interest rate. The company is only obligated to pay the stated interest rate to shareholders at stated intervals, but not the initial payment of funds to the company, which it may keep in perpetuity, unless it chooses to buy back the stock. There may also be conversion options, so that a shareholder can convert the preferred stock to common stock in some predetermined proportion. This type of stock is attractive to those companies that do not want to dilute earnings per share with additional common stock and that also do not want to incur the burden of principal repayments. Although there is an obligation to pay shareholders the stated interest rate, it is usually possible to delay payment if the funds are not available, though the interest will accumulate and must be paid when cash is available.

The third and final component of the cost of capital is *common stock*. A company is not required to pay anything to its shareholders in exchange for the stock, which makes this the least risky form of funding available. Instead, shareholders rely on a combination of dividend payments, as authorized by the board of directors (and which are entirely at the option of the board—authorization is not required by law), and appreciation in the value of the shares. However, since shareholders indirectly control the corporation through the board of directors, actions by management that depress the stock price or lead to a reduction in the dividend payment can lead to the firing of management by the board. Also, because shareholders typically expect a high return on investment in exchange for their money, the actual cost of these funds is the highest of all the components of the cost of capital.

When calculating the cost of debt, it is important to remember that the interest expense is tax deductible. This means that the tax paid by the company is reduced by the tax rate multiplied by the interest expense. An example is shown in Exhibit 16.1, where we assume that $1 million of debt has a basic interest rate of 9.5 percent and the corporate tax rate is 35 percent. The example clearly shows that the impact of taxes on the cost of debt significantly reduces the overall debt cost, thereby making this a most desirable form of funding.

If a company is not currently turning a profit and is therefore not in a position to pay taxes, one may question whether the company should factor the impact of taxes into the interest calculation. The answer is still yes because any net loss will carry forward to the next reporting period, when the company can offset future

EXHIBIT 16.1 Calculating the Interest Cost of Debt, Net of Taxes

$$\frac{(\text{Interest expense}) \times (1 - \text{Tax rate})}{\text{Amount of debt}} = \text{Net after-tax interest expense}$$

Or

$$\frac{\$95,000 \times (1 - .35)}{\$1,000,000} = \text{Net after-tax interest expense}$$

$$\frac{\$61,750}{\$1,000,000} = 6.175\%$$

earnings against the accumulated loss to avoid paying taxes at that time. Thus, the reduction in interest costs caused by the tax deductibility of interest is still applicable even if a company is not currently in a position to pay taxes.

Another issue is the cost of acquiring debt, and how this cost should be factored into the overall cost of debt calculation. When obtaining debt, either through a private placement or simply through a local bank, there are usually extra fees involved, which may include placement or brokerage fees, documentation fees, or the price of a bank audit. In the case of a private placement, the company may set a fixed percentage interest payment on the debt, but find that prospective borrowers will not purchase the debt instruments unless they can do so at a discount, thereby effectively increasing the interest rate they will earn on the debt. In both cases, the company is receiving less cash than initially expected, but still must pay out the same amount of interest expense. In effect, this raises the cost of the debt. To carry forward the example in Exhibit 16.1 to Exhibit 16.2, we assume that the interest payments are the same, but that brokerage fees were $25,000 and that the debt was sold at a 2 percent discount. The result is an increase in the actual interest rate. When compared to the cost of equity that is discussed in the next section, it becomes apparent that debt is a much less expensive form of funding than equity. However, although it may be tempting to alter a company's capital structure to increase the proportion of debt, thereby reducing the overall cost of capital, there are dangers involved in incurring a large interest expense.

Preferred stock stands at a midway point between debt and common stock. It requires an interest payment to the holder of each share of preferred stock, but does not require repayment to the shareholder of the amount paid for each share. There are a few special cases where the terms underlying the issuance of a particular set of preferred shares will require an additional payment to shareholders if company earnings exceed a specified level, but this is a rare

EXHIBIT 16.2 Calculating the Interest Cost of Debt, Net of Taxes, Fees, and Discounts

$$\frac{(\text{Interest expense}) \times (1 - \text{Tax rate})}{(\text{Amount of debt}) - (\text{Fees}) - (\text{Discount on sale of debt})} = \text{Net after-tax interest expense}$$

Or

$$\frac{\$95,000 \times (1 - .35)}{\$1,000,000 - \$25,000 - \$20,000} = \text{Net after-tax interest expense}$$

$$\frac{\$61,750}{\$955,000} = 6.466\%$$

Note: There also can be a premium on sale of debt instead of a discount, if investors are willing to pay extra for the interest rate offered. A premium usually occurs when the rate offered is higher than the current market rate or if the risk of nonpayment is so low that this is perceived as an extra benefit by investors.

situation. Also, some preferred shares carry provisions that allow delayed interest payments to be cumulative, so that they must all be paid before dividends can be paid out to holders of common stock. The main feature shared by all kinds of preferred stock is that, under the tax laws, interest payments are treated as dividends instead of interest expense, which means that these payments are not tax deductible. This is a key issue, for it greatly increases the cost of funds for any company using this funding source. By way of comparison, if a company has a choice between issuing debt or preferred stock at the same rate, the difference in cost will be the tax savings on the debt. In the next example, a company issues $1 million of debt and $1 million of preferred stock, both at 9 percent interest rates, with an assumed 35 percent tax rate.

Debt cost = Principal × (interest rate × (1 − tax rate))

Debt cost = $1,000,000 × (9% × (1 − .35))

$58,500 = $1,000,000 × (9% × .65)

If the same information is used to calculate the cost of payments using preferred stock, we have this result:

Preferred stock interest cost = Principal × interest rate

Preferred stock interest cost = $1,000,000 × 9%

$90,000 = $1,000,000 × 9%

This example shows that the differential caused by the applicability of taxes to debt payments makes preferred stock a much more expensive alternative. This being the case, why does anyone use preferred stock? The main reason is that there is no requirement to repay the stockholder for the initial investment, whereas debt requires either a periodic or a balloon payment of principal to eventually pay back the original amount. Companies also can eliminate the preferred stock interest payments if they include a convertibility feature in the stock agreement that allows for a conversion to common stock at some preset price point for the common stock. Thus, in cases where a company does not want to repay principal any time soon, but does not want to increase the amount of common shares outstanding, preferred stock provides a convenient, though expensive, alternative.

The most difficult cost of funding to calculate by far is common stock because there is no preset payment from which to derive a cost. Instead, it appears to be free money since investors hand over cash without any predetermined payment or even any expectation of having the company eventually pay them back for the stock. Unfortunately, the opposite is the case. Because holders of common stock have the most at risk (they are the last ones paid off in the event of bankruptcy), they are the ones who want the most in return. Any management team that ignores its common stockholders and does nothing to give them a return on their investments will find that these people either will vote in a new board of directors that will find a new management team, or else they will sell off their shares at a loss to new investors, thereby driving down the value of the stock and opening up the company to the attentions of a corporate raider who will also remove the management team.

One way to determine the cost of common stock is to estimate the amount of future dividend payments to stockholders and discount this stream of payments back into a net present value. The problem with this approach is that the amount of dividends paid out is problematic since they are declared at the discretion of the board of directors. Also, there is no provision in this calculation for changes in the underlying value of the stock; for some companies that do not pay any dividends, stock appreciation is the only way in which a stockholder will be compensated.

A better method is called the capital asset pricing model (CAPM). Without going into the very considerable theoretical detail behind this system, it essentially derives the cost of capital by determining the relative risk of holding the stock of a specific company as compared to a mix of all stocks in the market. This risk is composed of three elements. The first is the return that any investor can expect from a risk-free investment, which is usually defined as the return on a U.S. government security. The second element is the return from a set of securities considered to have an average level of risk. This can be the average return on a large "market basket" of stocks, such as the Standard & Poor's 500, the Dow Jones Industrials, or some other large cluster of stocks. The final element is a company's *beta*, which defines the amount by which a specific stock's returns vary from the returns of stocks with an average risk level. This information is provided by several of the major investment services, such as Value Line. A beta of 1.0 means that a specific stock is exactly as risky as the average stock, while a beta of 0.8 would represent a lower level of risk and a beta of 1.4 would be higher. When combined, this information yields the baseline return to be expected on any investment (the risk-free return), plus an added return that is based on the level of risk that an investor is assuming by purchasing a specific stock. This methodology is based totally on the assumption that the level of risk equates directly to the level of return, which additional research has determined to be a reasonably accurate way to determine the cost of equity capital. The main problem with this approach is that a company's beta will vary over time because it may add or subtract subsidiaries that are more or less risky, resulting in an altered degree of risk. Because of the likelihood of change, the equity cost of capital must be recomputed regularly to determine the most recent cost.

The calculation of the equity cost of capital using the CAPM methodology is relatively simple, once all the components of the equation have been accumulated. For example, if the risk-free cost of capital is 5 percent, the return on the Dow Jones Industrials is 12 percent, and ABC Company's beta is 1.5, the cost of equity for ABC Company would be:

$$
\begin{aligned}
\text{Cost of equity capital} &= \text{Risk-free return} + \text{Beta} \\
&\quad (\text{Average stock return} - \text{risk-free return}) \\
\text{Cost of equity capital} &= 5\% + 1.5\,(12\% - 5\%) \\
\text{Cost of equity capital} &= 5\% + 1.5 \times 7\% \\
\text{Cost of equity capital} &= 5\% + 10.5\% \\
\text{Cost of equity capital} &= \underline{15.5\%}
\end{aligned}
$$

Although the example uses a rather high beta that increases the cost of the stock, it is evident that, far from being an inexpensive form of funding, common stock is actually the *most* expensive form, given the size of returns that investors demand in exchange for putting their money at risk with a company. Accordingly, this form of funding should be used the most sparingly in order to keep the cost of capital at a lower level.

Now that we have derived the costs of debt, preferred stock, and common stock, it is time to assemble all three costs into a weighted cost of capital. The remainder of this section is structured in an example format, showing the method by which the weighted cost of capital of the Canary Corporation is calculated.

EXAMPLE

The chief financial officer of the Canary Corporation, Mr. Birdsong, is interested in determining the company's weighted cost of capital, to be used to ensure that projects have a sufficient return on investment, which will keep the company from going to seed. There are two debt offerings on the books. The first is $1 million that was sold below par value, which garnered $980,000 in cash proceeds. The company must pay interest of 8.5 percent on this debt. The second is for $3 million and was sold at par, but included legal fees of $25,000. The interest rate on this debt is 10 percent. There is also $2.5 million of preferred stock on the books, which requires annual interest (or dividend) payments amounting to 9 percent of the amount contributed to the company by investors. Finally, there is $4 million of common stock on the books. The risk-free rate of interest, as defined by the return on current U.S. government securities, is 6 percent, while the return expected from a typical market basket of related stocks is 12 percent. The company's beta is 1.2, and it currently pays income taxes at a marginal rate of 35 percent. What is the Canary Company's weighted cost of capital?

The method we will use is to compile the percentage cost of each form of funding separately and then calculate the weighted cost of capital, based on the amount of funding and percentage cost of each of the forms of funding discussed. We begin with the first debt item, which was $1 million of debt that was sold for $20,000 less than par value, at 8.5 percent debt. The marginal income tax rate is 35 percent. The calculation is:

$$\text{Net after-tax interest percent} = \frac{((\text{Interest expense}) \times (1 - \text{Tax rate})) \times \text{Amount of debt}}{(\text{Amount of debt}) - (\text{Discount on sale of debt})}$$

$$\text{Net after-tax interest percent} = \frac{((8.5) \times (1 - .35)) \times \$1,000,000}{\$1,000,000 - \$20,000}$$

$$\text{Net after-tax interest percent} = \underline{5.638\%}$$

We employ the same method for the second debt instrument, for which there is $3 million of debt that was sold at par. Legal fees of $25,000 were incurred to place the debt, which pays 10 percent interest. The marginal income tax rate remains at 35 percent. The calculation is:

$$\begin{array}{c} \text{Net after-tax} \\ \text{interest percent} \end{array} = \frac{((\text{Interest expense}) \times (1 - \text{Tax rate})) \times \text{Amount of debt}}{(\text{Amount of debt}) - (\text{Legal expense})}$$

$$\text{Net after-tax interest percent} = \frac{((10\%) \times (1 - .35)) \times \$3,000,000}{\$3,000,000 - \$25,000}$$

$$\text{Net after-tax interest percent} = \underline{7.091\%}$$

Having completed the interest expense for the two debt offerings, we move on to the cost of the preferred stock. As noted above, there is $2.5 million of preferred stock on the books, with an interest rate of 9 percent. The marginal corporate income tax does not apply because the interest payments are treated like dividends and are not deductible. The calculation is the simplest of all, for the answer is 9 percent since there is no income tax to confuse the issue.

To arrive at the cost of equity capital, we take from the example a return on risk-free securities of 6 percent, a return of 12 percent that is expected from a typical market basket of related stocks, and a beta of 1.2. We then plug this information into the next formula to arrive at the cost of equity capital:

$$\text{Cost of equity capital} = \text{Risk-free return} + \text{Beta}$$
$$(\text{Average stock return} - \text{risk-free return})$$
$$\text{Cost of equity capital} = 6\% + 1.2\,(12\% - 6\%)$$
$$\text{Cost of equity capital} = \underline{13.2\%}$$

Now that we know the cost of each type of funding, it is a simple matter to construct an exhibit such as the one shown in Exhibit 16.3 that lists the amount of each type of funding and its related cost, which we can quickly sum to arrive at a weighted cost of capital.

When combined into the weighted average calculation shown in Exhibit 16.3, we see that the weighted cost of capital is 9.75 percent. Although there is some considerably less expensive debt on the books, the majority of the funding is comprised of more expensive common and preferred stock, which drives up the overall cost of capital.

EXHIBIT 16.3 Weighted Cost of Capital Calculation

Type of Funding	Amount of Funding	Percentage Cost	Dollar Cost
Debt number 1	$ 980,000	5.638%	$ 55,252
Debt number 2	2,975,000	7.091%	210,957
Preferred stock	2,500,000	9.000%	225,000
Common stock	4,000,000	13.200%	528,000
Totals	$10,455,000	9.75%	$1,019,209

 DIVIDEND POLICY

Dividend policy is a factor to be considered in the management of shareholders' equity for four reasons:

1. Cash dividends paid are the largest recurring charge against retained earnings for most U.S. corporations.
2. The amount of dividends paid, which reduces the amount of equity remaining, will have an impact on the amount of long-term debt that can be prudently issued in view of the long-term debt to equity ratio that usually governs finance.
3. Dividend payout is an influence on the reception of new stock issues.
4. Dividend policy is an element in most loan and credit agreements, with restrictions on how much may be paid.

A certain company may not pay cash dividends on the basis that it can earn a higher return on reinvested earnings than can a shareholder by directly investing in new purchases of stock. This is not always true, so the issue is whether paying a dividend will increase the long-term return to the shareholder. The firm should consider the type of investors attracted to the stock and the expectation of the investors. In general, the ability to invest all the earnings at an acceptable rate of return is not a convincing reason to avoid paying a dividend. After all, a dividend is here and now, and future growth is more problematic. Other than in the case of a highly speculative situation or a company in severe financial difficulty, probably some dividend should be paid. This decision, however, is highly judgmental.

Dividend payments are determined by a number of influences, including:

- Need for additional capital for expansion or other reasons
- Cash flow of the enterprise

- Industry practice
- Shareholders' expectations

The amount to be paid is calculated either by the dividend payout ratio or as a percentage of beginning net worth each year. The most common practice is to measure dividends as a percentage of earnings. The payout ratio is calculated in this way:

$$\text{Payout ratio} = \frac{\text{Annual dividends paid to common shareholders}}{\text{Annual earnings available for common shareholders}}$$
$$\text{(after preferred dividends)}$$

Another way of calculating dividends, although less common than the payout method, is as a percentage of beginning net worth. The calculation is:

$$\text{Dividend payment ratio} = \frac{\text{Annual dividends paid to common shareholders}}{\text{beginning common shareholder book value}}$$

Dividend-paying practices send a message to the financial community, and investors and analysts accept the pattern as an indication of future payments. Hence, when a dividend payment rate is set, a dividend reduction should be avoided if at all possible. Dividend payments may follow any one of these patterns:

- A constant or regular quarterly payment
- A constant pattern with regularly recurring increases
- A constant pattern with irregular increases
- A constant pattern with periodic extra increases so as to avoid committing to regular increases

One type of dividend to be avoided is the special dividend. It does nothing to permanently increase the stock price since it represents a one-time outflow of cash, for which the stock price will promptly increase (when the dividend is announced) and then fall (after it is paid). Investors will assume that the special dividend will not be repeated, so they will not bid up the price of the stock in expectation of any additional special dividend on some unannounced date in the future.

LONG-TERM EQUITY PLANNING

For those companies with a practical financial planning system, the long-term planning sequence might be something like this three-step process.

EXHIBIT 16.4 Proposed Capital Structure

Segment	Preferred Structure	Minimally Acceptable Structure
Long-term debt	20.0%	25.0%
Shareholders' equity	80.0%	75.0%
Total	100.0%	100.0%

1. The company's financial management determines an acceptable capital structure and obtains the agreement of management and the board of directors.
2. As part of the long-range financial plan, the amount of funds required in excess of those available is determined, by year, in an approximate amount.
3. Based on projected needs over several years, the desired capital structure, the relative cost of each segment of capital (debt or equity), the cost of each debt issue, and any constraints imposed by credit agreements, or the judgment of management, the long-term fund requirements are allocated between long-term debt and equity.

Ordinarily the needs of additional equity capital are known some time in advance, and planning to take advantage of propitious market conditions and under generally acceptable terms results in a competitive cost of capital.

Now let us provide some illustrations of these points. Assume that the chief financial officer's recommendation has been approved by both the controller and company management and that the capital structure is as shown in Exhibit 16.4.

Moreover, Exhibit 16.5 presents the capital structure as it is expected to be at the end of the current year.

In the process of completing the strategic planning cycle and the related long-range financial plan, the required long-term funds, without designation as to type or source, are estimated to be $67 million in three years. This program

EXHIBIT 16.5 Projected Capital Structure

Long-term debt	31.5%
Shareholders' equity	68.5%
Total	100.0%

EXHIBIT 16.6 Long-Term Fund Requirements

| | Current Year | Plan Year | | | | | |
Item	(Estimated)	1	2	3	4	5	Total
Funds Required							
Working capital	$25	$30	$36	$ 42	$55	$ 30	$193
Long-term debt repayment	12	12	12	12	12	15	63
Fixed assets	15	14	40	50	15	40	159
Dividends	8	9	10	12	14	15	60
Total	$60	$65	$98	$116	$96	$100	$475
Internally Generated Funds							
Net income	$40	$45	$50	$ 60	$70	$ 75	$300
Depreciation	10	12	20	25	28	31	16
Total	$50	$57	$70	$ 85	$98	$106	$416
Funds required (excess)	$10	$ 8	$28	$ 31	$(2)	$ (6)	$ 59
Cumulative funds required (net)	$10	$ 8	$36	$ 67	$65	$ 59	

for substantial growth is reflected in Exhibit 16.6. Furthermore, after a slight hesitation in plan years 4 and 5, management thinks the cycle will be repeated.

There are a number of observations regarding the preceding funding plans, particularly in regard to the cost of equity, the separation between actual and budgeted debt/equity levels, and the need for different types of funding in the future. The observations follow.

■ *General.* Because the cost of equity capital is highest and issuance of new equity tends to dilute earnings, equity capital generally should be used sparingly, only to maintain the borrowing base and to attain and remain at the desired capital structure.

■ *Current year.* At the end of the current year, equity will provide only 68.5 percent of capital (see Exhibit 16.7), as compared to management's target of 80 percent and a minimally acceptable level of 75 percent. Obviously, the debt share of capitalization is too high.

■ *Plan year 20X5.* Given the start of an acceleration in annual earnings, management decides to hold the dividend payout ratio to 20 percent and to borrow under the term loan agreement (interest rate of 15 percent) the

EXHIBIT 16.7 Long-Term Fund Allocation ($ in Millions)

Year/Item	Beginning Balance	Net Income	Dividends	New Equity Offering	Ending Balance	Year-end % of Capitalization
Shareholders' Equity						
Current year	$260	$40	$ 8		$292	68.5%
Plan years						
20X5	292	45	9		328	72.0
20X6	328	50	10		368	72.0
20X7	368	60	12		416	72.0
20X8	416	70	14		472	76.0
20X9	472	75	15	$ 50	582	81.0
Contingency years						
20X0	582	80	16		646	80.0
20X1	646	85	17		714	83.0
Long-Term Debt						
Current-year, estimate						
Term loan	$100	$10	$—	$ 90		
Mortgage bond, present	46	2	—	44		
	146	12	—	134		
Plan Years						
20X5						
Term loan	$ 90	$10	$8	$ 88	31.5	
Mortgage bond, present	44	2	—	42		
	134	12	—	139		
20X6						
Term loan	$ 88	$10	$—	$ 78	28.0	

EXHIBIT 16.7 *(Continued)*

Year/Item	Beginning Balance	Net Income	Dividends	New Equity Offering	Ending Balance	Year-end % of Capitalization
Mortgage bond, present	42	2		40		
Mortgage bond, new	—	—	28	28	28.0	
	130	12	28	146		
20X7						
Term loan	$ 78	$10	$—	$ 68		
Mortgage bond, present	40	2		38		
Mortgage bond, new	28		31	59		
	146	12	31	165	28.0	
20X8						
Term loan	$ 68	$68	$ —	$ —		
Mortgage bond, present	38	2		36		
Mortgage bond, new	59		58	117		
	165	70	58	153	24.0	
20X9						
Mortgage bond, present	36	13		23		
Mortgage bond, new	117	2	—	115		
	153	15		138	19.0	
Contingency years						
20X0						
Mortgage bond, present	23	13	—	10		
Mortgage bond, new	115	10	—	105		
Debenture, new			50	50		
	138	23	50	165	20.0	
20X1						
Mortgage bond, present	10	10		—		
Mortgage bond, new	105	10		95		
Debenture	50	—		50		
	$165	$20		$145	17.0	

needed $8 million. Even so, the equity share of capitalization will increase from 68.5 percent to 72 percent.

▪ *Plan year 20X6.* With $28 million in new funds required, the company decides, in view of the heavy investment in fixed assets and a lower borrowing rate available, to issue a new mortgage bond. Some of the funds will be "taken down," or received, in this plan year and the balance in the next year. Despite the high level of borrowing, the equity share remains at 72 percent. The management decides it can live with such a level—for a temporary period, given the high volume of income.

▪ *Plan year 20X7.* The balance of the new mortgage bond proceeds covers the requirements with no reduction in the equity share of capitalization.

▪ *Plan year 20X8.* With net income now at a level of $70 million and a proposal by an insurance company to provide new funds through a new mortgage bond, management decides to accept this new loan of $58 million and pay off the more expensive term loan. Given the continued high level of earnings, equity capital at year-end will provide 76 percent of the capitalization. This is within the minimally acceptable standard used by the company.

▪ *Plan year 20X9.* In this last year of the five-year long-range plan, management believes the growth cycle is ready to start again. Without going through the complete long-range planning cycle again, it asks the financial vice president to estimate fund requirements for two more years—the "contingency" years. This quick review discloses that another $50 million will be needed in 20X0, with possibly a limited amount required also in 20X1. Accordingly, to raise the equity capitalization to the desired 80 percent level and to provide the needed equity base for expansion in future years, it plans for an issue of $50 million in equity funds.

The management and board of directors feel comfortable with the equity base; it is sufficiently large to provide reserves in the event of a downturn in business for a limited period, while still being in a position to borrow additionally if this becomes necessary. Exhibit 16.8 presents the summary of the planned debt reduction, new indebtedness to be incurred, shareholders' equity, and capitalization percentages.

In terms of management of shareholders' equity, the emphasis should be on planning, especially long-term planning, so as to achieve the proper capital structure and use it as the basis for prudent borrowing. Additionally, the many other aspects already discussed need to be reviewed, and policies and procedures developed or continued that will enhance shareholders' value. The

EXHIBIT 16.8 Summary of Planned Changes in Capital Structure ($ in millions)

Item	Interest Rate	Beginning Balance Amount	%	Increase/(Decrease) 20X5	20X6	20X7	20X8	20X9	Ending Balance Amount	%
Long-term Debt										
Term loan	15%	$ 90		$(2)	$(10)	$(10)	$(68)		$ —	—
Mortgage bond	14	44		(2)	(2)	(2)	(2)	$(13)	23	
Mortgage bond	12	—			28			(2)	26	
Mortgage bond	11.5	—				31	58		89	
Total		134	31.5	(4)	16	19	(12)	(15)	138	19.0
Shareholders' Equity										
Beginning balance		292							292	
Net income		—		45	50	60	70	75	300	
Dividends		—		(9)	(10)	(12)	(14)	(15)	(60)	
Net issue		—		—	—	—	—	50	50	
Subtotal		292	68.5	36	40	48	56	110	582	81.0
Total		$426	100	$ 32	$ 56	$ 67	$ 44	$ 95	$720	100

EXHIBIT 16.9 Annual Budget for Shareholder's Equity

Month	Beginning Balance	Estimated Net Income	Dividend Payments	Purchase of Treasury Shares	Estimated Dividend Reinvestments	Estimated Options Exercised	Ending Balance
January	$158,500	$ 2,650		$1,000			$160,150
February	160,150	2,410		1,000		$ 500	162,060
March	162,060	2,790	$1,720		$ 80		163,210
April	163,210	2,840					166,050
May	166,050	2,620		1,200		500	167,970
June	167,970	2,530	1,620		100		168,980
July	168,980	2,600		1,000			170,580
August	170,580	2,860				500	173,940
September	173,940	2,820	1,620		100		175,240
October	175,240	2,770		1,000			177,010
November	177,010	2,710				700	180,420
December	180,420	2,800	1,520		100		181,800
Total	$158,500	$32,400	$6,480	$5,200	$380	$2,200	$181,800

portion of the annual plan related to equity changes should be similar to that found in Exhibit 16.9.

REPURCHASING COMMON SHARES

Conceptually, a company is enfranchised to invest capital in the production of goods or services. Hence it should not knowingly invest in projects that will not provide a sufficiently high rate of return to adequately compensate the investors for the risk assumed. In other words, the enterprise should not invest simply because funds are available. Business management should identify sufficiently profitable projects that are consistent with corporate strategy, determine the capital required, and make the investment. Shareholders might interpret the repurchase of common stock as the lack of available investment opportunities. To some, the repurchase of company stock is not an "investment" but a return of capital. It is "disfinancing."

The next list presents some legitimate reasons for the repurchase of common stock.

- Shares may be needed for stock options or employee stock purchase plans, but management does not wish to increase the total shares outstanding.
- Shares are required in the exercise of outstanding warrants or for the conversion of outstanding convertibles, without issuing "new" shares.
- Shares are needed for a corporate acquisition.

Some guidelines in deciding to repurchase shares follow.

- If a company is excessively leveraged, it might do well to use cash to pay down existing long-term debt to reach the capital structure goal it envisions and not repurchase common shares.
- Management should examine its cash requirements for a reasonable time into the future, including fixed assets requirements, working capital needs, and other investment options, before it concludes that excess cash is available and that the equity capital genuinely is in excess of apparent long-term demands.
- The cash dividend policy should be examined to see that it helps increase the market price of the stock.
- Only after such a review should management decide to dispose of "excess equity" by purchasing company stock.

The best way to establish a strong case for a minimum stock price is for the board to approve a long-term stock repurchase program that allows for preapproved stock purchases at a specific trigger price. For example, if the board authorizes the company to buy back shares whenever the market price of its stock drops to $5, then this establishes a floor of $5, below which the stock's price is unlikely to drop. This tends to reduce the variability of the stock price, and may attract a group of investors who are less tolerant of risk. The key component of such a buy-back program is a long-term commitment to it since its nonrenewal may trigger a sudden price drop that will result in some investor turnover.

 ## CAPITAL STOCK RECORDS

An administrative concern in the management of shareholders' equity relates to the maintenance of capital stock records. In larger companies, the stock transfer agent keeps stock ledgers and transfer records. The information relative to payment of dividends on outstanding shares, for example, is secured from this source. The database is contained on computer files, and any number of sortings can produce relevant data regarding ownership, such as by geographical dispersion, the history and timing of purchases, market price activity, and the nature of the owners (e.g., individuals or institutions). Under these circumstances, the company merely maintains a ledger control account for each class of stock.

If a company has its own transfer department, then a separate ledger account must be maintained for each stockholder regarding each class of stock. The ledger must contain information such as the stockholder's name and address, the date of changes in holdings, the certificate numbers issued and surrendered, the number of shares in each transaction, and the total numbers of shares held. Optionally, the record may include a history of dividend payments. The stock ledgers should be supported by registration and transfer records that give the details of each transaction.

Management has an interest in monitoring, perhaps monthly, large holdings and the changes therein. Such a review may provide signals about possible takeover attempts. Companies may use outside consultants to perform this monitoring and to solicit proxies.

CHAPTER SEVENTEEN

Operational Accounting

T HIS CHAPTER FOCUSES ON how to upgrade the accounting function so that it runs as a world-class department should. First we define the jobs of everyone in the department, then describe the creation of a very specific work schedule and staff meetings to follow up on particularly difficult problems. Then we move on to the proper treatment of accounting errors and how to avoid them, followed by a lengthy discussion of how to use best practices to improve operations. We also review the pluses and minuses associated with outsourcing selected functions within the department. By following these guidelines, a controller can create a confident accounting department that is thoroughly capable of quickly and accurately processing all assigned tasks.

CREATE DEPARTMENTAL JOB DESCRIPTIONS

The first step in running an accounting department is to determine who is responsible for each task. Without such a determination, there is no way to control the flow of activities or to know whom to talk to about fixing problems. The typical departmental structure is for there to be one or more assistant controllers who are responsible for a selected set of functional areas, such as accounts payable and accounts receivable, or cost accounting and the general ledger. Below these personnel are a number of accountants and clerks. The organizational structure is similar to the one shown in Exhibit 17.1.

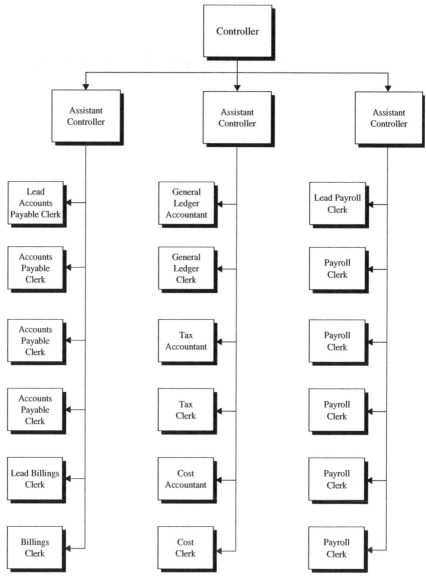

EXHIBIT 17.1   Accounting Department Organizational Structure

Once the controller has determined the reporting relationships of the accounting group, it is time to define the exact job description for each position. These descriptions should be set up in a standard format by job title, not by individual, since the descriptions must otherwise be constantly restructured as employees come and go or are promoted within the department. Detailed job descriptions for the billings clerk, collections clerk, payables clerk, and payroll clerk were noted in Chapter 1.

After each job description is created, the controller should review it in detail with each person whose job it describes since there may be missing line items that the controller has overlooked. Once it has been finalized, each employee should be given his or her own copy, and the controller or one of the assistant controllers should go over it with him or her at each performance review to ensure that all tasks are being completed and that the description is still accurate.

 ## CREATE A DEPARTMENTAL TRAINING PROGRAM

Once the controller has decided which employees are supposed to complete which tasks, it is time to see if they are capable of doing so. The best method is a combination of sitting with them to see how they complete work and reviewing their error rates and time needed for completed work. It takes time to form an accurate opinion of the abilities of each person, so a controller should allot at least a month, and probably longer, to this task. Once the controller has completed this initial review, the next step is to create a matrix of training programs needed to bring the accounting staff up to an expert level in all assigned areas of responsibility.

This matrix is an extremely important tool. It precisely delineates the training requirements for each person, as well as when the controller expects training to be completed. Exhibit 17.2 presents an example of such a training matrix. It lists the names of accounting employees across the top of the report and the names of training modules down the left side. The training grid has a shaded area for those training classes that have not yet been completed, with a due date inside it. For those training classes that an employee *has* completed, the shading is removed and the completion date is listed. For cases where the employee is not required to complete a class, there is no shading or due date.

An important point in regard to the use of a training program is that the required classes be targeted specifically at the current or prospective job

EXHIBIT 17.2 Sample Employee Training Matrix

[Correct score of at least 80% required to pass training]
[Shaded areas indicate required classes and due dates]

Training Description	Anderson, B. (Assistant Controller)	Draston, Q. (Cost Accountant)	Dudley, F. (Accounts Payable)	Ephraim, J. (Accounts Receivable)	Jones, J. (General Ledger)
Accounting Software Training:					
A/P - Entering a credit	July-01		July-01		
A/P - Entering an invoice	July-01		July-01		
A/P - Entering an invoice	July-01		August-01		
A/P - Matching documentation	July-01		August-01		
A/R - Applying cash	August-01			July-01	
A/R - Creating a credit	August-01			July-01	
A/R - Creating an invoice	August-01			August-01	
A/R - Deleting an invoice	August-01			August-01	
G/L - Alter report format	May-01				July-01
G/L - Create chart of accounts	May-01				August-01
G/L - Enter a journal entry	May-01	July-01			September-01
G/L - Enter the budget	May-01				October-01
Accounting Seminars:					
Acquisitions seminar	September-01				
Archiving	April-01				
Bank reconciliations	October-01				November-01
Closing the books	November-01				December-01
Consolidations	December-01				December-01
Cost accounting, activity-based	March-01	August-01			

[Correct score of at least 80% required to pass training]

[Shaded areas indicate required classes and due dates]

Training Description	Anderson, B. (Assistant Controller)	Draston, Q. (Cost Accountant)	Dudley, F. (Accounts Payable)	Ephraim, J. (Accounts Receivable)	Jones, J. (General Ledger)
Cost accounting, direct	March-01	August-01			
Cost accounting, job cost	March-01	September-01			
Cost accounting, process	March-01	September-01			
Foreign currency translation	January-02				
Incorporation documentation	February-02				
Outsourcing	March-02				
Payroll taxes	April-02				
Personal property taxes	May-02		September-01		
Sales taxes	June-02		October-01		
Target costing	March-01	October-01			
PC Software Training:					
Beginning Access			June-01		March-01
Intermediate Access	June-01	October-01			
Advanced Access	July-02	November-01			
Beginning Excel			May-01	April-01	July-01
Intermediate Excel	April-01	December-01		May-01	August-01
Advanced Excel	August-02	December-01			September-01
Beginning Word				August-01	
Intermediate Word	March-01			September-01	February-01
Advanced Word				October-01	

305

functions of each person. It is useless to force employees to train for a skill that they cannot use because they will forget the skill soon, and their time has been wasted. Similarly, if the controller expects employees to take on a new job function in the near future, the training should be assigned *immediately* prior to the assumption of the associated new job functions, so that the employees have no chance to forget what they have learned.

Training is made easier if there are prepackaged training programs available, either within the company or through an outside service, that meet the needs of the controller's training program. Because training for accountants frequently involves the company's accounting software, much of this training may be through seminars offered by the software provider. The other most common area of training for accountants is in specialized accounting topics, perhaps involving changes in Financial Accounting Standards Board (FASB) standards. For training updates in this area, it is best to arrange for seminar notifications from the local CPA organization or from the Institute of Management Accountants. If the staff needs to learn more about PC-based software packages, such as Excel, Word, or PowerPoint, many training organizations provide this service. Maintaining this list of possible training classes is an important part of the controller's training responsibilities.

Training is an area to which the typical controller assigns a low priority because the benefit may not be immediately obvious, and employees usually do not push for it either. However, given the long-term benefit of having a highly trained and competent staff, the controller should schedule some time once a month, on a recurring basis, to meet with the accounting staff and go over their training accomplishments from the last month as well as their goals for the next month. Only by ingraining training into the fabric of the department in this manner can the controller be assured that the staff will follow a consistent and targeted training program.

CLEAR OUT EXCESS DOCUMENTATION

For a new controller who is trying to attain control over an accounting department, the sheer quantity of paperwork can seem overwhelming—piles of documentation related to taxes, billings, supplier invoices, cash receipts, and on and on. There seems no end to the paperwork and nowhere to start. To avoid this problem, one of the very first acts of any controller should be to clear as much paperwork out of the department's confines as possible. This means going through every filing cabinet, every drawer, and every box, and determining the age and value of the papers contained inside. The main point is to get extra copies and information not currently needed off the premises, so that the controller can clearly see the tasks that still need to be done. This does *not* mean throwing out any documents. The objective is strictly to move out the documentation, not get rid of it permanently. Instead, box all the unneeded items, carefully label the boxes, and create an index that lists what is in every box, so that the accounting staff can easily find it again.

 ## STREAMLINE THE ACCOUNTING WORKFLOW

There is the potential for an endless series of improvement projects within the accounting department. Being a department that handles large quantities of paper, the accounting area can rapidly become choked with clutter, which greatly impedes the flow of work. Also, certain employees are more comfortable with clutter than others, and so will allow unusual quantities of materials to proliferate. The controller can attack this problem by focusing on the ongoing elimination of the following items, all of which interfere with the orderly flow of work:

- ▪ Unneeded chairs, desks, filing cabinets, and carts
- ▪ Unneeded computers, printers, phones, copiers, and fax machines
- ▪ Unneeded posted items, such as outdated labor law posters, white boards, corkboards, and old messages on those boards
- ▪ Excess quantities of office supplies at employee desks, such as printer paper, staplers, tape, and so on.

It is particularly important to search in all possible areas for these items: in corners and behind desks, and especially in drawers, cabinets, and closets, where such items tend to accumulate. To keep accumulation from occurring in these areas, consider removing all doors and drawers in the department. This means that all items are out in plain view, where they can be more easily monitored and therefore eliminated.

Whenever these items are removed from the accounting area, don't immediately throw them out or send them back to a storage area. Instead, pile them in a holding area that is readily accessible to the staff, so they have a few days to retrieve anything they really need. Then remove the remaining items from the holding area. It may be necessary to tag each item in the holding area, to identify where it came from and how long it should stay there until it is removed. If it is unlikely that an item in the holding area will be used within the next year, don't even consign it to storage—instead, put it in the trash or donate it. Otherwise the storage area will become excessively cluttered.

There is the particular problem of what to do about those employees who persist in piling up vast quantities of paperwork and supplies in their work areas. One possibility is the complete rebuilding of a work area. This involves *completely* emptying out someone's work area, even removing computer equipment and related cables. Then clean the entire area, and only put the most necessary items back. All other items are removed to a location well away from the employee, who then spends a week deciding how many items that were shifted elsewhere are actually needed. This process will likely liberate a startling number of supplies, and also allow a great deal of paperwork to be filed away.

This process is by no means an annual event—think more in terms of a weekly or monthly review of the accounting area. Clutter increases constantly, so only continual attention will keep it in check.

In addition to clutter reduction, consider reviewing work flows within the department. To do so, create a map of the department, noting all cubicles, office furniture, and equipment. Then note on it the travel paths taken by employees for *all* activities and note their frequency of travel. A likely result will be the repositioning or removal of furniture and equipment. Also, if the department relies on high-capacity, centralized office equipment, such as printers, faxes and copiers, it will likely make more sense to acquire a large number of lower-capacity units to position very close to individual employees or small groups of staff. Further, the map will clarify which employees need to be clustered together, along with certain document storage areas. By making these changes, travel times within the department can be substantially reduced.

A key detractor from optimum workflow is the filing cabinet. It is a central source of documentation, and because it is extremely heavy, it cannot be moved. Instead, employees must travel to it—possibly many times over the course of a day. An alternative is to buy a number of office carts with wheels; employees load these carts with the files they will need for that day, and position the carts nearby in their work areas. The amount of travel time reduction can be astonishingly high.

The cubicle can be a considerable detriment to an efficient department because it cannot be easily moved. Instead, swap out cubicles for desks, which can be easily reconfigured to match work flows. For example, group together the desks of the billing, cash application, and collection employees, so they can more easily discuss payment issues. If there is an increased need for more staff in this area, then simply move another desk into the group. If there is no way to avoid cubicles, then at least reduce their wall height, so that employees can more easily interact. High cubicle walls are the bane of employee communications.

Another issue that is frequently overlooked is the storage and replenishment of supplies. There is usually a central storage area for the department, but this is not always the best way to position supplies. For example, consider positioning printer and copier supplies right next to those items, so that users do not have to travel anywhere to find them. Also, assign replenishment responsibility to a single individual, and make sure that person uses a standardized checklist to update supplies on a daily basis. Otherwise, the department will lose valuable time searching for supplies that do not exist. The result of these activities should be a reduction in the accounting department's required amount of square footage, which in turn results in less travel time within the department. Thus, a good metric for departmental improvement is either total square footage or (better yet) square footage per person. This metric can be taken to an extreme since the staff could end up packed together like sardines in a can, so don't use it as an exclusive metric.

In summary, the accounting department can be continually streamlined to improve its efficiency. The top improvement considerations are to move high-usage items as close to the users as possible, and to remove anything that physically gets in the way.

DOCUMENT ALL MAJOR PROCESSES

Although the controller has now determined the skill levels of the accounting staff and organized them along functional lines, he or she still has no knowledge of how the department operates. This problem can be solved by undertaking an in-depth review and documentation of all processes.

The best way to begin a process review is to sit with the most knowledgeable person who is involved with each function and document every step of the process in great detail. The documentation should itemize the exact file locations used, both in the computer and in filing cabinets, as well as the precise keystrokes needed to complete each step. The reason for this level of detail is that the controller probably will incorporate the written procedure into a departmental procedures manual that will be used by new recruits who must learn the system from scratch. After the first draft is complete, review it with the most knowledgeable staff person and perhaps also distribute it through the department, with a request to highlight errors and then return the corrected document.

Once the initial process documentation is complete, review the workloads required to complete each process with either the assistant controllers or the most experienced staff people available, with a particular emphasis on peak work periods of the month, additional staffing requirements, particular areas in which errors are endemic, and changes that will smooth the flow of work. Of particular interest is the concept of process centering, which means that much of the move and queue time inherent in most processes can be eliminated by centralizing as much of the work as possible with one person, rather than only allowing one person to complete a small task out of the entire process, with many other people completing their small, specialized tasks later in the process flow. For example, the accounts payable process can switch to process centering by having a single person conduct all documentation matching, supplier contacts, research, and data entry, rather than keeping these functions separated among different specialists.

 ## SCHEDULE THE DEPARTMENT

Once the controller has outlined each person's job and has identified the major processes, it is time to create a schedule of activities for each position. This should be a simple calendar, such as the one shown in Exhibit 17.3 that lists the major activities that each person is to complete on a given date. Each person should have a different calendar that matches his or her job responsibilities. In order to maintain good control of daily activities, the controller should have a master calendar that notes all the activities of all personnel, which he or she can then use to walk through the department each day to ensure that tasks are being completed on time. There may be a few positions, such as the accounts payable clerical positions, where the job does not vary much per day, so a calendar is not necessary.

Activity calendars of this sort likely will require correction at least once a month, so it is best to hold brief staff meetings at the end of the previous month to go over these changes and to hand out new activity calendars. It is also useful to supplement these schedules with a vacation calendar, perhaps of the erasable whiteboard variety, that is posted in a visible spot in the department where employees can list their approved days off. This is a very useful tool for the controller because it clarifies those days on which backup support may be needed in order to complete assigned tasks.

Sunday	Monday	Tuesday	Wednesday	Thursday	Friday	Saturday
1	2 Month-end close Weekly statistics	3 Issue flash report	4 Department meeting	5 Collections review Check run	6 Financials due Executive committee	7
8	9 Weekly statistics	10 Quarterly staff review	11 Department meeting Target cost review	12 Collections review Check run	13 Executive committee	14
15	16 Weekly statistics	17	18 Department meeting ABC review	19 Collections review Check run	20 Executive committee	21
22	23 Weekly statistics	24 Inventory review	25 Department meeting Job cost review	26 Collections review Check run	27 Executive committee	28
29	30 Weekly statistics Pre-close meeting	31 Review accruals				

EXHIBIT 17.3 Activity Calendar for Controller

311

CORRECT THE UNDERLYING CAUSES OF ERRORS

Depending on the level of experience, training, and procedural accuracy in an accounting department, it is possible that the accounting staff spends up to 50 percent of its time just correcting errors from earlier transactions. For example, a fixed asset may have been recorded in the fixed asset register with an incorrect depreciation period, or an expense may have been charged to the wrong account number, or a customer may have been billed twice, or a supplier may have been paid twice. All of these transactions must be corrected, and each one may take hours to fix properly. Furthermore, because the adjustments are exceptions to the normal routine that someone (i.e., an auditor) may not understand when he or she reviews it at some point in the future, the reasons why the corrections have been made also must be fully documented, which takes up still more time. Finally, if the corrections are large enough, they may even have a material impact on the financial statements, which results in additional explanation as footnotes in the statements. This also takes time, not to mention being an embarrassment to the accounting department. Unless the controller corrects the core reasons why these errors continue to occur, the accounting department will never have time to work its way out from under the workload related to error correction.

When correcting errors, follow a specific set of steps that greatly assist in focusing attention on those errors that arise most frequently. The first step is to keep a log of all errors found. This log should include the nature of the error, when it occurred, who caused the error, and the underlying reason for the problem. Exhibit 17.4 shows an example of this log. Compiling this log can take some work, as the accounting staff may hide its errors from the controller and fix the problems without publicizing their mistakes. To find these errors, create error-spotting systems, such as a monthly review of all credits issued to customers, all journal entries, and all unvouchered accounts payable, which are the most common locations for error corrections. Then research each item found and insert it into the log. The next step is to create a Pareto analysis (i.e., 20 percent of the problems cause 80 percent of the total errors) that groups the errors by quantity of occurrences, so that the controller can see which problems arise the most frequently. Then target those errors causing the bulk of the problems, outline a correction plan, and implement it, which will rapidly reduce the incidence of errors. Error correction should be one of the key functions of the controller because it has such a major operational impact on the efficiency of the accounting department.

EXHIBIT 17.4 Example of an Accounting Error Log

Date Error Found	Date Error Occurred	Person Causing Error	Error Type	Cause of Error
06/11/11	03/04/11	Smith, J.	Incorrect pricing	Due to special deal by salesperson.
06/10/11	06/09/11	Novak, K.	Incorrect supplier cost	Due to incorrect accounts payable entry, shifting dollar amount by one decimal.
06/10/11	05/31/11	Orson, P.	Incorrect payroll accrual	Due to not using standard journal entry calculation to compile month-end expense.
06/09/11	06/09/11	Dudley, F.	Incorrect property tax accrual	Did not include cost of assets at secondary location.
06/09/11	06/01/11	Johnson, A.	Incorrect pricing	Due to customer service overriding standard price in computer.
06/08/11	02/28/11	Smith, J.	Incorrect cash book balance	Did not complete bank reconciliation last month.
06/08/11	01/13/11	Johnson, A.	Incorrect supplier cost	Due to incorrect accounts payable entry, shifting dollar amount by one decimal.
06/08/11	05/15/11	Anderson, L.	Tape inventory too high	Due to unit of measure change by engineering that switched tape quantity in inches to quantity in rolls.

An additional column that could be added to the example is one for the size of the error, in case the controller wants to focus on fixing problems of great magnitude, rather than those with the highest incidence of occurrence.

The reason for the "Date Error Occurred" column in the example is that the controller may have already fixed a problem that has only now been discovered. For example, if the error is dated three months previously, but the controller fixed the underlying problem the week before, then it can be safely ignored. However, if the problem occurred in just the past few days, then the underlying problem is clearly still an issue and requires further action.

It is also important to create a feedback loop to the accounting staff regarding the elimination of errors because this system will have a major negative impact on staff morale if it is not presented to them properly. To use a real-life example, a general manager created this technique to spot every conceivable problem in a company and used it to target employees for firing, rather than focusing on the problems that the system had highlighted. As a result, employee morale disintegrated, many staff left the company, and those remaining decided not to inform the general manager of any new problems since they eventually received the blame for the problems. A vastly better approach is to inform the accounting staff of what the process is designed to do and keep them informed during every phase of the system installation. Also, staff members should be included in the decision making for resolving errors; their participation will give rise to more fruitful ideas than any controller could originate alone.

 ## USE OF BEST PRACTICES

Even after documenting the accounting department's work flow, positioning employees in the correct jobs, and setting them up for the appropriate training programs, there is no assurance that the department will operate in a sufficiently effective manner. The controller may compare the work done by his or her accounting staff and find that it falls well behind the efficiency level of the accounting department of a competing company. The reason for the difference may be that the competition is using best practices to improve its operations. A best practice is any operational improvement that allows the accounting staff to generate more work with an equal or less amount of effort. A constant stream of innovation is coming out of companies all over the world, so there is no end to the number of best practices one can implement. The main problem is finding them. One source is the author's, *Accounting Best Practices* (Hoboken, NJ: John Wiley & Sons), for which a new edition is released every few years; the book lists and explains a large number of best practices, including implementation issues, control problems, and related costs.

Once a controller has discovered a best practice that may fit into his or her organization, it is very important to research the issue thoroughly to ensure that these points have been covered prior to commencing with an implementation:

- *Cost-benefit analysis.* A best practice may seem extraordinarily "sexy" in concept, but the controller always must ensure that the cost of installing it does not exceed the savings from using it. For example, a document imaging system may eliminate virtually all the paperwork from an accounting department, but the only identifiable savings from doing so may be the storage costs that are perhaps a few hundred dollars per month or year.

■ *Control issues.* A new best practice improvement may result in a major reduction in the volume of work, but it also may eliminate a key control point in the old system that is being replaced. If so, there is now a control risk that may result in a loss that greatly exceeds the potential savings from using the best practice. For example, using procurement cards to replace the bulk of a company's small purchases will avoid the use of purchase order authorizations, thereby allowing procurement card users to abuse small purchases, secure in the knowledge that no one is reviewing what they buy.

■ *Capacity.* If a controller is contemplating a mammoth project that will vastly improve the efficiency of the accounting department, it would be useful first to determine the capacity of the department to perform the installation because it must find the time among its other work to complete the project. It is unrealistic to assume that the existing staff, which is usually overworked, can also complete additional work related to best practice installations. Accordingly, often it is necessary to schedule additional help, either from other departments or consultants, who can assist with or even manage the work.

■ *Murphy's law.* The controller always should expect that something will go wrong with the installation of any best practice and be prepared for the worst possible case. For example, if switching to an automated vacation accrual tracking system that lists accruals on employee pay stubs, what must be done if some of the accruals are incorrect? The controller should prepare a plan for this contingency and expect to use it.

■ *Time requirements.* The longer an installation project runs, the worse its chances of succeeding because there inevitably will be other work that will take priority, the spirits of the implementation team will drop, and it will be more difficult to continue to obtain both funding and the support of senior management.

■ *Track record.* If the controller has a poor track record for installing best practices in the past, for whatever reason, it will be very difficult to convince the staff to participate in yet another project with any degree of enthusiasm. In such cases, it is best to start with an extremely small project that can be completed in the shortest possible time period, in order to build up the trust of the department.

■ *Personnel issues.* If a proposed best practice will require the approval or participation of someone who does not have a good record for assisting in previous implementations, then the controller must fix the problem with this person—through replacement, presenting a convincing argument, or shifting responsibility to a different person—before beginning to think about any other implementation-related issues. Without total personnel support, a best practice cannot be installed.

■ *Support by top management.* If a best practice can be installed without any involvement from other departments, then the chance of success is much higher than if another department must be brought into the process because this other group may have an entirely different agenda and therefore not want to cooperate. Given the level of difficulty when other departments are involved, the controller always should be sure that the top management group has fully bought into the best practice concept and will be fully supportive if other departments cause difficulties.

If the controller has reviewed the preceding items and finds no roadblocks that could seriously interfere with implementation efforts, it is time to determine which best practices to install first. The key issue here is to not immediately go after the one item with the biggest potential payback because it may be the most difficult or expensive one to implement. Instead, focus on creating an accounting organization that is used to always working on the implementation and maintenance of just a few best practices at a time, so that there is a tradition of improvement woven into the fabric of the department.

 ## OUTSOURCING SELECTED ACCOUNTING FUNCTIONS

Once the controller has straightened out the accounting process flow, eliminated recurring errors, and installed best practices, it may become evident that the department is spending too much of its resources on those accounting activities that do not create value for the company. For example, there may be a large workforce of hourly personnel that requires a numerous in-house payroll staff and lots of management attention, whereas the main value driver from the accounting perspective is generating cost accounting reports for the management team regarding the margins being earned on company products. In a situation such as this, the controller may want to review the cost-benefit of shifting some of the less important accounting functions to a supplier, who will run them on behalf of the controller.

All of the accounting functions can be outsourced, but the most common one by far is payroll. Such major suppliers as ADP, Paychex, and Ceridian perform the payroll processing for tens of thousands of companies. The reason why this function is commonly outsourced is that it is a combination of being a non–value-added activity and one that can result in significant government fines if tax remittances are not made by specified dates. Thus, with lots of downside risk and no upside potential for doing the job better, many controllers elect to hand this painful chore to a supplier. Other accounting functions are not so clear-cut, however. Smaller firms can have a supplier process their billings and accounts payable off-site, while outside bookkeepers can process the month-end close for a very small company. There are also a few cases where a supplier will take over the entire accounting department. However, there are also good reasons for treading carefully in these nonpayroll areas because the cost of using a supplier may greatly exceed the cost of performing the same tasks in-house. Also, relations between the company and its supplier can become strained if the outsourcing deal does not work out well, and the controller may be constantly bogged down in contract revisions, when he or she thought there would be more time available for other activities. Accounting functions that can be outsourced include:

- Bank reconciliations
- Check printing
- Collections
- Internal auditing
- Payroll
- Period closings
- Tax form preparation
- Transaction processing

If a controller decides to proceed with outsourcing an accounting function, there are several contractual issues to consider. In the case of payroll processing, the main variable is the price of the service, which is divided into a variable fee per person, plus a fixed monthly charge. Both fees are negotiable, although other terms do not vary much. The outsourcing of tax form preparation can be negotiated on the price of the service provided, as well as the specific people used by the supplier to complete the work. A controller usually can specify that the same group of people work on all tax forms, so that there is a base of experience and consistency. The main focus of collections outsourcing is the price, which can be either a fixed fee per invoice collected or more commonly a percentage of the dollars collected. Giving a supplier a higher volume of collections work can be used as leverage to reduce the per-invoice cost to the company. From a contractual standpoint, internal auditing is similar to tax form preparation in that the primary items for negotiation are the hourly rate and the personnel to be used. Another issue is what type of internal auditing methodology will be used, which the controller can specify. The contract for transaction processing requires the largest amount of negotiation. The single largest issue here is to avoid add-on fees (which tend to be very high) by rolling as many tasks into the monthly baseline fee as possible. Also, if company personnel are being transferred to the supplier, the minimum period for which they will be retained or the severance pay they will receive must be specified. In addition, the minimum period over which key personnel will be retained on the company's account before they can be moved to other supplier work sites must be determined—this keeps experienced personnel working on company business for as long as possible. Finally, the controller should be sure to retain approval control over any efficiencies the supplier wants to implement, because these may change the flow of information to other parts of the company and thus have political consequences. Given the number of negotiable items, it is apparent that a controller must be prepared to negotiate transaction outsourcing at some length in order to arrive at an advantageous contract with a supplier.

When outsourcing accounting functions, there are a few transitional issues to be aware of so that the shift to a supplier is as painless as possible. First, no matter what function is given to a supplier, there must be a functional coordinator who is in charge of the move, so that there is a single responsible person who can monitor the process. This person anticipates problems, deals with supplier and personnel issues, and tracks the progress of the transition against a time and activities budget. If payroll is being outsourced, then the key issue is the timing of the transition because it is easiest for the supplier if it takes place on January 1 of the new year, when the year-to-date records for all employees are reset to zero. Otherwise, the supplier cannot guarantee that the information that will appear on each employee's annual W-2 form will be correct. Also, a payroll supplier offers a number of add-on services, such as check stuffing, direct deposit, and automatic vacation accruals; however, it is best to transition to the most basic functions first to ensure that they work properly and then incrementally add on the other options later. If the controller is shifting the preparation of financial statements to a supplier, then the main issue is to verify with the supplier the individual accounts that will roll up into separate line items on the financial statements and to monitor this information for several months to ensure that the correct roll-up is occurring. When outsourcing the internal audit function, there are several extra steps to complete. Because the auditors will be meeting with many employees throughout the company, it is important to screen them for a minimum level of experience, then walk them through all relevant policies and procedures, train them in the use of the in-house auditing procedures (if they are to be used), negotiate the details of the audit plan for the upcoming year, and set up a monitoring plan to ensure that the audits are being conducted to the controller's satisfaction. Tax form preparation is much easier to begin because the controller only has to authorize the auditing firm to begin work, which it can then do based on the audit work papers it has already prepared; however, if the tax work is to be done by a different supplier, then the controller must send written permission to the auditing firm for it to copy all relevant audit work papers and send them to the tax preparation firm. The transition of transaction processing is the most difficult task of all. It involves transferring the accounting staff to the supplier, training any additional staff or supplier managers, either shifting the company's accounting database and application programs to the supplier's location or shifting the database to the supplier's software, and testing to ensure that the data have been moved successfully. The transition for transaction processing can be so complicated that a controller should assign one or more senior staff members to oversee this process.

Another part of outsourcing is maintaining proper control over the suppliers who are now running parts of the accounting department. A key issue is to keep the outsourcing of the internal audit function away from any suppliers who are handling other parts of the accounting department; otherwise, the supplier's auditors will be reviewing their own activities, which is a poor way to control the department. Another good control is to set up separate general ledger accounts for each supplier who is handling accounting department functions, summarize all their billed expenses through these accounts, and compare the expenses to the contractual amounts that were originally agreed on. Also, consider building bonus and penalty clauses into the contract with all suppliers, so that they have an incentive to complete required work both accurately and on time. Finally, there should be a periodic review meeting with supplier management, preferably quarterly, to go over problems that have arisen since the last meeting and how to resolve them. By keeping the lines of communication open between the controller and suppliers, most problems can be quickly resolved.

Setting up adequate controls over suppliers of accounting functions is not enough, however. The controller must be able to measure their performance to ensure that predetermined standards are being attained, which may result in bonus payments or penalties, depending on the outcome. In the case of collections, the controller's main concern is the supplier's ability to collect the highest possible proportion of overdue accounts receivable. Accordingly, the best measure is the percentage of collected funds from the dollars of billings that were assigned to the supplier. If a supplier is creating financial statements for the controller, the two main concerns are accuracy and timeliness. Accordingly, the controller should measure the accuracy of all accruals made, the number of material irregularities that must be adjusted in later financial statements, and the time required to issue the statements. If internal auditing is outsourced, then the controller should be most concerned with the supplier's ability to complete a high percentage of the audits that were originally agreed on. Another good measure is the average cost per audit. If payroll is being outsourced, then appropriate measures are the timeliness of the supplier in paying payroll taxes to the government, the average transaction cost per employee paid, and the number of payroll payments sent by the supplier to the wrong company locations. If a supplier is handling tax form preparation, then the controller certainly wants to know about any tax penalties paid that are due to incorrect or late tax filings. Finally, if the controller outsources transaction processing, several review measures should be used. The most important is the average cost per transaction, which should be compared to the cost prior to using the supplier, to ensure that costs are in line with expectations. Another is the supplier's error rate in completing transactions, although this is a difficult one to measure (because the supplier can easily cover up any errors). A major measurement from the perspective of the rest of the company is the supplier's timeliness in completing transactions, especially when this involves the processing and payment of employee expense reports. Finally, if the supplier is responsible for accounts payable, then a significant measure is ensuring that 100 percent of all possible early payment discounts have been taken. A controller should consider these measures to be nothing more than the bare minimum set of measures to use when dealing with suppliers; add as many as necessary to track their performance adequately.

A final issue is the management of outsourced functions. Although suppliers are technically responsible for their output, the controller is held responsible for all aspects of his or her department by senior management and so must stay in close touch with the activities of all suppliers. To do this, there must still be tight management control of the outsourced functions from within the company. This means that the controller should assign one or more assistant controllers the task of supervising all suppliers. These people should receive extra help from the company's legal counsel or purchasing staff in the matter of negotiating and reviewing contracts. Their typical job descriptions will be to: negotiate supplier contracts; authorize payments to suppliers; measure suppliers' performance; monitor supplier service levels and discuss any changes needed to improve them; review and approve all supplier outputs, such as financial statements or completed tax forms; and manage the transfer of functions to the suppliers. These are significant changes from the typical role of accounting managers, who tend to specialize in particular accounting areas, so some extra management training may be necessary for these employees before they are fully equipped to take on the task of managing the suppliers to whom accounting functions have been outsourced.

Outsourcing is a possibility for most accounting departments, but it must be investigated properly and used with care in order to achieve the maximum benefit at a minimal cost to the company.

CHAPTER EIGHTEEN

The Fast Close

O NE OF THE MOST common challenges for the controller is to close the month-end books and issue financial statements as fast as possible. The resulting statements are being demanded by corporate management, outside investors, and the Securities and Exchange Commission (for public companies) on the shortest possible timelines. However, the closing process has traditionally been a slow one—several surveys reveal that the average company requires about two weeks to close its subsidiary's books, followed by roughly another three weeks to roll up the results into corporate-level financial statements. Companies with more organized closing systems can reduce this process to about two weeks, while those companies with the best closing processes can reduce the entire interval to four days. These results represent a slight improvement in closing times over the past few years, but there is no massive improvement trend. Thus, companies are clearly having a difficult time shortening the closing process.

The text and exhibits in this chapter are adopted from the author's more comprehensive treatment of the fast close subject in *Fast Close*, Second Edition (Hoboken, NJ: John Wiley & Sons, 2009).

This chapter walks the reader through the process of closing the books and creating financial statements faster.

 ## DIFFERENT TYPES OF FAST CLOSE

Several variations on the fast close concept have appeared, causing some confusion about the nature of each one. The *fast close* is simply an acceleration of the standard closing process, resulting in approximately the same financial reporting package being issued (possibly somewhat stripped down). The focus of this approach is a careful examination of the closing process to strip out wait times, consolidate tasks, eliminate unnecessary functions, add transaction best practices, and selectively apply automation where necessary. It is a task in which an industrial engineer trained in efficiency improvements would feel quite at home.

The *soft close* is less labor-intensive than a regular close because it does not generate as much information. It is designed solely for internal corporate use, so its end product is only those management reports needed to run operations. With this reduced reporting goal in mind, the accounting staff can eliminate the use of overhead allocations. It may also be possible to stop some accruals and ignore the elimination of intercompany transactions, depending upon the level of reporting detail desired. The soft close is most commonly seen in companies that only issue quarterly or annual reports to outside entities, leaving all other months available for the soft close.

The *virtual close* involves the use of a largely automated accounting system, one that can produce required financial information at any time, on demand. This approach is rarely used, and only in the largest companies that can afford to install an enterprise resources planning (ERP) system that automatically consolidates and reports financial information. Also, the underlying transactions that feed into the ERP system must be essentially error-free, so an accurate virtual close is really the result of a hefty software investment as well as years of continual process improvements. The financial reports resulting from a virtual close tend to be stripped-down versions of GAAP-compliant reports since this approach avoids the need for such manual tasks as overhead allocation, accrual transactions, and the establishment of various reserves.

If achieved, a virtual close can be useful in fast-moving industries where financial results must be monitored on a frequent basis in order to make rapid-fire changes to a company's tactical or strategic direction, or at least to identify problem areas for fast management attention.

HOW TO ACHIEVE A FAST CLOSE

Reducing the time required to close the books is something that an industrial engineer can relate to—it is all about examining the existing process and finding ways to strip out unnecessary activities and perfect the completion of what is left. Since these activities have very little to do with the generally accepted accounting principles in which every accountant is trained, it should be no surprise that many controllers have no idea how to achieve a fast close. This section reveals how to do so.

Documenting the Existing Closing Process

The first step in achieving a fast close is the complete documentation of every step in the closing process. This should address all functional areas of the close, including payroll, invoicing, payables, inventory, cash, and the general ledger. Some companies in specialized industries may require additional closing tasks. The primary focus of this documentation should be a complete itemization of the nature of each task, who completes it, the time required to complete it, and any queue times that appear when a task is shifted to a different person within the process. An example of the resulting documentation for the payables process is shown in Exhibit 18.1.

The analysis in the exhibit shows a common state of affairs—lengthy queue times, a multitude of processing tasks, and high transaction error rates in some areas, all of which result in a payables closing process of four days.

When the documentation of all the closing processes is combined, it will reveal that most closing activities can be completed within one week of month-end. However, some activities cannot be started until other closing tasks are finished, which greatly increases the duration of the close. For example, if there are multiple company divisions, the additional tasks of currency conversion, mapping subsidiary entries to the corporate chart of accounts, and eliminating intercompany transactions will not begin until the subsidiaries have closed their books and forwarded their results to the corporate office. Also, even if a company only has a single location, it must prepare preliminary financial statements, review them for mistakes, create adjusting entries, add descriptive footnotes, and issue the resulting statements. These added tasks can easily extend the closing work into an additional week, as revealed by the closing timeline shown in Exhibit 18.2.

The closing timeline in the exhibit breaks down the most common closing tasks into four-hour increments. Some closing tasks may appear to require an

Inputs	Process Flow	Outputs	Wait Time	Process Time*	Responsibility	Error Rate*
Receiving log	Check off supplier invoices against receiving log	Payables ledger		2 hours	Payables clerk	1%
			0 hours			
Receiving log	Accrue unbilled supplier invoices			24 hours	Payables clerk	2%
			4 hours			
Payables ledger	Complete payables journal entry			1 hour	General ledger clerk	2%
			4 hours			
Payables ledger	Add purchases to fixed assets ledger	Fixed assets ledger		4 hours	Fixed assets clerk	1%
			0 hours			
	Calculate depreciation expense			1 hour	Fixed assets clerk	1%
			4 hours			
Payables ledger	Calculate overhead bases			2 hours	Cost accountant	5%
			0 hours			
	Allocate overhead costs			2 hours	Cost accountant	5%

Total Times: <u>12 hours</u>   <u>36 hours</u>

* Example only: varies by individual company

EXHIBIT 18.1 Payables Closing Analysis

---

excessive amount of time, such as the three days needed to complete a bank reconciliation. These long durations are typically caused by long queue times—for example, the bank reconciliation may only require an hour to complete, but the company must wait several days for the bank to deliver its bank statement, which causes the long task duration. Thus, the bulk of the eleven days of closing time in the exhibit is caused by queue time, rather than actual work.

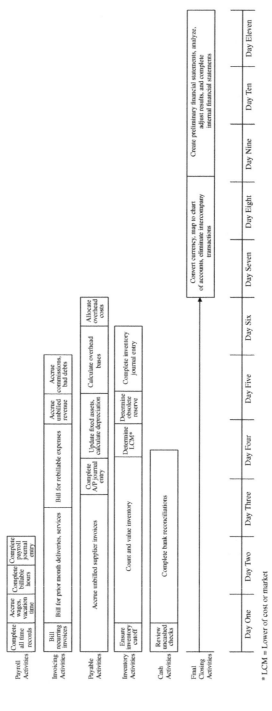

Payroll Activities

| | Complete all time records | Accrue wages, vacation time | Complete billable hours | Complete payroll journal entry |

Invoicing Activities

| Bill recurring invoices | Bill for prior month deliveries, services | Bill for rebillable expenses | Accrue unbilled revenue | Accrue commissions, bad debts |

Payable Activities

| Accrue unbilled supplier invoices | Complete A/P journal entry | Update fixed assets, calculate depreciation | Calculate overhead bases | Allocate overhead costs |

Inventory Activities

| Ensure inventory cutoff | Count and value inventory | Determine obsolete reserve | Determine LCM* | Complete inventory journal entry |

Cash Activities

| Review uncashed checks | Complete bank reconciliations |

Final Closing Activities

| Convert currency, map to chart of accounts, eliminate intercompany transactions | Create preliminary financial statements, analyze, adjust results, and complete internal financial statements |

| Day One | Day Two | Day Three | Day Four | Day Five | Day Six | Day Seven | Day Eight | Day Nine | Day Ten | Day Eleven |

* LCM = Lower of cost or market

EXHIBIT 18.2 Combined Closing Timeline

326

Alter the Timing of Closing Activities

The easiest and least expensive way to enhance the speed of the close is to shift work outside of the period traditionally reserved for closing activities. In most situations, controllers have grown accustomed to beginning their closing activities after the reporting period has been completed, and plowing through a fixed set of closing activities until the financial statements are completed many days later. A better approach is to review the closing activities to determine which ones can be shifted into the previous month, or delayed until after the close is completed. Here are a number of items to consider completing before the core closing period:

- *Bank reconciliation.* Most banks offer online access to transaction information that is accurate through the preceding business day. If so, get into the habit of updating the bank reconciliation every day, so there is no need to wait until month-end to receive a hard copy of the bank statement. Alternatively, request the bank to alter the period of the bank statement, so it closes several days prior to the company's reporting period. This means that the statement will arrive in time for reconciliation prior to the commencement of closing activities.
- *Overhead allocations.* The allocation of overhead costs is usually based on some activity measure, such as machine hours or labor hours. Since the activity measure is typically tracked outside of the accounting system, there is a tendency for it to be one of the last items available for closing calculations. To avoid this problem, consider using either the activity statistics from the preceding month for overhead allocations, or a rolling average of several preceding months.
- *Recurring invoices.* Some companies earn revenue from highly predictable billings, usually for some type of maintenance or subscription service. If this is the case, and the amount of each billing is already known well in advance of the invoicing date, consider shifting the billing activity into the week before the close. To avoid having the revenue be recorded in the wrong month, be sure to set the invoice date forward, to the date when the company customarily issues the invoices.
- *Bad debt reserve.* The reserve for bad debts is no more than an estimate of what bad debts are expected to be in the near future. That being the case, it is unlikely that updating the contents of the reserve a day or two prior to the end of the reporting period will have a significant incorrect impact on the size of the reserve.

▪ *Interest expense.* To complete an early accrual of the interest expense for the reporting period, the controller needs a good idea of whether debt levels are expected to change during the last few days of the reporting period, which is usually easy if there is an adequate cash forecasting system in place. Even if the anticipated debt level is incorrect, the amount of incorrectly accrued interest expense only covers one or two days, and so is sufficiently insignificant to have only a minor impact on the financial statements.

▪ *Unpaid wages.* If a company has mostly salaried employees, the unpaid wages accrual will only apply to a few employees, so estimates can safely be used to arrive at an approximate unpaid wage expense before the reporting period has closed. However, if there are many hourly employees, this may be quite a large accrual, where more accuracy is needed. If so, an early accrual is still possible if headcount levels are steady and employees work the same number of hours each day. A third alternative is to install a real-time timekeeping system, such as a computerized time clock, so that actual employee time worked is available with a delay of no more than one day. This allows the controller to only estimate the wage accrual for the last day of the reporting period—all other information used to create the accrual uses actual hours worked.

▪ *Vacation time.* The accrual for vacation liability is one that some controllers do not update frequently, on the grounds that headcount levels are stable, so the liability is easily estimated. However, in cases where headcount levels fluctuate, the size of the liability may also change to a considerable extent, and so may have a noticeable impact on financial results. If this is the case, update the vacation accrual as soon as the last payroll register of the reporting period has been completed. This document contains all the information needed to update the accrual and is usually available several days prior to the end of the reporting period.

▪ *Account reconciliations.* It is absolutely necessary to keep track of the contents of the larger asset and liability accounts, to ensure that costs are not inadvertently parked on the balance sheet instead of being charged to expense in the correct period. Though there is a risk that such items may be added to the balance sheet in the last day or two of the reporting period, it is usually a reasonable risk to complete account reconciliations a day or two early and simply adjust the accounts in the next reporting period for any late entries.

▪ *Depreciation.* Controllers usually wait until all accounts payable have been received before updating the fixed assets register and *then* calculating depreciation—which places it near the end of the closing process. However, it is quite possible to update the fixed assets register several days early and record the resulting depreciation before the core closing period. The main risk is that new fixed assets will be acquired in the last days of the reporting period, which means that their related depreciation expense will not be recorded. However, the additional depreciation (not normally a large amount) can be added to the next reporting period as a one-time adjustment, with the correction being made at some point outside of the other closing activities.

■ *Commissions.* If a company incurs a substantial commission expense, then the commission calculation is a key part of the closing activities, typically positioned right after final invoices are issued. To reduce the amount of calculation effort in the midst of the core closing activities, consider performing an early calculation of all other commissions that were earned on invoices issued earlier in the reporting period. This should leave only a few commission calculations for the smaller number of invoices issued at the end of the period. Also, the controller may be in the habit of waiting for the sales staff to review the commission calculations to ensure that the commission accrual is correct. However, this additional wait may not be necessary if the total amount of the commission will not change—only the salesperson being paid. Thus, waiting extra time for a commission calculation review may not be necessary.

■ *Financial statement error review.* The controller is usually under a great deal of pressure at the very end of the closing process to conduct a fast review of the financial statements, correct any obvious errors, and then immediately release the financials. This approach tends to ignore small errors and leaves little time to investigate the reasons for larger ones, so the causes of errors continue to exist. A better approach is to review the financials just before the end of the reporting period, when most of the underlying transactions have already been completed. This gives more time to create permanent fixes, and leaves only a few late transactions to review again once the financial statements have been created during the core closing period.

It is also possible to defer items until *after* the core closing period. Here are some areas in which a deferral makes sense:

■ *Rebillable expenses.* A major problem area for service-related companies is accumulating rebillable expenses from its employees (which can take days) in order to include these charges in the monthly billing to their customers. Waiting for these expenses can unduly delay the closing process. A better approach is to create an invoice at once that excludes the rebillable expenses, thereby allowing one to close the books. At this point, the company has the option of immediately issuing the invoices (for better cash flow) or of waiting for the employee expense reports to arrive and then retroactively adding them to the original invoices.

▪ *Invoice mailing.* The purpose of the close is to issue financial statements, not invoices. However, the mindset of many controllers is that they must first create invoices for the reporting period, then mail them, and then go back to the preparation of financial statements. Instead, create the invoices and then put them to one side until the financial statements have been released. Cash flow will suffer, but if a fast close is more important, then this is the correct approach.

▪ *Error investigation.* If errors in the financial statements are spotted, a detailed analysis of their causes in the midst of the close is a bad use of the accounting staff's time. Instead, make a list of the errors and then conduct a thorough investigation after the financials are issued. There is far less pressure once the close is completed, so a more thorough error analysis can be completed afterwards.

Revise the Financial Statement Contents

Sometimes the cause of a lengthy close is the nature of the financial statements being issued. There may be several variations of the reports, or they may include too much data of various types to make it possible to accumulate all the necessary information in a reasonably short period of time.

The controller may be issuing redundant financial statements. For example, one version goes to the manufacturing vice president, and contains information that is not included in the version going to the sales vice president, and so on. If there are a multitude of reports to issue, the controller will have a very difficult time releasing them without adding several days to the close. A better approach is to convince the report recipients that a single set of statements will suffice for all of them. If anyone insists on the inclusion of additional data, then ask if this data can be issued separately, after the primary financial statements have already been released.

Another problem with financial statements is the frequent inclusion of cost accounting and performance analysis metrics in the statements. This information usually includes some operational data that must be separately accumulated and manually reviewed, so it requires considerable extra time to collect and insert into the financials. A much better approach is to create a separate reporting package for this additional information that is released on a different schedule, so it does not interfere with the release of the primary financial statements. A likely outcome is that the additional information will be released more frequently, perhaps on a weekly schedule, so managers will receive more timely information as a result of this change.

Optimize the Use of Journal Entries

Manual adjustments to the financial statements are made through journal entries. Since they are manually created, they require additional time to complete and are subject to error. Therefore, reducing the number of journal entries and adding some elements of automation to any remaining entries will speed the closing process.

If the controller is excessively detail-oriented, she may have fallen into the habit of creating journal entries for extremely minor items that have no significant impact on the financial statements. For example, she could be creating an unpaid wages accrual when the number of hourly laborers is a tiny fraction of the total workforce, or spreading the cost of personal property taxes across the entire year, when the total amount of the expense does not justify the extra effort. These smaller entries could have been started when the related dollar amounts were larger, and then no one ever decided to cancel the entries once the need for them declined. The obvious solution is to review every journal entry made in the past month and see if any can be permanently eliminated without damaging the accuracy of the financial statements.

The controller should complete the same journal entries for every reporting period, so there is more consistency in the numbers presented. However, a more common state of affairs is for some journal entries to be inadvertently skipped in some reporting periods or even entered twice, resulting in clearly inaccurate financials that must be investigated and fixed—thereby lengthening the close. A better approach is to create a standard checklist of journal entries that includes a checkbox or space for initials to indicate the completion of each entry, as well as a reference number to show where the standard journal entry template is stored in the accounting software. This more methodical approach will ensure that the entries are used, every time.

The best way to handle journal entries is to convert as many as possible to recurring entries, so that a single entry at the beginning of the year will be automatically generated by the accounting software for all subsequent periods of the year. If entries are not sufficiently similar over multiple periods to be worth placing in a recurring entry, then at least standardize the entry by creating a journal entry template in the accounting software. By using the same entry format in every reporting period for the same journal entry, the controller avoids the errors that can arise when an entry is individually created in each period, probably resulting in some errors that require subsequent investigation and correction.

In larger companies, a number of people may be authorized to make journal entries. If so, there is a strong chance that employees may independently create the same entry, resulting in duplication that must be corrected—which slows down the close. In order to improve the quality of journal entries, consider limiting general ledger access to the smallest possible number of people, who can more easily track which entries have been made. Though this may appear to create a bottleneck that could lengthen the close, it avoids more time lost to error correction.

If a company has several subsidiaries, it may suffer from a wide array of local charts of accounts that must be manually mapped to the corporate chart of accounts as part of the closing process. This mapping approach can be automated with either customized software or through a mapping module that is available in high-end accounting software packages. An alternative that requires no automation is to force all subsidiaries to use the same chart of accounts, so no mapping is required. This approach will be time-consuming, so one can ensure that the data capture needs of each subsidiary are met, and may result in a rather large chart of accounts. However, the payoff is in a much easier consolidation process that will reduce the length of the close.

Centralize Accounting Activities

A major cause of closing problems in multilocation companies is differences in the way accounting transactions are processed in each location. This causes differences in local transactional training, makes it difficult to apply accounting best practices across the organization, and causes delays in the completion and forwarding of closing information to corporate headquarters. Also, if the headquarters staff detects problems with the forwarded information, it must send a request back to the subsidiary for an update, and wait for a reply—which takes more time.

There are several ways to address the problem of decentralized accounting. One approach is to keep accounting staff in all locations, but to issue a centrally promulgated series of accounting policies and procedures to those locations. If properly enforced, this gives the corporate controller assurance that all transactions are dealt with in the same manner in all locations. It has the additional benefit of allowing one to compare the closing performance of each location; since they are all using the same systems, they should be able to close at about the same time.

An alternative approach is to centralize all accounting operations in one location. This approach certainly reduces the total accounting headcount since the accounting managers required at each outside location are no longer needed. This also allows the company to concentrate all of its efforts on improving the efficiency of a single accounting operation, which usually results in a much faster rate of best practices adoption and, therefore, a faster closing speed. Another speed improvement results from the centralization of all error investigation and correction, thereby eliminating the extra queue built into a more diffused accounting environment where update requests are sent to outlying locations. This approach works best if the company has invested in an enterprise resources planning (ERP) system that is linked to all company locations; with such a system in place, the central accounting staff can more easily pull in operational information from outlying locations for a variety of purposes, which also contributes to a faster close. On the downside, consolidating accounting operations can run into considerable resistance from division managers, who like to keep an accounting staff close at hand.

Even if a company only has one location, it can still adopt the centralization approach to the faster close by concentrating closing activities with fewer people. By doing so, there is no need to hand off closing activities from one person to another, thereby eliminating queue times. Also, with fewer people involved, there is less chance that closing transactions will be misinterpreted, so there will be fewer errors to investigate and correct. Further, if some accounting staff are not involved in the close, this makes it easier to apportion all nonclosing actions to them, leaving the employees working on the close to devote virtually all of their efforts to this activity. The bottom line is that any level of increased centralization will improve the speed of the close.

Specific Improvements to Functional Areas

There are a number of best practices impacting specific functional areas that have the ancillary effect of improving the speed of the close. The following bullet points outline best practices by functional area that have this impact:

- *Inventory.* Without a doubt, the finest closing-related inventory best practice is to create an extremely accurate inventory tracking system.

As outlined more thoroughly in the author's *Inventory Accounting* (John Wiley & Sons, 2005), this involves proper labeling of all inventory items and rack locations, consolidating parts, assigning accurate part numbers, loading the resulting information into an inventory tracking database, and cycle counting the inventory repeatedly. By doing so, you can eventually gain complete comfort in the accuracy of the inventory without having to perform a physical count—and this saves an enormous amount of closing effort. Another best practice is shifting as much inventory as possible to the shop floor, where it is charged to expense in the current period. This reduces the amount of time-consuming inventory valuation work by the closing staff. Finally, there should be a long-range effort to shrink the total amount of inventory, thereby reducing the level of importance of this asset and the associated amount of closing activities. Inventory reduction activities can include the following:

- Reduce the length of supplier lead times
- Shift raw materials ownership to suppliers
- Drop ship inventory direct from suppliers to customers
- Schedule smaller production batches
- Produce to order rather than to stock
- Reduce machine setup times
- Reduce the number of products and product options
- Monitor and adjust safety stock levels on a frequent basis
- Monitor and disposition obsolete inventory on a frequent basis

- *Billing.* The creation of period-end invoices can occupy the largest part of the closing process in many companies. There are several ways to reduce the level of this invoicing activity. One is to shift the billing of recurring invoices into the preceding week; this is quite possible if the invoices are generated regularly and are always in the same amount. Another approach is to give the accounting staff direct access to shipping information by linking their computers to the those of the shipping department; this eliminates the wait time for shipping documents to be manually sent from the shipping to the accounting department. Yet another option is to eliminate invoices entirely by integrating electronic data interchange (EDI) billings with the company's computer systems; when a shipment occurs, the computer system sends an electronic invoice with no manual input from the accounting staff. Finally, consider referencing supporting documentation for an invoice with the words "billing as per the attached document," rather than laboriously transferring the information from the supporting documentation onto the invoice.

▪ *Payroll.* The expense related to salaries and wages may comprise a company's largest expense category, and so can occupy a considerable proportion of the closing process. There are several ways to streamline activities associated with this area. One is to simplify the commission structure. Commissions are usually calculated after the final invoices are generated for the month, and so are one of the last transactions to be compiled before the preliminary financial statements are issued. Thus, implementing a highly simplified commission structure can reduce the size of a bottleneck closing operation. Also, do not wait for the inevitable adjustments to the commissions by the sales staff to be received before closing the books—though the person receiving a commission may change, the total amount of the initial commission calculation is probably correct, so book the commission without further adjustment. It is also useful to implement both computerized time clocks (for in-house hourly staff) and Web-based timekeeping (for traveling employees). By doing so, the accumulation of timekeeping information becomes much simpler, both for the generation of an unpaid wages accrual, and for use in billing employee time to customers. An easy improvement is to place a cap on the amount of unused vacation time that employees are allowed to carry forward into the next year. By doing so, the vacation accrual becomes extremely simple, requiring only the recording of the maximum possible vacation carry forward as the ongoing accrual, rather than the detailed analysis that is normally required.

▪ *Payables.* Many controllers get into the habit of waiting up to a week after the period-end for supplier billings to arrive in the mail before they will even consider closing the books. With some up-front effort, it is possible to create a reasonably accurate accrual of supplier invoices that have not yet been received, thereby eliminating this extensive waiting period. There are two ways to eliminate the wait. One approach is to require that virtually all purchases above a minimum level be preauthorized with a purchase order. By doing so, the computer system can automatically compare the authorized purchase orders to received supplier invoices and received goods, yielding a list of authorized purchase orders for which there has been a receipt but for which no supplier invoice has arrived. The resulting report can be used as the basis for an unbilled payables accrual on the beginning of the first day of the closing process. An alternative approach for those companies not using purchase orders is to manually track the arrival dates and amounts of supplier invoices, so the controller can estimate the size of accruals for selected larger expenses. Though not as accurate as the purchase order approach, this alternative can be effective for smaller companies with lower purchasing volume.

A lesser concern in the payables area is the processing of supplier invoices that *do* arrive, but whose arrival is inconveniently at the end of the reporting period, when there is little time to properly process them. One way to reduce the volume of these invoices is to create a procurement card program within the company, whereby employees are encouraged to use credit cards for smaller purchases. Another approach is to use negative assurance to obtain payment approval—simply send an invoice copy to the invoice approver, and proceed with payment by assuming that they approve unless they say otherwise. Finally, a more advanced system requiring considerable custom programming is to have the receiving staff check off received items in the computer system for which a purchase order has already been created, with the computer system automatically scheduling payment without any operator intervention—this approach essentially eliminates all accounts payable labor, but is difficult to create and install.

▪ *Cash processing.* Though the processing of cash is part of the closing process, it occupies a relatively small place in the closing proceedings. As noted earlier, it is possible to use daily online bank reconciliations to avoid the period-end bank reconciliation. Also, to avoid spending time processing cash receipts at the end of the reporting period that could be used for other closing activities, consider using a lockbox where check images can be accessed online. By doing so, one can be assured that the lockbox operator is depositing cash receipts as rapidly as possible, while the logging of cash receipts into the computer system can be delayed until after the close is completed, using the online check images.

Though a considerable amount of time is required to implement some of the preceding best practices, their eventual implementation can lead to startling improvements in the duration of the closing process. In particular, the use of an inventory tracking system, electronic billings, computerized time clocks, and a payables accrual can lop multiple days off the duration of the close.

Incorporate Automation into the Closing Process

Few of the preceding suggestions require the use of advanced computer systems since much of the closing process really revolves around scheduling, error reduction and the content of the deliverables. Nonetheless, the following technologies are useful for squeezing some additional time from the closing process:

- *Workflow management system (WMS).* A WMS was originally designed to speed the flow of very large document volumes among large numbers of employees, and allocating work to those with the shortest backlog. This would appear to be at odds with the concept of the ideal closing team, which has very few members. However, it can be used to enforce the flow of closing activities in a specific order, which may support closing procedures that are being regularly tweaked to create better performance. It also tracks who worked on each activity and how long they needed to complete a task, which is useful for examining the performance of the closing team. It is also useful if the closing team is dispersed over several offices since it can coordinate their activities.

- *Consolidation software.* If there are multiple divisions to consolidate, then consolidation software is an alternative to a centralized accounting system. Consolidation software combines financial data from multiple entities, even if reported in different currencies, while also using accounting rules to account for the percentage of equity ownership. This software is very expensive, usually requires custom programming to link to the corporate accounting system, and is clearly designed only for large corporations. Consolidation is an integral part of the Oracle and SAP enterprise resource planning systems.

- *Data warehouse.* If there are many accounting databases throughout a company, one way to organize the data for easier financial querying and reporting is to construct a data warehouse. This is a central database that regularly extracts and consolidates data from a company's various computer systems. With it, the corporate staff can conduct drill-down analyses of the accounting data to find errors (depending upon how much data have been uploaded into the data warehouse), thereby reducing that portion of the closing process related to error investigation. However, data warehouses are very expensive and time-consuming to construct, requiring custom interfaces to every local database from which data are to be copied, and also require a great deal of ongoing maintenance to ensure that local system changes, deletions, and additions are reflected in the data warehouse.

- *Enterprise resources planning system (ERP).* An ERP system is a highly complex, interlocking set of databases and computer programs that are

Payroll Activities

| Calculate overhead bases | | Review billable hours | Accrue wages, vacation time | Complete payroll journal entry | Verify month-end time records |

Invoicing Activities

| Create preliminary commissions | Compare shipments to invoices | Accrue bad debts | Bill recurring invoices | Complete all billings; Accrue revenue |

Payable Activities

| Review re-billable expenses | Update fixed assets register | Calculate depreciation | Accrue unbilled supplier invoices | Complete A/P journal entry | Allocate overhead costs |

Inventory Activities

| Determine LCM* | Determine obsolete reserve | Count and value inventory |

Cash Activities

| Review uncashed checks | Daily bank reconciliation |

Final Closing Activities

| Complete reports in advance | Review statements for errors | → | Complete internal financial statements |

Prior to core closing period | Day One

* LCM = Lower of cost or market

EXHIBIT 18.3 Enhanced Closing Process

used to run essentially all company operations. It is very expensive, difficult to install, and requires altered company procedures to match those required by the ERP system. However, it also allows the closing staff to directly access accounting information anywhere in the company, and includes workflow management as well as consolidation modules.

With the exception of consolidation software, improving the speed of the close is almost never a sufficient reason to install any of the above systems. It is generally better to use nonautomation techniques to shrink the duration of the close to the greatest extent possible, and then see if the cost of the additional automation is worth the remaining reduction in the closing interval. Once all of the nonautomation closing improvements are implemented, a controller may find the remaining closing interval to be so short that the considerable additional cost of automation is not worth the investment.

 ENHANCED CLOSING PROCESS

If a controller follows the advice in the preceding sections, the result should be similar to the improved closing timeline shown in Exhibit 18.3.

The exhibit reveals that at least some portion of almost every closing activity can be shifted into the days prior to the core closing period. Cash-related activities should be completely removed from the core closing period. The sole major remaining functional area requiring considerable effort during the core close is the issuance of customer invoices, after which the only remaining closing task of substance is the assembly of the final financial statements. All other closing tasks in the core period relate to the review of information already entered prior to the end of the reporting period, or else the compilation of financial information for the final day or two before the period closed.

 SUMMARY

Closing the books can be a fascinating study in improving departmental efficiency—which is precisely what accountants are *not* trained in. They graduate from school with a fundamental knowledge of generally accepted accounting principles, but nothing about how to rapidly close the books. This chapter completed the required knowledge base by highlighting the workflow of the close; this simplifies what may initially seem to be an arcane, error-ridden process. In reality, given a considerable amount of analysis and ongoing process adjustments, it can become a relatively mechanical process that produces consistent results.

CHAPTER NINETEEN

SEC Filings

I F A CONTROLLER WORKS for a publicly held company, then there will be a multitude of ongoing report filings that are mandated by the Securities and Exchange Commission. Depending upon the size of the company and its activities, it may be necessary to have an entire group within the accounting department whose sole concern is this reporting. No matter who creates and files the reports, the controller will likely be deeply involved in this process.

This chapter describes the three most commonly filed reports, Form 8-K for undisclosed events, the Form 10-K annual report, and the Form 10-Q quarterly report. In addition, we cover several types of stock registration documents, as well as how to pay filing fees to the Securities and Exchange Commission. Securities attorneys are responsible for creating stock registration documents, but they will rely heavily upon information prepared by the accounting department.

FORM 8-K

A public company is required to file Form 8-K to report a material, undisclosed event. The form must be filed within four business days of the event. If the event occurs on a weekend or holiday, then the four-day rule shall begin on the next business day thereafter. A moderately active company will find itself filing this form quite frequently, possibly more than all other forms combined.

The SEC defines a number of types of material events that must be reported in a Form 8-K; they are described in the following table. For the more common Form 8-K disclosures, an example is also provided:

Section 1—Company's Business and Operations

Item 1.01   *Entry into a material definitive agreement.* This is for a material definitive agreement not made in the ordinary course of business. Disclose the date of the agreement, the parties involved, and a brief description of the agreement.

                Example: On[date] we entered into an amendment to our senior secured credit facility with ABC Bank. which amends the borrowing base definition. Under the terms of the amendment, the percentage of receivables to be included in the borrowing base is changed from 70% to 80%.

Item 1.02   *Termination of a material definitive agreement.* This is for the termination of a material definitive agreement not made in the ordinary course of business. Disclose the termination date, the parties involved, and a brief description of the agreement, as well as the circumstances surrounding the termination and any material early termination penalties incurred by the company.

                Example: On [date] the Company terminated its previously announcement Agreement and Plan of Merger, dated as of [date], with XYZ Company. The Company's board of directors did not believe that the merger could be finalized.

Item 1.03   *Bankruptcy or receivership.* This is for a company's entry into bankruptcy or receivership. Identify the proceeding, the identity of the court, the date that jurisdiction was assumed, and the identity of the receiver. If a plan of reorganization or liquidation has been entered, then disclose the court, confirmation date, and the material features of the plan.

                Example: On [date], ABC Company filed a voluntary petition for relief under chapter 11 of the United States bankruptcy code in the United States Bankruptcy Court, Southern District of New York (case number 01234). The Debtors will continue to operate the business as "debtors-in-possession" under the jurisdiction of the Court and in accordance with applicable provisions of the Bankruptcy Code and orders of the Court. The filing is attached hereto.

Section 2—Financial Information

Item 2.01   *Completion of acquisition or disposition of assets.* For the purchase or sale of a significant amount of assets, disclose the transaction date, the other party, the amount of consideration involved, and the source of funds used for an acquisition.

                Example: On [date], stockholders of ABC Company ("ABC") approved and adopted the Agreement and Plan of Merger, dated as of [date] by and among XYZ Company ("XYZ") and ABC, which contemplated that XYZ will merge with and into ABC, with ABC surviving the Merger as a wholly-owned subsidiary of XYZ. On [date], the Merger was consummated. Pursuant to the terms of the Merger Agreement, former ABC common stockholders are entitled to receive $1.15 in cash in exchange for each share of ABC common stock, outstanding immediately prior to the effective time of the Merger.

Item 2.02   *Results of operations and financial condition.* Note the date of the release of any material, nonpublic information regarding the company's results of operations or financial condition, and attach the text of the release.

Example: On [date], the Company announced its financial results for the quarter ended September 30, 20XX. The full text of the press release issued in connection with the announcement is furnished as an exhibit to this Form 8-K.

Item 2.03   *Creation of a direct financial obligation or an obligation under an off-balance sheet arrangement of a company.* When the company enters into a material obligation, disclose the transaction date and the amount and terms of the obligation.

Example: ABC Company ("ABC") will become obligated on material direct financial obligations pursuant to the Credit Agreement dated as of [date], among ABC and Big Bank ("Big"). Under the terms of the Credit Agreement, Big will make available to ABC up to a $100,000,000 term loan commitment and up to a $50,000,000 revolving loan commitment. Proceeds of the credit agreement may be used for general corporate purposes. The principal amount outstanding of all term loans and revolving loans is due and payable on [date]. Loans will bear interest at Big's base rate plus an applicable margin ranging from 0% to .2%, based upon ABC's credit rating. Interest on base rate loans is payable on a quarterly basis on the last day of March, June, September and December, and interest is payable at the end of the applicable interest period.

Item 2.04   *Triggering events that accelerate or increase a direct financial obligation or an obligation under an off-balance sheet arrangement.* If a triggering event occurs, note the date of the event and provide a brief description of it, as well as the amount of the obligation.

Example: On [date], the Company received notices from ABC Advisors, holder of the Company's convertible debentures, claiming that the Company was in default of the terms of the debentures for failure to maintain current financial statements in the registration statement relating to the sale of the Company's common stock issuable upon conversion of one of those debentures, and as a result that ABC Advisors was exercising its right to accelerate payment of the full principal amount of the debentures. Approximately $25 million, including interest, is currently outstanding on the debentures.

Item 2.05   *Costs associated with exit or disposal activities.* If the company commits to an exit or disposal plan, note the date of the commitment, the course of action to be taken, and the expected completion date. For each major type of cost, also estimate the range of amounts expected to be incurred.

Example: On [date], the Company committed to a restructuring plan that includes a reduction in force of approximately 500 positions. The

(Continued)

restructuring plan is intended to improve operational efficiencies. The Company anticipates that it will complete the restructuring by [date]. In connection with the restructuring, the Company expects to incur total expenses relating to termination benefits of $21 million to $24 million, all of which represent cash expenditures. The Company expects to record the majority of these restructuring charges in the quarter ending December 31, 20XX.

Item 2.06   *Material impairments.* If the company concludes that one or more of its assets are impaired, then disclose the date of the decision, describe the asset, and note the circumstances leading to the conclusion. Also note the amount of the impairment.

Example: During the quarter ended September 30, 20XX, as part of the Company's ongoing strategic review of the business, an impairment analysis was performed on the Aerospace segment goodwill and intangible assets. On [date] the Company concluded that non-cash goodwill and intangible asset impairment charges of $10 million were required and such charges were recorded in the quarter ended September 30, 20XX.

Section 3—Securities and Trading Markets

Item 3.01   *Notice of delisting or failure to satisfy a continued listing rule or standard; transfer of listing.* Disclose the date when the company received notice from a national exchange that a class of its common equity does not satisfy its continued listing, or that the exchange expects to delist it. Also note the rule being violated that led to the notification, and the action the company expects to take in response. If company has caused an exchange listing to be withdrawn, then describe the action taken and the date of the action.

Example: ABC Company today announced it has received notice from Nasdaq that its common stock is subject to potential delisting from the Nasdaq Capital Market because the bid price of the Company's common stock closed below the minimum $1.00 per share requirement for 30 consecutive business days prior to [date]. The Company has been granted an initial 180 calendar days, or until [date], to regain compliance.

Item 3.02   *Unregistered sales of equity securities.* In the event of an unregistered security sale, state the date of sale, the type and amount of securities sold, the consideration paid, the type of exemption from registration being claimed, and any convertibility terms. This report only need be filed if the shares issued are more than 1% of the shares outstanding. For a smaller reporting company, the reporting threshold is 5% of the shares outstanding.

Example: On [date], accredited investors purchased an aggregate of 25,000,000 shares of common stock at $2.00 per share for an aggregate purchase price of $50,000,000 from ABC Company ("ABC"). The funds raised will be utilized by ABC for working capital and research purposes. The shares were offered and sold to the accredited investors in a private placement transaction made in reliance upon exemptions from registration pursuant to Section 4(2) under the Securities Act of 1933. Each of the Investors are accredited investors as defined in Rule 501 of Regulation D promulgated under the Securities Act of 1933.

Item 3.03   *Material modification to rights of security holders.* Disclose the date of modification, the type of security involved, and the effect of the modification on the rights of the security holders.

Example: On [date], ABC Company entered into an amendment to its Preferred Stock Rights Agreement dated [date] with XYZ Trust Company to amend the exercise price of a right to purchase one share of its Series A Preferred Stock to $25.00 per share, and to make certain conforming changes related to the change in exercise price.

Section 4—Matters Related to Accountants and Financial Statements

Item 4.01   *Changes in the company's certifying accountant.* If the company's auditor resigns or is dismissed, disclose whether the change was a resignation or dismissal, and whether the auditor's report for either of the past two years contained an adverse opinion or disclaimer of opinion, or was qualified. Also state whether the change was recommended or approved by the company's board of directors or its audit committee, and whether there were any disagreements with the auditor during the two most recent fiscal years that were not resolved to the satisfaction of the auditor.

Example: On [date], our client-auditor relationship with XYZ Auditor ("XYZ") ceased. As of that date, ABC Company (the "ABC") had no disagreements with XYZ on any matter of accounting principles or practices, financial statement disclosure, or auditing scope or procedure. We have provided XYZ with a copy of the disclosures we are making in response to this Item 4.01. XYZ has furnished us with a letter dated [date], addressed to the Commission, and stating that it agrees with the statements made herein.

Item 4.02   *Nonreliance on previously issued financial statements or a related audit report or completed interim review.* If the company concludes that any previously issued financial statements cannot be relied upon because of an error, disclose the date of this decision, and describe the facts underlying the decision. There are multiple additional steps to be taken besides filing this Form 8-K.

Example: On [date], management of the Company, with concurrence of the Audit Committee of the Company's Board of Directors (the "Audit Committee"), concluded that the Company's previously issued financial statements for the three months ended March 31, 20XX (the "Financials") incorrectly valued an allowance against deferred tax assets. As a result, the Financials should no longer be relied upon. The Company intends to file amended financial statements in a Form 10-Q/A for the three month period ended March 31, 20XX no later than May 31, 20XX. During the first quarter of 20XX, in accordance with Statement of Financial Accounting Standards No. 109, "Accounting for Income Taxes" ("FAS 109"), the Company recorded a valuation allowance of $125 million to reduce certain net deferred tax assets to their anticipated realizable value. The Company later realized it had incorrectly determined the valuation allowance against deferred tax assets. The Company and its auditors have reached a preliminary conclusion that an additional valuation allowance of $45 million should have been recorded on March 31, 20XX.

(Continued)

Section 5—Corporate Governance and Management

Item 5.01   *Changes in control of the company.* Identify the person acquiring control of the company, the date of the change, and describe the transaction resulting in the change of control. Also note the amount of consideration used to effect the change, and the source of the person's funds to do so.

Example: On [date], Current Investor, the controlling shareholder of ABC Company ("ABC") entered into a Securities Purchase and Sale Agreement with XYZ Company ("XYZ"). Pursuant to the Securities Purchase and Sale Agreement, Current Investor agreed to sell all of his shares of the Company's common stock to XYZ. Upon the closing of the Securities Purchase and Sale Agreement on [date] (the "Closing"), a change in control of the Company occurred. Pursuant to the Securities Purchase and Sale Agreement, XYZ has acquired 5,000,000 shares of the Company's common stock from Current Investor. XYZ paid $15,000,000 to acquire such shares. Funds for the acquisition were from the working capital of XYZ. XYZ now owns 80% of ABC's issued and outstanding shares.

Item 5.02   *Departure of directors or certain officers; election of directors; appointment of certain officers.* If a director resigns, is removed, or refuses to stand for reelection because of a disagreement with the company, note the date of the event, the director's committee positions held, and describe the disagreement. If the director has provided any written correspondence related to the disagreement, then this must be attached as an exhibit.

Example: Mr. Alfred Director resigned as a director of ABC Company ("ABC"), effective on [date]. Mr. Director was a member of ABC's audit committee and governance committee. He gave no reason for his resignation.

Item 5.03   *Amendments to articles of incorporation or bylaws; change in fiscal year.* For such amendments that were not previously disclosed in a proxy statement, disclose the amendment date, and describe the change.

Example: On [date], ABC Company filed with the Secretary of State of the State of New York a Certificate of Amendment to its Certificate of Incorporation establishing the terms of a new class of Series A Preferred Stock.

Item 5.04   *Temporary suspension of trading under the company's employee benefit plans.* For such a suspension, note the reason for the blackout period, the plan transactions to be suspended, the class of equity securities affected, and the duration of the blackout period.

Example: On [date], the Audit Committee of the Board of Directors of ABC Company ("ABC") concluded that the Company's financial statements for one or more prior periods will likely need to be restated in conjunction with revising its sales return reserve calculations. Because of the potential restatement of this information and in order to ensure compliance with applicable securities laws, participants in the ABC Company 401k Plan (the "Plan") will be temporarily subject to a blackout period during which they will be precluded from acquiring beneficial ownership of additional interests in the Company's common stock fund under the 401(k) plan. During the blackout period, Plan participants will be unable to direct investments into the Company's stock fund under the Plan. The blackout period began at 7:00 a.m. Eastern time on [date] and is currently anticipated to end at 7:00 a.m. Eastern time on the day immediately following the day on which the restated financial statements are filed with the Securities and Exchange Commission.

Item 5.05   *Amendment to company's code of ethics, or waiver of a provision of the code of ethics. Note the date of any change that applies to the company's CEO, CFO, or principal accounting officer; the name of the person to whom it was granted, and describe the nature of the waiver.*
Example: On [date], the Board of Directors of the Company approved a Code of Business Conduct and Ethics, which covers all employees and directors of the Company. The new Code of Business Conduct and Ethics encompasses and supersedes the Code of Business Conduct and Ethics for the Company's Senior Officers, which has been posted on the Company's web site.

Item 5.06   *Change in shell company status. If a company is no longer a shell company, disclose the material terms of the transaction.*
Example: The disclosure regarding the reverse merger in Item 2.01 above is hereby incorporated by reference. Prior to the effective time of the reverse merger, ABC Company was a shell company.

Section 6—Asset-Backed Securities (ABS)

Item 6.01   *ABS informational and computational materials.* Report any information and computational material filed in, or as an exhibit to, this report.

Item 6.02   *Change of servicer or trustee.* If a servicer or trustee has resigned or been removed, or if a new servicer has been appointed, state the event date and the circumstances of the change.

Item 6.03   *Change in credit enhancement or other external support.* If the company becomes aware of any material enhancement or support regarding one or more classes of asset-backed securities, then identify the parties to the agreement causing the change, and describe its date, terms and conditions.

Item 6.04   *Failure to make a required distribution.* If a required distribution to holders of asset-based securities is not made, identify the failure and state the nature of the failure.

Item 6.05   *Securities Act updating disclosure.* If any material pool characteristic of the actual asset pool at the time of issuance differs by 5% or more from the description of the asset pool in the prospectus, then disclose the characteristics of the actual asset pool.

Section 7—Regulation FD

Item 7.01   *Regulation FD disclosure.* Disclose under this item only information that the company elects to disclose pursuant to Regulation FD.
Example: On [date], ABC Company ("ABC") will make a presentation to potential lenders. A copy of the slides to be used in the presentation is furnished herewith as an Exhibit.

(Continued)

Section 8—Other Events

Item 8.01   *Other events.* Disclose under this category any events that the company considers to be of importance to its securities holders.

Example: On [date], ABC Company ("ABC") entered into a Settlement Agreement with the United States Department of Justice to settle all outstanding federal suits against ABC in connection with claims related to the Company's alleged off-label marketing and promotion of its ABC Product® to pediatricians (the "Settlement Agreement"). The settlement is neither an admission of liability by ABC nor a concession by the United States that its claims are not well founded. Pursuant to the Settlement Agreement, the Company will pay approximately $10 million to settle the matter between the parties. The Settlement Agreement provides that, upon full payment of the settlement fees, the United States releases ABC from the claims asserted by the United States. As of [date], ABC accrued a loss contingency of $10 million for this matter.

ANNUAL 10-K AND QUARTERLY 10-Q REPORTS

Financial statements and supporting disclosures must be filed by publicly held companies with the SEC on a quarterly basis. Those statements issued for the first, second, and third quarters of a company's fiscal year are called 10-Q reports, while the year-end report is called a 10-K report. The 10-Q and 10-K reports include a company's basic financial statements, as well as the disclosures shown in the following table. *All* items must be included in the 10-K, and *indicated* items must be included in the 10-Q.

Item Header	Include in 10-Q	Description
Item 1. Business		Describes the company's general purpose, its history, business segments, customers, suppliers, sales and marketing operations, customer support, intellectual property, competition, and employees. It is designed to give the reader a grounding in what the company does and the business environment in which it operates.
Item 1A. Risk factors	Yes	An exhaustive compilation of all risks to which the company is subjected, and serves as a general warning to investors of what actions might negatively impact their investments in the company.

Item 1B. Unresolved staff comments		If an accelerated or large accelerated filer received written comments from the SEC at least 180 days before its fiscal year-end and those comments are unresolved, then disclose all material unresolved issues.
Item 2. Properties		Describes the company's leased or owned facilities, including square footage, lease termination dates, and lease amounts paid per month.
Item 3. Legal proceedings	Yes	Describes current legal proceedings involving the company, and the company's estimate of the likely outcome of those proceedings.
Item 4. Submission of matters to a vote of security holders	Yes	Describes any matters submitted to shareholders for a vote during the fourth quarter of the fiscal year.
Item 5. Market for company stock		Notes where the company's stock trades, the number of holders of record, and high and low closing prices per share, by quarter.
Item 6. Selected financial data		Provide in tabular comparative format, for the last five years, selected information from the company's income statement and balance sheet.
Item 7. Management's discussion and analysis (MD&A)	Yes	Involves multiple areas of required commentary, including opportunities, challenges, risks, trends, key performance indicators, future plans, and changes in revenues, cost of goods sold, other expenses, assets, and liabilities.
Item 7A. Quantitative and qualitative disclosures about market risk	Yes	Quantifies the market risk as of the end of the last fiscal year for its market risk-sensitive instruments. Several presentation formats are available.
Item 8. Financial statements and supplementary data	Yes	Includes all disclosures required by GAAP, including descriptions of acquisitions, discontinued operations, fixed assets, accrued liabilities, related party transactions, income taxes, stock options, segment information, and many other possibilities, depending on the nature of a company's transactions.
Item 9. Changes in and disagreements with accountants on accounting and financial disclosure		State the existence and nature of any disagreement with the company's auditors when the company elects to account for or disclose transactions in a manner different from what the auditors want.
Item 9A. Controls and procedures	Yes	A statement generally describing the company's system of internal controls, testing of controls,

(Continued)

Item Header	Include in 10-Q	Description
		changes in controls, and management's conclusions regarding the effectiveness of controls.
Item 10. Directors, executive officers and corporate governance		Identifies executive officers, directors, promoters, and control persons.
Item 11. Executive compensation		Itemizes various types of compensation received by company executives.
Item 12. Security ownership of certain beneficial owners and management and related stockholder matters		Notes the number of shares of all types owned or controlled by certain beneficial owners and management.
Item 13. Certain relationships and related transactions, and director independence		Describe any transactions with related parties during the past fiscal year involving amounts greater than $120,000.
Item 14. Principal accountant fees and services		Disclose the aggregate fees billed for each of the last two fiscal years for professional services rendered by the company's auditor for reviews and audits, for audit-related activities, taxation work, and all other fees.
Item 15. Exhibits and financial statement schedules	Yes	Item 601 of Regulation S-K requires the attachment of numerous exhibits to the 10-K, including such issues as a company's code of ethics, material contracts, articles of incorporation, bylaws, and acquisition purchase agreements.

TIMING OF ANNUAL AND QUARTERLY REPORT FILINGS

The 10-K filing deadline depends on the size of the company, as noted below:

- File within 60 days of the end of the fiscal year if the company is a *large accelerated filer*. This type of company must have an aggregate market value owned by nonaffiliated investors of at least $700 million as of the last business day of the company's most recent second fiscal quarter.

■ File within 75 days of the end of the fiscal year if the company is an *accelerated filer*. This type of company must have an aggregate market value owned by nonaffiliated investors of at least $75 million, but less than $700 million, as of the last business day of the company's most recent second fiscal quarter.

■ File within 90 days of the end of the fiscal year for all other companies.

The 10-Q filing deadline uses the same definitions to determine when the report must be filed:

■ File within 40 days of the end of the fiscal quarter for large accelerated filers and accelerated filers.

■ File within 45 days of the end of the fiscal quarter for all other companies.

 ## FORM S-1

The Form S-1 is the default stock registration form to be used if no other registration forms or exemptions from registration are applicable. The main informational contents of the Form S-1 are:

1. *Forepart of the registration statement.* Includes the company name, the title and amount of securities to be registered, and their offering price. Also describes the market for the securities, and a cross-reference to the risk factors section.

2. *Summary information.* Provides a summary of the prospectus contents that contains a brief overview of the key aspects of the offering, as well as contact information for the company's principal executive offices.

3. *Risk factors.* Discusses the most significant factors that make the offering speculative or risky, and explains how the risk affects the company or the securities being offered.

4. *Ratio of earnings to fixed charges.*

5. *Use of proceeds.* States the principal purpose for which proceeds from the offering are intended.

6. *Determination of offering price.* Describes the factors considered in determining the offering price, both for common equity and for warrants, rights, and convertible securities.

7. *Dilution.* Discloses book value per share information before and after the distribution.

8. *Selling security holders.* For those securities being sold for the account of another security holder, names each security holder, as well as

each person's relationship with the company within the past three years.

9. *Plan of distribution.* Describes information about underwriters, how securities are to be distributed, compensation paid to the sellers of securities, and stabilization transactions.

10. *Description of securities to be registered.* Describes such issues as the voting, liquidation, dividend, and conversion rights associated with the securities.

11. *Interests of named experts and counsel.* Identifies any experts and counsel that are certifying or preparing the registration document, or providing a supporting valuation, and the nature of their compensation relating to the registration.

12. *Information with respect to the registrant.* This section comprises the bulk of the document, and includes a description of the business and its property, any legal proceedings, the market price of the company's stock, financial statements, selected financial data, and management's discussion and analysis of the company's financial condition and its results of operations. It also requires disclosure of any disagreements with the company's auditors, market risk analysis, and several ownership and governance issues.

13. *Material changes.* Describes material changes that have occurred since the company's last-filed annual or quarterly report.

14. *Other expenses of issuance and distribution.* Itemizes the expenses incurred in connection with the issuance and distribution of the securities to be registered.

15. *Indemnification of directors and officers.* Notes the effect of any arrangements under which the company's directors and officers are insured or indemnified against liability.

16. *Recent sales of unregistered securities.* Identifies unregistered securities sold by the company within the past three years, and the use of proceeds.

17. *Exhibits and financial statement schedules.* Provides exhibits for such items as the underwriting agreement, consents, and powers of attorney.

FORM S-3

Form S-3 allows a company to incorporate a large amount of information into the form by reference, which is generally not allowed in a Form S-1. Specifically, the company can incorporate the information already filed in its latest Form 10-K, subsequent quarterly 10-Q reports, and 8-K reports, thereby essentially eliminating the "information with respect to the registration" that is needed for the Form S-1. Form S-3 is restricted to those companies meeting the following eligibility requirements:

- It is organized within and has principal business operations within the United States.
- It already has a class of registered securities, or has been meeting its periodic reporting requirements to the SEC for at least the past 12 months.
- It cannot have failed to pay dividends, sinking fund installments, or defaulted on scheduled debt or lease payments since the end of the last fiscal year.
- The aggregate market value of the common equity held by nonaffiliates of the company is at least $75 million.

If a company has an aggregate market value of common equity held by nonaffiliates of less than $75 million, it can still use Form S-3, provided that:

- The aggregate market value of securities sold by the company during the 12 months prior to the Form S-3 filing is no more than one-third of the aggregate market value of the voting and nonvoting common equity held by its nonaffiliated investors.
- It is not a shell company, and has not been one for the past 12 months.
- It has at least one class of common equity securities listed on a national securities exchange.

In addition, if the form is to be used to register nonconvertible securities, they must be rated "investment grade securities" by one of the nationally recognized statistical rating organizations.

 FORM S-8

This form allows a company to register securities that it offers to its employees and consultants under an employee benefit plan. Such a plan can involve a broad array of securities-related issuances, such as common stock, stock options, restricted stock units, and purchases under an employee stock purchase plan. People covered by this type of registration include employees, officers, directors, general partners, and consultants. Securities issued to consultants can only be registered through Form S-8 if they provide bona fide services to the company, and those services are not related to the sale of its securities, or making a market in them. Family members are also covered if they received company securities through an employee gift.

The form has the dual advantages of being effective immediately upon filing, and of being extremely simple to complete. The company must merely state that its regular periodic filings are incorporated by reference and note the manner in which the company indemnifies its officers and directors. There are a few other requirements that are generally not applicable. The principle accompanying document is the employee benefit plan.

This form of registration is only available if a public company has been current with its filing requirements for at least the past 12 months, and has not been a shell company for at least the preceding 60 days.

 ## FORMS REQUIRING PAYMENT TO THE SEC

Most ongoing informational reports filed with the SEC, such as Forms 10-Q, 10-K, and 8-K, require no fee. However, stock registration forms such as Forms S-1 and S-3 require a payment to the SEC. The SEC will not accept such filings if payment has not yet been received. Payments are made through the Fedwire system.

To calculate the fee to be paid to the SEC, instructions for every form requiring a payment begins with a table with calculation information, entitled "Calculation of Registration Fee." In it, the company itemizes the amount of securities to be offered, the proposed maximum aggregate offering price, and the amount of the registration fee. A sample table follows:

Title of each class of securities to be registered	Amount to be registered	Proposed maximum offering price per unit	Proposed maximum aggregate offering price	Amount of registration fee
Common stock, no par value under the ABC Company:				
20XX Employee Stock Purchase Plan	1,000,000	$2.50	$2,500,000	$100

To ensure that a company has paid in enough funds to process a filing, it should submit a test filing; the test will return whether there are sufficient funds on hand to complete the filing.

FEDWIRE PAYMENTS

To issue a wire transfer to the SEC, include in the wire instructions the American Bankers Association number for US Bank, which is 081000210. Then include the SEC's account number at US Bank, which is 152307768324, as well as the company's central index key (CIK). The SEC assigns a CIK to every company when it initially begins filing activities. The "CIK" designation should precede the CIK number; for example, the wiring instructions could read CIK0123456789. An example of the wiring instructions to the SEC follows:

Amount:	$10,000
Receiving bank ABA number:	081000210
Receiving bank name:	US Bank
Receiving account number:	152307768324
Receiving account name:	Securities & Exchange Commission
Originator to beneficiary information:	CIK0123456789

It is also possible to pay the SEC by check. To do so, make the check payable to the Securities and Exchange Commission. On the front of the check, include the SEC's account number (152307768324) and the company's CIK number. To send checks by overnight delivery service, mail to the following address:

U.S. Bank
Government Lockbox 979081
1005 Convention Plaza
SL-MO-C2-GL
St. Louis, MO 63101

To send checks by regular mail delivery, mail to the following address:

Securities & Exchange Commission
P.O. Box 979081
St. Louis, MO 63197-9000

The SEC occasionally changes these payment instructions, so be sure to verify the most recent information on the SEC web site, at www.sec.gov/info/edgar/fedwire.htm.

CHAPTER TWENTY

Performance Measurements and Trends

I F THE CONTROLLER IS to give quality information to management, then his or her ability to look objectively at the business is crucial. The controller must be familiar with its strengths and weaknesses and must understand the interrelationships of the functions of the organization. An important part of this knowledge revolves around the information provided by those ratios that describe the condition of the business as well as the trends of key operating statistics.

The board of directors and management use performance measures to judge and correct the performance of the company. Bank lending officers use financial ratios to determine how much funding the company is qualified to receive. Investors, suppliers, and securities analysts use the information to evaluate the creditworthiness and valuation of the company.

The use of a *few* sound relationships is recommended, rather than deluging top management with many ratios and trends. However, the controller should maintain an extensive set of performance measurements and trends to better explain to management the background and reasons for the conditions that exist in the company. In general, emphasis should be on *detailed analysis* by the controller and on *simplicity* in what is presented to management.

The performance measures described in this chapter tend to reflect patterns that are indicative not only of economic conditions, but also of stages in a company's growth. These stages can be start-up, rapid growth, maturity, and decline—ratios will vary considerably depending on the company's stage in this cycle. Thus, the relative "health" of a company's ratios may depend somewhat on a company's position within its growth cycle and not on the performance of the management team.

 ## PERFORMANCE MEASUREMENTS

Some of the more commonly used performance measures are discussed in this section. Not all of them will apply to every company, but if the controller selects those most applicable to his or her company, they will yield a good view of the firm's financial and operating performance. When the controller seeks to compare selected ratios of the company with those of particular competitors, much of the database can be secured from the annual report to shareholders or the Securities and Exchange Commission 10-K report, if the measurement is against a public company. Industry averages also may prove useful. Figures for this type of comparison can be secured from a number of sources, including the most recent *Almanac of Business and Industrial Financial Ratios, Dun & Bradstreet's Key Business Ratios*, the Federal Trade Commission's *Quarterly Reports*, SEC publications, and industry association releases. The performance measures follow.

Profitability Measures

These measures relate several profit factors to a significant base. Exhibits 20.1 and 20.2 present the calculations of profitability measures.

- *Percent return on net sales.* This indicates what share of the sales dollar is translated into profit. Industry averages are available from the Federal Trade Commission for comparison purposes.
- *Ratio of gross profit to net sales.* This is a key ratio; changes in the volume of sales, manufacturing costs, and the mixture of products sold will affect this ratio. A low margin may be evidence of intense price competition, poor pricing policies, or insufficient volume to cover fixed manufacturing costs. However, it may also indicate a shift in the classification of expenses between the cost of goods sold and administrative expenses.

EXHIBIT 20.1   Profitability Measures

Ratio	Derivation
Percent return on net sales	$\dfrac{\text{Net profit}}{\text{Net revenue}}$
Ratio of gross profit to net sales	$\dfrac{\text{Gross profit}}{\text{Net revenue}}$
Percent operating margin as related to sales	$\dfrac{\text{Operating margin}}{\text{Net revenue}}$
Percent return on assets employed	$\dfrac{\text{Net profit}}{\text{Total assets}}$
Percent return on shareholder equity	$\dfrac{\text{Net profit}}{\text{Shareholders equity}}$
Market value added	(Number of common shares outstanding × Share price) + (Number of preferred shares outstanding × Share price) − (Book value of invested capital)
Economic value added	(Net investment) × (Actual return on investment − Percentage cost of capital)
Percent return on total capital employed	$\dfrac{\text{Net profit}}{\text{Debt} + \text{Equity}}$
Book value per share	$\dfrac{\text{Total equity} - \text{Cost to liquidate preferred stock}}{\text{Total number of common shares outstanding}}$

- *Percent operating margin as related to sales.* This measures profitability unmarred by changes in the income tax rate or other income and expense.
- *Percent return on assets employed.* This measures how management has utilized the company's assets to produce a profit, and is considered by many to be the premier measure of a company's performance. Improvements in the ratio can occur either by improving earnings or by reducing the asset base, which includes both fixed assets and working capital.
- *Percent return on shareholder equity.* This is the other major measure of corporate performance. It reflects not only operating efficiency but also the impact of debt leverage, so that management has an incentive to use debt instead of capital as a source of operating funds. Excessive use of this metric as a corporate goal can lead to an excessive usage of debt, in order to maximize the return on shareholder equity.
- *Market value added.* This is a measure of wealth creation. It takes a firm's total market capitalization and subtracts from it the company's capital from debt and equity offerings, bank loans, and retained earnings. Any

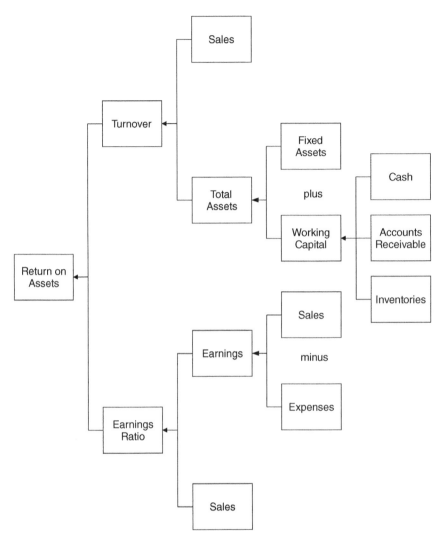

EXHIBIT 20.2 Components of Measurement of Percent Return on Assets Employed

excess amount indicates that the company has created more wealth than it has used.

▪ *Economic value added.* This is a company's after-tax net operating profit for the year, minus its cost of capital for that year. Any excess amount indicates that the company has created more wealth than it has used.

▪ *Percent return on total capital employed.* This measure does not distinguish between debt and capital.
▪ *Book value per share.* This measurement is used by investors to see if the market price of a share is in excess of or less than its book value. A higher market price indicates that investors have assigned extra value to a company, perhaps due to excellent management, product, and/or patents.

Measures of Growth

This information provides methods to determine a company's growth.

▪ *Percent increase in sales.* This measure can be compared to the size of the market to determine if the company has changed its percentage share of the market. It can also be reviewed for sales changes based on volume or price increases.
▪ *Percent increase in net income.* This measure is heavily used, but does not account for asset or equity usage; nor does it consider the impact of long-term research and development or other capital investment decisions.
▪ *Percent increase in earnings per share.* This measure indicates the avoidance of stock dilution, the use of debt, the use of retained earnings, or the acquisition of a company with a lower price/earnings ratio.

Liquidity Measures

These ratios measure the firm's ability to meet short-term obligations. Exhibit 20.3 shows calculations of liquidity measures.

▪ *Current ratio.* This is one of the most widely used ratios, particularly among credit people, to assess liquidity. It is calculated by dividing the total current assets by the total current liabilities. A ratio of 2 to 1 has long been considered as reflecting a satisfactory condition. When evaluating this ratio, the turnover rate of receivables and inventory should also be considered since low turnover rates actually contribute to an enhanced current ratio.
▪ *Quick ratio.* This is a supplement to the current ratio. It is defined as the relationship of cash, receivables, and investments to the current liabilities. This ratio excludes inventory on the assumption that inventory takes time to liquidate and so is not indicative of the firm's ability to meet its current obligations. A ratio of 1 to 1 is considered acceptable.

EXHIBIT 20.3 Liquidity Measures

Ratio	Derivation
Current ratio	$\dfrac{\text{Current assets}}{\text{Current liabilities}}$
Quick ratio	$\dfrac{\text{Cash} + \text{Marketable securities} + \text{Accounts receivable}}{\text{Current liabilities}}$
Cash ratio	$\dfrac{\text{Cash} + \text{Short-term marketable securities}}{\text{Current liabilities}}$
Working capital to debt ratio	$\dfrac{(\text{Cash} + \text{Accounts receivable} + \text{Inventory} - \text{Accounts payable})}{\text{Debt}}$
Days of working capital	$\dfrac{(\text{Accounts receivable} + \text{Inventory} - \text{Accounts payable})}{\text{Net sales}/365}$
Expense coverage days	$\dfrac{(\text{Cash} + \text{Short-term marketable securities} + \text{Accounts receivable})}{\text{Annual cash expenditures}/360}$
Risky asset conversion ratio	$\dfrac{\text{Cost of assets with minimal cash conversion value}}{\text{Total assets}}$
Liquidity index	$\dfrac{(\text{Accounts receivable} \times \text{Days to liquidate}) + (\text{Inventory} \times \text{Days to liquidate})}{\text{Accounts receivable} + \text{Inventory}}$
Altman's Z-score bankruptcy prediction formula	$(\text{Operating income}/\text{Total assets}) \times 3.3$ $+$ $(\text{Sales}/\text{Total assets}) \times 0.999$ $+$ $(\text{Market value of common stock} + \text{Preferred stock})/(\text{Total liabilities}) \times 0.6$ $+$ $(\text{Working capital}/\text{Total assets}) \times 1.2$ $+$ $(\text{Retained earnings}/\text{total assets}) \times 1.4$

■ *Cash ratio.* This is the most conservative measure of a company's ability to pay off its liabilities in the short term. It excludes the company's potential liquidation of any accounts receivable or inventory in order to meet that goal.

■ *Working capital to debt ratio.* This ratio can be used to see if a company could pay off its debt by liquidating its working capital. The measure is used only in cases where a debt must be paid off at once because eliminating a large amount of working capital makes it impossible to run a business and likely will lead to its dissolution.

■ *Days of working capital.* This ratio, when tracked on a trend line, is a good indicator of changes in the efficient use of working capital. A low number of days of working capital indicates a highly efficient use of working capital. However, a seasonal business may yield a highly variable metric, depending upon the time of year.

■ *Expense coverage days.* This calculation yields the number of days that a company can cover its ongoing expenditures with existing liquid assets.

The information is most useful for situations where the incoming cash flow is likely to be shut off, and management needs to know how long the company can continue to operate without an additional cash infusion.

▪ *Risky asset conversion ratio.* This measurement shows the proportion of a company's recorded assets that are unlikely to be easily converted into cash. This information is useful to lenders or acquirers because they need to know the underlying value of the company in which they are making an investment.

▪ *Liquidity index.* This measures the number of days it would take to convert accounts receivable and inventory into cash and is useful in determining a company's ability to generate sufficient cash to meet upcoming liabilities.

▪ *Altman's Z-score bankruptcy prediction formula.* This bankruptcy prediction mechanism combines five common business ratios, using a weighting system that was statistically calculated by Dr. Edward Altman to determine the likelihood of a company going bankrupt at some point in the future.

Debt Measures

The debt indicators measure the firm's ability to retain and pay for debt. Exhibit 20.4 presents calculations of debt indicators.

▪ *Borrowing base usage percentage.* This is an excellent measure for keeping track of the amount of debt that a company can potentially borrow, based

EXHIBIT 20.4 Debt Measures

Ratio	Derivation
Borrowing base percentage	$\dfrac{\text{Amount of debt outstanding}}{(\text{Accounts receivable} \times \text{Allowance percentage}) + (\text{Inventory} \times \text{Allowable percentage})}$
Debt coverage ratio	$\dfrac{\text{Earnings before interest and taxes}}{\text{Interest} + (\text{Scheduled principal payments}/(1 - \text{Tax rate}))}$
Times preferred dividends earned	$\dfrac{\text{Net income}}{\text{Preferred dividend}}$
Ratio of long-term debt to shareholders' equity	$\dfrac{\text{Total long-term debt}}{\text{Total shareholders' equity}}$
Number of times fixed charges are earned	$\dfrac{\text{Net profit}}{\text{Interest on debt including discount/premium amortization}}$

on that portion of its accounts receivable, inventory, and fixed assets that are not currently being used as collateral for an existing loan.

▪ *Debt coverage ratio.* This ratio compares reported earnings to the amount of scheduled after-tax interest and principal payments to see if there is enough income available to cover the payments.

▪ *Times preferred dividends earned.* This measurement is of most interest to the holders of preferred shares, who may want to know a company's ability to pay their dividends.

▪ *Ratio of long-term debt to shareholders' equity.* This relationship is an expression of the company's capitalization. Investors and bankers compare this ratio to acceptable norms for the industry. An excessive amount of long-term debt as related to net worth—for example, over 80 percent—raises questions of solvency in adverse times and usually heightens the cost of debt financing.

▪ *Number of times fixed charges are earned.* This ratio is used to indicate the margin of safety for the creditor. It is determined by dividing the net profit after taxes by the interest on fixed indebtedness, including discount amortization.

Activity Measures

The controller can measure the firm's ability to convert assets into sales or cash. Exhibit 20.5 presents calculations of the activity measures.

▪ *Receivables turnover.* This ratio is calculated by dividing net credit sales by the receivables at the end of the period. A proper turnover rate will depend

EXHIBIT 20.5 Activity Measures

Ratio	Derivation
Receivables turnover	$\dfrac{\text{Annualized credit sales}}{\text{(Average accounts receivable + Notes payable by customers)}}$
Inventory turnover	$\dfrac{\text{Cost of goods sold}}{\text{Inventory}}$
Inventory to working capital ratio	$\dfrac{\text{Inventory}}{\text{Accounts receivable + Inventory − Accounts payable}}$
Payables turnover	$\dfrac{\text{Total purchases}}{\text{Ending accounts payable balance}}$
Operating assets ratio	$\dfrac{\text{Assets used to create revenue}}{\text{Total assets}}$

on the industry's standard collection terms. For example, freight companies collect within 10 days, whereas credit card companies collect within 30 days. Lengthening turnover may be caused by overextension of credit, ineffective collection policies, too liberal a credit policy, or ineffective credit investigation.

▪ *Inventory turnover.* This ratio reveals how many times during the period the inventories are sold. It is calculated by dividing the cost of goods sold by the average inventory. Investigation into a poor turnover rate is necessary because it can be caused by lowered prices, slow-moving inventory, obsolete inventory, incorrect cost extensions, and so on.

▪ *Inventory to working capital ratio.* This ratio reveals if the proportion of inventory to working capital is too high, which indicates that a company may have difficulty converting its working capital to cash in the short term. Use the ratio alongside the inventory turnover metric since a high inventory turnover indicates that a company can indeed operate with a high inventory to working capital ratio and still be able to convert its inventory to cash in the short term.

▪ *Payables turnover.* This ratio reveals how rapidly the firm is paying its obligations. It can indicate that payables are being stretched too far or that apparently all discounts are being taken.

Operating Measures

By use of these ratios, the controller can express a relationship between items on the income statement and/or balance sheet. Exhibit 20.6 presents the calculations of operating measures.

▪ *Break-even point.* This calculation determines the exact sales level at which a company earns no profit. It is useful when making decisions about whether to add fixed costs, change product prices, or alter production capacity levels.

▪ *Margin of safety.* This calculates the amount by which a company's sales can drop before its break-even point is reached. It indicates the probability that a company may find itself in difficult financial circumstances caused by sales fluctuations.

▪ *Discretionary cost ratio.* This ratio is useful for determining if a company is capable of dispensing with certain discretionary costs in order to improve its financial results in the short term. A high ratio of discretionary costs to sales indicates that there are considerable opportunities for expense reductions.

EXHIBIT 20.6 Operating Measures

Ratio	Derivation
Break-even point	$\dfrac{\text{Total operating expenses}}{\text{Average gross margin percentage}}$
Margin of safety	$\dfrac{(\text{Current sales level} - \text{Break-even point})}{\text{Current sales level}}$
Discretionary cost ratio	$\dfrac{\text{Discretionary costs}}{\text{Sales}}$
Sales backlog ratio	$\dfrac{\text{Backlog of orders received}}{\text{Gross sales}}$
Fringe benefits to wages and salaries expense	$\dfrac{(\text{Life insurance} + \text{Medical insurance} + \text{Pension funding expense} + \text{Other benefits}}{(\text{Wages} + \text{Salaries} + \text{Payroll taxes})}$
Ratio of administrative expenses to sales	$\dfrac{\text{Total general and administrative expenses}}{\text{Gross sales}}$
Ratio of sales returns and allowances to gross sales	$\dfrac{\text{Total sales returns}}{\text{Gross sales}}$
Ratio of purchase discounts taken to total discounts	$\dfrac{\text{Total purchase discounts taken}}{\text{Total economical discounts available}}$
Ratio of repairs and maintenance to fixed assets	$\dfrac{\text{Maintenance and repair expense}}{\text{Total gross fixed assets}}$
Ratio of depreciation to fixed assets	$\dfrac{\text{Total accumulated depreciation}}{\text{Total gross fixed assets}}$
Ratio of fixed assets to shareholders' equity	$\dfrac{\text{Total gross fixed assets}}{\text{Total shareholders}}$

- *Sales backlog ratio.* This comparison of the current sales run rate to the current order backlog is a useful indicator of a company's ability to maintain its sales level. This ratio should be tracked on a trend line, so continuing upward or downward changes in the backlog level can more readily indicate probable changes in the sales level.
- *Fringe benefits to wages and salaries expense.* This measurement is useful for comparing differences in the benefits costs of an acquirer and acquiree because the acquirer's benefit plan may be imposed on the acquiree, resulting in the shifting of the acquirer's benefit cost structure to the acquiree.
- *Ratio of administrative expenses to sales.* This is a useful measurement for keeping track of the level of administrative overhead required to maintain a certain level of sales. It is particularly useful when tracked on a trend line, so steps can be taken to reduce expenses in proportion to any sales declines.

- *Ratio of sales returns and allowances to gross sales.* This reflects a cause of change in gross margin through reducing the sales income. It is an indication of the pressure on the sales force for price concessions and a weather vane of customer satisfaction. An increase in this ratio also indicates higher freight costs because of returns and increased expenses for adjusting and handling such matters.
- *Ratio of repairs and maintenance to fixed assets.* This ratio is a valuable guide for checking maintenance policy. In periods of low profits, some managements defer maintenance, allowing the equipment to fall into disrepair, in an effort to continue reporting profits. This policy tends to increase long-term maintenance expenses and probably property losses.
- *Ratio of depreciation to fixed assets.* This ratio is a rough check on the adequacy of the depreciation policy. It furnishes a simple means of comparison with other companies. Differences in accounting policy, maintenance policy, and the share of fixed assets owned have their effect on the ratio.
- *Ratio of fixed assets to shareholders' equity.* This relationship indicates if shareholders are contributing toward working capital, if the ratio of fixed assets to equity is less than 1. An excessively high fixed assets ratio may indicate an overinvestment in fixed assets, depending on the industry.

Cash Flow Measures

Cash flow ratios may be classified in two groupings: sufficiency ratios and efficiency ratios. The former category describes the adequacy of the cash flows in meeting the needs of the entity. The efficiency ratio indicates how well a company generates cash relative to selected measures. The ratios can be compared to other companies and to successive years in the same entity.

Exhibit 20.7 outlines the *sufficiency ratios.* Concerning these ratios, keep in mind that:

- The *cash flow adequacy ratio* measures the ability of the entity to generate sufficient cash to pay its debts, reinvest in its operations, and pay dividends to the owners. A value in excess of 1 over a period of years reflects an ability to satisfactorily cover these principal cash requirements.
- The next three ratios of *long-term debt repayment, dividend payout,* and *reinvestment* reflect the sufficiency of cash to meet each of these purposes. When added and expressed as a ratio, a percentage of the resulting number shows the share of cash required for these three purposes combined, without the need to borrow or use other sources of funds.

EXHIBIT 20.7 Sufficiency Ratios

Ratio	Derivation
Cash flow adequacy	$\dfrac{\text{Cash from operations}}{\text{Long-term debt paid} + \text{funds from assets purchased} + \text{dividends paid}}$
Long-term debt repayment	$\dfrac{\text{Long-term debt payments}}{\text{Cash from operations}}$
Dividend payout	$\dfrac{\text{Dividends}}{\text{Cash from operations}}$
Reinvestment	$\dfrac{\text{Purchase of assets}}{\text{Cash from operations}}$
Debt coverage	$\dfrac{\text{Total debt}}{\text{Cash from operations}}$
Fixed charge coverage	$\dfrac{\text{Fixed expenses} + \text{Fixed payments}}{\text{Cash flow from operations}}$
Cash to working capital	$\dfrac{\text{Cash} + \text{Short-term marketable securities}}{\text{Current assets} - \text{Current liabilities}}$

- The *debt coverage ratio* reflects how many years, at the current level of cash generation, are needed to retire all existing debt.
- The *fixed charge coverage ratio* reveals if a company must use a significant proportion of its available cash to cover fixed expenses, and can be an excellent indicator of future cash flow problems if sales decline in the future.
- The *cash to working capital ratio* is useful for determining the proportion of working capital that is made up of cash or investments that can be readily converted into cash. If the ratio is low, it may be an indication that a company will have trouble meeting its short-term commitments because of a lack of cash.

Exhibit 20.8 shows the three *efficiency ratios* growing in use. The cash efficiency ratios reflect the effectiveness or efficiency by which cash is generated from either operations or assets. Specifically:

- The *cash flow to sales ratio* reflects the percentage of each sales dollar realized as cash.
- The *cash flow return on assets* reflects the relative amount of cash that the assets (or assets employed) are able to generate.

EXHIBIT 20.8   Efficiency Ratios

Ratio	Derivation
Cash flow to sales	$\dfrac{\text{Cash flow from operations}}{\text{Sales}}$
Cash flow return on assets	$\dfrac{\text{Cash flow from operations}}{\text{Total assets}}$

Other Nonfinancial Measures

The nonfinancial measures in this section include ratios for shareholders, sales, marketing, inventory, production, and other key topics that have a considerable impact on a company's financial results. Exhibit 20.9 notes their calculations.

EXHIBIT 20.9   Other Nonfinancial Measures

Ratio	Derivation
Sales per employee	$\dfrac{\text{Annualized revenue}}{\text{Total full-time equivalents}}$
Transaction error rate	$\dfrac{\text{Number of errors}}{\text{Total number of transactions processed}}$
Time to produce financial statements	Financial statement issue date—First day of the month
Issued shares to authorized shares	$\dfrac{\text{Issued shares + Stock options +}}{\text{Stock warrants + Convertible securities}}$ over Total authorized shares
Employee turnover	$\dfrac{\text{Number of FTE employees who resigned}}{(\text{Total FTE employees at beginning of period} + \text{Total FTE employees at end of period})/2}$
Dividend yield ratio	$\dfrac{\text{Dividend per share}}{\text{Market price per share}}$
Insider stock buy-sell ratio	$\dfrac{\text{Number of stock sale transactions by insiders}}{\text{Number of stock purchase transactions by insiders}}$
Stock options to common shares ratio	$\dfrac{\text{Total stock options}}{\text{Total common shares outstanding}}$
	$\dfrac{\text{Total vested stock options}}{\text{Total common shares outstanding}}$
	$\dfrac{\text{Total vested options in the money}}{\text{Total common shares outstanding}}$

EXHIBIT 20.9 (*Continued*)

Ratio	Derivation
Percentage of existing parts reused in new products	$\dfrac{\text{Number of approved parts in bill of materials}}{\text{Total number of parts in bill of materials}}$
Ratio of actual to target cost	$\dfrac{\text{Total of actual product costs}}{\text{Total of target costs}}$
Warranty claims percentage	
Production schedule accuracy	$\dfrac{\text{Number of scheduled jobs completed}}{\text{Number of jobs scheduled for completion}}$
Obsolete inventory percentage	$\dfrac{\text{Cost of inventory items with no recent usage}}{\text{Total inventory cost}}$
Inventory accuracy	$\dfrac{\text{Number of accurate test items}}{\text{Total number of items sampled}}$
On-time shipment delivery percentage	Required delivery date–Actual delivery date
Constraint utilization	$\dfrac{\text{Actual hours used in constraint operation}}{\text{Total constraint hours available}}$
Degree of unbalance	
Break-even plant capacity	$\dfrac{\text{Current utilization} \times \text{total fixed costs}}{\text{Sales} - \text{variable expenses}}$
Average equipment setup time	(Start time for new production run) – (Stop time for last production run)
Unscheduled machine downtime percentage	$\dfrac{\text{Total minutes of unscheduled downtime}}{\text{Total minutes of machine time}}$
Scrap percentage	$\dfrac{\text{(Actual cost of goods sold)} - \text{(Standard cost of goods sold)}}{\text{Standard cost of goods sold}}$
Market share	$\dfrac{\text{Dollar volume of company shipments}}{\text{Dollar volume of industry shipments}}$
Customer turnover	$\dfrac{\text{Total number of customers} - \text{Invoiced customers}}{\text{Total number of customers}}$
Quote to close ratio	$\dfrac{\text{Dollar value of orders received}}{\text{Dollar value of quoted orders}}$
Sales per salesperson	$\dfrac{\text{Nonrecurring sales}}{\text{Number of FTE sales personnel}}$
Days of backlog	$\dfrac{\text{Dollar volume of sales backlog}}{\text{Average annual sales}/365}$

- ■ Accounting and Finance Measurements
  - ■ *Transaction error rate.* The accounting department must issue high-quality financial information in an efficient manner, which is driven to a large extent by its ability to process transactions accurately. This measurement tracks the proportion of transaction errors generated by the department.
  - ■ *Time to produce financial statements.* With the trend toward one-day financial statement issuance, controllers are increasingly subject to this measurement. The measurement can be subdivided into issuance time for consolidated statements and for the delivery of financial information from subsidiaries to the corporate parent. Another variation is to separately measure the time to issue financial statements to external constituencies, such as the Securities and Exchange Commission, which may require a substantial amount of preparation time.
  - ■ *Issued shares to authorized shares.* This measure tells the controller when it is necessary to go to the board of directors to ask for an additional authorization of shares.
  - ■ *Dividend yield ratio.* The return experienced by investors on company stock can be determined based on the stock's current market price. However, this assumes that investors just purchased stock at the current market price.
  - ■ *Insider stock buy-sell ratio.* Outside analysts use this measurement to determine if there is a disproportionate trend in stock ownership by insiders, perhaps caused by a belief within the company regarding the direction of company performance.
  - ■ *Stock options to common shares ratio.* Outside analysts use this measurement to determine if there is a significant risk of large numbers of options being converted into shares, thereby watering down the earnings per share for existing shareholders. This measure can be derived for all stock options, just those that have vested, or (most accurately) those vested options that are both vested and in the money, which are most likely to be converted into shares.
- ■ Human Resources Measurements
  - ■ *Employee turnover.* In a company with a highly skilled workforce, keeping employee turnover low is critical. This metric focuses on the number of full-time equivalent (FTE) employees, which includes part-time employees. This metric can be manipulated by shifting staffing needs to contractors, who are not usually included in the calculation.

- Engineering Measurements
  - *Bill of material accuracy.* The accuracy of all active bills of material is critical to the proper functioning of any materials planning system and can impact product costing, picking, assembly, and purchasing functions.
  - *Labor routing accuracy.* The accuracy of all active labor routing files is necessary for the proper planning of production capacity requirements, without which it is impossible to adhere to a production schedule.
  - *Ratio of actual to target cost.* This measure is used to determine the success of the engineering staff in creating products whose actual costs match or are less than their original target costs. This is a prime consideration in achieving long-term product profitability.
  - *Warranty claims percentage.* This measure can indicate product design flaws that are causing an unusual amount of product returns. However, a high warranty claims percentage can also be ascribed to issues outside of the engineering department, such as damage during shipping, or low-quality raw materials.
  - *Percentage of existing parts reused in new products.* This measure is quite useful for companies that have compiled an approved list of parts to be used in new product designs, which is a subset of all existing parts. By concentrating on the use of an approved parts list in new products, a company can incorporate high-quality, low-cost components for its products.
- Logistics Measurements
  - *Production schedule accuracy.* This measure is used to ensure that the jobs listed on the production schedule are completed in an orderly manner and in the scheduled sequence and quantities. Without this information, management cannot tell if orders are being delivered on time.
  - *Obsolete inventory percentage.* External auditors use this measurement to verify the size of the obsolete inventory reserve. Managers also can use the percentage to track their success in eliminating from inventory all obsolete items through such techniques as returns to suppliers, taxable donations, and reduced-price sales to customers.
  - *Inventory accuracy.* This is an extremely important measure for any company having a significant investment in inventory. It tells if additional control systems are needed to increase inventory accuracy levels to a sufficiently high standard to ensure that production planning, purchasing, and manufacturing activities can reliably depend on the inventory database.

- ▪ *On-time shipment delivery percentage.* This measure is most useful in situations where deliveries to customers are time-critical and can result in lost sales if the company cannot demonstrate reliable order fulfillment in a timely manner.
- ▪ Production Measurements
  - ▪ *Constraint utilization.* This measure is useful for tracking the usage level of the bottleneck operation. By increasing this operation's utilization level to as close to 100 percent as possible, a company can maximize its overall profitability (subject to the profitability mix of products run through the bottleneck operation).
  - ▪ *Degree of unbalance.* This refers to the amount of productive capacity in a production cell that cannot be utilized because of the presence of a production bottleneck. It is used by the production manager to adjust the layout and components of a production cell in order to achieve a higher rate of productive output for that cell. The metric is most useful for those cells having difficulty keeping pace with the level of demand.
  - ▪ *Break-even plant capacity.* This measurement reveals the point at which a facility's output exactly equals the expense associated with running it. It is particularly useful when making decisions regarding the replacement of labor-intensive activities requiring a variable labor rate with automated equipment requiring an additional fixed cost.
  - ▪ *Average equipment setup time.* This measurement is useful in situations where equipment is being run at maximum capacity, so it is critical to have the smallest possible amount of equipment down time between production runs. It is also useful in just-in-time production environments, where equipment setups occur frequently and can take up a large part of the time in a production process.
  - ▪ *Unscheduled machine downtime percentage.* This measure is used to track a company's ability to minimize unplanned machine downtime, which can play havoc with the production schedule, meeting promised delivery dates, short-term machine capacity utilization, and labor utilization.
  - ▪ *Scrap percentage.* Management should track this percentage closely because it is indicative of such problems as poor direct labor training, improper machine setups, materials handling problems, and the use of substandard raw materials.
- ▪ Sales and Marketing Measurements
  - ▪ *Market share.* This shows a company's share of sales in an entire market, which is a better measure of its success relative to its

competitors than any changes in sales are. For example, a company could erroneously think it is succeeding because it is increasing sales when the total market has grown so much that the company actually has lost some portion of its market share.

▪ *Customer turnover.* This measure is especially useful in situations where the cost of acquiring new customers is high, so the importance of retaining existing customers is paramount. A variation on this metric is to only track the turnover of the most profitable customers.

▪ *Quote to close ratio.* This reveals which sales personnel have the best ability to close a deal once it has been quoted.

▪ *Sales per salesperson.* This is the classic measure for determining the sales effectiveness of the sales staff, although it should be combined with a review of profits per salesperson to ensure that the sales staff is not selling low-margin products in order to make the measure look as high as possible.

▪ *Days of backlog.* The production department uses this measure to determine the amount of short-term manufacturing capacity required. It is also useful for sales forecasting because the amount of backlog has a direct bearing on a company's ability to generate sales. Finally, it can be used as the justification for outsourcing production work, in case the backlog is so large that it clearly overwhelms a company's short-term ability to meet demand.

 ## TRENDS

The controller is often so deeply engrossed in current problems that he or she fails to watch trends. Occasionally the use of trend analysis provides some very revealing figures with little expenditure of effort. Trend fluctuations should also be investigated in detail, so that the precise reason for change is examined and corrective action taken if necessary. Of course, it is easiest to keep historical records of all of the statistics and ratios mentioned earlier in this chapter; however, at a minimum, the controller should review these trends:

▪ *Trend of sales volume.* Trends here should be examined by territory and for each product.

▪ *Trend of gross margins.* The margins by product and volume should be investigated, so that the controller knows the source of the firm's contribution margin.

- *Trend of pricing.* The controller should be aware of changes in pricing and should track the sensitivity of sales volume to pricing changes.
- *Trend of product returns.* Sudden changes in product returns can signal a quality problem in the product or that the distribution pipeline is filled, and the company is forcing too much product onto its distributors.
- *Trend of cost of distribution channels.* The controller should periodically analyze the cost of various methods of selling (through distributors, direct sales, Internet sales, catalogs, etc.) versus the margin earned through each method of sale.
- *Trend of sales quotas.* Some sales managers predict higher sales without budgeting for increased sales staffs to bring in the business. The controller can discover such a problem by reviewing the trend in quotas per salesperson.
- *Trend of cost of sales calls.* The controller should see if the 80/20 rule applies to his or her company: Do 20 percent of the customers account for 80 percent of the business? If so, the controller can analyze the cost of servicing smaller accounts and recommend dropping certain accounts to improve the company's profitability.
- *Trend of cost of freight.* The company may extend into new geographical areas without considering the cost of shipping product into those areas. A review of the freight cost as a percentage of sales will spotlight this problem.
- *Trend of amount of utilized storage space.* This can be a major item because it can highlight a myriad of smaller problems, such as obsolete inventory, returned goods, scrapped parts, and excess finished goods.
- *Trend of utilized plant capacity.* This is a good indicator of the need for starting a second shift, for overtime pay, for increased maintenance costs, and for more facilities.
- *Trend of direct labor rates.* This trend can tell the controller if rates are too low compared to the local market rate (perhaps resulting in a disgruntled workforce), or that, during a layoff period, the average labor rate is rising because the lower-paid, lower-level people have been laid off.
- *Trend of the accuracy of inventory, bill of material, and labor routing information.* These three items are all required at levels of 98 percent accuracy or above in order to operate a material requirements planning (MRP) system. Accurate bills of material are required for a just-in-time (JIT) system.
- *Trend of ratio of overhead to production labor.* A company's overhead can balloon rapidly, and this is a primary means of detecting such a trend.
- *Trend of return on shareholders' equity and return on assets.* A significant decline in these measures signals reduced cash flow, more difficult

borrowing covenants, and many other problems, such as reduced margins and increased expenses.

INTERRELATIONSHIP OF RATIOS

The controller will find that focusing on a "problem" ratio and fixing the underlying issues can create problems with other related ratios. For example, a company's debt covenant may specify a current ratio of 2 to 1. If the ratio is 1.5 to 1, then the controller can borrow money and retain the cash to improve the current ratio. However, the controller's action could worsen the company's ratio of long-term debt to shareholder's equity. Exhibit 20.10 shows examples of the impact on related ratios of efforts by management to alter 10 key ratios.

JUST-IN-TIME RATIOS

The controller needs to use a different set of ratios when evaluating the performance of a JIT manufacturing system. A JIT system operates on the principle that the facility should receive only enough supplier components to build parts, produce only enough parts to build the desired number of products, and produce only enough products to meet demand. In order to produce with the exact number of required components from suppliers, the components must be delivered to the company on time, in the right quantities, and with perfect quality (no defective components). In order to produce only enough parts to build the desired number of products, setup times must be minimized, work-in-process (WIP) must be drastically reduced, and scrap must be tracked carefully. In short, the controller must devise data collection procedures for information that does not appear on the balance sheet or income statement. Inventory turnover is the only ratio related to JIT that can be derived from the balance sheet.

Exhibit 20.11 shows appropriate JIT measurements. Regarding these measurements, note that:

- The *on-time part delivery* measure should be tracked by supplier. The performance measure then should be graphed on a trend line and shared with the supplier, so that worsening trends can be discussed and corrected. The definition of "on time" will vary by company; some must have the product within a specified hour, while others can wait a day or more. Also,

EXHIBIT 20.10 Interrelationship of Ratio Changes

A Change in This Ratio	Affects These Ratios
Current ratio	Management improves the ratio by borrowing money and retaining the cash; the *ratio of long-term debt to shareholder's equity* worsens because debt has increased.
Ratio of long-term debt to shareholder's equity	Management improves the ratio by liquidating short-term investments to pay down the long-term debt; the *current ratio* worsens because investments have been reduced.
Ratio of net sales to receivables	Management improves the ratio by factoring receivables; the *ratio of net profits to net sales* worsens because there is a service charge associated with factoring the receivables.
Turnover of inventories	Management improves the ratio by selling off inventories; the *ratio of gross profit to net sales* worsens because management must pay premium prices to buy raw materials on short notice and ship it to the company by express freight.
Ratio of net sales to working capital	Management improves the ratio by extending payables; the *ratio of gross profit to net sales* worsens because suppliers will not ship additional raw materials, so management must pay premium prices to buy raw materials on short notice and ship it to the company by express freight.
Ratio of repairs and maintenance to fixed assets	Management improves the ratio by cutting the amount of maintenance work on equipment; *the ratio of net income to net sales* worsens because production capacity drops when equipment breaks down.
Number of times fixed charges are earned	Management improves the ratio by using cash on hand to pay down debt; the *current ratio* worsens because the cash is used.
Ratio of gross profit to net sales	Management improves the ratio by increasing prices; the *ratio of net income to net sales* worsens because fewer people buy the product at the higher price
Ratio of operating expenses to net	Management improves the ratio by reducing the accounting department's payroll; the *ratio of gross profit to net sales* worsens because there is no cost accountant to review increased product costs.
Ratio of net income to net sales	Management improves the ratio by selling manufacturing equipment and recording a gain on the sale; the *ratio of gross profit to net sales* worsens because production capacity is reduced, and production must be given to subcontractors at a higher cost.

EXHIBIT 20.11 Ratios Used to Measure Performance in a JIT Environment

Ratio	Derivation
On-time part delivery	$\dfrac{\text{Number of parts delivered on time}}{\text{Number of parts ordered for delivery date}}$
Part delivery in correct quantities	$\dfrac{\text{Quantity of parts delivered}}{\text{Quantity of parts ordered}}$
Quality of delivered parts	$\dfrac{(\text{Total number of parts}) - (\text{Number of effective parts})}{\text{Total number of parts}}$
Average setup time	Time from end of previous production run to start of next production run
Inventory turnover	$\dfrac{\text{Cost of goods sold}}{\text{Average inventory}}$
Amount of scrap	$\dfrac{\text{Dollar value of scrap}}{\text{Dollar value of production}}$

excessively early deliveries should not be considered on time, for then the company must store the materials longer than it should.

■ The *part delivery in correct quantities* measure should be tracked by supplier. Again, the measure should be graphed on a trend line and the information shared with the supplier. Excessive amounts of delivered quantities should be considered incorrect quantities because the company then must store and track the excess items.

■ The *quality of delivered parts* measure should be tracked by supplier. Again, the measure should be graphed on a trend line and the information shared with the supplier. The allowable tolerance limits used to define an item as being "within specifications" should be continually narrowed as the supplier attains the more generous tolerance goals, so that quality levels constantly improve.

■ The *average setup time* measure should be tracked by machine and plotted on a trend line. Management should closely follow the setup times of machines that cause bottlenecks and prioritize setup reduction analyses on those machines.

■ The *inventory turnover* measure should be broken down into raw materials, WIP, and finished goods, so that slow turnover areas can be highlighted more easily.

■ The *scrap* measure should be broken down into many categories, such as losses due to obsolescence, damage caused by material movement, and pilferage. Using such a detailed analysis, management can quickly focus on the most significant scrap problems.

CHAPTER TWENTY-ONE

Financial Analysis

T HIS CHAPTER EXPLORES A number of additional analysis techniques that will give a controller a much more comprehensive set of
tools for evaluating a company's various financial illnesses. Many
sections contain sample management reports that list not only the financial
analysis but also the controller's written evaluation, which is usually the most
read and influential of all the information released by the accounting
department.

ANALYZING FINANCIAL STATEMENTS

When the controller issues financial statements, the management team
probably will not have the time or the financial skill to review them in enough
detail to obtain sufficient knowledge about corrective actions to be taken. It is
the job of the controller to provide additional information about the financial
statements that reveals trends, risks, and opportunities for improvement.

The layout of the typical financial statement shows the current month's
performance as well as that of the previous month, plus year-to-date information. Unfortunately, this does not include a sufficient volume of information for

management to ascertain any trends in activity or profitability. An additional report is needed to present such information to management. Exhibit 21.1 presents an example of this report, where we itemize both the balance sheet and the income statement for a number of months. By using this format, managers can quickly scan through the information and determine trends in the major categories. However, the typical accounting system does not support this format, so the controller may have to authorize custom programming to create the report or else manually transfer the information into an electronic spreadsheet, which runs the risk of including typographical errors. If key line items in this full-year format are of particular importance to management, then the controller can convert them into a graphical presentation, which is easier to read. Exhibit 21.2 presents an example of graphical layouts, using the information from Exhibit 21.1. These layouts include separate graphs for the cash balance, revenue, and net profit.

In addition to trend information, the controller must provide the management team with information about the financial risks to which the company is currently subject. This information can include an analysis of how closely the company is coming to minimum loan covenants because dropping below them would give lenders the option to call their loans. Another good measure is a company's debt to equity ratio because a high ratio is indicative of an excessive degree of leverage that may be difficult to work off. A related measure is the number of times the interest expense is covered by current earnings because dropping below a ratio of 1 to 1 would mean that a company cannot pay for, and therefore will probably default on, its debts. Other useful risk measures are the current and quick ratios because they compare the amount of a company's current assets to its current liabilities. If the ratio is near or below 1 to 1, a company may have difficulty paying its liabilities. Exhibit 21.3 notes these ratios using the same full-year format used in Exhibit 21.1. The exhibit clearly shows any positive or negative trends. It is very useful to include the formulas for each ratio in this analysis (as is demonstrated in the example), so management can then see for itself exactly how the numbers come together to form each ratio.

The metrics report in Exhibit 21.3 reveals a great deal of information about a company. In the example, we see a company that is heavily burdened by debt, and that achieves a minuscule return on assets and net profit. However, its sales have surged as the year has progressed, which has slightly increased its profitability. Also, it has gradually reduced its investment in working capital, which has allowed it to pay off a modest amount of debt. However, there is still far too much interest expense, and a lender must wonder how long the

EXHIBIT 21.1   Full-Year Presentation of Financial Results

Balance Sheet by Month

Feb	Mar	Apr	May	Jun	Jul	Aug	Sep	Oct	Nov	Dec
-525,509	-494,706	-438,354	-157,490	-156,705	-156,044	-155,979	-155,519	-155,266	-155,154	-155,084
2,450,378	2,042,165	3,035,957	2,997,925	2,983,026	2,970,431	2,969,194	2,960,432	2,955,618	2,953,493	2,952,163
2,273,238	2,418,776	2,715,241	2,587,566	2,574,708	2,563,838	2,562,770	2,555,207	2,551,052	2,549,217	2,548,069
4,198,107	3,966,235	5,312,844	5,428,000	5,401,029	5,378,225	5,375,985	5,360,120	5,351,405	5,347,556	5,345,148
5,091,069	5,004,064	4,949,893	4,873,264	4,796,635	4,720,006	4,643,377	4,566,748	4,490,119	4,413,490	4,336,861
97,042	97,042	35,113	45,676	52,019	48,442	49,503	50,026	51,247	52,068	53,006
9,386,218	9,067,341	10,297,850	10,346,940	10,249,683	10,146,673	10,068,865	9,976,894	9,892,771	9,813,114	9,735,015
1,862,154	1,671,275	2,575,146	2,585,191	2,675,719	2,682,612	2,739,248	2,747,322	2,787,249	2,816,385	2,841,512
277,914	273,981	244,332	330,597	342,169	343,050	350,293	351,325	356,431	360,157	363,370
2,140,068	1,945,256	2,819,478	2,915,789	3,017,894	3,025,668	3,089,547	3,098,654	3,143,687	3,176,548	3,204,889
7,138,983	7,004,849	7,347,400	7,289,850	7,091,621	6,967,058	6,811,315	6,696,395	6,552,842	6,425,603	6,304,912
15,000	15,000	15,000	15,000							
92,167	102,236	115,972	126,302	140,168	153,947	168,003	181,845	196,242	210,963	225,214
107,167	117,236	130,972	141,302	140,168	153,947	168,003	181,845	196,242	210,963	225,214
9,386,218	9,067,341	10,297,850	10,346,940	10,249,683	10,146,673	10,068,865	9,976,894	9,892,771	9,813,114	9,735,015

EXHIBIT 21.1 (Continued)

					Income Statement by Month					
Feb	Mar	Apr	May	Jun	Jul	Aug	Sep	Oct	Nov	Dec
1,497,352	1,432,057	1,700,024	1,776,442	1,809,052	1,825,056	1,840,723	1,872,154	1,895,003	1,913,457	1,925,665
759,157	619,133	869,053	902,280	917,189	925,303	933,247	949,182	960,767	970,123	976,312
225,446	201,941	240,561	238,054	236,986	239,082	241,135	245,252	248,245	250,663	252,262
445,763	490,262	467,053	519,050	528,243	532,916	537,491	546,669	553,341	558,729	562,294
66,986	120,721	123,357	117,058	126,634	127,754	128,851	131,051	132,650	133,942	134,797
89,554	103,940	100,463	99,841	103,524	104,789	105,423	107,982	108,654	109,408	111,045
−22,568	16,781	22,894	17,217	23,110	22,965	23,428	23,069	23,996	24,534	23,752
−9,027	6,712	9,158	6,887	9,244	9,186	9,371	9,228	9,598	9,814	9,501
−13,541	10,069	13,736	10,330	13,866	13,779	14,057	13,841	14,398	14,720	14,251

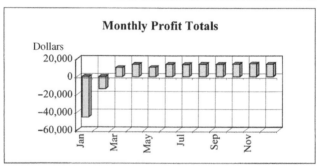

EXHIBIT 21.2 Graphical Presentation of Financial Trends

company can continue to take funds from working capital to pay off its debt, especially since there is more than twice as much debt as working capital. Finally, the lender must be waiving all covenant requirements because the company is unable to meet any of them. In short, the ratio analysis reveals a company trying to pull itself out from under a monstrous load of debt with only the slightest of profit margins, but one that is using its assets wisely to improve its financial position toward the end of the year.

EXHIBIT 21.3 Full-Year Presentation of Risk and Financial Ratios

					Metrics							
	Jan	Feb	Mar	Apr	May	Jun	Jul	Aug	Sep	Oct	Nov	Dec
Loan Covenants (required):												
Quick ratio (1.0:1)	1.2	0.9	1.0	0.7	0.7	0.7	0.7	0.6	0.6	0.6	0.6	0.6
Current ratio (1.5:1)	2.5	2.0	2.0	1.9	1.9	1.8	1.8	1.7	1.7	1.7	1.7	1.7
Debt/Equity (1:1)	62.7	66.6	59.8	56.1	51.6	50.6	45.3	40.5	36.8	33.4	30.5	28.0
Times Interest Earned (2:1)	-0.8	-0.3	0.2	0.2	0.2	0.3	0.3	0.3	0.3	0.3	0.3	0.3
Financial Risk Measures:												
Inventory turnover	8.9	7.6	6.5	7.0	7.7	7.8	7.9	8.0	8.2	8.3	8.4	8.4
Accounts receivable turnover	8.2	7.3	8.4	6.7	7.1	7.3	7.4	7.4	7.6	7.7	7.8	7.8
Employee turnover (annualized)	14%	16%	21%	27%	23%	24%	21%	19%	18%	21%	23%	25%
No. of employees	160.0	163.0	165.0	168.0	172.0	184.0	188.0	191.0	199.0	203.0	204.0	206.0
Revenue per employee	$112,723	$110,235	$104,150	$121,430	$123,938	$117,982	$116,493	$115,648	$112,894	$112,020	$112,556	$112,175
Total working capital (000s)	$3,053	$2,861	$2,790	$3,176	$3,000	$2,882	$2,852	$2,793	$2,768	$2,719	$2,686	$2,659
Return on assets (annualized)	-5.8%	-1.7%	1.3%	1.6%	1.2%	1.6%	1.6%	1.7%	1.7%	1.7%	1.8%	1.8%
Gross margin percentage	1.0%	4.5%	8.4%	7.3%	6.6%	7.0%	7.0%	7.0%	7.0%	7.0%	7.0%	7.0%
Net profit percentage	-3.0%	-0.9%	0.7%	0.8%	0.6%	0.8%	0.8%	0.8%	0.7%	0.8%	0.8%	0.7%

(Continued)

EXHIBIT 21.3 *(Continued)*

							Metrics					
	Jan	Feb	Mar	Apr	May	Jun	Jul	Aug	Sep	Oct	Nov	Dec

Measurement Descriptions:

Quick ratio	(Cash + Accounts Receivable)/(Current Liabilities)
Current ratio	(Current Assets)/(Current Liabilities)
Debt/Equity	(Short-Term Debt + Long-Term Debt)/(Total Stockholder's Equity)
Times interest earned	(Net Profit Before Interest Expense)/(Interest Expense)
Inventory turnover	(Cost of Goods Sold × 12)/(Inventory)
Accounts receivable turnover	(Revenue × 2)/(Accounts Receivable)
Employee turnover (annualized)	(Total Departed Employees)/(Total Employees at Beginning of Year × 12)
No. of employees	Total Full Time Equivalents
Revenue per employee	(Monthly Revenue × 12)/(No. of Employees)
Total working capital	(Accounts Receivable + Inventory − Accounts Payable)
Return on assets (annualized)	(Net Profit/Total Assets) × 12
Gross margin percentage	(Gross Margin)/(Revenue)
Net profit percentage	(Net Profit)/(Revenue)

The second half of the example in Exhibit 21.3 includes a listing of ratios that show developing changes in the financial condition of the company. These are useful leading indicators of potential problems that the management team should address as soon as possible. For example, the amount of sales per employee signals a change in the efficiency of the company in generating sales. The same measure is later applied to gross margins and net margins. Also, an increase in the annualized rate of employee turnover will possibly result in a later drop in the efficiency of the company because new employees must go through a learning curve before they can become as productive as the employees they replaced. The exact measures used will vary by business since each one operates in a different environment and therefore requires different leading indicators of its financial activity.

Once a controller has assembled all this information, the management team should have sufficient information available to form conclusions regarding the financial condition of the company, its prospects in the near term (based on current trends), and what actions to take to improve the business. However, this information is still largely numerical, which may not be the best way to present information to the management team. Accordingly, the controller should attach a written executive summary to the financial statement package that itemizes the main issues. In order to lend some organization to this presentation, it is best to set up standard categories in which the controller can insert information, such as the main line items in the balance sheet and income statement plus information about working capital, capital expenditures, and loans.

ANALYZING WORKING CAPITAL

A company can experience excellent profitability and still go bankrupt for lack of cash. This event is caused most commonly by increases in accounts receivable and inventory or a decline in accounts payable. The first two are the primary operating investments that a company must make in order to support sales to customers, while the last is a key source of funding for operations. The management team can be taken by surprise by sudden shifts in these cash flows unless the controller keeps a watchful eye on the company's investment in working capital and relays reports on changes.

The main tasks for the controller are not only to track the dollar amount of working capital, but also to conduct a sufficiently detailed investigation into the causes of variations to write a detailed analysis of any problems, along with recommendations for changes. In order to conduct such an in-depth analysis, it is first necessary to understand the reasons why there are changes in working capital:

▪ *Accounts receivable—poor collection efforts.* The investment in accounts receivable will rise if the collections staff does not actively investigate all overdue invoices, contact customers regarding the reasons, and correct any problems that are preventing the customers from paying. Dunning letters or even lawsuits may be required to collect the funds.

▪ *Accounts receivable—poor credit setting standards.* The investment in accounts receivable will rise if the finance department is issuing excessively high credit levels to customers who do not have the financial capacity to pay for such large purchases (or at least not for a long time). A secondary problem may be that the sales staff is selling to new customers in advance of their having been approved for credit and then is using the customer purchase orders as a tool for pressuring the finance staff into granting excessively high levels of credit. The best way to avoid this difficulty is to set new customer credit standards in advance and to regularly review credit ratings for old customers.

▪ *Accounts receivable—delivery problems.* The investment in accounts receivable will increase if there are delivery problems to the customer, such as incorrect products or quantities, as well as product quality issues or damage due to incorrect packaging or shipping. In all these cases, customers will refuse to pay for billed amounts. The only way to resolve these issues is for the collections staff to investigate each one, collect evidence from the customers, and issue them credits, which is a very time-consuming process. To correct these problems, the controller must collect the error information forwarded by the collections staff and meet with the related departments (e.g., warehouse, production, engineering, and quality) on a regular basis to determine and implement corrective actions, based on this information.

▪ *Accounts receivable—billing problems.* The investment in accounts receivable will increase if there are problems with the invoices sent to customers, such as an address that routes it to the wrong customer location, incorrect unit pricing, missing customer purchase order numbers, or any other incorrect or missing information. As was the case with delivery problems in the preceding point, the collections staff must research these problems with the customer; but in this case, a new invoice is sometimes issued, which requires extra transit and processing time and greatly lengthens the interval before the customer pays for each invoice. To avoid these problems, the controller should actively investigate all billing problems uncovered by the collections staff, correct them, and watch for any repeat incidents that will need additional corrective action.

- *Inventory—excessive purchasing.* The investment in inventory will increase if the purchasing staff buys an excessive quantity of parts. This is a common problem when the purchasing department is focusing on being efficient by reducing the number of purchase orders, which results in buying many months' supply of parts. It is also caused by the use of economic order quantities, which generally results in large-quantity purchases. This approach also keeps the purchasing staff from absorbing blame for running out of parts because they always keep too much on hand. A better approach is to use just-in-time (JIT) purchasing techniques or a material requirements planning (MRP) system without economic order quantities that details the precise part quantities needed. It is also helpful to avoid any purchasing department ranking systems that alter purchasing behavior in the direction of buying too much inventory.

- *Inventory—excessive quantities forecasted.* The investment in finished goods inventory will increase if the sales and marketing staff forecasts an excessive amount of unit sales because the production department will build to this forecast, which will result in a major increase in finished goods inventory. The best way to mitigate this problem is to keep very close track of unit sales, perhaps as frequently as on a weekly basis, and to notify the management group as soon as it appears that sales forecasts will not be matched by actual sales. However, this is a difficult issue for products with strongly seasonal sales because nearly all product sales may occur in such a short time frame that there is no way to modify the production schedule. In such cases, it may be best to use a substantial markdown of the inventory in order to clear it from stock; otherwise, there may be a risk of product obsolescence.

- *Inventory—excessive quantities produced.* The finished goods and work-in-progress (WIP) inventory investment will increase if the production department runs excessively long runs. This is a common situation because the production department wants to create as much product as possible before it tears down an equipment setup that may have taken hours to complete. To avoid this situation, the controller can suggest measuring the production department on the leanness of its WIP inventories or switching to just-in-time (JIT) production cells that use kanban pull systems.

- *Inventory—premature engineering changes.* The raw materials inventory investment will increase if the engineering staff institutes an engineering change order on a product that requires the replacement of existing component parts with different parts. If there are quantities of the old part in stock at the time of the changeover, and if those parts cannot be used on other products, then they will automatically become obsolete. The best way to avoid this problem is to set up a procedure that requires the engineering staff to check on existing part quantities prior to implementing an engineering change order, as well as involving the purchasing staff members in all engineering changes, so they will know when to stop buying the parts that are to be eliminated.

- *Inventory—distribution issues.* The WIP and finished goods inventory investment will increase if there are problems with the distribution system. For example, if the company has decided to add several new warehouses to improve the delivery time to customers, then each one requires an investment in inventory. Also, if the company shifts its WIP to a different location for final assembly, there may be a large buffer stock of inventory at that location, which is used to keep the assembly operation running in case deliveries do not arrive on time. This problem can also arise if the production department is producing on a different schedule from the one used by the assembly department. These problems are best resolved by closely reviewing the cost-benefit analysis for each additional warehouse, as well as by more closely meshing the production operation and any downstream departments that rely on its output, perhaps by using a kanban pull system.

- *Accounts payable—use of early payment discounts.* The funding available from accounts payable will decline if the controller elects to take all early payment discounts that are allowed by suppliers. Although this is for a good cause, and will result in reduced expenses on the items purchased for which deductions are being taken, it also means that the company will have a smaller float on the money being loaned to it by suppliers. One way to mitigate this issue is to determine the corporate cost of capital and make sure that all discounts taken will result in savings exceeding that cost.

- *Accounts payable—changes in supplier payment terms.* The funding available from accounts payable will decline if suppliers reduce their days of payment terms. This happens either when the purchasing staff negotiates better prices in exchange for a reduction in payment terms, or because the company's payments have previously been so overdue that the suppliers' credit departments are forced to cut back on their terms. If the cause is related to a price reduction negotiated by the purchasing department, then the controller should review the pricing change to verify that the savings from the cost reduction exceeds the added funding cost resulting from a more rapid payment to the supplier.

▪ *Accounts payable—changes to new suppliers.* The funding available from accounts payable will also decline if the purchasing staff switches to new suppliers who have shorter payment terms than the ones they are replacing. There may be good reasons for the switch, such as lower prices, better product quality, or more reliable delivery service. Once again, the controller should compare the savings from using the new supplier to the cost of losing supplier funding. Because the purchasing staff usually does not change suppliers without good reason, there is not normally a good alternative to using a new supplier.

▪ *Accounts payable—paying suppliers too early.* The funding available from accounts payable will decline if there is a problem in the accounting department that results in early payments to suppliers. This may be caused by poor training of the accounting staff, pressure from suppliers for early payment, or payment procedures that result in very infrequent check runs, so that the accounting staff feels obligated to make some early payments rather than waiting several weeks for the next check run. This area is entirely within the controller's area of responsibility and can be quickly influenced by procedural or training improvements. If there is pressure from other departments to make early payments to suppliers, the controller should obtain high-level management support of a policy that suppliers will not be paid early.

Given the large number of possible reasons why a company's working capital investment is increasing and the number of departments that could be involved in the increase, it is evident that the controller should conduct more than a superficial investigation of causes, so that an explanation can accompany the working capital report to management that clearly defines the issues and recommends solutions. Otherwise, management will know only that there is a problem, not how to fix it. Exhibit 21.4 is an example of a working capital trend line report that includes both a graphical representation of a company's working capital investment and a further breakdown of the components of the total. In addition, Exhibit 21.5 contains a sample set of controller's notes to management that itemize the precise problems that have caused the changes in working capital and that include specific recommendations for modifications. This type of format is necessary for management to fully understand the

EXHIBIT 21.4 Sample Working Capital Analysis

Date	Total Working Capital	Inventory	Accounts Receivable	Accounts Payable
January	1,700,000	2,000,000	1,500,000	1,800,000
February	1,825,000	2,050,000	1,650,000	1,875,000
March	1,875,000	2,100,000	1,700,000	1,925,000
Week 1	2,075,000	2,200,000	1,775,000	1,900,000
Week 2	2,250,000	2,275,000	1,850,000	1,875,000
Week 3	2,400,000	2,350,000	1,900,000	1,850,000
Week 4	2,575,000	2,450,000	1,925,000	1,800,000
Week 5	2,800,000	2,550,000	2,000,000	1,750,000

EXHIBIT 21.5 Sample Controller's Notes on the Working Capital Analysis in Exhibit 21.4

The company's working capital investment has increased by $1,200,000 in the past three months. This is due to several factors, one of which is the conversion to a new motor for the Roto-Wash clothes washer before the old stock had been fully depleted. The inventory investment in the old motors is $250,000. Also, the production department made an excessively long production run on the Roto-Wash, resulting in an excess finished goods inventory of $300,000. Further, our accounts receivable from CAS (Central Appliance Stores) are overdue by $500,000, which was caused by the preplacement of a $500,000 customer order prior to approval by the credit department, with override approval by the executive committee. Finally, the controller chose to take early payment discounts that resulted in a net decrease in accounts payable of $50,000. Since the company has now used up its entire line of credit and has no spare cash, we recommend the following actions to reduce the company's investment in working capital:

- Reverse the engineering change order for Roto-Wash motors until the old stock has been depleted, which should be three months, based on current sales levels, and which is subject to the following item.
- Stop production of the Roto-Wash for two months, which will allow demand to catch up with current finished goods inventory stocks.
- Put an immediate credit hold on Credit Appliance Stores until its $500,000 overdue invoice is paid, followed by the imposition of a revised $100,000 credit limit.
- Stop taking early payment discounts of all kinds until the working capital investment allows enough excess cash flow to begin taking them again.

reasons for changes in working capital as well as the ramifications of what will happen if the problems are not fixed.

Note that the working capital analysis in Exhibit 21.4 lists the month-end working capital for each of the past three months as well as for the five weeks of the current month. This gives the controller a good feel for how the working capital investment has been tracking over the short term. In some situations, it may also be necessary to add prior-year figures, which yields a longer trend line. This latter approach is most useful for companies with very slow growth rates because current operating conditions will be very comparable to those of previous years.

 ## ANALYZING FINANCING OPTIONS

Sometimes the controller is called on to give recommendations regarding the types of financing that a company should use, especially when there is no chief financial officer to fill this function. This is a key issue because each type of financing carries with it certain unique risks and benefits that other members of the management team may not be aware of, risks and benefits that can have a significant impact on a company's financial risk and return on equity.

There are two basic types of funding: debt and equity. Debt is an agreement to pay interest on a loaned sum, which eventually must be returned to the creditor. It may also be collateralized against certain company assets in the event of default. Some variations on this concept are the balloon payment loan, which requires minimal periodic payments and a large final payment; the lease, which is a loan targeted at a specific asset and under which the creditor may continue to own the asset; and preferred stock, which is a crossover instrument that requires period interest payments, but has no provision for paying back the initial principal payment. A variation on the loan from a lender is a bond issuance, in which a company issues debt directly to individual investors, and which results in similar costs and terms as a bank loan, although the costs tend to be somewhat lower. The interest rate on all these types of debt will be lower if there is associated collateral because the lender has minimized its risk by having the option to sell company assets to pay itself back. However, the interest rate can be extremely high if there is no collateral because the lender has a much higher degree of nonpayment risk. Also, if the form of debt is a lease, there are so many variables involved in the determination of lease rates (current and ending asset valuations, maintenance and tax costs, and interest rates) that a company can end up paying a very high interest rate unless it is extremely careful in analyzing all components of each lease deal. Thus, the cost of a lease option can vary considerably with the terms of the debt.

Equity funding is the payment made by an owner to purchase common stock. The company need not pay back the owner, nor is there any stated interest rate. However, a company should never think that this is "free money." Quite the contrary—because owners have no collateral in the business, they expect outsized returns in exchange for their investments. Accordingly, the company either must issue board-authorized dividends or else increase the company valuation to such an extent that owners can sell their shares for a substantial profit. There is also a major risk to management in issuing common stock because owners control the board of directors, which in turn can hire or fire the management group. Some variations on the equity concept are preferred stock, which involves the nonredeemable purchase of preferred stock, and stock rights, which are rights for current stockholders to purchase additional shares in proportion to their current holdings. Finally, there are warrants, which are rights to buy common stock at attractive prices and which are attached to debt instruments, such as bonds, to make the purchase of the debt instruments more attractive.

A variation on both the debt and equity concepts is the convertible security, which is a debt instrument that the holder can convert over to equity at a fixed price. This is an attractive option if the actual share price is much higher than the fixed price at which a lender is allowed to purchase stock—the difference between the two prices is a pure profit to the lender when converting from debt to equity.

When considering which of these options to recommend, the controller must understand the cost and risk of each type of funding. Except for the most highly leveraged situations, the incremental cost of debt is always less than the cost of equity. This is because interest payments to lenders are tax deductible, which substantially reduces the cost of debt, whereas dividend payments to the holders of common stock are not. In addition, lenders take no ownership interest in a company, so there is no risk that they will unseat the management group; this is not at all the case if the company sells common stock. However, there is a risk in procuring too much debt because the amount of interest payments can eat up all excess cash flow. Such a situation can force a company into bankruptcy if cash flow declines for any reason whatever, such as during a business downturn. Accordingly, lenders frequently insist that a company not exceed a specified debt/equity ratio, which forces a company to obtain some equity from investors at regular intervals. Also, lenders can require onerous loan covenants that require a company to obtain lender approval for special activities, such as the sale or purchase of assets or special distributions to

EXHIBIT 21.6 Summary of Financing Option Advantages and Disadvantages

Financing Option	Advantages	Disadvantages
Leasing	Good for replacement of assets that wear out quickly; the sale-and-lease back option makes available a large amount of cash.	Can be very expensive unless all components of the transaction are carefully evaluated and negotiated.
Loans	Least expensive form of funding.	May require assets as loan collateral, as well as loan covenants, some control over operations, and first call on the results of asset sales in the event of a liquidation.
Common stock	Can raise substantial amounts of funds, and there is no need to pay back the capital.	Shareholder expectations for returns are very high, and it also gives shareholders the ability to oust the board of directors and (indirectly) the management team if performance expectations are not met. Also, dividend payments are not tax deductible.
Convertible securities	Can avoid paying off bond debt, as well as reducing interest payments and improving the debt/equity ratio.	Reduces the earnings per share and weakens the control of current shareholders, but only if conversion to shares occurs.
Preferred stock	Can avoid paying back the principal.	Interest expense is not tax deductible.
Stock rights	Simple way to raise funds from existing shareholders.	Will not necessarily retain ownership interests in the same proportions as prior to the stock rights offering.
Warrants	Can reduce bond interest rates.	Dilutes earnings per share and may weaken owner control of the company.

Source: Reprinted with permission from *Financial Analysis: A Controller's Guide, Second Edition* (Hoboken, NJ: John Wiley & Sons, 2006).

shareholders; these covenants are essentially designed to ensure that the lenders are paid back and not that the company will use the funds most effectively, so there is some conflict in how the loaned money will be used.

Exhibit 21.6 summarizes the advantages and disadvantages of each type of debt and equity. When choosing financing options from among the list, the controller should remember that the correct option will vary over time because the correct mix of debt and equity, with their associated levels of cost and risk, will vary from year to year in response to changes in the organization's cash flow, the willingness of lenders to provide more debt, and stated changes in the targeted rate of return to shareholders. Consequently, the correct type of financing must be constantly reevaluated based on changing circumstances.

 ## SERVICES PROFITABILITY ANALYSIS

In the services industry, employee billable hours constitute the prime criterion for overall corporate profitability. Financial analysis should encompass the following three factors, which encompass the primary determinants of profitability in the services sector:

- Percentage of time billed
- Full labor cost per hour
- Billing price per hour

The percentage of time billed can be easily tracked with a spreadsheet, such as the one shown in Exhibit 21.7, where billable employee time is listed by week, with a month-to-date billable percentage listed not only by employee, but also for the entire company. This approach easily highlights any staff who are not meeting minimum billable targets.

In the exhibit, note the "work days" row at the bottom, which indicates the number of standard working days in each week of the report, as well as the

EXHIBIT 21.7　Billable Hours Report

| Name | Week Ending | | | | Hours | Billable % |
	07 Feb.	14 Feb.	21 Feb.	28 Feb.		
Abrams, J.	40	30	0	0	70	46%
Barlow, M.	40	32	27	39	138	91%
Chubby, T.	48	32	42	43	165	109%
Totals	128	94	69	82	373	82%
Billable %	107%	98%	58%	68%	82%	
Work Days	5	4	5	5		

EXHIBIT 21.8 Full Labor Cost per Hour Calculation

Name	Labor Rate per Hour	Payroll Taxes	Pension Matching	Medical Insurance	Long-Term Disability	Full Labor Cost/Hour
Abrams, J.	**$17.50**	$1.37	$0.05	$2.93	$0.04	**$21.89**
Barlow, M.	29.32	2.30	0.05	5.17	0.03	**36.87**
Chubby, T.	41.07	3.22	0.05	2.93	0.04	**47.31**

maximum number of hours that employees can bill during the month. The exhibit shows that more than 100 percent of possible employee hours were billed during the first week of February, due to the billable overtime hours worked by T. Chubby. However, J Abrams later becomes unbillable, resulting in only a 46 percent billable percentage for that employee by the end of the month. In total, the group has an 82 percent billable percentage during the month.

The full labor cost per hour encompasses not only the hourly rate paid per employee, but also the hourly cost of payroll taxes, various types of insurance, and other benefits (net of deductions paid by employees). Exhibit 21.8 shows the calculation of the full labor cost per hour for several employees.

A key consideration is that, if the employees providing services are being paid on a salary basis, then any overtime hours worked by them that are billable to customers represent a pure profit increase since there is no offsetting labor cost.

The price billed per hour means little unless it is compared to the full labor rate cost per hour, thereby arriving at the margin being earned on each hour worked. Otherwise, a high hourly cost could entirely offset an otherwise impressive billing rate, resulting in no profitability for the company. Exhibit 21.9 shows how the billing rate, full labor cost per hour, and billable percentage can be combined to reveal a complete picture of profitability for billable employees.

EXHIBIT 21.9 Employee Profitability Analysis

Name	Billing Rate Per Hour	Billable × Percentage =	Net Billing Rate per Hour	Full Labor − Cost/Hour	Gross = Margin
Abrams, J.	$45.00	46%	$20.70	$21.89	($1.19)
Barlow, M.	55.00	91%	50.05	36.87	13.18
Chubby, T.	60.00	109%	65.40	47.31	18.09

EXHIBIT 21.10 Breakeven Billable Percentage Calculation

Name	Full Labor Cost/Hour	/	Billing Rate Per Hour	=	Breakeven Billable %
Abrams, J.	$21.89		$45.00		49%
Barlow, M.	36.87		55.00		67%
Chubby, T.	47.31		60.00		79%

In the exhibit, the billable percentage for J. Abrams has dropped so low that the net billing rate per hour is less than that employee's fully burdened labor cost per hour; the solution is to either increase the billing rate, increase the billable percentage, reduce the employee's cost, or terminate the employee. The situation for the third employee on the list, T. Chubby, is somewhat different. We assume that Chubby does not receive extra overtime pay; if this were not the case, then the labor cost per hour in the exhibit would increase substantially to include the cost of an overtime premium.

The analysis in Exhibit 21.10 could also include a charge for a commission percentage, on the grounds that a salesperson is being paid a commission for having obtained the services contract under which the employee is now billable.

Another use for Exhibit 21.9 is to calculate the breakeven billable percentage for each employee, which management can then use as a minimum billable target. This information can be determined by shifting the information in the exhibit slightly and revising the calculation, as shown in Exhibit 21.10.

The analysis in Exhibit 21.10 reveals a different aspect of the situation; though J. Abrams is currently not profitable, a relatively low billing percentage of 49 percent will result in a profit. Conversely, though T. Chubby is currently profitable on an hourly basis, the break-even analysis reveals that a much higher billable percentage is required to maintain this situation because the margin on Chubby's services is lower than for the other two employees.

The analysis of profitability for services is nearly complete, and only excludes the consideration of corporate overhead. The gross margins noted for employees in Exhibit 21.9 must be extrapolated by the total number of hours worked in the reporting period to arrive at the grand total gross margin earned during the period. Overhead expenses are then compared to this figure to determine the profit or loss for the period, as shown in Exhibit 21.11. The

EXHIBIT 21.11 Corporate Profitability Analysis

Name	Gross Margin Per Hour	×	Hours Worked In Period	=	Total Gross Margin
Abrams, J.	($1.19)		70		($83.30)
Barlow, M.	13.18		138		1,818.84
Chubby, T.	18.09		165		2,984.85
			Total gross margin		$4,720.39
			Overhead expenses		($9,425.00)
			Net loss		($4,704.61)

exhibit reveals that the company must either pare overhead expenses drastically, obtain additional billable staff, or greatly increase the gross margin per hour of the existing employees in order to earn a profit.

THE THROUGHPUT ANALYSIS MODEL

The primary focus of throughput analysis is on how to force as much throughput dollars (sales minus totally variable expenses) as possible through the capacity constraint (i.e., the bottleneck operation). It does this by first determining the throughput dollars per minute of every production job scheduled to run through the capacity constraint, and rearranging the order of production priority so that the products with the highest throughput dollars per minute are completed first. The system is based on the supposition that only a certain amount of production can be squeezed through a bottleneck operation, so the production that yields the highest margin must come first in order of production scheduling priority, to ensure that profits are maximized. The concept is most easily demonstrated in the example shown in Exhibit 21.12.

In the example, we have four types of products that a company can sell. Each requires some machining time on the company's capacity constraint, which is the circuit board manufacturing process (CBMP). The first item is a 19″ color television, which requires four minutes of the CBMP's time. The television sells for $100.00, and has associated direct materials of $67.56, which gives it a throughput of $32.44 (the price and direct materials cost are not shown in the exhibit, only inferred). We then divide the throughput of $32.44 by the four minutes of processing time per unit on the capacity constraint to arrive at the throughput dollars per minute of $8.11 that is

EXHIBIT 21.12 Throughput Model

Product Name	Throughput $$/minute of Constraint	Required Constraint Usage (min.)	Units of Scheduled Production	Constraint Utilization (minutes)	Throughput per Product
1. 19" Color television	$8.11	4	500/500	2,000	$16,220
2. 32" LCD television	7.50	6	350/350	2,100	15,750
3. 50" High-definition TV	6.21	10	150/150	1,500	9,315
4. 42" Plasma television	5.00	12	180/400	2,160	10,800
		Total planned constraint time		7,760	—
		Maximum constraint time		8,000	—
			Throughput total		$52,085
			Operating expense total		47,900
			Profit		$4,185
			Profit percentage		8.0%
			Investment		$320,000
			Return on investment[*]		15.7%

[*]Annualized

shown in the second column of the exhibit. We then calculate the throughput per minute for the other three products and sort them in high-low order, based on which ones contribute the most throughput per minute. This leaves the 19″ color television at the top of the list. Next, we multiply the scheduled production for each item by the time required to move it through the constrained resource. We do this for all four products and verify that the total planned time required for the constraint operation is equal to or less than the actual time available at the constraint, as shown in the "Total planned constraint time" row. In the exhibit, the maximum available constraint time is listed in bold as 8,000 minutes, which is the approximate usage level for an eight-hour day in a 21-day month of business days, assuming 80 percent efficiency. This number will vary dramatically, depending on the number of shifts used, scrap levels, and the efficiency of operation of the constrained resource.

A key concept is that the maximum number of units of the highest throughput-per-minute item (in this case, the 19″ color television) are to be sold, as well as the maximum volume for each product listed below it. Only the production volume of the product listed at the bottom of the table (in this case, the 42″ plasma television) will be reduced in order to meet the limitations of the constrained resource. The amount of planned production as well as the amount of potential sales are shown in the "Units of Scheduled Production" column of the throughput model. For example, "500/500" is shown in this column for the 19″ color television, which means that there are 500 units of potential sales for this product, and the company plans to produce all 500 units. Only for the last product in the table, the 42″ plasma television, do the units of production not match the potential sales (180 units are being produced instead of the 400 units of potential sales). By doing so, a company can maximize throughput.

Then, by multiplying the throughput per minute by the number of minutes for each product, and then multiplying the result by the total number of units produced, we arrive at the total throughput for each product, as shown in the final column, as well as for the entire production process for the one-month period, which is $52,085. We must still subtract from the total throughput the sum of all operating expenses for the facility, which is $47,900 in the exhibit. After they are subtracted from the total throughput, we find that we have achieved a profit of 8.0 percent and a return on investment (annualized since the results of the model are only for a one-month period) of 15.7 percent.

When reviewing a proposal with this model, one must review the impact of the decision on the incremental change in net profit caused by a change in throughput minus operating expenses, divided by the change in investment. If there is an incremental improvement in the model, then the proposed decision should be accepted. The model makes it easy to determine the exact amount of system improvement (or degradation) occurring by incrementally changing one element of the production system.

PRODUCTION OUTSOURCING DECISION

The proper analysis of this question surrounds whether a company can earn more throughput on a combination of the outsourced production and the additional new production that will now be available through the constrained resource.

The traditional cost accounting approach would have stated that profits would be lowered by accepting an outsourcing deal that clearly cost more than the product's internal cost. However, by using this deal to release some capacity at the bottleneck, the company is able to earn more money on the production of other products.

EXAMPLE

To continue with the information in the original throughput example, one of the company's key suppliers has offered to take over the entire production of the 50" high-definition television, package it in the company's boxes, and drop ship the completed goods directly to the company's customers. The catch is that the company's throughput per unit will decrease from its current $62.10 to $30.00. The cost accounting staff would likely reject this deal, on the grounds that profits would be reduced. To see if this is a good deal, we turn once again to the throughput model, which is reproduced in the following table. In this exhibit, we have removed the number from the "units of scheduled production" column for the high-definition television since it can now be produced without the use of the capacity constraint. However, we are still able to put a cumulative throughput dollar figure into the final column for this product since there is some margin to be made by outsourcing it through the supplier. By removing the high-definition television's usage of the capacity constraint, we are now able to produce more of the next product in line, which is the plasma television set. This additional production allows the company to increase the amount of throughput dollars, thereby creating $3,885 more profits than was the case before the outsourcing deal.

Product Name	Throughput $$/ minute of Constraint	Required Constraint Usage (min.)	Units of Scheduled Production	Constraint Utilization (minutes)	Throughput per Product
1. 19" Color television	$8.11	4	500/500	2,000	$16,220
2. 32" LCD television	7.50	6	350/350	2,100	15,750
3. 50" High-definition TV	3.00	10	150/150	N/A	4,500
4. 42" Plasma television	5.00	12	325/400	3,900	19,500
		Total planned constraint time		8,000	—
		Maximum constraint time		8,000	—
			Throughput total		$55,970
			Operating expense total		47,900
			Profit		$8,070
			Profit percentage		14.4%
			Investment		$320,000
			Return on investment[*]		30.3%

[*] Annualized

NEW PRODUCT DECISION

When adding a new product that requires use of the constrained resource, management may be startled to find that profits actually decline as a result of the introduction because the new product eliminated an old product that yielded more throughput per minute. The traditional cost accounting system will not spot this problem because it focuses on the profitability of a product, rather than the amount of the constrained resource needed to produce it.

EXAMPLE

The company's engineers have designed a new, lower-cost 32" LCD television to replace the existing model. The two products are compared in the following table:

	32" LCD Television (New)	32" LCD Television (Old)
Price	$400	$400
Totally variable costs	$340	$355
Throughput	$ 60	$ 45
Overhead allocation	$ 35	$ 35
Profit	$ 25	$ 10
Required constraint usage	10 minutes	6 minutes
Throughput per minute of constraint	$ 6.00	$7.50

The traditional cost accountant would review this comparative exhibit and conclude that the new model is clearly better since it costs less to build, resulting in a profit $15 greater than for the old model. However, the new model achieves less throughput per minute because its larger throughput is being spread over a substantial increase in the required amount of time on the constrained resource. By replacing the old model with the new model, we arrive at the results shown in the next table:

(Continued)

The New Product Addition Decision (Lower Cost)

Product Name	Throughput $$/minute of Constraint	Required Constraint Usage (min.)	Units of Scheduled Production	Constraint Utilization (minutes)	Throughput per Product
1. 19" Color television	$8.11	4	500/500	2,000	$16,220
2. 50" High-definition TV	6.21	10	150/150	1,500	9,315
3. 32" LCD television **(new)**	6.00	10	350/350	3,500	21,000
4. 42" Plasma television	5.00	12	83/400	996	4,980

Total planned constraint time	**7,996**	—
Maximum constraint time	**8,000**	—

Throughput total	**$51,515**
Operating expense total	47,900
Profit	$3,615
Profit percentage	8.0%
Investment	$320,000
Return on investment[*]	13.6%

[*]Annualized

The model shows that profits have declined by $570 because the new model has used up so much constraint time that the company is no longer able to produce as many of the 42" plasma televisions. Furthermore, the throughput per minute on the new product has declined so much that it is now ranked as the third most profitable product, instead of occupying the number two position, as was the case for its predecessor product.

Let us now modify the analysis so that the company's product engineers have spent their time reducing the required amount of constraint time for the 32" LCD television, rather than in reducing its cost. In fact, let us assume that they *increase* the product's cost by $5 while *reducing* the amount of required constraint time from six minutes to five minutes, which increases its throughput per minute to $8.00. The result is shown in the following table, where the company's total throughput has increased because more time is now available at the constrained resource for additional production of the plasma television. However, this new product introduction would almost certainly have been cancelled by the cost accountants because the cost per unit would have increased.

(Continued)

The New Product Addition Decision (Higher Throughput/Minute)

Product Name	Throughput $$/minute of Constraint	Required Constraint Usage (min.)	Units of Scheduled Production	Constraint Utilization (minutes)	Throughput per Product
1. 19" Color television	$8.11	4	500/500	2,000	$16,220
2. 32" LCD television (new)	8.00	5	350/350	1,750	14,000
3. 50" High-definition TV	6.21	10	150/150	1,500	9,315
4. 42" Plasma television	5.00	12	229/400	2,748	13,740
		Total planned constraint time		**7,998**	—
		Maximum constraint time		**8,000**	—
			Throughput total		**$53,275**
			Operating expense total		47,900
			Profit		**$5,375**
			Profit percentage		10.1%
			Investment		$320,000
			Return on investment[*]		20.2%

[*] Annualized

CHAPTER TWENTY-TWO

Cost Reduction

T HE TYPICAL CORPORATION GOES through cycles of growth and contraction. During a contraction phase, the controller will inevitably be asked which expenses should be reduced. The worst possible recommendation is to recommend an across-the-board cost reduction since it impacts both key areas and less crucial ones equally. A better approach is to undertake a carefully targeted analysis that results in the selective pruning of only those costs that a company can most easily afford to lose. This chapter describes various techniques for cost reduction analysis, including spend analysis, supplier consolidation, and workforce reduction. It also provides an overview of a number of analysis tools, including check sheets, Ishikawa diagrams, and value stream mapping.

TYPES OF REPORTS USED FOR COST REDUCTION ANALYSIS

A cost reduction analysis project should start with a general overview of the target area that results in a graphical presentation of potential cost reductions. The format in Exhibit 22.1 shows the potential cost reduction impact of

Do Not Pursue

○ Commission restructuring

○ Banking fees

○ Security guard reduction

High Payback, But Difficult

○ Office merger

○ Sell subsidiary

○ Supplier consolidation

○ Advertising cutback

○ Generic office supplies

○ Cancel office parties

Low Payback, But Easy

○ Single MRO distributor

○ Layoff

○ Procurement card program

Best Implementation Option

Implementation Difficulty

Cost Reduction Impact

EXHIBIT 22.1 Cost Reduction Payoff Matrix

numerous projects across the bottom axis and implementation difficulty on the vertical axis. Cost reductions in the lower right corner are "low-hanging fruit" that generate significant returns in exchange for a modest effort. Conversely, items in the upper left corner require a great deal of effort and produce minimal returns. This format is a good guideline for deciding which projects to address first, and which can safely be delayed.

In the exhibit, the commission restructuring in the upper left corner is projected to have such a low payback and high difficulty of implementation that it is not worth doing, whereas the procurement card program is highly worthwhile since it has the reverse characteristics.

A variation on the cost reduction payoff matrix is one that itemizes a number of additional factors, such as the risk of project failure, implementation duration, and level of support. If any prospective project has a high-risk score in any category, then the project manager should either consider alternative projects or work on risk mitigation strategies. A sample risk matrix is shown in Exhibit 22.2. In the exhibit, the riskiest project appears to be the office merger, which contains three high-risk scores, while the single MRO (maintenance, repair, and operations) distributor option is the safest, with four low-risk scores.

Exhibits 22.1 and 22.2 only provide an overview of potential cost reduction projects. The next step in an organized cost reduction system is to generate greater detail regarding potential reductions. The format is shown in Exhibit 22.3, which begins with the general topics already shown in the

EXHIBIT 22.2 Cost Reduction Risk Matrix

	Cost Overrun	Customer Turnover	Extended Implementation	Management Support	Project Failure
Advertising cutback	1	4	3	2	1
Layoffs	2	1	2	4	1
Office merger	3	1	4	5	4
Single MRO distributor	1	1	4	1	2
Supplier consolidation	2	1	5	1	3
Scoring	1 = low risk 5 = high risk	1 < 1 month 5 > 1 year	1 < 1 month 5 > 1 year	1 = high 5 = low	1 = low risk 5 = high risk

EXHIBIT 22.3 Cost Reduction Itemization Matrix

Topic Area	Opportunity	Action	Implementation Difficulty	Cost Reduction (000s)
Advertising cutback	All of advertising is spent on NASCAR sponsorship	Drop sponsorship and switch to mix of Internet and magazine advertising	Low	$380
Cancel office parties	Currently have Christmas and summer parties for 14 offices	Eliminate all summer office parties	Low	170
Generic office supplies	Using brand names for 140+ types of office supplies	Standardize on generic office supplies	Low	30
Layoff	10% of production staff is currently idle	Conduct a layoff of 5% of the production staff, leaving the remainder on staff to maintain capacity	Low	490
Procurement card program	Purchase orders used for virtually all purchases	Implement a procurement card program, and mandate its usage for purchases under $500	Low	640
Single MRO distributor	Currently use 15 MRO distributors	Centralize orders and shift to standard generic supplies	Low	520
		Total Cost Reduction		**$2,230**
Banking fees	Currently paying account fees for a separate bank account for each office, and not aggregating cash for investing purposes	Switch all accounts to a single bank, and roll all cash into an investment account, using zero-balance accounts.	High	40

(Continued)

EXHIBIT 22.3 *(Continued)*

Topic Area	Opportunity	Action	Implementation Difficulty	Cost Reduction (000s)
Commission restructuring	Junior-level base pay is 25% higher than comparable rates in the market	Drop base pay to market rate for all new hires	High	75
Office merger	The Denver and Boulder offices service approximately the same group of customers	Eliminate the Boulder office, sublease the space, and shift staff to the Denver office	High	390
Security guard reduction	Currently have evening on-site security guards for all 14 offices	Switch to a private contractor that patrols the area periodically	High	85
Sell subsidiary	The Wynona Brewery is the only brewery still owned by the company	Sell the subsidiary	High	790
Supplier consolidation	Have over 1,000 suppliers for 5,400 stock-keeping units	Consolidate the supply base to 300 suppliers, and realize a 3% overall cost reduction	High	500
			Total Cost Reduction	**$1,880**

cost reduction payoff matrix, and then notes and quantifies specific opportunities. The matrix is split into two pieces, with those projects estimated to have low levels of implementation difficulty listed at the top, and those with more difficult implementation difficulty listed at the bottom.

SPEND ANALYSIS OVERVIEW

Spend analysis is the process of organizing procurement information by suppliers and commodities, and then using this information to achieve volume discounts and rebates with a reduced number of suppliers. A spend analysis system requires the creation and enhancement of a spend database as the source of a spend analysis, followed by the gradual concentration of ordering volume with a select group of suppliers; this is followed by continual efforts to monitor the company's compliance with the new system. This lengthy process can result in major cost reductions.

 SPEND DATABASE

The spend database is a highly organized cluster of files containing key information about *what* a company buys, *how much* it spends, and *who* it buys from. The database needs input feeds from the procurement systems of every company subsidiary, which should be updated on at least a quarterly basis. By aggregating all of this purchasing information, a company can see cost saving opportunities at the corporate level that would not have been present at the subsidiary level.

Next, the information must be *cleansed* and *enriched*. Cleansing is improving upon and correcting the information already contained within a database, while enrichment is adding new information to the database. As an example of cleansing, the same supplier may be recorded under a slightly different name in the feeds coming from different subsidiaries, such as International Business Machines, IBM, and I.B.M. When this happens, it is difficult to determine the amount of a company's total spend with a specific supplier. To fix the problem, the spend database should link all of the name variations for a single supplier to a single parent-level supplier name. For example, IBM could be used as the parent supplier name, and I.B.M. and International Business Machines are linked to it.

A considerable amount of cleansing may be required for item descriptions. An identical item listed in the item master records of five subsidiaries can easily have five wildly different descriptions, and it can be very difficult to match them. One way to correct the situation is to load supplier part numbers and part descriptions into the spend database, so that a part number arriving through a feed from a subsidiary will automatically pull in the correct part description.

Part of the database enrichment process includes adding commodity codes to each purchase. A commodity code assigns a general spend category to a supplier. The company can then aggregate purchase dollars for each commodity code to see where it is spending the bulk of its money, and use this information to negotiate volume purchase discounts with suppliers.

It may also be useful to enrich the spend database with a supplier credit rating. This information is periodically updated through an input feed from a third-party credit rating agency. The spend analysis system then issues reports containing just those suppliers whose credit ratings indicate that they are in financial difficulty, which the company uses to re-source with different suppliers.

Another possible enrichment is to periodically update the spend database with the company's in-house supplier ratings. These are useful for steering more work toward those suppliers that consistently have high ratings on such issues as quality and on-time performance.

A fully loaded spend database is not usable unless it has an excellent report writing package since the ability to drill down through the data is of paramount importance to spend management. Consequently, the database should be equipped with a report writer that can report on information at multiple levels, including by subsidiary, commodity code, and geographic region.

 ## SUPPLIER CONSOLIDATION ANALYSIS

The primary spend analysis strategy is to consolidate purchases in order to increase buying volume with a smaller number of preferred suppliers. These consolidation activities should be based on the number of available suppliers and the dollar volume of goods purchased. If there are few suppliers available, then single-sourcing in exchange for a cooperative approach to cost reduction may be the only cost reduction strategy. However, if there are many suppliers available and the dollar volume of purchased quantities is high, then a company can engage in a global search for the lowest-cost provider, or reverse auctions to bid down prices. If there are many suppliers but dollar volumes are low, then global sourcing is probably not cost-effective, but sourcing through a single distributor may yield the lowest overall cost. These options are shown in the cost reduction strategy matrix in Exhibit 22.4.

If a company elects to follow a global sourcing strategy, this will yield the greatest cost reductions if products have a very high labor content; international suppliers typically have access to labor rates far below those in the domestic market. Global sourcing does not work as well for raw materials since international suppliers probably have no better access to low-cost raw materials than do domestic suppliers (and must incur higher freight costs to deliver to the company).

As a company gradually shifts its business toward its preferred suppliers, its spend analysis will focus on the remaining nonpreferred suppliers. This will be a substantial list, but one toward which an ever-shrinking proportion of the company's spend is directed. The most cost-effective approach is to continually

Commodity Purchases

High dollar value, many substitutes and suppliers
Invest in global sourcing if high labor content, otherwise e-auctions for high material content

Strategic Partnerships

High dollar value, few suppliers or substitutes
Use sole source, cooperative cost reduction

Low-Value Expendables

Low dollar value, many substitutes and suppliers
Non-strategic, so use e-auctions, distributors

Key Purchases

Low dollar value, few suppliers or substitutes
Use sole source, cooperative cost reduction

Purchase Value

Alternate Sourcing Difficulty

EXHIBIT 22.4 Cost Reduction Strategy Matrix

review the highest-dollar commodities that have not yet been addressed, to pick a preferred supplier within each one, and direct the bulk of the business in that commodity to that supplier.

PARTS CONSOLIDATION ANALYSIS

Spend analysis highlights problems with parts duplication. This issue arises when different subsidiaries use slightly different versions of the same parts. If the parts description fields in the spend database have been normalized so that descriptions are comparable, the spend analysis team can spot opportunities for standardizing on a smaller number of parts. If essentially the same part is coming from different suppliers, then immediate consolidation of parts with a single supplier is possible. However, this analysis may also call for a longer-term solution, which is designing parts standardization into new versions of the company's products. In the later case, cost savings may take years to realize.

Parts duplication analysis tends to be a distant second effort behind supplier consolidation, but it can provide significant savings. For example, if a smaller firm can standardize its parts, it can order the remaining parts in greater volumes; its cost per unit may therefore decline to the point where it can effectively compete on price against a much larger competitor that has not taken advantage of parts standardization. This effect comes from buying large quantities of a smaller number of items.

MAINTENANCE, REPAIR, AND OPERATIONS ITEM ANALYSIS

Maintenance, repair, and operations (MRO) items are typically bought in great variety and very small quantities, which makes them difficult to consolidate for volume purchases. Instead, enroll the services of a distributor in examining the company's MRO purchases. The distributor can recommend replacing SKUs with less expensive ones, or which can be shipped at lower freight expense, or have lower support costs. The distributor deals with these MRO items every day in much greater volumes than the company does, and so has greater knowledge of cost-effectiveness. Distributors will perform this service if the company consolidates its MRO purchases with them.

This is the single most important MRO cost reduction initiative because a company can essentially shift a large part of its investigative labor to a third party.

 ## SPEND COMPLIANCE

The end result of spend analysis is a much greater concentration of a company's spend with a much smaller number of preferred suppliers. However, given the multitude of locations from which a large corporation can initiate purchases, and its ever-changing needs, it can be quite difficult to keep this small and select supplier base from rapidly expanding again, thereby diluting the effort of the original spend analysis. There are a number of ways to improve compliance with a completed spend analysis project, which are:

- *Contracts database.* The foundation for spend compliance is to construct a database containing all contracts that the company has entered into with its approved suppliers. This database is used to match subsequent purchasing information against what should have been purchased through these key suppliers, and the terms at which items were purchased from them. As an example of how the contracts database can be used, Contractor ABC has agreed to issue Smith Company a 2 percent rebate once Smith purchases 30,000 widgets from ABC. The company matches its purchases against the contracts database, and finds that Contractor ABC did not issued to Smith the rebate once the 30,000-unit threshold was surpassed. Smith contacts ABC and extracts not only the rebate, but also interest income for the delayed payment.
- *Incumbent rebates and discounts.* The contracts database can be loaded immediately with any existing supplier contracts; by doing so, and matching it against the spend database, a company may realize an immediate benefit, which is that suppliers may not have issued rebates and discounts based on *existing* contracts and purchase volumes.
- *Maverick spenders.* Some employees do not route purchase requests through the purchasing department, and they do not purchase through the approved corporate online purchasing catalog. Their mind-set is to either buy their favorite brand or to use their favorite supplier. By doing so, they reduce a company's purchase volumes with preferred suppliers, which results in fewer rebates and discounts. Some ways to deal with maverick spenders include bringing their activities to the attention of

senior management, including maverick spending in their annual performance reviews, and charging their departments for lost savings.

 SPEND ANALYSIS REPORTS

There is no better spend analysis report than one that clearly states exactly how much money a company can save if only it complies with directing orders to the lowest-cost supplier. The table shown in Exhibit 22.5 for a single part number illustrates the concept. The exhibit shows the lowest (and approved) price in the top row, and then the various prices being paid to other suppliers (and even the same supplier by a different subsidiary (!)—see the fourth row), along with the additional costs being incurred by continuing to use the other suppliers. This is a powerful argument for showing exactly how to reduce expenses for each subsidiary, supplier, and component.

Commodity codes are multilevel, and reporting only at the topmost level may not provide a sufficient level of detail regarding the volume of spend or the number of suppliers. If so, the report shown in Exhibit 22.6 drills down through multiple levels of commodity codes to provide this additional detail.

Another useful report is to show a quarterly trend of spend with the company's suppliers. Not only does it show the ongoing concentration of spend with top suppliers, but (of more importance) it can be used in ongoing negotiations to obtain further price reductions, discounts, and rebates as

EXHIBIT 22.5 Compliance Profit Impact

Widget, Part #123

Subsidiary	Supplier	Approved?	Unit Price	12-Month Purchase Volume (Units)	Variance from Approved Unit Price
Northridge	J.C. Hammonds	×	$1.00	25,000	—
Sonoma	Dithers & Sons		1.05	15,000	$750
Denver	Arbuthnot Corp.		1.08	18,000	1,440
Atlanta	J.C. Hammonds		1.10	42,000	4,200
Birmingham	Checkers Ltd.		1.15	15,000	2,250
				Total profit impact	**$8,640**

EXHIBIT 22.6 Multilevel Commodity Spend Report

Level 1 Commodity	Level 2 Commodity	Level 3 Commodity	Total Suppliers	Total Spend (000s)
Metal manufacturing	Steel product	Iron and steel pipe	8	$13,540
		Rolled steel	4	4,710
		Steel wire	3	3,900
	Steel product total		15	$22,150
	Aluminum product	Aluminum sheets	2	2,370
		Extruded aluminum	9	970
		Other aluminum	11	320
	Aluminum product total		22	$ 3,660
	Nonferrous metal	Extruded copper	14	1,900
		Copper wire	2	1,110
		Other nonferrous	5	880
	Nonferrous metal total		21	$ 3,890
Supplies total			50	$29,700

the company directs more business toward its top suppliers. The report also shows the remaining spend *not* with the top suppliers, which shows the company the extent of additional spend concentration that it can achieve. An example is shown in Exhibit 22.7.

EXHIBIT 22.7 Supplier Spend Trend Report

Ranking	Supplier Name	Spend (000s)			
		Quarter 1	Quarter 2	Quarter 3	Quarter 4
1	Columbus Framing	$ 17,980	$ 18,020	$ 18,400	$ 18,940
2	Masonic Metalcastings	9,730	10,030	10,170	10,500
3	Jacobean Fittings	7,090	7,260	7,605	7,865
4	Bricklin Supply	5,995	6,190	6,430	6,990
5	J.C. Hammonds Corp.	5,450	5,780	6,000	6,150
	Subtotals	$ 46,245	$ 47,280	$ 48,605	$ 50,445
Remaining suppliers		90,410	89,045	86,830	84,060
	Grand totals	$136,655	$136,325	$135,435	$134,505
Remaining suppliers percent of total		**66%**	**65%**	**64%**	**62%**

EXHIBIT 22.8 Preferred Supplier Concentration by Commodity

	20x1		20x2		20x3	
Commodity	Preferred Supplier Spend (000s)	Percent of Total Spend	Preferred Supplier Spend (000s)	Percent of Total Spend	Preferred Supplier Spend (000s)	Percent of Total Spend
Facilities	$1,400	14%	$1,623	18%	$2,044	29%
Fittings	170	3%	350	8%	482	11%
Fixed assets	13,079	32%	16,080	39%	15,750	37%
Materials	2,450	10%	5,030	20%	5,850	24%
Supplies	–	0%	80	4%	130	10%

It is also possible to aggregate information at a considerably higher level to see what proportion of total spend has been shifted to approved suppliers by commodity type. The purpose of this report is to measure progress toward gradually shifting spend into a small cluster of preferred suppliers. It does not measure cost savings, focusing instead on general levels of concentration. An example is shown in Exhibit 22.8.

An overall result of spend analysis is to reduce the number of suppliers. At a general level, it is useful to aggregate this information to see how much concentration is occurring. The intent is not to shift *all* spend into a small number of suppliers since it is not cost-effective to spend time eliminating the smallest tier of suppliers. Instead, the focus of the report is to highlight the *proportion* of spend concentrated in the top tier of suppliers. An example is shown in Exhibit 22.9.

The example spend concentration report reveals that the company has a considerable amount of supplier consolidation work to do; the number of suppliers with 80 percent of total spend in each commodity category comprise

EXHIBIT 22.9 Spend Concentration Report

For the Year Ended December 31, 20x3

	Facilities	Fittings	Fixed Assets	Materials	Supplies
Total spend (000s)	$7,048	$4,382	$42,568	$24,375	$1,300
Total suppliers	108	240	42	289	98
Suppliers with 80% of spend	22	50	10	63	25
Suppliers with 90% of spend	51	82	18	90	31
Suppliers with 95% of spend	73	129	25	135	43

roughly 20 percent of the total number of suppliers, which does not depart appreciably from what a Pareto analysis would reveal. In other words, the supplier distribution does not depart significantly from what would be expected if the company had taken no action at all to concentrate its spend with preferred suppliers.

 ## WORKFORCE REDUCTION ANALYSIS

The first step in workforce cost reduction is to determine the cost directly attributable to each employee. Exhibit 22.10 shows a good format for this calculation. From left to right, it shows base-level annual compensation, followed by all related payroll taxes and net benefit costs. It then continues with several additional expenses that can be directly traced to each employee. The Social Security tax is only applicable below a certain maximum wage level, which is noted in the lower left corner of the exhibit. The 401k pension withholding for each employee is not an expense, but is included in order to show the company 401k match, which *is* an expense. The exhibit is sorted in alphabetical order by employee last name.

Overhead costs should be considered if a sufficient number of positions are eliminated to also trigger an immediate overhead reduction. Exhibit 22.11 uses the same format as Exhibit 22.10, but now the assumption is that by laying off entire *groups* of employees, a block of clearly identifiable overhead expenses can be eliminated. In the exhibit, employees are now sorted by store location, so that the elimination of an entire group of employees and their associated overhead costs can be clumped together. The cost reduction decision point is no longer the individual employee, but rather an entire company location.

Thus far, the analysis has only addressed the cost of each employee or group of employees, but does not incorporate any revenue that employees may directly generate, such as in a service environment. Without this information, a company may lay off its most expensive employee, without considering that the same person also generates a great deal of revenue for the company.

Exhibit 22.12 shows a breakdown of both revenue and cost for employees, so that profitability can now be ascertained on an individual level. The exhibit compresses the level of expense detail, thereby making room for revenue and profit information. The exhibit includes a column for a commission expense, which is subtracted from the revenues to arrive at a net revenue amount for each employee.

EXHIBIT 22.10 Employee Cost Rollup

Employee Name	Annual Pay	Social Security	Medicare	401K Withhold	50% 401K Match	Medical	Medical Deducts	Annual Phone	Annual T&E	Total Cost
Andrews, Bill	$ 42,750	$ 2,651	$ 620	$ 4,000	$ 2,000	$ 14,185	$ (5,242)	$ 1,200	$ 5,000	$ 63,163
Brennan, Charles	$ 125,000	$ 6,622	$ 1,813	$ 16,500	$ 8,250	$ 17,265	$ (6,780)	$ –	$ –	$ 152,169
Cantor, David	$ 80,000	$ 4,960	$ 1,160	$ 7,250	$ 3,625	$ 6,175	$ (1,225)	$ 1,200	$ 8,500	$ 104,395
DiMaggio, Earnest	$ 77,500	$ 4,805	$ 1,124	$ 2,500	$ 1,250	$ 17,265	$ (6,780)	$ 1,450	$ 500	$ 97,114
Entenmann, Franklin	$ 142,500	$ 6,622	$ 2,066	$ 16,500	$ 8,250	$ 17,265	$ (6,780)	$ 1,200	$ 18,500	$ 189,623
Fairview, George	$ 37,500	$ 2,325	$ 544	$ 500	$ 250	$ –	$ –	$ 1,200	$ 1,250	$ 43,069
Gorman, Hercules	$ 225,000	$ 6,622	$ 3,263	$ 16,500	$ 8,250	$ –	$ –	$ 1,200	$ 32,750	$ 277,084
Henderson, Ian	$ 85,000	$ 5,270	$ 1,233	$ 4,000	$ 2,000	$ 17,265	$ (6,780)	$ 1,200	$ 1,750	$ 106,938
Innes, Julie	$ 73,000	$ 4,526	$ 1,059	$ –	$ –	$ –	$ –	$ –	$ –	$ 78,585
Jackson, Kari	$ 119,000	$ 6,622	$ 1,726	$ 14,250	$ 7,125	$ 6,175	$ (1,225)	$ –	$ –	$ 139,422
Klerk, Larry	$ 170,000	$ 6,622	$ 2,465	$ 16,500	$ 8,250	$ 14,185	$ (5,242)	$ 1,450	$ 800	$ 198,530
Lincoln, Mandy	$ 95,000	$ 5,890	$ 1,378	$ 9,000	$ 4,500	$ 6,175	$ (1,225)	$ 1,200	$ 4,250	$ 117,168
Masters, Nancy	$ 62,500	$ 3,875	$ 906	$ 1,000	$ 500	$ 14,185	$ (5,242)	$ 1,200	$ –	$ 77,924
	$ 1,334,750	$ 67,410	$ 19,354		$ 54,250	$ 130,140	$ (46,521)	$ 12,500	$ 73,300	$ 1,645,182
Percent of total	81%	4%	1%		3%	8%	-3%	1%	4%	100%

		Social Security	Medicare	401K Withhold
	Tax percentage	6.20%	1.45%	None
	Maximum cap	$ 106,800		

418

EXHIBIT 22.11 Employee Cost Rollup with Overhead

Napa Store:	Annual Pay	Social Security	Medicare	401K Withhold	50% 401K Match	Medical	Medical Deducts	Annual Phone	Annual T&E	Total Cost
Andrews, Bill	$ 42,750	$ 2,651	$ 620	$ 4,000	$ 2,000	$ 14,185	$ (5,242)	$ 1,200	$ 5,000	$ 63,163
Entenmann, Franklin	$ 142,500	$ 6,622	$ 2,066	$ 16,500	$ 8,250	$ 17,265	$ (6,780)	$ 1,200	$ 18,500	$ 189,623
Jackson, Kari	$ 119,000	$ 6,622	$ 1,726	$ 14,250	$ 7,125	$ 6,175	$ (1,225)	$ –	$ –	$ 139,422
Klerk, Larry	$ 170,000	$ 6,622	$ 2,465	$ 16,500	$ 8,250	$ 14,185	$ (5,242)	$ 1,450	$ 800	$ 198,530
Lincoln, Mandy	$ 95,000	$ 5,890	$ 1,378	$ 9,000	$ 4,500	$ 6,175	$ (1,225)	$ 1,200	$ 4,250	$ 117,168
Masters, Nancy	$ 62,500	$ 3,875	$ 906	$ 1,000	$ 500	$ 14,185	$ (5,242)	$ 1,200	$ –	$ 77,924
										$ 785,830
									Annual Rent:	$ 156,000
									Annual Utilities:	$ 28,000
										$ 969,830
Santa Rosa Store:										
Brennan, Charles	$ 125,000	$ 6,622	$ 1,813	$ 16,500	$ 8,250	$ 17,265	$ (6,780)	$ –	$ –	$ 152,169
Cantor, David	$ 80,000	$ 4,960	$ 1,160	$ 7,250	$ 3,625	$ 6,175	$ (1,225)	$ 1,200	$ 8,500	$ 104,395
DiMaggio, Earnest	$ 77,500	$ 4,805	$ 1,124	$ 2,500	$ 1,250	$ 17,265	$ (6,780)	$ 1,450	$ 500	$ 97,114
Fairview, George	$ 37,500	$ 2,325	$ 544	$ 500	$ 250	$ –	$ –	$ 1,200	$ 1,250	$ 43,069
Gorman, Hercules	$ 225,000	$ 6,622	$ 3,263	$ 16,500	$ 8,250	$ –	$ –	$ 1,200	$ 32,750	$ 277,084
Henderson, Ian	$ 85,000	$ 5,270	$ 1,233	$ 4,000	$ 2,000	$ 17,265	$ (6,780)	$ 1,200	$ 1,750	$ 106,938
Innes, Julie	$ 73,000	$ 4,526	$ 1,059	$ –	$ –	$ –	$ –	$ –	$ –	$ 78,585
										$ 859,353
									Annual Rent:	$ 172,000
									Annual Utilities:	$ 32,500
										$ 1,063,853

EXHIBIT 22.12 Employee Profitability Calculation

Employee Name	Revenues			Annual Pay	Expenses		Total Cost	Profit	Profit %
	Annual Revenues	Commission	Net Revenues		Payroll Taxes	Benefits			
Andrews, Bill	$ 101,890	$ 4,076	$ 97,814	$ 42,750	$ 3,270	$ 17,143	$ 63,163	$ 34,651	35%
Brennan, Charles	$ 234,750	$ 9,390	$ 225,360	$ 125,000	$ 8,434	$ 18,735	$ 152,169	$ 73,191	32%
Cantor, David	$ 119,250	$ 4,770	$ 114,480	$ 80,000	$ 6,120	$ 18,275	$ 104,395	$ 10,085	9%
DiMaggio, Earnest	$ 142,120	$ 5,685	$ 136,435	$ 77,500	$ 5,929	$ 13,685	$ 97,114	$ 39,321	29%
Entenmann, Franklin	$ 267,040	$ 10,682	$ 256,358	$ 142,500	$ 8,688	$ 38,435	$ 189,623	$ 66,736	26%
Fairview, George	$ 71,020	$ 2,841	$ 68,179	$ 37,500	$ 2,869	$ 2,700	$ 43,069	$ 25,110	37%
Gorman, Hercules	$ 203,150	$ 8,126	$ 195,024	$ 225,000	$ 9,884	$ 42,200	$ 277,084	$ (82,060)	-42%
Henderson, Ian	$ 173,350	$ 6,934	$ 166,416	$ 85,000	$ 6,503	$ 15,435	$ 106,938	$ 59,479	36%
Innes, Julie	$ 123,950	$ 4,958	$ 118,992	$ 73,000	$ 5,585	$ –	$ 78,585	$ 40,408	34%
Jackson, Kari	$ 225,290	$ 9,012	$ 216,278	$ 119,000	$ 8,347	$ 12,075	$ 139,422	$ 76,856	36%
Klerk, Larry	$ 274,040	$ 10,962	$ 263,078	$ 170,000	$ 9,087	$ 19,443	$ 198,530	$ 64,549	25%
Lincoln, Mandy	$ 92,650	$ 3,706	$ 88,944	$ 95,000	$ 7,268	$ 14,900	$ 117,168	$ (28,224)	-32%
Masters, Nancy	$ 129,740	$ 5,190	$ 124,550	$ 62,500	$ 4,781	$ 10,643	$ 77,924	$ 46,626	37%
	$ 2,158,240	$ 86,330	$ 2,071,910	$ 1,334,750	$ 86,763	$ 223,669	$ 1,645,182	$ 426,728	21%

WORKFORCE REDUCTION ISSUES

A workforce reduction is designed to save money, but it may do the reverse in the short term since there are a number of expenses associated with it. Here are several expenses to consider, followed by several ways to mitigate them:

- *Severance package.* The most minimal severance package is simply severance pay, but can also include a number of other costs, such as benefits continuation, the use of a company phone or computer, and outplacement services. Severance pay is typically linked to the number of years of employee service, so the payout can be severe if the workforce reduction includes personnel with high seniority.
- *Accrued vacation.* If an employee has not used any portion of his or her earned vacation, the company must pay it to the employee at the time of the workforce reduction.
- *Stock grant acceleration.* If an employee is part of a stock grant program, the program will likely have an award acceleration clause, where vesting in the shares is accelerated in the event of a change in control of the company. If the employee is being laid off because of the change in control, it is likely that he or she will receive the stock grant at termination. If so, the company must record a noncash expense at the time of vesting to reflect the recognition of all remaining expense associated with the stock grant.
- *Unemployment insurance.* If a company continually lays off its employees, they in turn will draw down the state's unemployment fund, which the state government must replenish by increasing the company's unemployment contribution rate in the following year.
- *Potential lawsuits.* There is always a risk that some employees will sue the company for wrongful termination. Even if there is no likelihood of a payout, the company must still pay legal fees to defend its position. To avoid this issue, make any severance payment conditional upon employee agreement not file a claim against the company.

The severance and vacation expenses noted above can be mitigated to some extent by paying them out based on an average of an employee's pay for the past few years, rather than on the final pay level (which is presumably higher). This pay calculation should be fully documented in the employee manual.

WORKFORCE REDUCTION ALTERNATIVES

Many companies try to avoid a workforce reduction. However, there are still prospects for reducing payroll costs. The following techniques are still available:

- *Review overtime pay.* There should be a formal supervisory review of all overtime hours claimed, which can be triggered by an automated time-keeping system. Better yet, an analyst should review the reasons why the bulk of the overtime hours were incurred, and see if there are any alternatives that can avoid the future incurrence of this cost.
- *Use vacation time.* By encouraging its staff to take unused vacation time, a company still incurs a cash outflow to pay for the vacations, but this may also soak up a considerable amount of unused vacation time, so that employees will be more available later, when they may be needed for revenue-generating activities.
- *Delay new hires.* If there is a reasonable expectation that business will improve shortly, then hold off on making offers to new hire candidates. If offers have already been extended, then consider delaying their start dates, while paying them a stipend and moving expenses.
- *Attrition.* The most noninvasive form of workforce reduction is simply to not replace employees when they retire or leave the company for other reasons. This is a long-term solution since employee departures may occur over quite a few years before a company has reduced its headcount to its targeted level.
- *Delay or reduce scheduled pay raises.* If a medium-term business downturn is expected, then management can authorize a significant delay in scheduled pay raises, or reduce the amount of raises that will be granted. This approach should be shared by all, to gain acceptance.
- *Require unpaid days off.* There may be cases where occasional unpaid days off for the entire workforce will resolve financial difficulties. If so, reduce the sting for employees by allowing them to pick which days to take off. For example, the days off may coincide with school vacations or be adjacent to federal holidays.
- *Shorten the work week.* If there is not enough work for a large part of the company, then the company can elect to shorten the work week for some period of time, with reduced pay to match the shorter work period. This alternative works best for a single-day reduction from a five-day to a four-day work week since the result is a 20 percent pay cut for everyone in the company.

- *Shorten working hours.* In a retail environment, it may make sense to determine when the bulk of customers are shopping, and then contract store hours to match.
- *Use unpaid leaves of absence.* An unpaid leave of absence only encourages employees to look for new jobs, and so will likely result in a very high turnover level in the near term. However, if the company offers to continue paying benefits to employees during their leaves of absence, they may be more inclined to stay out of work longer, and still return to the company at the end of their leaves of absence.
- *Offer paid sabbaticals.* If the business downturn is expected to be extensive, then management can offer a sabbatical with a moderate rate of pay to those employees judged to have sufficient seniority. The amount paid can be viewed as a retainer for consulting services, which the company can exercise by occasionally calling in employees on sabbatical to assist during high-volume periods.
- *Freeze pay.* The workforce may accept a complete pay freeze for a limited period of time, if they understand that the situation is caused by economic conditions that put the company at risk. This approach works best if everyone is included in the pay freeze.
- *Implement a pay cut.* A more drastic alternative is to mandate a pay cut. If implemented, this should be universal, so that no charges of favoritism can be levied. Further, the pay cut should be even greater for the management team, which creates a solid reason for the management group to work the company back into profitability.

If the company enacts either a shorter work week or fewer working hours during the business day, then this will also reduce the amount of vacation and sick hours accrued, so there is a cumulative cost reduction effect.

 ## 5S ANALYSIS

The 5S system is about organizing the workplace in order to eliminate waste. From a cost reduction perspective, it promotes workplace efficiency. As the name of this tool implies, there are five steps, and their names all begin with "S." They are:

1. *Sort.* Review all the items within a work area, retain those needed for daily operations, and dispose of all other items.

2. *Straighten.* Reposition furniture and equipment to best serve the process flow, and move all other items out of the way.
3. *Scrub.* Clean the area completely.
4. *Systematize.* Establish schedules for repetitively cleaning the area.
5. *Standardize.* Incorporate the 5S system into standard company operations, so that it is performed on an ongoing basis. This should include a formal system for monitoring the results of the program.

A company should not embark upon a 5S clean sweep of an entire company at the same time since that would create a great deal of disruption. Instead, this is a methodical process that is used to gradually address all locations, after which it starts over again in a continual cycle.

 ## CHECK SHEETS

The check sheet is a structured form used for the collection and analysis of data. Its most common application is for the collection of data about the frequency or patterns of events. Data entry on the form is designed to be as simple as possible, with check marks or similar symbols. The check sheet is most frequently used in a production setting, but can be easily applied anywhere in a company.

For example, what if the controller is trying to increase the efficiency of the cash application process? Her first step is to determine the frequency of various issues impacting the process, so that she can focus her efforts on efficiency improvement. She discusses the project with the cash application staff, and uses their input to construct the check sheet shown in Exhibit 22.13. The cash application staff fills it in during a one-week period, resulting in the determination that unauthorized payment deductions are the most frequent problem encountered during cash application, followed by missing remittance detail information. This information can then be used to prioritize efficiency improvement (and the resulting cost reduction) activities.

 ## ERROR QUANTIFICATION

Any error that results in a scrapped or reworked product or document is piling up costs. A company can create an information tracking system to aggregate error information, which is then summarized into a report such as the one shown in Exhibit 22.14. The report notes the number of incidences of an error

Reason	Day					
	Mon.	Tue.	Wed.	Thu.	Fri.	Total
Customer double pay		‖		│		3
No remittance advice enclosed	│	╫	‖	│	‖‖‖	13
Pays with multiple checks			│		│	2
Unauthorized deductions taken	╫	╫‖‖	‖‖‖	╫‖‖	‖	25
Total	6	14	7	9	7	43

EXHIBIT 22.13 Cash Application Check Sheet

EXHIBIT 22.14 Error Quantification Report

Error Type	Number of Incidents	Lost Throughput per Incident	Total Lost Throughput	Total Rework Time	Total Rework Cost
Rework—Adjust paint gaps	14	$11.14	$155.96	3:30	$70.00
Rework—Cut off excess trim	29	8.23	238.67	5:00	100.00
Rework—Redrill unaligned hole	8	4.88	39.04	2:00	40.00
Rework—Smooth rough edges	11	7.35	80.85	1:00	20.00
Scrap—Broken base unit	10	19.20	192.00	–	–
Scrap—Crushed packaging	4	6.10	24.40	–	–
Scrap—Dented electronics	17	12.05	204.85	–	–

event during the measurement period. It also notes the lost throughput of each item. If an item is scrapped, then the associated throughput (revenue minus totally variable costs) is lost forever. If an item is reworked, then the cost of the rework labor is offset against the lost throughput to yield a reduced level of throughput. Further, the report indicates the time and labor cost required for rework.

The error quantification report example reveals that the worst scrap issue to investigate is dented electronics since the company loses the most throughput dollars from this problem. Among the rework issues, the cost of additional labor must be offset against the potential lost throughput to see if rework is worthwhile. The redrilling work is costing more to fix than the throughput that would otherwise be lost, so these items can be scrapped instead. The other rework efforts all yield a higher throughput than would be the case if no rework were done.

 FIXED COST ANALYSIS

A common decision point is whether to incur a large fixed cost (such as a high-capacity machine) in order to achieve higher margins through greater production efficiency. The answer, in many cases, is no. The reason is that a large fixed cost increases a company's break-even point, so that it must make more sales before it can begin to earn a profit. This can be a risky scenario in a volatile market. The issue can even be reversed—should existing fixed costs be eliminated in exchange for variable costs that result in somewhat lower margins? In many cases, yes. It is worthwhile to be somewhat less profitable in exchange for having a more flexible company that can earn a profit over a broader range of revenues and margins. This issue can extend to a variety of nonproduction issues, such as leasing office space rather than buying a building.

ISHIKAWA DIAGRAMS

The Ishikawa diagram reveals the causes of a specified event. The diagram, as shown in Exhibit 22.15, has the general appearance of the bones of a fish. The problem to be solved lies at the head. Major bones represent groups of major causes, while minor bones represent subcauses. An Ishikawa diagram is an excellent starting point for a cost reduction analysis since solving the issues listed along the various branches of the diagram will likely solve the initial problem, which may have been a source of considerable expense.

The exhibit shows the categories of issues causing late product deliveries to customers. The issues are clustered under general categories, such as Policy, Product, and Machine. For example, under the Machine category, incorrect machine setups are delaying the production of goods, as well as inadequate preventive maintenance that is increasing machine down time. Each of the items on the diagram can be addressed in order to ultimately reduce the incidence of late product deliveries to customers.

There are a large number of major causes under which subcauses can be clustered. Possible headings include environment, equipment, inspection, manpower, materials, maintenance, management, policies, prices, procedures, processing, products, promotions, and suppliers.

VALUE STREAM MAPPING

Value stream mapping (VSM) focuses on the identification of waste across an entire process. A VSM chart identifies all of the actions required to complete a process, while also identifying key information about each action item. Key information will vary by the process under review, but can include total hours worked, overtime hours, cycle time to complete a transaction, error rates, and absenteeism.

The VSM chart shown in Exhibit 22.16 addresses the entire procurement cycle, from the initial placement of a requisition through processing of the

EXHIBIT 22.15 Ishikawa Diagram

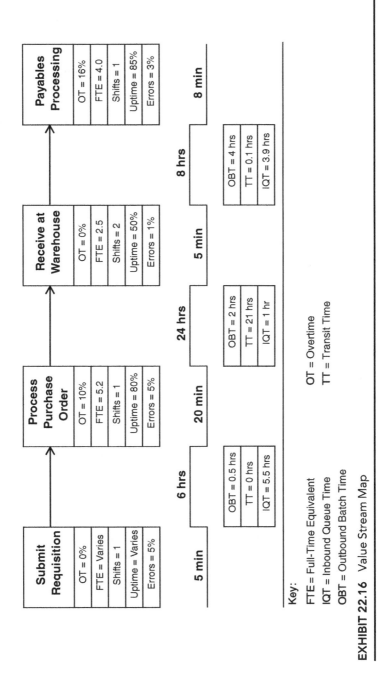

Submit Requisition

OT = 0%	
FTE = Varies	
Shifts = 1	
Uptime = Varies	
Errors = 5%	

Process Purchase Order

OT = 10%	
FTE = 5.2	
Shifts = 1	
Uptime = 80%	
Errors = 5%	

Receive at Warehouse

OT = 0%	
FTE = 2.5	
Shifts = 2	
Uptime = 50%	
Errors = 1%	

Payables Processing

OT = 16%	
FTE = 4.0	
Shifts = 1	
Uptime = 85%	
Errors = 3%	

5 min — 6 hrs — 20 min — 24 hrs — 5 min — 8 hrs — 8 min

OBT = 0.5 hrs	
TT = 0 hrs	
IQT = 5.5 hrs	

OBT = 2 hrs	
TT = 21 hrs	
IQT = 1 hr	

OBT = 4 hrs	
TT = 0.1 hrs	
IQT = 3.9 hrs	

Key:

FTE = Full-Time Equivalent
IQT = Inbound Queue Time
OBT = Outbound Batch Time

OT = Overtime
TT = Transit Time

EXHIBIT 22.16 Value Stream Map

resulting supplier invoice. Under each processing step, the VSM chart itemizes the amount of overtime, staffing, work shifts, process uptime, and transaction error rate. The chart then shows the total time required for each processing step, as well as the time required between steps, and also identifies the types of time spent *between* steps (e.g., outbound batching, transit time, and inbound queue time).

The chart reveals that most of the procurement cycle time is used between processing steps, especially in the transit time of orders from suppliers to the company. If total cycle time is an issue, then a reasonable conclusion would be to either source locally or expend more for faster delivery services. However, if the emphasis is on speedier in-house processing, then the chart shows that the purchase order processing stage is the most time-consuming; it is also probably a bottleneck operation, given the amount of overtime incurred. Likely conclusions would be to reduce the error rate in the purchasing area by working on a reduction of errors in the upstream requisitioning area, offloading purchasing work with procurement cards, or bolstering capacity by adding purchasing staff.

Another option for shrinking the long cycle time is to have the receiving staff send receiving documents to the payables department more frequently than once every four hours; cutting the outbound batch time in half would eliminate two hours from the total cycle time.

VSM works best in highly focused, high-volume processes where it makes sense to spend time wringing a few seconds out of repetitive processes.

 ## WASTE ANALYSIS

Cost reduction can be performed simply by identifying the various types of waste, and then working to reduce them. Here are seven types of waste to be aware of:

1. *Additional processing.* This is any production process that does not directly add value to a product, such as a quality control review.
2. *Defects.* Any processing that destroys or harms production that has already passed through the bottleneck operation is a form of waste because it eliminates valuable throughput and may require additional expenditures for rework.
3. *Inventory.* Inventory of all types requires a working capital investment, incurs storage costs, and is at risk of obsolescence. It also hides other cost issues, such as production imbalances and poor work practices.

4. *Motion.* Any motion by employees that does not add value is a waste. This includes any equipment setup time.

5. *Overproduction.* Any production exceeding specific customer orders is a waste because it uses materials and other resources, which then incur storage costs and are subject to obsolescence.

6. *Transportation.* This is the movement of materials between any operations that transform the materials, such as between workstations in a production process. The more something moves, the more opportunity there is to damage materials. Spending on materials handling equipment or conveyor belts is also a form of waste.

7. *Waiting.* Any time when a machine or its operator is waiting is considered a waste of that resource. Waiting can be caused by unbalanced workloads, overstaffing, materials shortages, and so forth.

23

Taxes

T
HE REPORTING REQUIREMENTS OF all governmental agencies have increased significantly and have become more complex. This is particularly true of the reporting requirements for federal and state taxes. The endless rules and regulations are always changing to be consistent with national policy and economic objectives. It is mandatory that business develop and maintain adequate records to meet the requirements of these widely diverse patterns of federal and local tax laws. If the records and reporting systems are not properly planned, a company will be subject to considerable financial exposure. Emphasis must be placed on the proper recording of financial transactions, accuracy in preparing data for tax reports, and timely reporting to concerned taxing authorities.

Some companies follow a practice of referring federal tax matters to public accountants or tax attorneys. There are, of course, times when such assistance is desirable and necessary. However, the tendency to place such responsibility in hands outside the home organization carries with it certain disadvantages. The application of tax laws to a specific business situation requires an intimate knowledge of the business and its transactions—something the external tax advisor cannot gain through an occasional or annual visit. More than this, the application of the tax laws must be considered in many day-to-day operating decisions. In addition, the controller has as a primary function the determination of the periodic and annual earnings, and federal laws are an important factor in such determination. The controller, then, has a fundamental responsibility to be fully informed on tax matters, particularly federal income taxes, and to use this knowledge to avoid paying excess taxes.

In summary, the controller should be able to check the more important tax computations. The entire accounting staff should have a general understanding of the tax laws and should be sufficiently aware of tax implications to inquire into, and secure an answer to, the probable tax results of any given transaction.

TAX STRATEGY

The obvious objective of tax strategy is to minimize the amount of cash paid out for taxes. However, this objective directly conflicts with the general desire to report as much income as possible to shareholders because more reported income results in more taxes. Only in the case of privately owned firms do these conflicting problems go away because the owners have no need to impress anyone with their reported level of earnings and would prefer to retain as much cash in the company as possible by avoiding the payment of taxes.

For those controllers who are intent on reducing their corporation's tax burdens, there are five primary goals to include in their tax strategies, all of which involve increasing the number of differences between the book and tax records, so that reportable income for tax purposes is reduced. The five items are:

1. *Accelerate deductions.* By recognizing expenses sooner, expenses that would otherwise be deferred can be forced into the current reporting year. The primary deduction acceleration involves depreciation, for which a company typically uses the Modified Accelerated Cost Recovery System (MACRS) (an accelerated depreciation methodology acceptable for tax reporting purposes), and straight-line depreciation, which results in a higher level of reported earnings for other purposes.

2. *Take all available tax credits.* A credit results in a permanent reduction in taxes and thus is highly desirable. Unfortunately, credits are increasingly difficult to find, though a company might qualify for the research and experimental tax credit, which is available to those companies that have increased their research activities over the previous year. The only type of

expense that qualifies for this credit is that which is undertaken to discover information that is technical in nature, and its application must be intended for use in developing a new or improved business component for the taxpayer. Also, all of the research activities must be elements of a process of experimentation relating to a new or improved function, or that enhance the current level of performance, reliability, or quality. A credit cannot be taken for research conducted after the beginning of commercial production, for the customization of a product for a specific customer, the duplication of an existing process or product, or research required for some types of software to be used internally.

There are more tax credits available at the local level, where they are offered to those businesses willing to operate in economic development zones or as part of specialized relocation deals (which are normally available only to larger companies).

3. *Avoid nonallowable expenses.* A few expenses, most notably meals and entertainment, are completely or at least partially not allowed for purposes of computing taxable income. A key company strategy is to reduce these types of expenses to the bare minimum, thereby avoiding any lost benefits from nonallowable expenses.

4. *Increase tax deferrals.* In a number of situations taxes can be shifted into the future, such as payments in stock for acquisitions or the deferral of revenue received until all related services have been performed. These deferrals can shift a large part of the tax liability into the future, where the time value of money results in a smaller present value of the tax liability than would otherwise be the case.

5. *Obtain tax-exempt income.* The controller should consider investing excess funds in municipal bonds, which are exempt from both federal income taxes and the income taxes of the state in which they were issued. The downside of this approach is that the return on municipal bonds is less than the return on other forms of investment, due to their inherent tax savings.

TAX ORGANIZATION

The responsibility for the tax activities should be placed with a financial executive who understands the relationship of the accounting function to the tax laws and compliance. As the tax function affects cash flows and accounting determinations, it is a controller's function.

The increasing importance of taxes as a cost of doing business and the significant number of taxing authorities to be considered make it imperative that the administration of tax matters be regarded as a separate function in the organization. The plan of organization in most companies gives formal recognition to the tax function. In some companies with complex tax problems and worldwide business interests, management considers taxes important enough to appoint a vice president of taxation. In other situations, a separate department is established, headed by a manager responsible for all facets of taxes. Depending on the complexity and size of the tax problems, the tax department may be organized according to the types of taxes, such as federal income taxes, state income taxes, sales taxes, property taxes, and payroll taxes.

A prime consideration in organizing and staffing a tax department is the degree of centralization concerning the administration of tax matters. This is particularly important when a company has several plants, branches, operating units, and international operations. Normally, a centralized tax organization will exercise control over all tax policies and procedures within the company. In addition, it will manage the home office tax organization and in some cases direct the day-to-day activities of the decentralized tax people. However, in any event, functional control over the field tax organization should be vested in the corporate tax manager.

There are some advantages to having local personnel handle certain tax functions because of the relationships with the local taxing authorities, as in the case of property taxes. The corporate tax manager should make periodic reviews in these instances.

The preparation of tax returns can be centralized or decentralized, depending on the circumstances and economics. If the data are in the local office, it may be advantageous to have the return prepared locally, with appropriate review by the tax manager's staff. The records to be maintained should be prescribed by the corporate tax department. Some companies, for example, have the payroll department of each entity prepare payroll tax returns since the detail information is readily available from the payroll records. However, the tax manager will review and probably sign and file the returns.

As in any function, there are advantages to the centralization of tax responsibilities. It is more economical, permits a higher degree of specialization, is a more efficient use of tax resources (e.g., a centralized tax library), promotes uniformity, and allows more flexibility in handling the workload. There can also be disadvantages to a centralized tax function, such as the lack of sufficient contact with local taxing authorities. In those cases where decentralization is used, the central tax department should still provide guidance, instruction, and review services.

 ## ROLE OF THE TAX MANAGER

The functions of the tax manager will vary with the organization. The next list is an indication of the extent of responsibilities assigned to the tax department in a large company.

- Develop, recommend, and implement approved plans for an effective tax management program applicable to all elements of the corporation. Ensure that the company complies with all applicable laws, rules, and regulations pertaining to taxes.
- Select personnel, assign duties, and establish appropriate control over activities.
- Plan for the administration of local or branch office tax functions.
- Maintain adequate tax records, prepare forms and working papers, and establish designation of the files.
- Prepare a tax manual establishing procedures and responsibilities.
- Evaluate the effect of tax laws, regulations, rulings, and court cases on the company's tax liabilities and potential business activities.
- Develop policies and procedures to minimize the company's tax liability.
- Determine that the company has filed all tax returns, reports, and declarations required by law.
- Recommend action concerning all tax adjustments proposed by the various taxing authorities or by the company's independent public accountants and represent the company, or cause the company to be represented, in all negotiations affecting the company's tax liabilities.
- Initiate action to obtain IRS approval, when required, with respect to changes in accounting methods and procedures and matters pertaining to retirement or savings plans.
- Prepare and prosecute in cooperation with counsel, formal protests, claims, petitions, or court actions with respect to disputed tax matters involving the company, coordinating all such activities with other concerned functions, such as legal and accounting.
- Initiate action, when required, to obtain IRS rulings regarding the company's tax liability.

■ Analyze the tax implications of proposed acquisitions to determine present or potential problems and examine tax carry-back or -forward possibilities.

■ Provide information concerning federal, state, local, and foreign tax matters, based on the advice of counsel where necessary.

■ Analyze the tax effect of legal documents affecting the company and render advice regarding appropriate action to minimize the company's tax liabilities with respect thereto.

■ Review the annual and strategic plans to develop the tax liabilities for each period and incorporate the results into the approved plan.

■ Research the foreign tax consequences of the business plan; the company is entitled to a credit against its federal income tax liability for any foreign income tax paid.

It is imperative that the tax department communicate with all units of the organization. To be effective, the tax department should be involved in management decisions on business acquisitions, pension plans and fringe benefit programs, financing agreements, establishment of foreign entities, including their location and form, contract terms related to taxes, divestitures of business units or products, location of facilities, and various kinds of business arrangements such as joint ventures or consulting agreements. Tax planning includes making all levels of management aware of the significance of tax considerations in the decision-making process. An effective tax manager will create the opportunity to present sound and creative tax ideas to members of the management team on a regular basis.

The tax manager must have an intimate knowledge of the company and its products, services, and general business operations. To achieve this, he or she must be in touch with all concerned and develop a network of communications sensitive to situations having tax implications.

 ## TAX RECORDS

The tax laws are so complex, so great in number, and of such differing natures that it is not practical to know all the provisions of the laws and all the facts of the business that have a direct bearing on taxability. Consequently, the company must have the necessary records if adequate tax planning is to be completed, if management is to have a clear view of the tax situation, or if any degree of administrative control is to be successful. The penalties for oversight or incompetence are heavy.

EXHIBIT 23.1   Tax Calendar

Event	J	F	M	A	M	J	J	A	S	O	N	D
Estimated payments for the year				15		15			15			15
Mail Y/E tax packets to subs	15											
Federal use tax							31					
Federal excise quarterly return	31			30			31			31		
Federal excise monthly prepay #2	31	28	31	30	31	30	31	30	30	31	30	31
Federal excise monthly prepay #1	15	15	15	15	15	15	15	15	15	15	15	15

The nature of the records will be governed by the relative complexity of the tax problem. Broadly speaking, however, certain records are needed for administrative control purposes, to support the tax returns, and to meet the specific requirements of the law. Tax records are grouped into four major classifications:

1. *Tax calendar.* A schedule that serves as a reminder regarding the due dates for filing tax returns, preparing reports, paying tax bills, hearing dates, audit dates, assessment dates, and any other key tax event. When computerized, this schedule can automatically remind the staff of upcoming deadlines. Exhibit 23.1 presents an abbreviated tax calendar.
2. *Information records.* This is a summary of the tax law and related matters as they affect the business. This record is used as a reference when preparing the tax return. Exhibit 23.2 presents a sample tax information record. The information to be recorded about each tax includes:
   ▪ Name of the tax
   ▪ Description of the tax
   ▪ Basis
   ▪ Tax rates
   ▪ Exemptions from the tax
   ▪ Time of the filing return
   ▪ Return form number and name
   ▪ Approximate time required for preparation

EXHIBIT 23.2 Tax Information Record

Information Needed	Federal Income Tax
Description and type	Income
Locations covered	All except foreign legal entities
Who must file	All domestic legal entities, consolidated
Where filed (address)	IRS—Salt Lake City, Utah
Form number	1120, plus any other applicable forms
Period(s) covered	20XX
Due dates	3/15/XX (Extensions through 9/15/XX)
Rate or basis of tax	34%
Approximate amount of tax	$5,000,000
Information required	Detailed income statement, balance sheet, and comprehensive analysis of differences between book income and taxable income. Calculation of alternative minimum tax (AMT).
Source of data	Books and records of the various profit centers
Account charged	Number 260
File index	Federal file #3, drawer #2
Comments	Revise scheduling for asset depreciation range and guideline depreciation

- To whom the return is sent, and when
- Source of the data for preparing the return
- Why the company is subject to the tax
- The tax accounting
- The procedure, including any special instructions
- Penalties for nonpayment

3. *Working paper files.* These files contain the facts incident to the year-to-year returns. These operating files are of an infinite variety and are perhaps comparable to the permanent files and working paper files created in connection with an audit. Essentially, the files must contain a complete and orderly record of this information, plus additional material that may vary by type of tax:
   - Record of payments
   - Record of assessments
   - Reconciliation of tax data to the records
   - Copies of the return

- Refund record, including basis
- Correspondence on the tax

4. *Supporting ledgers.* These are the accounting records maintained by the accounting department. The tax manager should be closely involved in the construction of a chart of accounts that records information needed to file tax returns, in order to avoid the laborious manual compilation of information.

TAX VERSUS BOOK ACCOUNTING

The principal source of information required for federal income tax returns is the regular accounting records of the company. However, although tax accounting and book accounting are generally the same, they differ in three important respects:

1. *Income and expenses specifically excluded for tax purposes.* Examples include the tax-exempt income from government bonds or contributions in excess of the allowable maximum. These data are not difficult to account for; they appear on the reconciliation, and that usually ends the matter.
2. *Differences resulting from the recognition of the time when losses or income may be recognized.* The reserve positions and related charge-offs are included in this group. Supplementary worksheets are sufficient records for this information, and separate ledgers need not be maintained.
3. *Differences in cost bases.* This general category includes differences in depreciation rates and bases, treatment of maintenance and repair costs, and inventory valuation. Major information recording problems can arise in relation to different cost bases. It is necessary to determine whether a separate series of supplementary accounts needs to be maintained. For example, where substantially different depreciation bases and rates are used, separate ledgers may be required.

An important schedule for the controller's review is the reconciliation of net income contained in the federal income tax return. This schedule reveals the major differing points between tax and book accounting.

The controller and tax manager are faced with the problem of how these differences should be treated in the records. It is obviously necessary to maintain a running record of these differences and to reconcile book and tax figures if a company is to secure full tax benefits. The maintenance of such records is essential to ensure that the company will not overlook a tax deduction to which it could properly be entitled in a subsequent year. However, it does not follow that a completely independent set of books need be maintained for tax purposes.

SALES AND USE TAXES

Sales taxes are imposed at the state, county, and city level—frequently by all three at once. It is also possible for a special tax to be added to the sales tax and applied to a unique region, such as for the construction of a baseball stadium or to support a regional mass transit system. The sales tax is multiplied by the price paid on goods and services on transactions occurring within the taxing area. However, the definition of goods and services that are required to be taxed will vary by state (not usually at the county or city level), and so must be researched at the local level to determine the precise basis of calculation. For example, some states do not tax food sales, on the grounds that this is a necessity whose cost should be reduced as much as possible, while other states include it in their required list of items to be taxed.

A company is required to charge sales taxes to its customers and remit the resulting receipts to the local state government, which will split out the portions due to the local county and city governments and remit these taxes on the company's behalf to those entities. If the company does not charge its customers for these taxes, it is still liable for them and must pay the unbilled amounts to the state government, though it has the right to attempt to bill its customers after the fact for the missing sales taxes. This can be a difficult collection chore, especially if sales are primarily over the counter, where there are few transaction records that identify the customer. Also, a company is obligated to keep abreast of all changes in sales tax rates and charge its customers for the correct amount; if it does not do so, then it is liable to the government for the difference between what it actually charged and the statutory rate. If a company overcharges its customers, the excess must also be remitted to the government.

The state in which a company is collecting sales taxes can decide how frequently it wants the company to remit taxes. If there are only modest sales, the state may decide that the cost of paperwork exceeds the value of the remittances and will only require an annual remittance. It is more common to have quarterly or monthly remittances. The state will review the dollar amount of remittances from time to time and adjust the required remittance frequency based on this information.

All government entities have the right to audit a company's books to see if the proper sales taxes are being charged, and so a company can theoretically be subject to three sales tax audits per year—one each from the city, county, and state revenue departments. Also, since these audits can come from any taxing jurisdiction in which a company does business, there could literally be thousands of potential audits.

The obligation to collect sales taxes is based on the concept of *nexus*, which occurs if a company is located within the boundaries of the taxing government, or if its employees live there, or when it ships goods into that area with its own transportation. If nexus exists, then sales taxes must be collected by the seller. If not, the recipient of purchased goods instead has an obligation to compile a list of items purchased and remit a use tax to the appropriate authority. The use tax is in the same amount as the sales tax. The only difference is that the remitting party is the buyer instead of the seller. Use taxes are also subject to audits by all taxing jurisdictions.

If the buyer of a company's products is including them in its own products for resale to another entity, then the buyer does not have to pay a sales tax to the seller. Instead, the buyer will charge a sales tax to the buyer of *its* final product. This approach is used under the theory that a sales tax should only be charged one time on the sale of a product. However, it can be a difficult chore to explain the lack of sales tax billings during an audit, so sales taxes should only be halted if a buyer sends a sales tax exemption form to the company, which it should then keep on file. The sales tax exemption certificate may be named a resale certificate instead, depending upon the issuing authority. It can also be issued to government entities, which are generally exempt from sales and use taxes. As a general rule, sales taxes should always be charged unless there is a sales tax exemption certificate on file—otherwise, the company will still be liable for the remittance of sales taxes in the event of an audit.

PROPER CLASSIFICATION OF ACCOUNTS

When designing the accounting records and account structure or chart of accounts, the controller should be aware of and consider the accounting data required for the preparation of tax returns. If provision is made in the establishment of the accounting records, the orderly storage of tax-related information can facilitate the tax work and protect the interests of the company from a tax viewpoint.

It is desirable to include in the account structure the capability for detailed analysis of various items such as repairs and maintenance, so it can be readily demonstrated that additions to a plant have not been expensed. Also, where practical, a segregation of nontaxable income or nonallowable deductions should be made in the accounts. Such an account structure will save valuable time in making costly analyses at critical times and make less likely the possibility of not including those items in the tax return.

CHAPTER TWENTY-FOUR

Selecting a Financial Information System

THE CONTROLLER IS PRIMARILY responsible for seeing that the financial information system meets the needs of those who receive and use its output: management, shareholders, creditors, suppliers, customers, government agencies, and stock exchanges as well as the general public.

This chapter contains a proven approach to selecting and implementing an automated financial information system (FIS). It includes an overview of reasons why financial system software should be purchased instead of developed in-house, an explanation of how to thoroughly define systems requirements, an approach to preparing a request for proposal (RFP), and ways to evaluate software, hardware, and the vendors who sell it. Selection and implementation of an FIS are extremely important to an organization's financial operation. As a result, the organization must be willing either to devote a substantial amount of time and effort to these activities or to hire outside consultants to assist in the process.

For the purposes of this chapter, it is assumed that the selection process includes both computer hardware and software. Many selecting organizations already have computer hardware in place. However, where possible, it is recommended that an organization select software that best meets its needs without being constrained by the hardware currently in place.

REASONS TO PURCHASE SOFTWARE

In general, it is recommended that software packages be purchased, instead of developed in-house, to meet the needs of an organization's financial operations. The reasons include:

- *Implementation speed.* Packaged software generally can be implemented much more quickly than software developed in-house.
- *Fewer software problems.* Packaged software normally already has been thoroughly tested and debugged before it is sold.
- *Lower overall cost.* The total cost of packaged software tends to be significantly less than the cost of software developed in-house.
- *Software vendor assistance.* Most software vendors, especially those in the midrange (microcomputer) and mainframe market, provide ongoing support and maintenance for their software.
- *Package enhancements.* To maintain market position and sales, software vendors generally provide enhanced functionality and new modules.
- *Documentation.* Most software packages come with a variety of manuals, including user, technical, and operations.
- *Training.* The vast majority of software vendors provide a variety of training classes for users and technical personnel.
- *Research and development.* Software vendors are in the business of selling system solutions. To maintain (and improve) a competitive market position, they must invest a substantial amount of money in research and development (R&D).
- *Information systems support.* In general, it is much easier to locate personnel who are familiar with packaged software and can support it than to find good support for in-house systems.
- *User group.* Packaged software vendors tend to support and encourage user groups. Participation in these groups can be an effective means of identifying ways in which to use the system more efficiently.

DEFINING SYSTEMS REQUIREMENTS

Before software is selected, the specific requirements need to be defined precisely. The application areas typically included in an FIS are budgeting, purchasing, accounts payable and check reconciliation, general ledger, accounts receivable and revenue accounting, fixed assets, cost accounting, inventory, and order entry and billing.

If application requirements are not thoroughly defined and documented, the software selected probably will not meet the organization's needs. It will be useful to develop a systems requirements definition (SRD) document that:

- Serves as the basis for the RFP
- Communicates the organization's requirements to the vendors
- Helps the selected software meet the organization's current and future needs
- Enhances the organization's understanding of each application area (e.g., accounts payable and accounts receivable) and how automation can assist in improving access to information in that area
- Prioritizes the application areas to be automated
- Matches requirements against the software's capabilities to determine where it is deficient and where modifications must be developed

A number of approaches may be used to develop FIS requirements. These approaches include questionnaires, executive interviews, document reviews, and outside sources.

Questionnaires

Questionnaires may be used to develop a general understanding of an organization, its objectives, and the environment in which it operates. They also may be used to define major financially oriented tasks, analyze transactions, determine major systems interfaces, and assist with the development of FIS requirements. Exhibit 24.1 illustrates the types of questions that can appear in the questionnaire.

Executive Interviews

The purposes of conducting executive interviews include:

- Developing an overall understanding of the organization—its strategies, environment, and objectives
- Defining the executive's information needs
- Determining the executive's opinions on the current system
- Identifying the organization's goals, objectives, and critical success factors
- Identifying the executive's system expectations
- Predicting growth areas or new needs that must be planned for by the information systems (IS) department
- Improving the executive's buy-in to the selection process

EXHIBIT 24.1 Sample Questionnaire for Defining Application Requirements

1. For what functions are you responsible?

2. What are the primary goals of your job?

3. With what other departments do you interface?

4. What major tasks do you perform?

5. What reports do you prepare? (Please attach a sample of each report.)

6. What forms do you use? (Please attach a sample of each form.)

7. Where do these forms originate?

8. Where do these forms go when you complete them?

9. What financial information do you receive from other departments?

10. What changes do you predict will occur in your job over the next one to three years?

11. What additional information could you use?

12. What automated system do you currently utilize?

Executive interviews should not be designed to elicit detailed information on systems specifications. Rather, they should help elicit general information needs and the strategic goals and objectives of the organization.

It is important that the information and reporting needs of executives be emphasized and identified early in the selection process. Too frequently, only the needs of staff and middle management are incorporated. The resulting FIS frequently does not provide executives with the reports necessary for effectively managing the application areas.

Document Reviews

Another way to develop systems requirements is to review input forms and reports. Doing so provides the organization with a listing of its current data elements and helps to define the minimum reporting requirements of the proposed FIS.

Outside Sources

Another source of requirements that should be included in an SRD is the environment in which the financial organization exists. Economic trends, changes in laws and practices, and revisions to governmental regulations all may affect the reporting requirements of an FIS and, therefore, should be reviewed.

There is a cost involved in collecting systems requirements. As a result, an organization should not spend an excessive amount of time documenting these requirements because if it does so, it may never get to the point of selecting software.

Vendor Demonstrations

A final source of requirements is through software vendor demonstrations. These demonstrations can provide organizations with new information about system features.

 EXISTING SYSTEM DOCUMENTATION

After the questionnaires and executive interviews have been completed and the other sources of information reviewed, it is critical that the existing manual and/or automated financial systems be documented. These factors should be included in this documentation:

- The key objectives of the system (e.g., to maintain the general ledger and produce financial reports)
- Who supports the system
- The major system inputs, edits, controls, and outputs (reports)
- All system interfaces and special features
- The volume of transactions processed by the system
- The approximate costs of operating the system

In addition, if the system is automated, it is important to note the hardware platform on which it operates, the language in which it is written, its age, and the approximate amount invested in the system.

 ## JOINT SESSIONS

An effective and efficient means of ensuring a thorough system requirements survey is by conducting joint sessions with the employees who will be using and supporting the system. The benefits of conducting joint sessions include development of a more complete SRD and an improved user buy-in. The steps required to conduct a joint session include:

- Prepare "straw man" requirements for each application. These requirements generally are based on research previously conducted by the organization or information obtained from software vendors, computer-related literature, or IS consultants.
- Distribute the requirements document to the employees interested in or affected by the specific application.
- Conduct a joint session for each application area. During these sessions, which generally are facilitated by a selection team member or a consultant, the participants are asked to:
  - Prioritize each requirement (state whether the requirement is required, desired, optional, or not applicable)
  - Identify additional requirements

After the current financial systems are documented and the joint sessions conducted, it is time to finalize the SRD. The purpose of the SRD, which will become part of the RFP, is to communicate to software vendors the organization's systems requirements and allow the vendors to identify software products that can meet those requirements. The SRD should be divided by application area (general ledger and accounts payable). The application area should be further divided into these topics: general systems narrative, processing requirements, inquiry requirements, reporting requirements, and data requirements.

The requirements should be stated as a single sentence. Exhibit 24.2 gives an abbreviated example of these factors for an accounts receivable system.

EXHIBIT 24.2 Accounts Receivable System Requirements

The accounts receivable system should be designed to handle all of the organization's receivables and collection requirements. The system must interface both with the order entry system to obtain billing information and with the general ledger system to post billings, cash receipts, and bad-debt journal entries.

Processing Requirements

The accounts receivable system should be able to perform these functions:

• Post to different revenue accounts depending on the type of service performed.

• Enter nonaccounting data to the master file online.

• Disallow the deletion of data with an account balance greater than zero.

• Interface with the order entry/billing system.

Inquiry Requirements

The accounts receivable system should include these inquiry features and capabilities:

• Online review of billing and payment history

• Inquiry as to the status of a bill using a variety of data elements including:

Customer name

Customer number

Invoice number

Reporting Requirements

The accounts receivable system should produce these reports:

• *Accounts receivable aging report*—a report indicating the amount of time an accounts receivable balance has been outstanding.

   Frequency: weekly and on demand

• *Cash receipts register*—a register containing information on:

Date of receipt

Check number

Customer name and number

EXHIBIT 24.2 *(Continued)*

Dollar amount

Invoice number applied to

General ledger account posted to

  Frequency: daily and on demand

Data Requirements

The Customer Master File should contain these data elements:

Customer Name—60 alpha/numeric characters

Customer Number—20 alpha/numeric characters

Customer Address I

—Street—60 alpha/numeric characters

—City—20 alpha characters

—State—20 alpha characters

Customer Address 2

—Street—60 alpha/numeric characters

—City—20 alpha/numeric characters

—State—2 alpha characters

Customer Contact I

—Name—40 alpha/numeric characters

—Phone number—9 numeric characters

—Street—60 alpha/numeric characters

—City—20 alpha characters

—State—2 alpha characters

System requirements documents (SRDs) may be from 5 to well over 100 pages per application, depending on the number and the level of detail desired. Be careful not to overdefine the requirements or make the SRD so general that it allows all software packages to meet its needs.

After completing the SRD, the prioritization of the applications should be performed. It is vital for an organization to clearly define each application in the order of importance, to help it evaluate the completed FRP and identify the factors on which the software selection will be decided. Factors to consider when assigning priorities of applications to be automated include:

The impact of the system on the organization and its customers

The costs and benefits of the system

The demand for the system

The dependence of the system on other systems

PREPARING THE REQUEST FOR PROPOSAL

An RFP is used to effectively communicate the FIS's requirements to software and/or hardware vendors. It is prepared after the SRD and serves these purposes:

- Communicates the organization's systems requirements to vendors and facilitates a uniform response to those requirements.
- Requests specific commitments from vendors, such as the system's functionality, the level of support and documentation provided, the costs, and contractual arrangements.
- Serves as a tool for effectively comparing vendors. The RFP should be designed in a way that allows the selecting organization to compare the proposals of various vendors easily.

Depending on the organization's situation, RFPs may be prepared for software, hardware, or both. However, no matter what style the organization selects, the RFP must be well structured and precise in order to elicit a clear and concise response from vendors. A vague and poorly organized RFP is likely to result in proposals that are too general and difficult to compare and are lacking details in many areas. Exhibit 24.3 shows a typical contents page for an RFP.

Cover Letter

The cover letter notifies the hardware and/or software vendor that the organization is requesting a proposal for specific applications and/or hardware. In addition, the cover letter should contain this information: important deadlines (i.e., the date of the bidders conference and when the proposal is due) and the projected installation and implementation dates; the overall objective of the

EXHIBIT 24.3 RFP Table of Contents

I.	Cover Letter
II.	General Information/Proposal Guidelines
III.	Background Material
IV.	Vendor Questionnaire
V.	Vendor Cost Summary
VI.	System Requirements

RFP; the individual within the organization to contact with questions; and the format and content of the RFP.

General Information/Proposal Guidelines

The general information/proposal guidelines section contains information on how the proposal is to be completed, how the selection process will be conducted, and the importance of a concise and timely response. Also included in this section is whether site visits will be made by the organization, plus statements that the cost of preparing the proposal is entirely the vendor's responsibility, the organization reserves the right to reject any and all proposals, and the confidentiality of the material contained in the RFP is assured.

Background Material

The background material includes information about the organization that is of interest to the vendor. Generally included in this section is a description of the organization's different business functions currently being performed and by which departments; volume statistics (e.g., the number of payroll and accounts payable checks issued per month and the number of general ledger transactions); the current hardware, financial system software and modules, and operating system, if any; and the hours of operation. This information is very useful for vendors when preparing their proposals.

Vendor Questionnaire

The vendor questionnaire asks a variety of questions on the vendor's background, clients, training, and growth; systems reliability, security, and performance; how modifications are handled; how reports are produced; acceptance testing and implementation schedule; data control; staffing; R&D expenditures; documentation; and hardware proposed, if any. The answers to these questions will assist the organization in selecting the final vendor. This section must be extremely well constructed and the questions concisely formulated. (See Exhibit 24.4 for examples of vendor evaluation criteria.)

Vendor Cost Summary

In the vendor cost summary, the vendor is requested to complete a cost schedule specifying the costs of the proposed FIS. Each vendor generally is asked to provide information on recurring and nonrecurring costs over a five-year period and supplemental schedules to explain the derivation of all costs

---

EXHIBIT 24.4 Vendor Evaluation Criteria

Key factors to consider when evaluating vendors:

Product Support
- Location of nearest sales and support office
- Size of the support staff at nearest service office and their qualifications.
- Availability of remote diagnostics
- Availability of 24-hour support and associated cost
- Guaranteed response time for system problems
- Preventive maintenance approach and policies
- Problem resolution procedures
- Availability of installation and implementation support
- Existence of and level of support of a user group
- Existence of complete user and technical documentation
- Frequency of documentation and system updates

Reputation and Stability
- Number of years in the computer industry
- Number of similar installations of the particular system still operating
- Sales growth rate of applications being reviewed
- Financial condition of the vendor and/or its parent company
- Research and development budget and number of staff

---

and what is included in such items as installation and maintenance fees. Exhibit 24.5 is an example of a vendor cost summary schedule.

System Requirements

The system requirements section sets forth the processing, inquiry, reporting, and data requirements developed during the systems requirement definition process. Each vendor is asked to complete a matrix that contains all application requirements. Vendors are asked to respond to the next categories for *each* requirement:

- Whether the current system can satisfy the requirement. The only acceptable response is yes or no.
- Cross-Reference (X-REF). Where in the vendor's documentation is the requirement described?
- Comments. Any comments the vendor may have regarding the specific requirement.

Exhibit 24.6 reproduces a page from an accounts payable information requirements section, together with a possible vendor response.

EXHIBIT 24.5 Vendor Cost Summary

| | Year | | | | | |
---	1	2	3	4	5	Total
Recurring costs						
Hardware						
CPU lease	\$___	\$___	\$___	\$___	\$___	\$___
Terminal lease	___	___	___	___	___	___
Printer lease	___	___	___	___	___	___
Other lease	___	___	___	___	___	___
CPU maintenance	___	___	___	___	___	___
Terminal maintenance	___	___	___	___	___	___
Printer maintenance	___	___	___	___	___	___
Other maintenance	___	___	___	___	___	___
Software						
Software license	___	___	___	___	___	___
Software support	___	___	___	___	___	___
Other fees	___	___	___	___	___	___
Supplies						
Disks, tapes	___	___	___	___	___	___
Ribbons, paper	___	___	___	___	___	___
Other	___	___	___	___	___	___
Total	\$___	\$___	\$___	\$___	\$___	\$___
Nonrecurring costs						
Hardware						
CPU purchase	\$___	\$___	\$___	\$___	\$___	\$___
Terminal purchase	___	___	___	___	___	___
Printer purchase	___	___	___	___	___	___
Other purchase	___	___	___	___	___	___
Software						
Software purchase	___	___	___	___	___	___
Installation						
Freight	___	___	___	___	___	___

(Continued)

EXHIBIT 24.5 (*Continued*)

	Year					
	1	2	3	4	5	Total
Cabling	——	——	——	——	——	——
Site preparation	——	——	——	——	——	——
Training	——	——	——	——	——	——
Customization	——	——	——	——	——	———
System initializing	——	——	——	——	——	——
Installation	——	——	——	——	——	——
Other	——	——	——	——	——	——
Total	$___	$___	$___	$___	$___	$___
TOTAL	$___	$___	$___	$___	$___	$___

EXHIBIT 24.6 Completed Accounts Payable System Requirements

	Response			
Requirement	Yes	No	X-REF	Comments
1. Enter invoices online.	X		User Manual pp. 5–22	
2. Enter vendor credit memoranda for future payments.	X		User Manual pp. 6–21	$5,000 additional fee
3. Write checks automatically based on invoice date and a predefined pay period (e.g., 30 days from invoice date).	X		User Manual pp. 3–22	
4. Automatically process recurring payments.		X	User Manual pp. 2–10	
5. Process and post manual checks to correct vendor and general ledger account.	X		User Manual pp. 3–12	
6. Automatically interface with general ledger system.	X		User Manual pp. 7–12	
7. Edit for duplicate invoice numbers to the same vendor.	X		User Manual pp. 6–10	$3,000 additional fee
8. Allow for standard discount terms (e.g., 1/10 net 30).	X		User Manual pp. 3–20	

DISTRIBUTION OF THE REQUEST FOR PROPOSAL

Once the RFP is completed, the organization must determine the vendors to whom it will be sent. With over 50,000 software packages available, narrowing the field can be a difficult task. However, there are some basic factors to consider.

- *Geographic location.* The ability to receive timely support is extremely critical. Because many software vendors may not have offices located near the organization, this factor can be used to eliminate many vendors.
- *Hardware considerations.* Many software programs run only on certain hardware configurations (e.g., IBM or H-P hardware only). Therefore, if the organization owns hardware or has a preference for a certain manufacturer, the software options are reduced significantly.
- *Organization size.* The size of the organization influences the size of the computer system that must be acquired. Software generally is designed to run on microcomputers, midrange systems, or mainframes. As a result, the software vendors to which the organization may send the RFP are limited.
- *Organizational preference.* Some organizations prefer to deal with firms that develop software only. Other organizations prefer to deal with turnkey vendors that supply both hardware and software. The organization's decision in this area will influence the number of vendors to which the RFP can be sent.
- *Vendor characteristics.* Often it is possible to prescreen vendors to determine if it is appropriate to send them an RFP. This can be accomplished by calling a vendor representative, reviewing vendor literature, or discussing vendors with organizations similar to yours. When prescreening a vendor, look at factors such as the vendor's stability and related experience, list prices, and flexibility.

Other means of identifying vendors that should receive the RFP include engaging a consultant experienced in hardware and software selections, reviewing computer-oriented magazines, contacting hardware vendors for lists of potential software suppliers, and networking with other organizations.

In general, the RFP should be sent to between 5 and 10 vendors; any more than that, and the process becomes cumbersome; any fewer, and the choices become too limited. The vendor should be given sufficient time—three to six weeks—to complete the RFP accurately and thoroughly.

REVIEW OF THE VENDOR'S COMPLETED PROPOSAL

When the proposals are returned, they should be given an initial brief review. This brief review will most likely eliminate the proposals that do not meet the organization's minimum critical needs.

In general, systems decisions should be more heavily influenced by the software, not the hardware. Therefore, the organization should review the vendors' software proposals first. The goal of this review is to determine the two or three finalists.

The organization needs to evaluate two types of software: application and systems. Application software is the software that performs the functions needed by the end user, such as generating invoices, preparing financial statements, and recording cash receipts. It is used to perform specific processing or computational tasks. Examples of application software include accounts payable, accounts receivable, and general ledger systems. Systems software makes it possible to utilize the application software. Included in this broad category are operating systems, database management systems, report writers, database compilers, and debugging aids. Organizations use the system requirements section of their RFPs to review the vendor's application software. As mentioned, each vendor is asked to respond to each requirement. The selecting organization should tabulate these responses to determine how well the vendor's software meets the organization's needs. These five guidelines should be used:

1. Prepare a spreadsheet listing all of the requirements. The spreadsheet should look exactly like the information systems requirement section displayed in Exhibit 24.6.
2. Determine the number of points a response is worth. For example, a "yes" response may be worth 10 points to a "Required" requirement, but only 6 points on a "Desired" feature. (A sample scoring scheme follows.)
3. Tally the vendor's responses.
4. Total the score by application area.
5. Determine the vendor's total score.

Response	Required	Desired	Optional
Yes	10	6	4
No	0	0	0

The spreadsheet should look exactly like the information systems requirement displayed in Exhibit 24.6. The rating sheet in Exhibit 24.7 can be effective

EXHIBIT 24.7 Application Software Rating Sheet

Requirement	Required or Desired	Response Yes	No	Comments
1. Enter invoices online.	R			
2. Enter vendor credit memoranda online and apply credits to future payments.	R			
3. Write checks automatically based on invoice date and a predefined pay period (e.g., 30 days from invoice date).	R			
4. Automatically process recurring payments.	R			
5. Process and post manual checks to correct vendor and general ledger account.	R			
6. Automatically interface with general ledger system.	R			
7. Edit for duplicate invoice numbers.	R			
8. Allow for standard discount terms (e.g., 2/10 net 30).	D			

in evaluating the vendor responses. In addition, the organization should review the next characteristics of each vendor's application software.

- *Flexibility.* Is the software very easy to modify? Will it handle the organization's needs five years from installation? Is it easy to debug?
- *Documentation.* Is it easy to use? Is it accurate and thorough? Is it regularly updated? Does it describe all error messages? Are all screen formats presented? Does it clearly describe recovery procedures? Are terms defined? Who maintains it?
- *Controls.* Is a clear audit trail of all transactions available? Are data validated before files are updated? Does password security exist? Are all errors flagged? Is a listing of log-on attempts provided? Are different authorization levels available? Can check digits be used? Are batch totals available?

Analyzing systems software can be more difficult than analyzing application software, because system software is harder to quantify. However, these guidelines can be useful:

- *Determine the systems software factors to be evaluated.* For example, it is likely that the selecting organization will want to review:
  - The operating and database management system
  - Multiuser capabilities
  - Programming language utilized
  - Compilation speeds
  - Systems utilities, such as file maintenance programs, backup and restore programs, and sorting and text editors
  - Systems support software, such as file management processors, password protection, screen formatters, report writers, and print spoolers
  - Compatibility of the system with other software products
  - Interactive and communications capabilities
  - Ease of operation
- *Once the factors have been determined, prioritize and assign numeric values to them.*
- *Review the vendor's proposal and assign a score to each factor.* Assigning scores is a somewhat subjective process. However, it is important that it be performed.
- *Total the vendor's score in this section.* Exhibit 24.8 provides an example of how systems software can be prioritized and scored.

As mentioned, the software decision usually takes precedence over the hardware decision. However, a thorough review of the proposed hardware is

EXHIBIT 24.8 Scoring for Systems Software

Factor	Points Assigned	Vendor A Score
1. Operating system	18	16
2. DBMS	12	12
3. Multiuser capabilities	10	6
4. Programming language	6	6
5. Compilation speed	6	2
6. Systems utilities	8	6
7. Systems support software	10	7
8. Compatibility	8	8
9. Interactive and communications capabilities	10	9
10. Ease of operations	12	8
Total Points	100	80

extremely important to ensure that the FIS will meet the organization's needs. The size of the proposed hardware system depends on three factors:

1. The volume statistics listed in the background section of the RFP
2. The organization's projected growth rates
3. The vendor's experience with similar clients

Acquiring a system that meets the organization's current and future needs is extremely important. Either an in-house IS specialist or an experienced IS consultant must review the capabilities and flexibility of the proposed hardware configuration. Other hardware factors to review include:

▪ Central processing unit
▪ Peripheral devices (i.e., disk and tape drives)
▪ Remote devices (i.e., communications support equipment)
▪ Environmental considerations
▪ Flexibility and expandability
▪ Systems reliability

Once the hardware evaluation factors have been identified, they should be prioritized and assigned a numeric value. (This is similar to the method recommended for reviewing systems software.) Then each vendor's proposal should be reviewed and assigned a score on each factor. The total score on hardware is then determined.

After the hardware and software have been evaluated, the next step is to evaluate the vendor(s). Depending on the system desired, this may involve reviewing a software vendor and a hardware vendor. The primary factors to consider when evaluating a vendor are:

▪ Product support
▪ Reputation and financial stability
▪ Experience
▪ Product availability and enhancements
▪ Documentation
▪ Training

Once the software, hardware, and vendor have been evaluated thoroughly, the selection of the finalist vendors can occur. The finalists are then analyzed further by means of reference calls, attendance at vendor demonstrations, and site visits. Because substantial amounts of time and money are invested in reviewing the finalist vendors, it is vital that the selecting organization choose vendors who actually can provide it with an FIS that meets its needs.

REFERENCE CALLS

One of the most important aspects of the systems selection process is making reference calls to existing systems users. Reference calls are a means by which an organization can find out what a vendor may not want them to know. For example, the organization may discover that a vendor's documentation and support are not as good as its sales literature claims.

The questions asked during a reference call should be both fact- and opinion-oriented. The users should be asked to list the software implemented and their overall opinion of the software. Topics to cover when making a reference call include:

- Type of organization
- Volume statistics
- Software packages purchased
- Software packages implemented
- Ease of installation
- Operating system
- Database management system
- Hardware installed
- Hardware dependability
- Systems security
- Response time
- Quality of reports
- Approach to system selection
- Why vendor(s) were chosen
- Ease of operation
- Quality of training
- Quality of documentation
- Modifications made
- Quality of support
- Vendor dependability
- Unforeseen costs

- User group membership/satisfaction
- Overall satisfaction
- Names of other users

The names of other systems users are important because frequently vendors provide only the names of satisfied users. Asking a user for names of other users may lead to one who is not pleased with the system.

 ## DEMONSTRATION

After the reference calls have been completed, the organization should consider attending vendor demonstrations to obtain additional information on the software and vendor, see how the software operates, and review the look and feel of the system, its ease of use, and the level of complexity.

Prior to attending the vendor demonstration, the organization should prepare an agenda for the vendor to follow, develop a feedback form for the attendees to rate various aspects of the software and the vendor (e.g., screen layout and ease of use), and prepare a list of questions and sample transactions for the vendor to enter into the system (e.g., matching a purchase order and invoice).

It is important to remember that the vendors obviously will be presenting their software in its best light. Those attending the demonstration must be in a position to evaluate this information.

 ## SITE VISITS

After the reference calls have been made and demonstrations have been attended, the organization should arrange to see the system at a working installation, not at the vendor's headquarters. The purpose of the site visits include:

- Viewing the system in a real-life environment
- Answering questions that may have arisen during the selection process
- Assisting the organization in deciding whether the system will meet its current and future needs

The site visit should take place at a user's place of business and should be on a live rather than demo system so that the vendor has no opportunity to manipulate the demonstration to its advantage. Although the majority of vendors are ethical, manipulation of potential customers is not unheard of.

The individuals present at the demonstration should include in-house IS personnel; potential system users, such as the accounts payable supervisor; and the IS consultant, if one is being used. The visit should take no more than a day to complete. The selecting team representatives should come prepared with a set of questions to ask the other organization and a feedback form on which to record ratings of the vendor.

If possible, the organization should arrange to make site visits within a two-week period to more easily compare the systems.

 ## COST OF THE SYSTEM

The costs of purchasing hardware, software, and implementation support can be a very critical factor in a selection process and should be analyzed carefully. The vendor cost summary portion of the RFP may be used to compare the costs of proposed systems. However, other cost factors need to be clarified before comparing the total costs of the proposed systems. Consider:

- What will the proposed enhancements cost?
- How will the cost of future enhancements be determined?
- Is there an additional fee for installation?
- Is there an additional fee for training?
- How much does maintenance cost?
- Is there an additional fee for 24-hour support?
- Is there a charge for system updates?
- Will the organization receive a discount if it purchases other applications?
- Does the software license allow for the use of the software at multiple sites? If not, what is the charge for the other sites?
- How much does the warranty cost and how long is it in effect?
- When does the warranty go into effect? (Ideally, the warranty should go into effect on the date the system is accepted, not on the date the system is installed.)
- Does the vendor guarantee in writing a full refund if the software does not perform as promised?
- Is the price of documentation included in the total price?
- Can the organization duplicate the documentation, or must it pay for additional copies? If so, what is the cost for additional copies?
- Is the source code (a copy of the programs) included in the system's price? If not, what is the charge for the source code?

FINAL SELECTION

Once the software, hardware, and vendor have been thoroughly reviewed and the reference calls, demonstrations, and site visits have been completed, the organization is in a position to select the system. If the organization has completed the steps outlined in this chapter, it should find itself with an FIS that meets current and future needs. Once the final selection has been made, the organization is in a position to begin contract negotiations.

CONTRACT NEGOTIATIONS

After the software and hardware have been selected, preparation for contract negotiations between the organization and the vendor(s) should ensue. The objectives of contract negotiations are to:

- Define the organization's expectations clearly to avoid misunderstandings
- Define precisely what remedies are available if the vendor fails to perform as promised
- Protect the organization against unexpected occurrences, such as the bankruptcy of the vendor
- Ensure the best terms possible for the organization

Negotiating a contract can be a long and costly process. When negotiating, there are several points to remember:

- Do not accept the vendor's standard contract.
- Negotiate with someone with the authority to bind the vendor.
- Never accept oral promises.
- Do not make unreasonable demands.
- Obtain advice from a professional experienced in contract negotiations.

Four specific steps are essential for effectively negotiating a mutually beneficial contract:

1. Choose a negotiating team to represent the selecting organization, including an IS specialist, an individual who will be using the system, an attorney or consultant with significant computer-related contract experience, and a purchasing department representative.

2. Determine the specific objectives of the negotiations and prepare a plan of action to take if the negotiations fail.
3. Review the standard contract terms offered by the vendor and identify problem areas and points that are missing.
4. Meet with the vendor to negotiate the contract.

The contract should clearly specify the costs for hardware, software, maintenance, installation support, modifications testing, and upgrades. The organization should attempt to ensure that it is protected from any price increases without its written consent. The contract should also clearly identify the terms of payment. The organization should hold back a substantial portion of the purchase price (10 percent to 30 percent) until the system is fully operational for a specified period of time and has passed all acceptance tests.

 POSTIMPLEMENTATION REVIEW

After a system has been implemented, a postimplementation review (PIR) should be completed. It should have these objectives:

▪ Determining if the anticipated results of the selection and implementation process have been attained
▪ Comparing the original cost estimate to the actual costs
▪ Identifying weaknesses in support, documentation, training, and functionality
▪ Reviewing the adequacy of reports, security, and ease of use
▪ Identifying additional systems enhancements that may be required
▪ Reviewing the timeliness of report preparation and distribution

The best time to perform a PIR is approximately 6 to 18 months after the system is installed. During this period, users have become familiar with the new system. This timing also allows significant system problems or issues to surface. Conducting the review earlier than six months will not allow time for people to relinquish old habits. The areas to be reviewed during the PIR include:

▪ How successfully the system has been implemented
▪ The efficiency and effectiveness of the system
▪ How well the system is being utilized
▪ If system features exist that have not been implemented or used

- If user's needs are being met
- If the system is sufficiently secure

The five steps to be taken to perform a PIR include:

Step 1. Reviewing the statement of requirements, RFP, and the selected vendor's proposal
Step 2. Interviewing key individuals from the selection committee, implementation team, IS staff, user group, and internal audit
Step 3. Reviewing the system's implementation, training, documentation, support, security, operations, input forms, and reports
Step 4. Evaluating the implementation process
Step 5. Formulating the findings, conclusions, and recommendations in a report

The benefits of performing a PIR include:

- Detecting issues related to the system
- Evaluating the effectiveness of training and determining whether additional training is required
- Determining whether additional documentation is necessary
- Determining whether the expected benefits have been realized
- Preparing recommendations for improvements to the system to maximize its use
- Providing guidance and insight for future systems implementations

New Controller Checklist

A PERSON WHO HAS been newly hired into the controller position may feel overwhelmed by the vast number of tasks to be completed and may wonder where to begin. The attached list gives some guidance about the priority of tasks.

The first few priorities are heavily stacked in favor of creating and improving the accuracy of a cash forecasting system, which requires a detailed knowledge of payables, receivables, debt payments, contracts, and capital expenditures. The new controller must have a firm grasp of this information before proceeding to any other steps, because a company without cash will not survive long enough for the controller to address anything else.

A key priority falling immediately after the cash forecasting system is a detailed review of all current contracts. The controller should read these personally, with the objective of finding any contract terms that have a potential to put the company in jeopardy or at least have a significant downward impact on its profitability.

The next group of priorities involves the establishment of measurement systems, so the controller can see what problems are likely to arise and how this can impact the priority of his or her future activities.

Adapted with permission from Appendix A of Steven M. Bragg, *The CFO Financial Leadership Manual*, Third Edition (Hoboken, NJ: John Wiley & Sons, 2010).

Next in line is a complete review of the controller staff's capabilities, work schedules, and training requirements. Although an inexperienced controller may be tempted to advance this task to the topmost priority, it is listed lower here because staff development is more of a midrange to long-term goal. It has little impact on the very short-term performance of the controller's assigned areas, whereas the preceding items must be completed very quickly, so the controller can see which areas are at risk and require the most immediate attention.

Activities following the staff development priorities can be shifted in priority, depending on the company-specific situation. However, it is highly recommended that the controller follow the exact priorities through and including the staff development action items, because completing these tasks will likely give him or her the best possible handle on the critical short-term needs of the organization.

Priority	Action	Description
1	Forecast cash	Any other action is useless if the company runs out of money, so immediately create a cash forecast and initially revise it on a weekly basis. Continually modify the model to improve its accuracy.
2	Establish daily bank reconciliations	The cash forecast will not be too accurate if the underlying bank balances are inaccurate, so arrange to have Internet access to daily bank balances and ensure that a daily reconciliation is made with this information.
3	Review payables	Not only go over all current payables, but conduct a full one-year review of the vendor ledger with the payables staff. The objective is to understand the nature, amount, and timing of payments. This information is very useful for increasing the accuracy of the cash forecast.
4	Review collections	Go over all current accounts receivable with the collections staff, and then expand the review to all major customers, even if there are no receivables currently outstanding. This gives an excellent overview of cash inflows for the cash forecast.
5	Review debt agreements	Personally review the debt agreements to verify the dates when payments come due, the applicable interest rates, and particularly any covenants that can result in the debt being called by the lender. This knowledge prevents any unexpected surprises from occurring in the cash forecasting system.

6	Review capital expenditures	The last priority that feeds into the cash forecasting system is capital expenditures. This has the lowest priority of the cash-related activities, since typically this is a discretionary payment. The controller should be aware of which expenditures are critical short-term items that probably cannot be delayed and which potentially can be shifted farther into the future.
7	Review contracts	The controller and legal counsel should obtain copies of all current contracts and review them in great detail to ensure that there are no hidden surprises, such as unexpected liabilities or potential lawsuits. Unexpected contractual pitfalls are a problem in a large number of situations, and are worthy of review very early in a controller's tenure.
8	Establish metrics	Establish a set of initial metrics on a multimonth trend line in order to determine the company's performance in a number of areas, including days of receivables, payables, and inventory, as well as gross and operating margins, the overall break-even point, and any metrics required by loan covenants. The exact measures used will vary by industry. The intent is to give the controller early knowledge of potential performance issues.
9	Create sales report	The controller must be aware of anticipated sales for at least the current month, as well as changes in the backlog. This information should be included in a weekly sales report that goes not only to the controller but to the entire management team.
10	Create flash report	The controller should incorporate the total periodic sales listed on the sales report in a flash report that itemizes the latest expectation for total financial results for the reporting period. Like the sales report, this report should be issued weekly and should go to the entire management team. By completing these top 10 priorities, the controller has gained a knowledge of all aspects of cash flow, any contractual problems, and short-term financial results.
11	Review the staff	With short-term issues taken care of, it is now time to deal with the controller's primary long-term asset: the staff. This review should include an examination of all resumes for employees reporting either directly or indirectly to the controller, face-to-face meetings with them, and group sessions. The outcome should be a clear understanding of each person's capabilities and aspirations, training needs, and weaknesses.

(Continued)

Priority	Action	Description
12	Review department efficiencies	Develop metrics for those functions reporting to the controller, and determine where efficiencies are in the most need of improvement. Based on the initial staff review, create a plan to improve efficiency levels and begin its implementation.
13	Initiate accounts payable best practices implementations	Accounts payable activities likely require a large proportion of staff time, so installing best practices here can yield large efficiencies. Common best practices include the use of procurement cards, auditing expense reports, using signature stamps, sending standard adjustment letters to suppliers, and assigning staff to specific supplier accounts.
14	Initiate collections best practices implementations	If the billing and collection process requires too much staff time or yields slow payments, the installation of best practices is in order. These should include the preapproval of customer credit, e-mailing invoices to customers in PDF format, simplifying the product pricing structure, assigning customers to specific collections staff, and issuing billings early for recurring invoices.
15	Initiate payroll best practices implementations	If there is a large company staff, improving the payroll staff's efficiency with best practices can result in significant labor savings. Typical best practices include the minimization of payroll deductions, posting payroll forms on the company intranet, requiring direct deposit, outsourcing payroll processing, and consolidating payroll cycles and systems.
16	Establish training schedules	Based on the staff review and departmental efficiency plans, create a training schedule for each employee that is tailored precisely to how that person fits into the controller's plans for increasing departmental efficiency.
17	Delegate tasks	Based on information gleaned from the last three tasks, the controller should consider a gradual shifting of selected tasks to subordinates, allowing him or her more time to delve into the priorities yet to come. If there are no competent staff members to whom anything can be delegated, the next step will be staff replacement in order to upgrade staff quality.

		With these basic staff management priorities initiated, the controller can shift to the identification and resolution of risk issues.
18	Review auditors' management letter	Outside auditors usually issue a letter to management at the conclusion of each audit that itemizes control and other problems that they feel should be addressed. This letter is an excellent source of information for the new controller who wants a quick grasp of potential problem areas.
19	Review internal audit reports	Internal audit reports are similar to the auditors' management letter in providing information about potential areas of risk, although many firms do not have internal audit teams or target the activities of their teams at only a small number of areas each year. If these reports are available, the controller should obtain and read them.
20	Review controls	The controller should conduct a general overview of all financial controls, based on the information contained in the last two priority items, plus an examination of control flowcharts for all key accounting and financial processes. This overview should result in the identification of control weaknesses that the controller can fix.
21	Review financial disclosures	If the company is publicly held, the controller should compare all current SEC filing requirements to what the company is actually reporting and adjust reports as necessary. This chore can be given to a qualified subordinate or even to outside auditors.
22	Revise management reports	The controller should now have enough preliminary knowledge of company operations to see if the management reports being issued by the accounting and finance departments contain the right kind of information needed to run the company properly. Likely a substantial overhaul of the existing reporting system will be necessary.
23	Review computer system requirements	The creation of new management reports may uncover flaws in the underlying computer systems, such as data storage capacity problems or the inability to collect various types of key information automatically. This is a good time for the controller to assess the requirements of these systems and initiate their long-term overhaul, if necessary.

(Continued)

Priority	Action	Description
24	Conduct cost review	The controller should use group and individual sessions with the accounting staff and with most department managers to walk through the entire income statement and devise both short- and long-term plans for reducing costs.
25	Create budgeting process	The priority for budgeting may be accelerated if the controller begins work near or in the midst of the standard budgeting period. This process should include an evaluation of how well the process has worked in the past, how it supports company strategy, and how it supports the management compensation plan. A key aspect is the creation of a financing plan, so the controller has some idea of the timing and amount of funds that may be needed.
26	Review inventory aging	If the company has substantial assets tied up in inventory, the controller should take a significant amount of time to physically review the state of the inventory, where it is stored, how old it is, and how much appears to be reduced in value. These steps are necessary because inventory is subject to reporting fraud and shrinkage, can be grossly overvalued, and can cause reporting nightmares for the controller if not properly kept track of.
27	Install inventory best practices	If the inventory carries a high valuation, the controller should install several key best practices to ensure that the valuation does not incorrectly fluctuate, resulting in incorrect financial statements. These best practices should include the use of cycle counting, eliminating periodic physical counts, and periodically measuring inventory accuracy levels.
28	Review document retention systems	Last in priority is a review of document retention systems. Some controllers ignore this item entirely, but inadequate paperwork storage can cause major problems in the event of any type of audit, which may result in fines by government entities. Although a low priority, document retention systems must be reviewed at some point.

This priority list should not lead a controller to believe that once an item is completed, it does not have to be addressed again. On the contrary, the completion of each priority item likely will reveal additional problem areas that will require additional work to address. In addition, any system is likely to degrade over time, requiring repeated reviews by the controller to ensure that it is operating properly. In short, the new controller will find that he or she will cycle through this list repeatedly.

About the Author

Steven Bragg, CPA, has been the chief financial officer or controller of four companies, as well as a consulting manager at Ernst & Young and auditor at Deloitte & Touche. He received a master's degree in finance from Bentley College, an MBA from Babson College, and a bachelor's degree in economics from the University of Maine. He has been the two-time president of the Colorado Mountain Club and is an avid alpine skier, mountain biker, and certified master diver. Mr. Bragg resides in Centennial, Colorado. He has written the following books published by John Wiley & Sons:

Accounting and Finance for Your Small Business
Accounting Best Practices
Accounting Control Best Practices
Accounting Policies and Procedures Manual
Billing and Collections Best Practices
Business Ratios and Formulas
Controller's Guide to Costing
Controller's Guide to Planning and Controlling Operations
Controller's Guide: Roles and Responsibilities for the New Controller
Controllership
Cost Accounting
Cost Reduction Analysis
Essentials of Payroll
Fast Close
Financial Analysis
GAAP Guide
GAAP Policies and Procedures
GAAS Guide
Inventory Accounting
Inventory Best Practices

Just-in-Time Accounting
Management Accounting Best Practices
Managing Explosive Corporate Growth
Mergers & Acquisitions
Outsourcing
Payroll Accounting
Payroll Best Practices
Revenue Recognition
Running a Public Company
Running an Effective Investor Relations Department
Sales and Operations for Your Small Business
Throughput Accounting
The Controller's Function
The New CFO Financial Leadership Manual
The Ultimate Accountants' Reference
Treasury Management
The Vest Pocket Controller
The Vest Pocket IFRS

Free Online Resources by Steve Bragg

Steve issues the Accounting Best Practices podcast, which you can access at www.accountingtools.com or iTunes.

Index

Printed and bound by CPI Group (UK) Ltd, Croydon, CR0 4YY

23/04/2025

14661005-0005